A Practical Guide to

Beauty Therapy

for NVQ Level 2

3rd edition

revised

Janet Simms

Nelson Thornes

a Wolters Kluwer business

Published in 2006 by:
Nelson Thornes Ltd
Delta Place
27 Bath Road
CHELTENHAM
GL53 7TH
United Kingdom

06 07 08 09 10 / 10 9 8 7 6 5 4 3 2 1

A catalogue record for this book is available from the British Library

ISBN 0 7487 9772 6

Illustrations by Oxford Designers and Illustrators, IFA Design, Peter Cox, Linda Herd, Lorraine White and John Taylor
Page make-up by IFA Design Ltd, Plymouth, Devon

Printed and bound in China by Midas Printing International Ltd

Contents

Foreword

I am delighted with the continuing success of my book, which, to date, has helped thousands of students working towards a qualification in Beauty Therapy. The format of the book has been well received due to the order, depth and breadth of its content, and the style of presentation. I am fortunate to have met many students from all over the UK who have used the book and fed back to me the value it has brought to their training. Many qualified beauty therapists who used the book during their training even bought later editions of the book to keep themselves updated and train others once they entered employment. Praise indeed! It makes all the hard work involved in producing the book worthwhile.

This edition includes chapters on Nail Art and Spa Treatments, and provides the underpinning knowledge required for students and practitioners providing general beauty therapy, make-up and nail services. Faithful regard has been paid to providing the underpinning knowledge required for successful completion of each unit in the level 2 award. Colour photographs, self-checks and practical learning and assessment activities are included throughout the book and, at the beginning of each chapter, there is revision guidance and referencing to the NVQ standards. Key skills have been given greater coverage in Chapter 2 and the activities designed in to each chapter provide opportunities for generating key skills assessment evidence.

Students and trainees are required, increasingly, to undertake more study in their own time, away from their workplace, college or training centre. It has become even more important for them to have a book that guides them steadily through the learning process, whether working independently or with friends or colleagues studying in a similar way. This was my aim when writing the book and I hope it proves to fulfil it.

I hope you get as much pleasure using the book as I have had in writing it. I wish you success. Enjoy learning, set yourself high standards and never be afraid to question!

Janet Simms

Acknowledgements

Janet Simms

I would like to give special thanks to my family and friends who supported and encouraged me with this book. In particular, thank you to my boys Adam and David, and my parents. Also, in recognition of their technical and professional contributions to this new addition, Catherine Peel, Melle Stripp, the Four Seasons Spa team at the Airport Marriott Hotel Manchester, and Bryn Williams of Sterling Supplies Ltd. Thank you also, to Roger and Nagwa Stanforth, whose contribution on sugaring in an earlier edition has stood the test of time.

Last, but not least, I would like to thank Claire Hart and the team at Nelson Thornes who kept me going and did such a wonderful job of turning my work into a real book. Very many thanks for all your help.

For further information about NVQs in Beauty Therapy in your region, contact your local Learning and Skills Council, HABIA (The Hairdressing and Beauty Industry Authority) or College of Further Education.

One person who definitely is very much part of the nail industry is Melle Stripp. I am very grateful to Melle for working with me on the nail art chapter and contributing her designs. Melle's story may be an inspiration to you.

Melle Stripp

Melle's career as a nail artist started in 1996 with evening classes in manicure. Just one hour of the whole course was given to nail art but it was enough to get Melle 'hooked'! Since then, her passion for nails and nail art has grown. Starting with freehand nail art products, she created designs for herself and her family. Word spread as her designs became more elaborate and the nails got longer! The next level she studied was airbrushed nail art. Now running her own successful business 'All Things Nails', which provides airbrush and nail art equipment, and tuition for nail technicians across the UK and Europe, Melle has had her work displayed in publications and the media throughout the world, including Italian *Vogue*, on Sky TV, at London Fashion Week with Alexander McQueen and all of the nail industry magazines in the UK and USA. Her website is www.AllThingsNails.co.uk.

Staff at The Four Seasons Spa, Manchester Airport Marriott Hotel: Lisa Bennett, Charlotte Corby, Sam Llewellyn, Jenni Horsfield, Ian Wakefield.
Photographer: Martin Sookias.
Models: Veena Bedi, Chris Carr, Suzy Carr, Will Davies, Theodore Fadle, Kath Lucas, Victoria Lucas, Russell Moores, Bello Nelson, Robert Paterson, Emmaline Tsui. Heather Williams and Tina Baker, and all at Martin & Phelps.

Photo credits
- Advertising Archive (p.102)
- Alessandro (p.97, p.347 bottom, p.350, p.362, p.401)
- American Express (p.89 right)
- Aston & Fincher (p.270, p.306 bottom, p.313 bottom, p.314, p.369)
- Robert Baran (p.336 bottom)
- Caflon (p.431, p.433, p.435)

- Cetuem (p.405, p.407, p.408, p.413)
- Chubb Fire (p.44)
- Clynol (p.184, p.234 middle right and right)
- Corel 554 (NT) (p.243)
- Corel 664 (NT) (p.302)
- Creativ Collection/EWI (NT) (p.86)
- Designer Nails UK Ltd (p.408, p.423, p.424)
- DK Images (p.218, p.465)
- Elemis (p.166 top)
- Finders Health (p.471)
- Floatworks (UK) Ltd (p.452, p.458)
- Getty Images (p.71 top)
- GiGi (p.306)
- Grafton International (p.348 bottom, p.366, p.368)
- Guinot (p.166 bottom, p.245)
- HSBC (p.87, p. 88, p.89 left)
- Image Source 2 (NT) (p.70 bottom)
- Instant Art/Signs (NT) (p.49)
- Jane Iredale (p.251)
- JICA (p.167, p.177, p.234 middle left, p.330 right)
- La Remedi (p.356, p.364 top and bottom left)
- Manchester Airport Marriott Hotel (p.442 top)
- Natural Nail Company (p.347 top, p.356, p.358, p.364 top and bottom left)
- OPI (p.71 bottom, p.330 left, p.346 bottom, p.349, p.359)
- Photodisc 75 (NT) (p.157, p.180, p.183, p.210, p.234 left, p.278 right)
- Powerstock/Dinodia (p.438)
- Prestige Medical (p.58)
- Rex Features/Brian Rasic (p.278 left)
- Science Photo Library (p.47, p.57, p.58 top, p.121, p.133, p.134, p.135, p.136, p.137, p.138, p.139, p.140, p.141, p.142, p.144, p.212 bottom, p.333, p.334, p.335, p.336 top and middle, p.337, p.338, p.339, p.340, p.464)
- Martin Sookias (p.2, p.6, p.17, p.24, p.26, p.29, p.36, p.39, p.69, p.70 top, p.74, p.79, p.96, p.106, p.111, p.151, p.176, p.178, p.186, p.188, p.189, p.190, p.191, p.192, p.199, p.200, p.201, p.202, p.203, p.204, p.205, p.212 top, p.215, p 219, p.223, p.236, p.248, p.249, p.255, p.256, p.260, p.262, p.268, p.270, p.273, p.281, p.282, p.284, p.286, p.288, p.294, p.295, p.297, p.311, p.312, p.313, p.325, p.354, p.355, p.357, p.363, p.364 right, p.370, p.371, p.372, p.373, p.392, p.404, p.415, p.416, p.417, p.449, p.450, p.452 top, p.453, p.465, p.466, p.468)
- Sorisa (p.58 bottom, p.193, p.195, p.307 bottom, p.309)
- Sukar (p.307 top, p.316, p.321, p.322)
- Melle Strip (p.378, p.380, p.381, p.382, p.383, p.393, p.394, p.395)
- Thalgo (p.181, p.442, p.454, p.470)
- Virgin Vie (p.257, p.280)
- Zen (p.62)

A PRACTICAL GUIDE TO BEAUTY THERAPY

Chapter 1 Employment standards

Legal and professional framework

After working through this chapter you will be able to:

- appreciate the importance of professional standards
- understand the laws relating to beauty therapy
- describe professional standards of hygiene and appearance
- give clients a positive impression of yourself and your organisation.

To be a successful beauty therapist you need to operate within the professional and legal frameworks of the industry. These set the standards required for employment. High standards are essential for earning the trust and confidence of the public. They also earn you the respect of colleagues and other professionals who contribute to the success of the business.

Professional associations

It will be worth your while joining one of the **professional associations** that represents you and your industry. A range of services and support will be available to you including:

- technical and product updating
- business advice
- news bulletins
- special rates for insurance cover
- membership badge and display materials.

Also, you will benefit by being able to meet up regularly and speak with other professionals in the beauty industry at meetings, exhibitions and social events. Professional associations are committed to advancing beauty therapy and maintaining high standards in the profession. They provide maximum protection for the public and will work hard on your behalf. In return, you must always conduct yourself according to their code of ethics and maintain high standards of professional practice in all aspects of your work.

Meet the professionals

Professional code of ethics

Each professional organisation produces its own code of practice based on expected standards of behaviour. These standards are referred to as a professional code of ethics. Whichever organisation you decide to join, you will have to sign a written declaration that you will:

- always work within the law
- never treat or claim to be able to treat a medical condition
- respect client confidentiality at all times
- show respect for other professions by referring clients appropriately, for example to general practitioners, chiropodists, physiotherapists
- maintain high standards of hygiene and safety in all aspects of your work
- apply certain treatments only with the written permission of the client's general practitioner
- support, help and show loyalty to other professional beauty therapists
- never 'poach' another member's clients or criticise their work
- uphold the honour of the profession at all times, for example when working on members of the opposite sex.

A PRACTICAL GUIDE TO BEAUTY THERAPY

Activity 1.1: Professional associations

1   Send off for information from at least two professional associations. You will find their details in the professional beauty journals. Compare their terms and conditions of membership and find out what they have to offer. Decide which association you are going to join.

2   Complete an application form. Ask your supervisor to check the completed form, then make a photocopy before you send it off.

Legal framework

All businesses are required to work within a legal framework, which protects the interests of everyone associated with the business. You will need to know about the laws relating to beauty therapy and how they affect your work, in particular those relating to health and safety, consumer protection and employment.

Types of legislation

The law is made up of different types of legislation: Acts, which are written in broad terms; and regulations, which are more specific and expand on details of the Acts. The law in the United Kingdom is influenced, increasingly, by the European Union (EU). The EU is working towards harmonising the laws in the European Union member states. When new directives are issued, regulations are produced to 'tighten up' the laws in the UK.

Be proud of your profession! Project an image that instils trust and confidence in both clients and colleagues. Always treat other people as you would wish to be treated yourself.

Activity 1.2: Working in Europe

You may, one day, like the idea of working in another European country.

1   Gather information about each of the countries in the EU and compare the types of beauty therapy jobs available.

2   Find out what additional qualifications or skills you might need to work in the European country of your choice.

Your library or study centre will be able to help you. Professional associations, the internet, beauty recruitment agencies and trade journals are also sources of information.

Health and safety legislation

The law demands that every place of work is a healthy and safe place to be, not only for the people who work there but also for clients and other visitors. This even includes trespassers!

The main responsibilities for health and safety lie with the employer, who must ensure that:

- appropriate health and safety policies are in place
- the premises are clean and safe
- all staff are trained in health and safety procedures.

Beauty salons, by the nature of their business, offer a wide range of services. Most of these require the therapists to work in very close personal contact with their clients.

As an employee, you have rights and responsibilities not only to your employer, but also to your clients, customers and colleagues. Failure to comply with the law can have very serious consequences.

Many of them involve the use of potentially dangerous equipment and chemicals. There are considerable risks of spreading infection or causing personal injury if correct procedures are not followed.

Health and safety legislation is part of criminal law. Failure to comply with the law has serious consequences and can be very expensive for the business, resulting in:

● claims made by injured staff

● claims made by injured clients

● prosecution and fines

● closure of the business

● loss of trade through bad publicity

● loss of staff through damaged reputation.

Would you want to work for a salon that neglected the health and safety of its clients and staff?

Health and safety

Health and Safety Executive

The **Health and Safety Executive** (HSE) is the 'lead' authority on health and safety. The HSE provides information and gives advice through its area offices. It also enforces health and safety legislation by sending inspectors from the local authority to check up on standards of health and safety. The inspectors are usually **Environmental Health Officers**. They have considerable powers, including the right to carry out, at almost any time, an inspection of the premises or an investigation into a complaint.

If the inspectors are not satisfied with the standards of health and safety, they will issue either an improvement notice or a prohibition notice.

Improvement notice
This will allow the employer 21 days or more to make specified improvements; an employer who fails to comply with the notice by the given date can end up in court.

Prohibition notice
This is very serious; the risks to health and safety are so severe that the business has to close down until the improvements have been made. The business will not be allowed to start operating again until the inspectors are satisfied that all problems have been dealt with to the required standards. An inspector will come back to check compliance with the notice. Failure to comply with the notice can result in prosecution.

Activity 1.3: Health and Safety Executive

1 Find out the address of your local Health and Safety Executive (HSE) office from the library and contact them for up-to-date publications and information. Keep a copy of the letter you send. Alternatively, use the internet website www.hse.gov.uk.

2 Once you have the information, highlight specific details relating to beauty therapy and keep it safely for reference.

The Health and Safety at Work Act 1974

This Act covers all aspects of health, safety and welfare at work. It identifies the responsibilities of employers and employees to provide a safe working environment, not just for themselves but for anyone present on the business premises.
In 1992 EU directives resulted in strict regulations being introduced. These 1992 regulations became known as the 'six pack' and have been incorporated into the Health and Safety at Work Act.

The Management of Health and Safety at Work Regulations 1999

Employers have responsibility for safeguarding, as far as possible, the health, safety and welfare of themselves, their employees and members of the public. This means that health and safety must be integrated into all other aspects of planning, managing and organising the business. The employer is responsible for ensuring that there are rules and codes of practice in place, and that these are monitored, reviewed and complied with by all staff.

The employer must:
- make suitable and sufficient assessments of the risks to health and safety of employees and others
- record the significant findings of risk assessments
- instruct and train employees exposed to risks, on the appropriate protective and preventative measures
- display the statutory poster 'Health and Safety Law – What you should know'
- consult with employees on matters affecting their health and safety
- provide safe access to and exits from the place of work
- ensure all substances are stored, handled, disposed of and transported safely
- keep all equipment up to standard
- ensure that the environment is free from toxic fumes
- have safety equipment checked regularly
- make sure that all staff know the safety procedures
- provide safety information and training
- ensure safe systems of work
- maintain records of injuries and first-aid treatment
- report notifiable accidents, diseases and dangerous occurrences in the workplace
- monitor and review health and safety arrangements as necessary
- ensure employees are competent.

Accidents can happen at any time!

REMEMBER

Employees have a duty always to work without endangering themselves or others. You must not misuse or interfere with anything provided for your health, safety or welfare.

REMEMBER

In most cases, separate toilet facilities must be available for men and women. However, in a small salon, men and women can use the same facilities as long as each WC is in a separate room which can be locked from the inside.

Wearing disposable apron and gloves for depilatory waxing

The Workplace (Health, Safety and Welfare) Regulations 1992

● These regulations have tightened up those aspects of the Offices, Shops and Railways and Premises Act 1963 and the Health and Safety at Work Act 1974 relating to business premises and safety facilities.

● The employer must provide:

   ● a clean and tidy workplace with appropriate heating, lighting and ventilation; waste material must not be allowed to accumulate and should be stored and disposed of safely

   ● toilets for staff and clients with washing facilities provided next to every WC, and a supply of hot and cold water, soap and clean towels (or the equivalent)

   ● safe floors, staircases and passageways, which are free from obstruction

   ● fixtures, fittings and floorings, which are in good condition and secure

   ● resting, eating and drinking facilities for staff who are required to stay on the premises at break times

   ● fire exits and fire-fighting equipment

   ● secure storage space for outdoor and protective clothing.

The Provision and Use of Work Equipment Regulations 1998

The employer must ensure that all equipment at work is properly constructed, suitable for its purpose and kept in a good state of repair. This applies to both new and secondhand equipment. All employees must be trained to use and maintain the equipment properly and written records must be kept of any maintenance work.

REMEMBER

You are not qualified to use a piece of equipment until you have received proper training.

The Personal Protective Equipment (PPE) at Work Regulations 1992

It is the employer's responsibility to ensure that all employees who may be at risk of being exposed to health risks or injury are provided with appropriate protective equipment.

Activity 1.4: Personal protective equipment

Ask your supervisor which treatments and procedures in your salon require you to wear protective equipment. Find out what the equipment is and where it is kept.

REMEMBER

As a beauty therapist, it is unlikely that you will spend much time working at a computer. However, if you work for a large company, there will probably be administrative staff who do. The Health and Safety (Display Screen Equipment) Regulations will apply to them.

The Health and Safety (Display Screen Equipment) Regulations 1992

Employees who use a visual display unit (VDU) more or less continuously in their job must be protected from possible adverse health effects. Eye troubles, headaches, back pain, stress and fatigue can all be caused by working at a word processor all day. Employers have to assess the risks to their own employees and take steps to deal with them, for instance by fitting blinds to eliminate glare, adjusting the position of the screen, providing a more suitable chair set at the right height.

GOOD PRACTICE

While you are in training, be aware of the possible effects of spending too much time working at the computer when completing assignments. Give yourself regular breaks, preferably involving some exercise.

The Manual Handling Operations Regulations 1992

Many injuries to the back, hands, arms, legs and feet occur as a result of incorrect lifting, carrying and handling techniques. Some sprains and strains build up over a period of time, others occur as the result of a single incident. Employers are required to make an assessment of the risks to their employees and make sure that they provide appropriate training. Sometimes, the working environment may need adapting, for instance by reorganising shelves and storage space in stockrooms.

Incorrect lifting and carrying can cause serious injuries

The Local Government (Miscellaneous Provisions) Act 1982

Local authorities have powers to inspect and register businesses which practise beauty therapy treatments. They are concerned particularly with treatments such as ear piercing, electrical epilation and micro-pigmentation. These treatments involve the use of needles or sharp implements and, therefore, carry a higher risk of cross-infection and skin damage. The salon must demonstrate that correct hygiene practices are used for storing, using and disposing of sharp implements.

REMEMBER

You need a basic knowledge of first aid so that you can assist with minor accidental injuries or unexpected situations that can happen from time to time in the salon. If you are interested in becoming a qualified first aider, details of courses and examinations can be obtained from your local college or by contacting the British Red Cross, St John Ambulance or St Andrew's Ambulance Association.

REMEMBER

A fire can close the business temporarily or permanently, destroying important papers and records at the same time. It can cause extensive damage to property and result in serious injuries or even death. Everybody in the business must know how to prevent a fire from happening and how to deal with a fire if one happens.

GOOD PRACTICE

A Certificate of Means of Escape in Case of Fire should be displayed. The local fire authority will issue this once they have inspected and approved the escape routes. A certificate of registration or licence is awarded by the local authority, who may charge a fee.

HEALTH MATTERS

'Manual handling' means any transporting or supporting of a load, including lifting, putting down, pushing, pulling, carrying or moving by hand or bodily force. You must be able to identify 'safe' weights for lifting and know how to adapt your posture to avoid injury.

The Act states that:

● a person may not carry out their practice unless registered by the local authority

● premises have to be registered to carry out treatments.

To become registered, a salon must show that its standards conform to the rules and regulations issued by the local council. These are contained in by-laws and cover:

● the cleanliness of the premises and fittings

● the cleanliness of persons registered and their assistants

● the cleansing and sterilisation of instruments, materials and equipment used.

The Health and Safety (First Aid) Regulations 1981

These lay down the minimum requirements for the provision of first aid in the workplace. The requirements vary according to the number of employees and the type of business. A well-stocked first-aid kit must be readily available. Staff should know who is responsible for first aid, what the first-aid kit looks like and where it is kept. The reception is usually the best place. A qualified first aider is always an asset but it is not compulsory for a small business to employ one.

The Fire Precautions Act 1971, The Fire Precautions (Workplace) Regulations 1999

All workplaces must carry out a fire risk assessment and have regular fire drills. All staff must be trained in fire and emergency evacuation procedures, and the premises must have adequate means of escape in cases of fire:

● room contents should not obstruct access to the escape routes

● fire exit doors should be clearly marked and kept closed to prevent a fire from spreading

● fire exit doors should remain unlocked from the inside to enable a quick exit in an emergency

● there must be adequate fire fighting equipment which is in good working order

● the equipment must be readily available and suitable for the different types of fire that could possibly occur

● staff should be trained in fire drill procedures and notices of the drill should be displayed.

The Reporting of Injuries, Diseases and Dangerous Occurrences Regulations 1995

Known as **RIDDOR**, these regulations identify the work-related incidents which need reporting and how they should be reported. If any staff or members of the public suffer from a personal injury at work, it must be reported in the salon's Accident Book. This is to inform the employer and ensure that serious injuries get reported to the enforcement officer at the local council.

Activity 1.5: RIDDOR

1 Get hold of a copy of 'Everyone's guide to RIDDOR', a short booklet, which may be obtained free of charge from your local HSE.

2 Ask your supervisor if you can have a look at your salon's Accident Book to see what has occurred in the last 12 months. Note the follow-up action that was taken. Make recommendations on how the accidents could have been avoided.

REMEMBER

The four main ways by which a substance may harm the body are by:

- entering the eyes
- inhalation
- swallowing
- skin contact (by either absorption or entry through a break in the skin).

The employer needs to consider these when assessing the risks in the salon. Effective controls can then be introduced, backed up with staff training.

The Control of Substances Hazardous to Health Regulations 2002 (COSHH)

The **COSHH** regulations require employers to control people's exposure to hazardous substances in the workplace. Some of the products used in the salon are safe in normal use, but become hazardous under certain conditions. Staff must be trained so that they understand the risks associated with different substances and are able to take the appropriate safety precautions.

REMEMBER

The **Working Time Regulations 1998** specify the maximum weekly working hours and entitlements to rest periods and holidays. Your employer will have considered these when setting out your terms and conditions of employment.

REMEMBER

The **Health and Safety (Training for Employment) Regulations 1990** extend the coverage of health and safety legislation to people receiving 'relevant training' in the workplace. This includes school pupils and college students on training schemes or work experience placements.

Know how to protect yourself from potentially hazardous substances

Activity 1.6: Hazardous substances

1 Obtain a copy of 'A Guide to Health and Safety in the Salon', which has been produced by The Hairdressing Manufacturers and Wholesale Association Ltd (WHMA) and the Cosmetic, Toiletry and Perfumers Association. Either of the associations or your wholesaler should be able to provide you with a copy.

2 Read through the guide. It explains about potential hazards with products used commonly in the salon. Highlight the information about treatments offered in your salon.

If you spot an electrical
fault or potential electrical
hazard in the salon, report
it to your supervisor. Never
use equipment or an
appliance that you know
is unsafe.

The Environmental Protection Act 1990

This Act links in to the COSHH regulations. Anyone using hazardous substances must ensure that the disposal of them does not cause harm to the environment or to anyone else. Waste chemicals must be disposed of safely.

The Electricity at Work Regulations 1990

Every electrical appliance at work must be tested at least once a year by a qualified electrician. A written record must be kept of these tests and be available for inspection by the Health and Safety authority. Regular inspections should be carried out to detect simple faults, such as cracked plugs, frayed cables and damage to external casings. Any faulty equipment identified must be clearly marked and taken out of use until it is repaired.

The Employers' Liability (Compulsory Insurance) Act 1969

The **Employers' Liability** (Compulsory Insurance) Act 1969 requires that employers have everyone on their payroll covered by employers' liability insurance and that a current certificate of insurance is displayed at the place of work. The insurance provides cover for claims that might arise when an employee suffers injuries or illness as the result of negligence by either the employer or another employee. Employees who are injured as a result of their own negligence are not covered by the Act.

REMEMBER

Only people who are electrically qualified should deal with electrical faults and installations.

Public liability insurance

Injuries that are proven to be caused by professional negligence can result in very expensive fines and claims for compensation. **Public liability** insurance is not a legal requirement, but it should be taken out by employers to cover them for claims made by members of the public as a result of injury or damage to personal property caused by the employer or employee at work.

REMEMBER

Failure to insure for employers' liability is a serious offence which carries very heavy financial penalties.

A special professional indemnity insurance extends this liability to cover named employees against claims, by clients, of personal injury resulting from a treatment. All employees who give treatments should be covered by professional indemnity insurance. This is particularly important in respect of 'higher risk' treatments such as ear piercing, wax depilation and electrical epilation.

**GOOD
PRACTICE**

Hopefully, you will never have to answer to a client's claims of injury resulting from one of your treatments. However, accidents do happen. You must make sure you are protected, financially, by **professional indemnity** insurance. Your professional association will provide you with details.

It is a good idea to display your qualifications and your public liability insurance certificate in the salon

Health and safety legislation

1 Give four reasons why an employer should ensure that the business complies with health and safety legislation.

2 List four areas of health and safety in the salon, for which the employee (you) is (are) directly responsible.

3 Name and describe two types of notice that could be issued by an Environmental Health Officer following an inspection of the salon premises.

4 What actions should be taken when an employee suffers injuries following an accident in the salon?

5 List six requirements of the Fire Precautions Act 1971.

6 Name each of the regulations introduced in 1992, making up the EU 'six pack', which became incorporated into the Health and Safety at Work Act 1974.

7 Why does the law require staff to be trained in correct manual handling techniques?

8 Give two reasons why beauty therapists and salons need to be registered with their local authority.

9 State the four main areas of risk that need to be considered for COSHH assessments.

10 Give (a) two requirements of the employer and (b) one requirement of the employee (you) in order to comply with the Electricity at Work Regulations 1990.

11 Distinguish between employers' liability, public liability and professional indemnity insurance.

12 Give one reason why a professional association might refuse to pay out insurance on behalf of one of its members.

Mobile beauty therapists do not have as many regulations to comply with, but they must ensure that they are registered, if necessary, with their local council. They must provide a first-aid kit, records of electrical safety tests of their equipment and evidence of appropriate hygiene procedures.

GOOD PRACTICE

The **Health and Safety (Information for Employees) Regulations 1989** require employers to display a poster telling employees what they need to know about health and safety.

Consumer protection

You must ensure that your clients have realistic expectations from their treatments and that they understand how to get the best results from products they purchase for home care. This avoids disappointment later and also helps to develop the clients' confidence in your advice. As consumers of your products and services, clients have legal rights. There are a number of organisations and regulations dealing with consumer protection.

The Office of Fair Trading (OFT)

This organisation helps protect consumers by:

- encouraging trade associations to set up voluntary codes of practice
- prosecuting traders who break the law
- advising on the need for new legislation
- issuing information and publications.

Environmental Health and Trading Standards (EHTS)

Environmental Health departments deal with hygiene and food quality. Trading Standards departments handle complaints on weights and measures and trade descriptions. Trading Standards Officers are employed by local authorities to investigate consumer complaints. Having investigated the complaint, they have the power to take the business to court.

The Advertising Standards Authority (ASA)

Financed by the advertising industry, the ASA oversees much of the advertising in the UK. Its voluntary British Code of Advertising Practice states that advertisements should be 'legal, decent, honest and truthful'. The work of the ASA is influenced by the European Union and UK legislation.

The ASA and beauty products

The Advertising Standards Authority has a special set of guidelines for companies promoting beauty products. Its British Code of Advertising and Sales Promotion states that when a claim is made about the action of a product on the skin, it must distinguish between the effects that are due to the composition of the product and the effects that are brought about by the way the product is applied, for example by massage.

The ASA has also identified the need for realistic claims about the effects of 'anti-ageing products'. Advertisements can refer to the temporary prevention, delay or masking of premature ageing, but far-reaching claims about the effects of the products on the ageing process must be avoided. The ASA says that, although lines and wrinkles can be reduced, it has not seen evidence that they can be permanently removed by cosmetic products.

The British Standards Institute (BSI)

The BSI is an independent body that sets voluntary standards of reliability and quality. Its objectives are to:

- establish quality standards
- promote health and safety
- protect the environment.

Manufacturers submit their products for testing voluntarily. The test covers such things as safety, strength and quality, depending upon the type of product. A product that has been tested and approved by the BSI is eligible to carry the 'Kitemark'. The BSI has been involved with developing common quality standards in the Single European Market.

The Consumers' Association

Best known for its *Which?* series of magazines, the Consumers' Association campaigns for consumer rights, and researches into the quality and standards of consumer products and services.

Consumer protection legislation

A business that denies its clients and customers (consumers) their rights will, inevitably, face legal action. UK governments and the EU have passed a range of laws to protect the consumer – the most important are listed on the next page.

The Sale and Supply of Goods Act 1994

This identifies the contract that takes place between the seller (in this case, your salon) and the customer (client) when a product is purchased. Once the contract has been made between the seller and the buyer, this Act can be enforced. The Act makes the seller responsible for ensuring that the goods are sold free from defects. It covers all goods, regardless of where they were purchased. Under the terms of the Act, the seller has to ensure that the goods are:

- of satisfactory quality – this is defined as the standard regarded by a reasonable person as satisfactory, having taken into account the description of the goods, the price and any other relevant circumstances
- reasonably fit – the goods must be able to do whatever the seller claims they do.

The Sale and Supply of Goods Act 1994 has replaced the Sale of Goods and Services Act 1982. The part of the Act relating to services is particularly important for a beauty salon because of the treatments offered. The Act requires that the person giving the service must do so with reasonable care and skill, within a reasonable time and for a reasonable charge.

The Trades Descriptions Act 1968 and 1972

This Act makes it a crime to describe goods falsely and to sell, or offer for sale, goods that have false claims made about them. It covers many things such as advertisements, display cards and oral descriptions, and applies to quality, quantity, fitness for purpose and price. The part of the Act passed in 1972 deals with the labelling of the country of origin: a product must be clearly labelled so that the consumer can see where it was made.

ACTIVITY

Activity 1.7: Trades descriptions

Do you think advertisements can be misleading?

1 Go through some magazines, journals and information leaflets which promote skin-care products. Look closely at what it is claimed the products can do. Pick out any examples of adverts that you think could be misleading. Look closely at the language and images used. What exactly are the adverts saying?

2 Working in a small group, make a five-minute presentation of your findings to your supervisor and colleagues. Use visual materials and examples from your research.

The Resale Prices Act 1964 and 1976

This Act prevents manufacturers from forcing retailers to sell their products at a certain price. They can, however, recommend a retail price.

The Consumer Protection Act 1987

This Act was passed following EU directives to safeguard the consumer against unsafe products. The Act covers product liability, general safety requirements and misleading prices.

HEALTH MATTERS

In November 1997, the testing of cosmetic products on animals was banned in the UK. The ban has yet to extend to the testing of individual ingredients in cosmetic products.

REMEMBER

Verbal and written contracts are both classed as valid contracts. A buyer is entitled to a refund or to have the goods replaced if the contract is broken. They do not have to accept a credit note. It is up to the seller to resolve the customer complaint and then to take issue with their suppliers if the goods are found to be defective.

REMEMBER

When you buy goods from a supplier or directly from a manufacturer, you have the same legal rights as a customer who makes a purchase from you.

REMEMBER

EU directives have resulted in strict regulations about cosmetic products. Where a company claims specific effects of a product due to a named 'active' ingredient, there must be scientific evidence that the product is capable of having those effects with the amount of 'active' ingredient contained.

REMEMBER

A client who suffers an adverse reaction to a product used during their treatment or purchased from you, may make a claim against you or the salon. **Product liability** insurance provides cover against such claims. Your professional association will provide details.

The Cosmetic Products (Safety) Regulations 1989

These link in with the Consumer Protection Act and require that cosmetics and toiletries have safe formulations and that the products are tested as being safe for use.

REMEMBER

Be very careful when completing client records. Information must be accurate and written in professional language. A client is entitled to see their records and they may be required as evidence if a claim is brought against the salon.

The Data Protection Act 1984

This Act requires businesses that store details about clients on computer to register with the **Data Protection** Registrar and to comply with a Code of Practice. The Act does not apply to records that are stored manually. Registration forms are available from the post office. They require information on what is stored on the computer, its uses, sources and to whom the data may be disclosed.

SELF-CHECKS

Consumer legislation

1 What is the role of a Trading Standards Officer?

2 State the two main responsibilities of the 'seller' under the terms of the Sale and Supply of Goods Act 1974.

3 What are the two alternatives you must offer a customer if they are found to have made a justified complaint against a product purchased in your salon?

4 Name the main Act concerned with standards of advertising.

5 How has recent European legislation 'tightened up' on claims by the manufacturer about 'active' ingredients contained in their cosmetic products?

6 State two ways of ensuring that clients are not misled about the prices of products in your salon.

REMEMBER

Respect client confidentiality at all times. Never repeat anything told to you or discussed by you both during a treatment, and do not discuss the client or their treatments with any other clients.

Employment legislation

Once you have become employed, you will have certain statutory rights under **employment legislation**. These are legally binding and include the following:

- a detailed pay statement showing what you have earned and what deductions have been made from your earnings
- equal pay for equal work
- no discrimination on the basis of gender, race, disability or marital status
- at least one week's notice of dismissal if you have been employed for at least two months

- statutory sick pay and maternity pay
- a healthy and safe working environment
- the right to redundancy payment if you have been employed by the company for at least two years
- the right to complain to an industrial tribunal if you feel you have been unfairly dismissed
- the right to retain employment under the same conditions if the business is taken over by another company.

The Employment Rights Act 1996

Under this Act you are entitled to ask for a written statement of the terms and conditions of your employment after you have been employed for a month. You also have the right to receive the written statement after two months of commencing employment. The statement should include:

- details of your salary or wages, including commission arrangements
- hours of work
- notice entitlements and obligations
- holiday entitlement
- date of commencement of employment
- job description
- workplace location.

If your employer does not provide you with a written statement, then you have the right to apply to an industrial tribunal, which can order the employer to produce one.

Contract of employment

The written statement of employment is often referred to as the '**contract of employment**'. However, under employment law, the contract is actually made when the employer offers you the job and you accept it. This can be done verbally. It does not have to be written down. A written 'contract of employment' provides legal protection for both the employer and the employee.

The Sex Discrimination Acts 1975, 1986 and the Race Relations Act 1976

The aim of these Acts is to prevent the employer from discriminating against job applicants, either directly or indirectly, on the basis of their race, gender or marital status. The Equal Opportunities Commission investigates complaints of discrimination and monitors the wording of job advertisements.

The Disability Discrimination Act 1995

This Act makes it unlawful for an employer of 20 or more staff to discriminate against a current or prospective employee because of a reason relating to their disability. If an employee or applicant is competent to do the job required, then the employer is responsible for making reasonable changes to the working environment and general employment arrangements so that the employee with a disability is not disadvantaged.

Job competence

When you apply for a job, you must provide evidence that you are competent. This means showing that you have the skills, knowledge and understanding to be able to perform all aspects of the job to the required standard. The competencies required should be contained in a detailed job description and person specification. Copies of your qualifications, references, your curriculum vitae or record of your achievements will provide important information that will help an employer to make judgements about your competence.

REMEMBER

Health and safety legislation requires employers to ensure that all their staff are competent to do the jobs they are employed to do.

As part of the selection process, you may be required to undertake a 'trade test' where your technical and interpersonal skills will be assessed by a senior member of staff. This is not unusual when recruiting beauty therapists and provides further evidence of your competence for the job and suitability for employment in the salon.

GOOD PRACTICE

Sometimes you will be required to take further training so that the salon can offer new treatments or services. Be grateful for the chance to learn new techniques – the more you can do, the more valuable you become as an employee!

SELF-CHECKS

Employment legislation

1 State five legal entitlements of an employee.

2 List six things you should ask an employer before accepting a job offer.

3 Give two reasons why it is important to have a written statement of the terms and conditions of employment.

4 Give three areas of discrimination covered by Equal Opportunities employment legislation.

5 State three reasons why it is important for employers to ensure that all staff are competent to do their jobs.

6 List three ways of providing evidence for an employer that you are competent to do a job that has been advertised.

Professional image

The effort you put into getting ready for work reflects your pride in the job. Clients will initially judge your professionalism on how you present yourself. This is known as your **professional image**. You are in an industry where image and appearance are important. It is fine for you to have your own individual look provided that you appreciate that there are professional standards of dress and appearance that must be followed.

Appearance and personal hygiene

Your appearance should reflect your professional skills and knowledge. Clients will have confidence in your abilities if you always look smart, clean and well groomed. Good personal hygiene is essential as your work will bring you into very close contact with clients and colleagues. Good personal hygiene also helps to keep the body healthy. Here are some general rules.

Body freshness

Have at least one daily bath or shower. This removes the build-up of sweat and loose, dead skin cells. Bacteria thrive in warm, moist areas of the body such as the armpits and feet. If you do not wash the bacteria away regularly, they produce unpleasant body odour (BO), which everybody notices but no one likes to mention!

Use an antiperspirant. This has a cooling, astringent (tightening) effect, preventing the build-up of sweat which causes body odour. Most antiperspirants are also bactericidal. Under normal circumstances, antiperspirants stay effective all day, but it is a good idea to keep one at work just in case.

HEALTH MATTERS

Deodorants are not generally as effective as antiperspirants. Although most have some bactericidal properties, they really only mask smells. They do not deal with the real cause of the problem, which is a build-up of sweat. Some people, however, prefer to use a deodorant as their skin can be sensitive to the extra ingredients contained in an antiperspirant.

Wear clean, fresh underwear every day. If you wear an underskirt make sure that it does not show below your overall.

Overall

Wear a clean, well-pressed overall each day. Your overall will probably be made of cotton or maybe polycotton, which is easier to launder. These fabrics are lightweight and comfortable to wear for working. Make sure your overall is not too tight. It should be loose enough for air and moisture to circulate. This helps to keep the body cool and fresh.

Make sure your overall is not too short. Knee length is usually the most appropriate. Your overall should be long enough to look respectable when you sit down or if you need to stretch or lean across a client. Try and avoid travelling in your overall and do not wear it anywhere it might pick up unpleasant smells.

REMEMBER

A brisk rub with the towel after a bath or shower helps to stimulate the circulation and perk up the body – particularly useful if you have difficulty getting going in the mornings!

REMEMBER

Sweat evaporates freely from skin that is exposed to the air, but not from areas where two surfaces of skin meet or where clothes and shoes fit tightly.

Jewellery

Keep jewellery to the minimum: ideally a pair of small earrings and, if you are married, a flat wedding ring. Avoid wearing bracelets and watch straps, which can get

Jenny – Nail Technician

Ian – Leisure Manager

Sam – Spa Manager

Lisa – Beauty Therapist

Vicky – Beauty Therapist

REMEMBER

Any jewellery you wear must look appropriate for work and not interfere with your professional image.

REMEMBER

If your hands are well groomed, this sets a good example for your clients and helps to promote the salon's products and treatments.

GOOD PRACTICE

Always wear a protective apron or tabard when preparing or giving treatments where a spill could stain or damage your overall.

GOOD PRACTICE

Wear a nurse's 'fob' watch pinned to your overall. This will help you to keep an eye on the time when giving treatments, while keeping your wrist free from jewellery.

REMEMBER

The smells of cigarettes, garlic and other strongly flavoured foods stay on the breath for some time. Others can smell them long after you have tasted them!

in the way during treatments or which may 'catch' the client's skin. Do not wear loose-fitting chains and necklaces which could make contact with the client's skin during treatment. This is both unhygienic and uncomfortable for the client.

Hands

Keep your hands clean and smooth. Wash your hands regularly throughout the day. Breaks in the skin provide a route for bacteria. Use hand cream regularly to prevent the skin from cracking. Wear protective gloves when cleaning and when mixing chemicals.

Keep your nails clean and short. Use a nail brush as part of your regular cleansing routine. Nails trap dirt underneath them. The shorter the nails are, the easier they are to keep clean. Wear enamel on your finger nails only if you are employed as a manicurist or nail technician.

HEALTH MATTERS

If you work as a beauty therapist, treating the face or body, you must not wear nail enamel. This is for two reasons:

● your nails may come into direct contact with the skin and the client may be allergic to your nail enamel; this would produce an unpleasant reaction

● nails that are free from enamel can be seen to be clean; this is very reassuring for a client and inspires confidence.

Feet

Wear correctly fitting shoes. You will spend a lot of time on your feet. Shoes that fit properly provide space for your feet and toes to spread, and will prevent them from getting too hot and uncomfortable. Wear low-heeled shoes that are clean, smart and comfortable, and appropriate for wearing with your overall.

Use foot sprays and medicated foot powders. These help to keep the feet cool and dry. A clean pair of tights or stockings should be worn each day. They should be a natural colour, plain and not pulled or laddered. Keep a spare pair at the salon for emergencies.

Oral hygiene

Brush your teeth thoroughly after every meal as well as in the morning and last thing at night. Rinse the toothbrush well afterwards. Use dental floss regularly to remove plaque from between your teeth and under your gums. Keep a spare toothbrush at work and have a breath freshener or mouthwash on hand just in case.

HEALTH MATTERS

Bad breath results from the decay of food particles left on the teeth. This is one reason why frequent brushing is so important. A build-up of food, particularly sugars, will eventually cause tooth decay and other dental problems. Stomach disorders can also cause bad breath.

Hair care

Have clean, shiny hair, dressed in a smart, manageable style. Make regular visits to the hairdresser to keep your style in shape. Your hair should not fall over your face or the face of your client when you are working. This is unhygienic and irritating for the client. Long hair should be dressed up or secured back off the face.

Brush your hair daily to remove dust, scurf and parasites, which could otherwise accumulate on the hair. Wash and disinfect combs and brushes regularly to avoid a build-up of grease, loosened hair and other debris. Infection can occur if the scalp is scratched with dirty hair equipment.

Make-up

Always wear make-up for work. A light application is all that is required to project a professional image and set a good example to clients. Refresh your make-up during the day if necessary. This can help to give you a boost when you are getting tired. A fresh application of lipstick always brightens up the face.

GOOD PRACTICE

Ideally, you should wear make-up products that are available for purchase in the salon. This helps to advertise the products and promote retail sales.

SELF-CHECKS

Professional image

1 Explain the cause of body odour.

2 State the main difference between a deodorant and an antiperspirant.

3 Give three reasons for wearing an overall.

4 What are the main reasons for not wearing jewellery at work?

5 Give two reasons why nail enamel should not be worn when giving a facial treatment.

6 Why should long hair be styled off the face?

7 Give three reasons why make-up should be worn for work.

8 In your own words, explain what 'having a professional image' means.

REMEMBER

Every salon has its own rules on dress, which reflect the professional image of the business. Always stick to the rules! Do not try changing them without consulting your supervisor first.

ACTIVITY

Activity 1.9: Professional image

How strict is your salon about the appearance of the staff? How important do you think it is to have rules about dress? Have a small group discussion. Look at yourself and your colleagues. Is there room for improvement? Does everyone present a professional image? Do you all look as if you are working for the same business? Be diplomatic with your comments!

MULTIPLE CHOICE QUIZ

Legal and professional framework

There may appear to be more than one correct answer. Read each question carefully before making your final decision. Discuss your answers with colleagues and your supervisor and see if you all agree. If you do not, talk through the issues raised and let your supervisor have the last word!

1 During a beauty treatment, the safety of a client is the responsibility of the:
(a) employer
(b) client
(c) supervisor
(d) employee (you).

2 Bad publicity is expensive for a salon because:
(a) advertising has to be paid for
(b) clients are put off coming to the salon

(c) other salons pinch the clients
(d) the staff have to be paid more.

3 The main role of the Health and Safety Executive is to:
(a) provide information and advice on health and safety
(b) write health and safety legislation
(c) carry out health and safety inspections
(d) prosecute employers in breach of health and safety.

4 The safety of a salon's electrical equipment is the responsibility of the:
(a) electrician
(b) employer
(c) employee (you).

Legal and professional framework

5 The COSHH Regulations were introduced to:
(a) ban hazardous substances from the workplace
(b) prevent abnormal reactions to hazardous substances in the workplace
(c) control exposure to hazardous substances in the workplace
(d) control the number of hazardous substances in the workplace.

6 Details of abnormal reactions or problems with treatments should be recorded so that:
(a) the treatment is no longer offered in the salon
(b) accurate information is available for insurance purposes
(c) the salon cannot be held responsible for accidents
(d) the manufacturer can be informed.

7 The Employers' Liability (Compulsory Insurance) Act covers claims that may arise from:
(a) injury to the employer in the workplace
(b) injury to a client in the workplace
(c) injury to an employee in the workplace
(d) any accidents that may happen in the workplace.

8 Professional indemnity insurance covers employees against claims of:
(a) professional negligence
(b) damage to property
(c) injury to a client
(d) damage to reputation.

9 Long nails are less hygienic than short ones because:
(a) they spread infection easily
(b) they are more prone to infection
(c) they collect more germs underneath
(d) they can break and cause germs to enter.

10 An overall should be loose enough to:
(a) disguise figure faults
(b) prevent body odour
(c) prevent sweating
(d) allow air and moisture to circulate.

11 Good personal hygiene is essential for:
(a) creating a professional image
(b) avoiding the spread of infection
(c) removing surface bacteria
(d) improving personal appearance.

12 Antiperspirants help to prevent body odour because:
(a) they smell fresh
(b) they prevent sweating
(c) they kill bacteria
(d) they have a cooling, astringent effect.

KEY TERMS

You should now understand the following words or phrases. If you do not, go back through the chapter and find out what they mean:

Professional association	**Professional code of ethics**	**Health and Safety Executive**
Environmental Health Officer	**RIDDOR**	**COSHH**
Public liability	**Professional indemnity**	**Employers' liability**
Product liability	**Employment legislation**	**Contract of employment**
Professional image	**Data protection**	**Client confidentiality**

Chapter 2 Roles and responsibilities

Develop and maintain your effectiveness at work

After working through this chapter you will be able to:

- understand the importance of team work
- understand the value of key skills
- communicate effectively with others
- deal with difficulties at work
- plan and manage your time
- plan and manage your personal development plan
- identify learning opportunities
- monitor your own learning and performance.

Before you work through this chapter: Be wise and revise!
Revision topics to help you achieve this unit:

Develop and maintain your effectiveness at work

TOPIC	CHAPTER	PAGE
Professional associations	1	1
Professional code of ethics	1	2
Job competence	1	16
Professional image	1	16

Everyone wants to work for a successful business so it is important that they work well together and know what they have to do to make their own contribution. This involves agreeing targets, creating action plans and working to agreed deadlines. These do not necessarily have to be written down. They occur as a result of good salon management, effective communications, and conscientious and committed staff.

REMEMBER

Staff make the greatest contribution to the atmosphere of the salon. If clients enjoy their salon visits and are satisfied with the treatment they receive, they will stay loyal and become very important to the success of the business.

Team work

A successful business employs committed, hard-working staff who pull together as a team and are motivated towards the same goals. A good employer spends a lot of time and thought recruiting new people to the business, making sure that all new employees fit in with the rest of the team, ensuring effective **team work**.

Professional relationships

Most people behave slightly unnaturally at interview and it is not until they have worked in the salon for a time that their true character and personality are revealed! Most good working relationships develop easily. Some have to be worked at. Whatever the personal feelings of individuals towards one another, clients must never sense a bad atmosphere in the salon because of friction between staff.

REMEMBER

Skimping or leaving jobs lets down the rest of the team and lowers professional standards. A bad impression reflects on everybody.

REMEMBER

It can be hard sometimes, but you must learn to leave your personal problems at home and always be cheerful with your clients and colleagues. Friends will want to share your problems, but not during working hours.

You will spend a lot of time in the company of the people you work with. You will not always like everyone, but that does not really matter. You must accept that people are different and that, at work, mutual respect is more important than being the best of friends.

REMEMBER

You may be needed to help with outside demonstrations and other promotional activities, which help to make the business a success.

If you can be described as the following, you will not have too much trouble earning the respect of your colleagues (and you will probably be very popular as well!):

- conscientious – working to the best of your ability and being thorough in everything you do
- dedicated – showing commitment to the job and being prepared to put in extra time when required
- self-motivated – keeping yourself busy and not always needing to be told what to do
- determined – wanting to succeed and taking every opportunity to improve your professional skills and knowledge of the job
- responsible – not needing to be constantly supervised or watched over, having the confidence of your colleagues to get on with the work
- well presented – appearing smart and professional, always projecting a good image of the salon
- sensitive – accepting that there is room for different views and opinions, never making tactless remarks that could offend
- reliable – arriving in good time for work and not taking time off unnecessarily
- co-operative – being helpful and supportive, making a positive contribution to the team effort
- flexible – taking things in your stride, adapting to different situations and circumstances without complaining or showing resistance
- warm and friendly – making everyone feel that you really enjoy your work and that you have a genuine interest in others.

REMEMBER

Working closely with others can sometimes have its frustrations and tensions. You should always try to be sensitive to the feelings of others and act accordingly.

A PRACTICAL GUIDE TO BEAUTY THERAPY

Everyone who works in a salon contributes to its success. Cleaners, receptionists, therapists, technicians and management all have roles that are different yet essential to the operation. Take pride in your own work and value that of others. Once you have proved yourself as a member of the team you will have earned the respect of colleagues and the loyalty of your clients.

ACTIVITY

Activity 2.1: Team work

Working with a colleague, imagine a typical day in the salon. Think of six ways in which you could use your initiative to help out generally or support a member of your team if a problem occurs. Compare your list with those produced by other team members and discuss the results.

ACTIVITY

Activity 2.2: Face the music!

Sometimes it can be very difficult to make judgements about ourselves. Being an effective team member really has more to do with how others see us, whether in employment or during training.

Working in a small group, agree an appropriate rating scale for grading each other's professional qualities. For example, you may decide to use a scale of 1–5, where 1 is disastrous and 5 is excellent! Use this scale to grade each member of your group against the following attributes:

- conscientious
- self-motivated
- responsible
- well presented
- sensitive
- reliable
- co-operative
- flexible
- friendly.

Talk quite openly about the scores you give. Justify the grades you award and be positive with the advice you give colleagues on how they might improve their team-working skills. It is important to listen to what is said about you! Accept any criticism in the spirit in which it is given and treat it as a valuable aid to learning.

Key skills

Many of the skills that you need for being a successful beauty therapist are not specialist, technical skills, for example those required to perform a massage routine or apply make-up; they are personal skills, which, although being essential for work, can be transferred to many different situations in life. These transferable, personal skills are known as '**key skills**'.

Accrediting key skills

The portfolio of assessment evidence that you collect for your NVQ Beauty Therapy will contain evidence that can also be used to accredit you with NVQ key skills. Discuss the best way of collecting and cross-referencing portfolio evidence with your supervisor.

Key skills cover a broad range of skills needed in everyday situations:

- communication
- application of number
- information technology
- working with others
- improving own learning and performance
- problem solving.

Many of the activities included in this book will give you the opportunity to use one or more key skills. When you have completed the activity, keep the evidence for your portfolio of assessment.

Communication skills

Good communication skills are essential for building up successful relationships. A breakdown in communication always creates problems and, in business, this can have serious consequences.

Whether dealing on a one-to-one basis, for example with a colleague or client, or with a group of people, possibly your audience at a demonstration event, you must always be able to communicate effectively. To be accredited with this key skill, you will need to show evidence that you can:

- contribute to discussions
- give a short talk
- produce and interpret written and spoken communications
- understand and use images.

Good communication skills help to build trust and develop loyal customers

REMEMBER

Good communication is about always understanding and being understood by others. Learn to ask the right sort of questions to get the information you want and make sure you really do 'listen' to the answers.

Reading, writing, speaking and listening are essential skills for ensuring effective communications in the salon. When communications break down, problems occur. Everyone working in the salon must have good communication skills.

You must be able to:

- read information that is essential for carrying out your work safely and effectively – identify those details that are important
- write clearly in the appropriate format – check that what you have written can be read by others and makes sense
- speak clearly and confidently – make sure that information is accurate and explained well
- listen carefully and 'hear' what is being said – be sure of the facts.

REMEMBER

Reading is not just about understanding written words. Sometimes instructions are given using symbols and diagrams. These can often be more effective than using words, particularly for people who have difficulty reading or understanding the language.

Reading

Some of the information you need will be written down. You will not be able to use the information unless you can first make sense of it! Effective reading involves selecting and reading for a particular purpose, getting the information you need, checking your understanding of what you have read and summarising the information obtained. The following are examples of written information you will need to read in the salon. Can you think of any more?

- Appointment details
- Client records
- Product labels
- Treatment information
- Price lists
- Promotional material
- Instruction leaflets
- Journals.

ACTIVITY

Activity 2.3: Using symbols and diagrams

1 Think of three different examples in the salon where symbols or diagrams are used to give instructions. State how effective you think each of your examples is and explain why.

2 Create three new symbols or diagrams that could be used in the salon. They might be used for display as notices or included in salon literature or instruction leaflets for use by clients or staff. Compare your ideas with those of your colleagues. Decide which ones are worth producing on a computer for use in your salon.

Writing

Any written information you provide must be clear, accurate and easily understood by other people. This way, misunderstandings are avoided. At work, you may have to adapt your writing to suit different purposes and know how to use different types of written material for obtaining, providing and keeping information. Sometimes this will mean using abbreviations or codes, for example when making an entry in the appointment book or filling in a client's record card. Always follow the salon's procedures. Do not introduce abbreviations or codes that only you understand!

GOOD PRACTICE

Always read back over what you have written. Check that it contains all the relevant information and that it makes sense. This is particularly important when taking messages and dealing with information over the telephone. Here are some examples of activities that require good writing:

- entering details in the appointment book
- making out appointment cards
- filling in client record cards
- writing out a bill
- passing on a message
- writing up a report.

Communicating over the telephone at reception

GOOD PRACTICE

It will help you both as a speaker and a listener to learn how to 'paraphrase'. Paraphrasing is summarising in your own words what was said. This is not the same as repeating exactly what someone else has said. Paraphrasing gives you the opportunity to clarify things and check that there are no misunderstandings.

Speaking

During a normal working day, you will speak to many different types of people about a wide range of things. It is important that you do this well. Good speaking skills are essential for keeping up the salon's image with clients, suppliers, members of the public and other professional colleagues. Most of your speaking will take place on a one-to-one basis, either directly or indirectly over the telephone. At other times, you may be speaking to a group of people or a larger audience.

Whatever the situation, you will need to:

- speak clearly
- use language that is appropriate
- emphasise key points
- ask the right sorts of questions
- know how to respond to others
- say things that are relevant to the subject
- say things that keep the discussion going
- check and show understanding of what has been said.

Listening

Listening is quite a hard thing to do. This is because we can think much faster than we can speak. There is a time delay between someone's speech and our mental thought processes when we are listening. If we allow ourselves to get distracted from what someone is saying, by thinking of other things, we stop listening and information gets 'lost'.

REMEMBER

It is much easier to give the speaker your attention when dealing with them face to face. Body language and facial expressions help you to pick up things that are more difficult to grasp on the telephone (when you cannot see the speaker). During a phone conversation you have to work harder at listening and checking your understanding of what is being said.

Here are some pointers to help you become a good listener:

- be interested in what is being said – even if it doesn't sound interesting, it might turn out to be!
- concentrate on what the speaker is saying
- resist the temptation to anticipate what is going to be said
- do not interrupt, but wait until there is a pause or you are asked to speak
- ask questions to check your understanding of what has been said
- take notes if necessary.

Listening carefully to a client asking advice

Things to avoid when listening:

- being too tired to pay attention properly
- deciding in advance that there is no point in listening
- external noises and distractions
- switching off because of 'information overload'
- listening only for the bits you want to hear
- switching off because you think you know where the conversation is going
- thinking of what you are going to say when it is your turn.

Asking questions

All information passed on and used in the salon must be accurate and relevant. This is particularly important, for example, when advising clients about the best choice of treatments and products or needing a colleague to help you with a problem. The way you ask questions will determine the usefulness of the information you get back.

Examples of 'open' questions:

- When are you available on Monday?
- What treatments have you had at the salon before?
- How do you normally look after your nails?
- Why have you been using this skin treatment cream?

Examples of 'closed' questions:

- Are you available at 10 o'clock on Monday morning?
- Have you had treatment at the salon before?
- Do you have a regular nail care routine?
- Does your skin normally feel dry?

What you must do:

- use 'closed' questions only to get short, straightforward answers (usually yes or no). Closed questions do not check understanding. They just help to confirm or eliminate ideas
- use 'open' questions to get fuller and more detailed answers. Open questions are good because they help to develop the conversation and provide more information. Open questions give the person more room to say whatever they need to say. They often begin with how, what, when, where, who or why
- ask probing questions – 'Tell me more about ...' or, 'So, why was that?' These questions also tend to include how, what, when, where, who and why
- ask one question at a time
- wait for a good time to ask a question
- ask questions sensitively to avoid embarrassment or reluctance by the person to give you a full or honest answer
- wait for the answer before asking another question
- keep asking questions until you are satisfied with the answer.

ACTIVITY

Activity 2.4: Asking questions

Compare the above examples of closed and open questions. Decide which version of each question is the more useful, the closed question or the open question. It could be that both types are useful, but in different circumstances. Explain your answers.

Body language

The way you present yourself is a form of communication. Always project a professional image. This helps to develop trust and confidence in your work.

- Stand or sit 'tall', that is with your back straight and your head held up. Apart from being good for your posture, it shows that you are confident. Clients trust a person who appears confident. People who slouch give out the wrong 'signals'.

Crowding over somebody can be very intimidating!

- Use positive hand movements and open gestures. These are friendly and welcoming. Avoid finger pointing or folding your arms across your chest. These can be considered aggressive.

- Keep your facial expressions relaxed, and smile genuinely and often. People always feel better and respond well to a smile. It is very difficult not to smile back at someone who is smiling at you!

- Always face the person and maintain good eye contact when speaking or listening. People who avoid eye contact or look down give the impression of being dishonest.

- Tilt your head slightly and nod occasionally when listening. This shows that you are concentrating and are interested in what is being said.

- Try to move smoothly in a relaxed manner. People who are confident use steady, unhurried movements.

- During a conversation, keep a reasonable space between yourself and the other person. Crowding over somebody when speaking to them can feel very intimidating.

ACTIVITY

Activity 2.5: Communication skills

Working with a colleague, read a current copy of one of the professional journals. Your library or study centre should have one if you don't own one yourself. Pick a topic which interests you, plan some additional research and then write a short report of what you have learned. Prepare a five-minute presentation about your chosen topic to a small audience, using notes and images to help you. Ask your audience questions to check that they have been listening. Listen and respond to their answers to check that they have understood.

Application of number

Many of the tasks you undertake at work will require you to be competent when working with numbers, for example when dealing with money, measuring out quantities, estimating amounts, working out your commission. To be accredited with this key skill, you will need to show evidence that you can work with numbers when:

- collecting and recording information
- interpreting and presenting information
- carrying out calculations.

If maths was never your best or favourite subject at school, don't worry! This key skill is about the way you work with and use numbers every day in your job, often without thinking about it.

Information technology

Computers are used widely in business. A lot of important information can be produced, stored and retrieved on a computer. Records can be kept and databases created. Dealing with financial information becomes much easier and less time consuming using a computer. Business letters and promotional materials can also be produced. To be accredited with this key skill you will need to show evidence that you can:

- find, explore and develop information
- process and present information
- evaluate the use of information technology.

The skills needed to operate the salon's computerised systems may seem daunting to anyone who has not received basic IT (information technology) training, but, for example, once you have learned how to use a computerised appointment system or have entered client details into the salon's database, you will soon begin to appreciate the importance of computers to the efficiency and effectiveness of the business.

Receptionist inputting sales information into client database

Working with others

A successful business employs committed, hard-working staff who pull together as a team and are motivated towards the same goals.

To be accredited with this key skill, you will need to show evidence that you can take responsibility for work you have agreed as an individual and also as a member of a team. This will involve:

- identifying collective goals and responsibilities
- working to collective goals.

Discussing targets at a staff meeting

A well-managed business will have a very clear idea of where it is going, and when and how it is going to get there. 'Where' it is going will be written into the business's strategic plan. 'How' it is going to get there will be written into the business's operational plan. Operational plans are concerned with the day-to-day activities, which keep the business moving, growing and becoming more successful.

Successful operational plans rely on the support and commitment of the people who work in the business. A good business will ensure that there are clear lines of communication between managers, supervisors and staff and that regular, effective supervision meetings take place to ensure that everyone is working to their potential towards the same goals.

People who don't 'pull their weight', or are sloppy in their work, let down the team and threaten the success of the business. There should be procedures in place to deal with competence and behavioural issues at work. These will include **capability**, grievance and **appeals procedures**, details of which should be included in the company's staff handbook or be available from your supervisor:

- capability – consistently performing to the required standards; where a person is found 'not' to be capable, depending on the problem, they may need additional training and support or, in more serious cases, dealing with through **disciplinary procedures**
- grievance – where a person feels they are being treated unfairly and makes a complaint; the **grievance procedure** sets out how the complaint will be investigated, by whom, by when and the alternative possible outcomes
- appeals – a person who has been disciplined or has had a grievance proven against them may appeal against the decision using the 'appeals' procedure; there are usually set timescales involved and if the appeal cannot be resolved satisfactorily, it may be necessary to go outside the business for help.

Improving own learning and performance

If you are clear about where you want to go and what you have to do to get there, you will find it much easier to achieve your personal goals. Improving own learning and performance is about recognising your personal strengths and weaknesses, and putting together an action plan for building on the strengths and tackling the weaknesses. You may already have started this process. If not, your NVQ training programme is an ideal starting point. By reviewing your progress periodically with your supervisor and setting new targets, you should, ultimately, achieve your career aims. Hopefully you will get good advice and lots of encouragement on the way. To be accredited with this key skill you will need to show evidence that you can:

- identify targets
- follow a schedule to meet targets.

REMEMBER

Good employers understand the importance of getting good staff 'on board' and keeping them. Make sure you understand where the business is going, and what you and your team have to do to help it get there.

The growth and development of a business is very much dependent on the growth and development of the people who work in it. Hopefully, while you are working for someone else, you will have employers who understand the importance of investing in the ongoing training and development of their staff. Make it your business to seek out learning opportunities and let your employer know what your ambitions are and how they can help you. If they are ambitious for their business and they feel that your ambitions 'match' their ambitions, they should be only too happy to co-operate with your **personal development plan**. Regular supervision and appraisal processes help to keep your personal development plan under review.

GOOD PRACTICE

It is important that you establish good working relationships with your supervisor. Ultimately, your supervisor is the person you go to when things go wrong or when you have a problem. In these situations, what you learn is essential to your continuing learning and development. You need to reflect on what has happened and what you have learned.

Supervisions and appraisals

In a well-managed business, you will have regular **supervisions** with your line manager. Supervisions are progress reviews. Their effectiveness relies on the competence of your line manager to understand your job role and know how you are performing in that role. You should come out of your supervisions being clear about what you are doing well and where you need to improve. The advice you get will often be linked to **productivity targets** set by your supervisor. These might identify the number of clients you are expected to treat over the week, the amount of income you are expected to generate through treatments and retail sales, and other targets related to your job. Regular **appraisals** will identify the further training or learning you need in order to develop in line with the needs of the business. Sometimes, tight deadlines for training might be imposed, depending on the timescales involved.

ACTIVITY

Activity 2.6: Improving own learning and performance

Using the computer, create a table entitled 'My personal development plan'. Use it to map out your productivity and learning targets for the next month. Make it clear when and how you are going to achieve your targets. Discuss your plan with your supervisor and make sure you are realistic about what you can achieve. Arrange a date and time to review your progress. Remember: plan, do, review!

Time management

Time management is an important part of being successful both at work and in your personal life. These days people have to 'juggle' in order to achieve a balance between work, family commitments, leisure and learning opportunities. A balanced life is a healthier life, so, if you have lots of different commitments, you need to map them out over the time you have available and, within the map, set yourself appropriate and realistic targets. Planning the achievement of your NVQ qualification is a good start! If it all feels a bit too much, get family, friends, colleagues and your supervisor to help you.

REMEMBER

Plan, do, review! This is useful advice for managing your time both at home and at work.

Managing your time at work

Your effectiveness at work relies, in part, on good time management skills. This means not just arriving on time, but also organising your roles and responsibilities efficiently and effectively within the working day. Also, you need to make the best use of quieter times, perhaps by reading up on new products and treatments or helping out colleagues who would benefit from your assistance. To some extent, the management of your time is influenced by the nature of the services offered and their associated **commercial timings**. These will have been considered by the receptionist when filling in your column in the appointment book and may vary slightly between businesses, depending on the specialist nature of the treatments.

The range of standard service times for NVQ Level 2 Beauty Therapy

	SERVICE (EXCLUDING CONSULTATION AND PREPARATION)	MAX TIME (MINUTES)
1	Eyebrow shape	15
2	Eyelash tint	20
3	Facial	60
4	Make-up	45
5	Manicure	45
6	Pedicure	60
7	Eyebrow wax	15
8	Underarm wax	15
9	Half leg wax	30
10	Bikini-line wax	15
11	Arm wax	30
12	Full leg wax	45
13	Half leg, bikini, underarm	45
14	Full leg, bikini, underarm	60
15	Facial, including eyelash tint and eyebrow shape	75
16	Eyebrow shape and eyelash tint	30
17	Eyebrow tint	10
18	Eyebrow tint, eyebrow shape and eyelash tint	30
19	Ear piercing	15
20	Nail art	5–10 per nail
21	Facial and make-up	90
22	False eyelashes	15

This table has been produced by HABIA (Hairdressing and Beauty Industry Authority)

Problem solving

Your day-to-day work will require you to make decisions and tackle a range of problems, most of which are fairly routine. Your beauty therapy training will provide you with the skills and knowledge to deal with many of the problems that are likely to occur. The salon's policies and procedures will provide further guidelines to help you with others. To be accredited with the key skill 'Problem solving', you will need to show evidence that you can:

● use established procedures to clarify routine problems
● select standard solutions to routine problems.

As you become more experienced, you will probably be given more responsibility. This will inevitably mean you will have a greater range of problems to deal with. Learn from people who are more senior in the business. See how they tackle different sorts of problems and ask their advice.

A PRACTICAL GUIDE TO BEAUTY THERAPY

Activity 2.7: Key skills

From this list of work-related activities, try to identify which of the six key skills you would need to do the job properly. Remember that there may be more than one key skill involved. In each case, discuss the best way of producing assessment evidence:

- selling skin-care products to a client
- giving a talk and make-up demonstration to a women's group
- creating and sending out a 'special offer' mail shot
- working on reception during a busy period
- conducting a client consultation
- cashing up at the end of the day
- making out a spreadsheet to show the daily takings
- checking off a new delivery of stock.

If you are having a personal problem with the behaviour of a colleague at work, it is always best to tackle it tactfully, as soon as possible and directly with the person concerned. If the problem continues and it becomes a professional problem, impacting on the business, you should report it to your supervisor.

MULTIPLE CHOICE QUIZ

Develop and maintain your effectiveness at work

There may appear to be more than one correct answer. Read each question carefully before making your final decision. Discuss your answers with your colleagues and see if you all agree. If you don't, talk through the issues raised.

1 It is important that everyone at work:
(a) likes each other
(b) tolerates each other
(c) respects each other
(d) understands each other.

2 A person who keeps themselves busy is:
(a) determined
(b) conscientious
(c) reliable
(d) self-motivated.

3 Key skills are:
(a) personal and non-transferable
(b) technical and transferable
(c) personal and transferable
(d) technical and non-transferable.

4 Employers need people with effective key skills because they:
(a) help make the business successful
(b) help promote the business
(c) are flexible
(d) are reliable.

5 One example of a communication skill is:
(a) listening
(b) problem solving
(c) working with others
(d) being warm and friendly.

6 Regular supervision meetings ensure that:
(a) problems with individuals are dealt with immediately
(b) people can air their grievances
(c) everyone is working effectively towards their targets
(d) everyone is working as hard as they can.

7 Details of the company's standards and procedures should be contained in the:
(a) staff handbook
(b) staff training plan
(c) contract of employment
(d) written terms and conditions of employment.

8 The main purpose of an appraisal is to:
(a) review progress since the last supervision
(b) prepare for the next supervision
(c) identify training and development needs
(d) identify key skills development needs.

KEY TERMS

You should now understand the following words or phrases. If you do not, go back through the chapter and find out what they mean:

Key skills	Productivity targets	Team work
Personal development plan	Supervisions	Appraisals
Time management	Grievance procedure	Commercial timings
Appeals procedure	Capability	Disciplinary procedure

Chapter 3 Health and safety

Ensure your own actions reduce risks to health and safety

After working through this chapter you will be able to:

- identify and report potential hazards in the workplace
- assess and reduce risks to health and safety
- control the salon environment
- carry out emergency procedures
- carry out sanitisation and sterilisation procedures
- carry out security procedures
- understand workplace policies relating to health and safety.

Before you work through this chapter: Be wise and revise!
Revision topics to help you achieve this unit:

Ensure your own actions reduce risks to health and safety

TOPIC	CHAPTER	PAGE
Health and safety executive	1	4
Health and safety legislation	1	3
Environmental Protection Act 1990	1	10
Employer's liability	1	10
Public liability	1	10
Appearance and personal hygiene	1	17

Although the employer is legally accountable for the health and safety of people working in or visiting the salon, it is the staff who, on a day-to-day basis, are at the forefront of business operations. All employees have a professional responsibility for ensuring high standards of health and safety. The standards should be set out in the salon's policies and procedures.

Controlling the salon environment

The salon must offer the same high standards of hygiene, safety and comfort throughout the working day. This is to ensure that all clients receive the same quality of service, whatever the time of their appointment. At all times, the salon must be:

- clean and tidy
- maintained at a reasonable temperature
- well ventilated
- well lit.

Maintaining a clean and tidy salon

REMEMBER

Cleaning products contain chemicals, therefore the COSHH regulations apply (see page 9). Always read and follow the manufacturers' instructions carefully when preparing, using and disposing of cleaning solutions.

If careful thought has gone into designing the salon, all work surfaces, wall and floor coverings, furniture and fittings will have been chosen not only to look attractive, but also to be fit for purpose and easy to clean. This is particularly important for items that will be coming into direct contact with clients or with materials and equipment that will be used during treatments.

Couches, stools and worktops should be wiped over regularly with a mild liquid detergent which cleans, deodorises and disinfects. Most products of this type are safe for use on plastics and metal, and can also be used effectively for cleaning other surfaces such as countertops, sinks, workstations, footbaths, tanning beds and telephones.

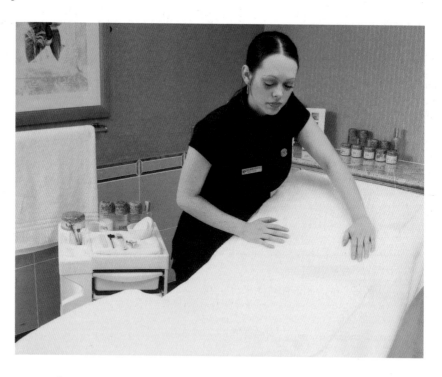

The treatment area must look and be scrupulously clean and tidy for each client

What you must do:

- make sure you know the salon's cleaning policy and follow the procedures
- practise quick but effective tidying and cleaning routines in between clients
- know which cleaning methods are used in your salon and for what purpose
- understand the special care that must be taken when using different types of cleaning products.

A PRACTICAL GUIDE TO BEAUTY THERAPY

Dealing with waste

Waste should be dealt with promptly. It should not be allowed to build up on trolleys and work surfaces.

What you must do:

- dispose of waste in a covered bin
- remove salon waste daily
- place contaminated needles in a yellow 'sharps' container: when full, this should be disposed of by a reputable hygiene disposal company, as advised by the local environmental health department
- clear away and dispose of broken glass carefully after an accident.

> ## GOOD PRACTICE
>
> When dealing with broken glass:
>
> - clear it away immediately
> - try and avoid handling broken glass; use a dustpan and brush
> - if you have to touch broken glass, wear strong gloves to protect your hands
> - ensure broken glass does not cause injury to anyone else once you have disposed of it; wrap it up securely in several layers of newspaper before placing in a waste bin.

> ## GOOD PRACTICE
>
> If a spillage occurs, wipe it up immediately and make sure the floor is dry to prevent slipping.

> ## GOOD PRACTICE
>
> Make sure that the waste resulting from your treatments is placed directly into a lined container and disposed of in a large, sealed refuse sack with other salon waste.

ACTIVITY

Activity 3.1: Maintaining a clean and tidy salon

Cleaning and tidying procedures vary between different areas of the salon, depending on the nature of the services provided and the way the area is designed, furnished and fitted to provide those services.

Produce a booklet for new trainees, which gives clear instructions on the cleaning and maintenance policy for your salon. Your booklet should cover each of the functional areas, for example: reception, facial room, waxing area, sun bed and should include:

- details of all cleaning procedures including their frequency, the materials and products used with special instructions for their use (COSHH)
- advice on the removal of waste; the type of waste may vary in different areas of the salon
- clear guidelines on how the area should be maintained during and between treatments.

Your booklet should measure 148 mm × 210 mm (A5 size). Give the booklet a title and include a contents page. Each page should be numbered. Your booklet will look more professional if you produce it on a computer.

Water supply

The salon needs a constant supply of clean hot and cold water. Problems with plumbing and drains may mean that treatments have to be delayed or even cancelled. This can cause financial loss to the business.

Do not waste water. It is becoming increasingly expensive and, in some areas of the country, less plentiful in supplies. Water is heated up by either gas, oil or electricity, all of which have to be paid for. Heating costs are a major expense for the salon. Wasting hot water is literally pouring money down the drain!

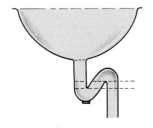

The S-bend waste trap beneath a wash basin

What you must do:

- report a blocked sink immediately to your supervisor
- do not leave the hot water tap running longer than necessary; this is both wasteful and expensive
- do not flush solid or semi-solid materials down the sink; they may cause a blockage in the pipes that carry water away from the salon to the drains outside
- in the event of a pipe bursting, turn off the water at the stopcock; this will stop the supply of water to the salon from outside
- if water that comes out of the tap is discoloured or smells strange, report it to your supervisor who should contact the local water authority for advice.

HEALTH MATTERS

Do not delay in attending to a blocked sink. Waste water that is left standing smells unpleasant. Also, bacterial growth increases and this may spread disease.

HEALTH MATTERS

In the event of a water pipe bursting, it is advisable to turn off the electricity as well as the water. Until you have done this, you should not touch any light switches or electrical appliances. You could get electrocuted.

The plumbing beneath the basin has a waste trap which holds water and stops gases and smells from the drains travelling back up the pipes. If a small object accidentally falls through the plug hole, the waste trap can be investigated to see if it has settled there.

Heating and ventilation

The working temperature of the salon should be 16 °C (60–80 °F) after the first hour. Thermostatically controlled heating systems keep the salon at a comfortable temperature. They have a device that switches off the heat when the required temperature has been reached and then turns it on again as the temperature begins to fall. The heating method should not give out dangerous or offensive fumes.

There should be enough ventilation to keep the air fresh and to prevent the build-up of fumes. Extractor fans and open windows help to remove pungent smells, for example those produced by solvent-based manicure preparations and some nail technology products.

A full air-conditioning system is ideal for keeping the salon comfortable and fresh. This method recirculates air and replaces it with clean, fresh air heated to the correct temperature. It also helps to control humidity levels where there is water vapour being produced, for example by a steam bath or shower.

HEALTH MATTERS

Too much exposure to pungent smells can cause nausea and headaches. Where possible, the layout of the salon should ensure that treatments creating fumes take place near an open window.

What you must do:

- know how to control the heating and ventilation systems in your salon
- if possible, open a nearby window when using products that smell strongly.

Lighting

The lighting in the salon should be bright enough for everyone to move around safely but not so bright as to create glare.

Adequate and suitable lighting is needed in order to:

- enable people to see what they are doing and where they are going
- show up potential hazards such as a step
- encourage and highlight cleanliness
- prevent eye strain.

Natural daylight is the best sort of light and has the advantage of showing up 'true' colours. Artificial lighting often distorts colours. Warm white fluorescent tubes are nearly as good as daylight for colour matching. The special lighting needed for close work is usually provided by a magnifying angle-poise lamp containing a circular fluorescent tube.

What you must do:

- always make sure that you have enough light to work safely and accurately
- ensure that neither your client nor you are dazzled by a bright light
- report glaring light bulbs and flickering tubes to your supervisor so that they can be checked or replaced.

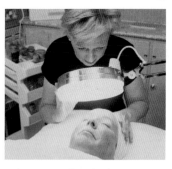

Using an anglepoise lamp to examine the skin

Health and safety

Under the Health and Safety at Work Act 1974, everyone is obliged always to work safely and to have consideration for their colleagues at work. You need to know the possible risks to safety in your salon and how to prevent anything that could result in personal injury or damage to property. Should an emergency occur, you need to be able to do whatever you can to protect yourself and others.

What you must do:

- take reasonable care to avoid injury to yourself and others
- co-operate with others in matters of safety
- avoid interfering with or misusing anything provided to protect your health and safety
- take part in all health and safety training provided by your employer
- read and make sure you understand all safety information provided for you
- know the salon's health and safety procedures.

Physical safety

Accidents can happen, not just when you are treating clients, but also when taking breaks, returning equipment to store, dealing with stock, cleaning up or even just moving around the salon. The employer is responsible for ensuring that the layout of the salon is safe and that staff have been trained to protect themselves from physical injury. Accidents are far less likely to occur in a 'safe' working environment. The main cause of accidents is negligence.

What you must do:

- keep alert; as soon as you spot a potential danger, either do something about it or report it to someone who can
- be conscientious in all aspects of your work; protect yourself and those around you.

REMEMBER

A *hazard* is something with the potential to cause harm, for example a trailing cable from a piece of electrical equipment.

A *risk* is the likelihood of the hazard's potential being realised, for example if the cable is trailing across the floor where it is likely to trip someone up. Ensuring the cable runs along a wall, out of the way, reduces the risk.

Lifting and handling

Serious injuries can result from lifting, carrying and moving heavy loads. You must be able to identify 'safe' weights for lifting and know how to adapt your posture to avoid straining your back. This is particularly important when moving equipment, assisting clients on and off the beauty couch, and when dealing with stock.

What you must do:

- ensure your route is clear
- grasp the load firmly with the palms of your hands (not fingertips)

A PRACTICAL GUIDE TO BEAUTY THERAPY

- hold the load close to your body
- do not change your grip while carrying
- let your legs, not your back, take the strain
- keep your spine straight
- avoid jerking; never twist your body while picking up a load
- lift in easy stages, eg floor to knee to start with
- avoid over-stretching.

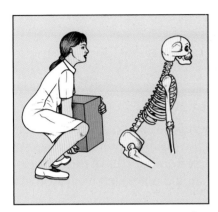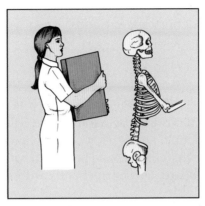

Correct lifting and carrying technique; avoid straining your back when moving heavy stock

ACTIVITY

Activity 3.2: Accident report form

1 Design an accident report form for use in your salon. Make sure the layout is clear and that it covers all of the necessary information. Provide enough space for details to be written in by hand. When you are happy with your basic design, produce the final report form using a computer.

2 Working with a colleague, create a case study of an accident occurring in a salon. Feel free to use your imagination! Ask your colleague to write a report of the accident using your form.

3 Decide how effective your report form is and suggest improvements that could be made.

4 Discuss the legal implications of the accident you have used for your case study and suggest what follow-up action you think would be most appropriate.

SELF-CHECKS

Physical safety

1 Give two responsibilities of the employer for ensuring the safety of staff.

2 State four responsibilities of the employee for ensuring the safety of themselves and others.

3 When are accidents most likely to occur in the salon?

4 List four ways of avoiding back strain when lifting and carrying a heavy load.

5 Name three pieces of legislation that cover the health and safety of clients in the salon.

6 Distinguish between a hazard and a risk. Give one example to explain your answer.

Fire safety

A fire can close the business temporarily or permanently, destroying important papers and records at the same time. It can cause extensive damage to property and result in serious injuries or even death. Everybody in the business must know how to prevent a fire from happening and how to deal with a fire if one happens. This is described as **fire safety**.

The common causes of fires are:

- electrical faults
- smouldering cigarette ends
- open flames
- matches
- heaters.

All electrical work in the salon should be undertaken by a qualified electrician. Ideally, smoking should not be allowed anywhere on the business premises. Main supplies of flammable materials should be stored well away from sources of heat in a closed, metal cupboard. Loose paper and cardboard should not be left lying around.

What you must do:

- keep flammable products away from sources of heat
- avoid overloading electrical circuits
- never leave the flex of an electric heater trailing where it could be tripped over
- switch off and disconnect electrical appliances after use
- do not smoke or allow smoking except in specially designated areas
- avoid placing towels over electric or gas heaters
- use a safety lighter in preference to matches for lighting a gas heater
- before leaving at night, check that bins are emptied and that all electrical appliances are unplugged.

Fire-fighting equipment

A fire should be detected and tackled within a few minutes of it breaking out. Employees should be trained in the correct use of fire-fighting equipment. This may be used to put out a small fire but, more usually, it helps to keep control of the fire until the fire brigade arrives.

The local fire authority will provide advice regarding the best locations and types of equipment for the business.

Fire extinguishers

There are different types of extinguishers for different types of fires. Using the wrong type could make the fire worse.

A PRACTICAL GUIDE TO BEAUTY THERAPY

Know your fire extinguisher colour code

	RED	**BLUE**	**CREAM**	**BLACK**	**GREEN**
Contains	Water	Dry powder	Foam	CO_2 (carbon dioxide)	Vapourising liquids
Safe for electrical fires?	Unsafe all voltages	Safe all voltages	Unsafe all voltages	Safe all voltages	Safe all voltages
Use on	Wood, paper, textiles etc.	Flammable liquids	Flammable liquids	Flammable liquids	Flammable liquids

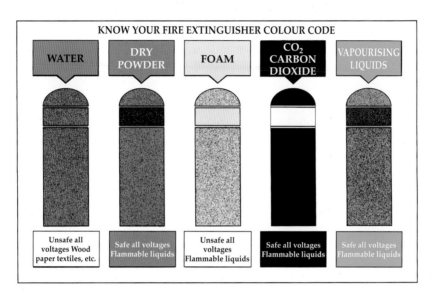

Colour-coded fire extinguishers

GOOD PRACTICE

The layout of the salon should be designed to limit the spread of fire. Treatments that use highly flammable substances or heating processes should be kept in a special area of the salon, away from the main activities.

Fire blanket
A blanket is used to smother a small, localised fire or if a person's clothing is on fire.

Sand
A bucket of sand is used to soak up liquids that are the source of a fire and, also, to smother the fire.

Water hoses
Hoses are used to extinguish large fires, for example those fuelled by paper. Buckets of water may be used to extinguish a small fire fuelled by paper.

Evacuating the salon
Once it has started, a fire can rip through the premises in minutes. The most important thing is to get away from the fire to safety. This means getting everybody out of the salon, even if they are in the middle of a treatment. If it is safe to do so, a designated person should take the appointment book and visitor's book with them as they leave the building. When everybody is outside, they should gather at a muster point. Their names should be checked against the names in the books. The emergency services must be told if anyone is missing.

GOOD PRACTICE

If you have time, shut windows and doors and turn off electric and gas appliances. This will help to prevent the fire from spreading.

Fire-fighting equipment

What you must do:

● never ignore the smell of burning: if there is a fire, the sooner you know the better

● sound the fire alarm if there is one

● know where the fire-fighting equipment is kept and how to use it

● know the emergency evacuation procedures for your salon

● know the location of the nearest fire exit

● know where to assemble outside the building on evacuation

● check for injuries and continue to take care of your client and others while you wait for the emergency services to arrive

● know how to call the emergency services

● find out where the nearest phone is.

Calling the emergency services

It is very important to try not to panic and to speak clearly and not too fast when calling for help from the emergency services.

What you must do:

● dial 999

● tell the operator you want the Fire Service

● give your telephone number and location. If you are in a public telephone box, these details will be displayed

● wait for the Fire Service to come on the line

● give the full address of the emergency and other relevant details of the fire

● report any injuries

● listen carefully to any questions you are asked and answer them calmly

● listen very carefully to any instructions you are given

● after the call, replace the receiver and wait with the others, in a safe place, for the Fire Service to arrive.

ACTIVITY

Activity 3.3: Fire safety

1. Draw a scale floor plan of the salon, indicating the position of doors and windows. On the plan, show the location of the fire-fighting equipment. Clearly label the type of fire-fighting equipment present.
2. Using colour, indicate the fire exit routes from each area of the salon.
3. Identify the specific location of the 'muster' point outside the business premises.

SELF-CHECKS

Fire safety

1. State two of the most likely causes of fire in the salon.
2. Name two types of fire extinguisher normally recommended for salon use. State the colour of each of these types of extinguisher.
3. What is the purpose of a fire blanket?
4. What steps should be taken to ensure that there is no one left in the salon after a fire has started?
5. State two ways of preventing a fire from spreading.
6. Name the three emergency services. State the telephone number that should be dialled to contact the emergency services.

Electrical safety

All electrical items must be tested for **electrical safety** at least once a year by a qualified electrician. Records should be kept of the tests. The main risks associated with unsafe electrical equipment are **electric shock** and fire.

REMEMBER

You must not treat clients with any piece of electrical equipment for which you have not received training. A record must be kept of when the training took place.

Electric shock

If a fault develops in an electrical appliance, the outer casing may become live. This may cause anyone using or touching the appliance to receive an electric shock. The current will pass straight through the body from the mains to earth, contracting the muscles in its path. The muscles may stay contracted, causing breathing and the heart to stop. A mild electric shock is unpleasant. A severe electric shock can be fatal. For the treatment of electric shock, see the table on page 48.

Fire

A fire can occur as the result of poor electrical maintenance, for example faulty or damaged flexes, plugs and switches; also, if the electrical circuit becomes overloaded. This can happen when two or more machines are being operated from one socket using an adaptor. If the correct fuse is not fitted, the socket may become overloaded with current and get dangerously hot.

REMEMBER

Electrical safety is just as important in the staff room as it is in the salon. A kettle that is unsafe can present as big a risk to health as a faulty piece of salon equipment.

Electrical precautions

Basic safety checks should be carried out before using any piece of electrical equipment. Machines should be handled carefully and stored safely between treatments.

When using any electrical appliance or piece of equipment, always check that:

- cables and flexes are in good condition with no signs of fraying or worn insulation
- there are no trailing flexes that could cause someone to trip
- the plug is intact; if cracked or broken it must be replaced
- there are no loose connections; leads should feel firmly attached and switches should be secure
- the appliance is on a level and stable base
- there is no water in the immediate area
- the appliance is switched off and disconnected from the mains after use
- the appliance is left clean and stored properly
- cables and flexes are wound up and secured to avoid them becoming damaged in between uses
- sockets are not overloaded or broken.

You should know how to wire a plug:

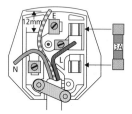

1 Cut away the outer cable, unscrew the cable grip and insert the cable

2 Cut away the insulation using wire strippers

3 Twist the copper strands together

4 Insert each wire into the correct pin

5 Tighten all the screws and the cable grip. Attach the plastic backplate

Wire a plug

ACTIVITY

Activity 3.4: Electrical safety

Modern electrical appliances have built-in safety features which prevent the current from 'straying' if there is a fault. Plugs, flexes and sockets also have safety features that give some protection against damage from electrical 'overload'.

1 Find out about five safety features common to all electrical appliances. Write short notes on each one.

2 With a friend or colleague, study one piece of electrical salon equipment in detail. Read the literature supplied with the machine and discuss the safety features you find. Identify any signs or symbols showing that the appliance has met the minimum safety standards.

Identifying and reporting faulty equipment

Once you have been trained on a piece of equipment, you will know the characteristic features that show the machine is working properly. Having carried out the basic safety checks, you should always test the equipment on yourself in front of the client. This is particularly important if the client has not had the treatment before and is feeling a little nervous. If anything feels, sounds, smells or appears wrong to you when testing the equipment, do not proceed with treatment. Take the faulty equipment out of use immediately and report it to your supervisor.

SELF-CHECKS

Electrical safety

1 What are the two main risks associated with electrical equipment?

2 Give four indications that a piece of electrical equipment is not safe to use.

3 Explain the action that should be taken if a machine develops a fault.

4 Why are electrical appliances 'earthed' for safety?

5 Name the main piece of legislation that applies to the safety of electrical equipment in the salon. Outline the main requirements of this legislation.

GOOD PRACTICE

It is advisable to keep in the first-aid box a card listing the names, addresses and telephone numbers of local health centres and hospitals. If you have any doubt about an injury, always seek medical advice from a doctor or nurse at a health clinic or the casualty department at a hospital.

First aid

You need a basic knowledge of first aid so that you can assist with minor accidental injuries or unexpected situations that happen from time to time in the salon. More serious injuries, for example those involving acute pain, loss of consciousness or serious bleeding, should be dealt with by a qualified first aider, doctor or nurse.

First-aid kit

Health and safety regulations require the salon to have a first-aid kit readily available. All staff should know what the first-aid box looks like and where it is kept. It is recommended that the box is green with a white cross marked on it, and that it is dust proof and free from damp. The contents should be sufficient to cover most emergency situations. Essential items are:

- a first-aid guidance card
- 10 assorted plasters (preferably waterproof)
- different sizes of sterile dressings: three medium, one large, one extra large
- one sterile eye pad
- two triangular bandages
- two crêpe roller bandages
- six safety pins
- disposable gloves.

Useful additions to this list are:

- surgical adhesive tape and lint
- antiseptic liquid or cream
- an eye bath
- gauze
- antihistamine cream
- cotton wool
- medical wipes.

If the salon has a fridge with a freezer compartment, it is a good idea to keep an ice pack for injuries that produce swelling.

First-aid box

GOOD PRACTICE

Disposable gloves should be worn when dealing with cuts or open wounds and when getting rid of materials that have been contaminated with blood. Gloves give some protection from hepatitis B and AIDS. Dispose of contaminated cotton wool and dressings in a plastic bag which has been tied up. (For more information on AIDS and hepatitis B, see page 56.)

PROBLEM	PRIORITY	ACTION
Minor cuts	To stop the bleeding and minimise risk of infection	Apply pressure over cotton wool taking care to avoid contact with the blood (see AIDS and hepatitis, page 56).
Severe cuts	To stop the bleeding and minimise risk of infection	Keep applying pressure over a clean towel until qualified help arrives. Put on disposable gloves as soon as possible.
Electric shock	To remove from source of electricity	Do not touch the person until they are disconnected from the electricity supply. If breathing has stopped, artificial respiration will need to be given by a qualified person. Ring for an ambulance (see Calling the emergency services, page 44).
Dizziness	To restore the flow of blood to the head	Position the person with their head down between the knees and loosen their clothing.
Fainting	To restore the flow of blood to the head	Lie the person down with their feet raised on a cushion.
Nose bleed	To constrict the flow of blood	Sit the person up with the head bent forward. Loosen the clothing around the neck. Pinch, firmly, the soft part of the nose, until the bleeding has stopped. Make sure breathing continues through the mouth during this period. If bleeding has not stopped after half an hour, medical attention must be sought.
Burns	To cool the skin and prevent it from breaking	Hold the affected area under cold, running water until the pain is relieved. Serious burns should be covered loosely with a dry sterile dressing and medical attention sought.
Epilepsy	To prevent self-injury and relieve embarrassment after an attack	Do not interfere forcibly with a person during an attack. Gently prevent them from injuring themselves. Ensure the person's airways are clear and wipe away any froth which forms at the mouth. After the attack, cover with a blanket, comfort and give reassurance until recovery is complete.
Objects in the eye	To remove the object without damaging the eye	Expose the invaded area and try stroking the object towards the inside corner of the eye with a dampened twist of cotton wool. If this is not successful, help the person to use an eye bath containing clean warm water.
Falls	To determine if there is spine damage. To treat minor injuries if the fall is not serious	If the person complains of pains in the back or neck, then do not move them: cover with a warm blanket and get medical aid immediately. For less serious falls, treat the bruises, cuts, sprains or grazes as appropriate.
Bruises	To reduce pain and swelling	Apply cold compresses for 30 minutes using a towel wrapped round an ice-pack or soaked with very cold tap water. Keep the compress in place with a bandage. Replace it if it dries out.
Grazes	To clean wound and prevent infection	Soak a pad of cotton wool with antiseptic and gently clean the graze, working outwards from the centre. Replace the cotton wool regularly throughout the cleaning. Apply a sterile gauze dressing, preferably a non-adherent type, to protect the wound as it heals. If dirt or foreign matter has become embedded in the graze, the person should be referred to a doctor who may want to give a tetanus injection.
Sprains	To reduce swelling and pain	Apply cold compresses to the area (see treatment for bruises) and support the affected joint with a bandage firmly applied. Refer the person to a doctor.

First aid

1 Why should the first-aid kit contain an antiseptic?

2 Why should disposable gloves be worn when treating an open wound?

3 What help should be given to a client who is feeling dizzy?

4 What is the cause of fainting?

5 What is the correct treatment for a nose bleed?

6 What immediate action should be taken following a burn to the hand?

7 Whenever possible, why should furniture be removed from the area where a person is having an epileptic fit?

8 What should an eye bath contain to flush out the eye?

9 What are the signs that a person may have damaged their spine following a fall?

10 For what reason might an ice pack be used when giving first aid?

ACTIVITY

Activity 3.5: First aid

1 Find out where the first-aid kit is kept in your salon and who is in charge of first-aid procedures. Ask if you can have a look at the first-aid kit. Check the contents to see if there is anything missing. If there is, inform your supervisor.

2 Working with a partner, role play the first-aid procedures for each of the following:
   (a) a nose bleed
   (b) dizziness
   (c) object in the eye
   (d) fainting.

Product safety

Many of the products used in the salon are safe under normal use but can become unsafe if not stored, handled or disposed of properly. This is because of the chemical ingredients they contain, which require particular conditions to keep them safe. Specific hazard warning symbols and guidance phrases have been introduced for labelling products. These show, at a glance, what the dangers are. Products may be very toxic, toxic on contact with skin, by inhalation or if swallowed.

Safety signs are the subject of EU legislation

REMEMBER

The employer is required, by law, to assess the risks with chemical products used in the salon, and to provide guidance and training for staff. Trainees must always be supervised when carrying out treatments using dangerous substances.

Hazardous substances

Hazardous substances may enter the body by inhalation through the nose, by ingesting through the mouth, by absorption or penetration through the skin and via the eyes.

What you must do:

- know the potential hazards in your salon and carry out the necessary safety precautions
- always read labels and make sure the guidance on them does not get worn off or covered
- read any leaflets provided by manufacturers and keep them for reference
- check with your supplier if you are unsure about a product
- mix products in a well-ventilated area
- try not to breathe in dust, vapour or spray
- wear protective clothing where necessary
- dispose of waste chemicals and unused mixtures safely: small amounts may be rinsed away down the sink to dilute and remove them
- ensure that damaged and leaking containers are handled with care when disposing of them.

As with all beauty products, substances that are hazardous should be stored in an area which is:

- secure
- inaccessible to children and other unauthorised people
- dry and well ventilated
- away from sources of ignition
- cool (room temperature or slightly cooler)
- away from direct light.

Handling and disposing of hazardous substances

PRODUCT TYPE	HEALTH HAZARD	USE/HANDLING	STORAGE	DISPOSAL	CAUTION
Aerosols: spray cleaners, nail dry sprays	Flammable: contents are under pressure and can cause an explosion or fire.	Use in well-ventilated area. Do not smoke while using. Keep away from eyes. Do not inhale. Do not spray near naked flame or on hot surfaces. Keep cans cool.	Cool, dry place away from sunlight.	Do not pierce or burn aerosol container.	In case of fire, evacuate quickly areas known to contain aerosols and let Fire Service know of their location.
Cuticle remover	Caustic: can burn the skin.	Keep away from eyes. Follow the instructions for use. Do not use on damaged or sensitive skin.	Cool, dry place.	Wear gloves. Mop up spills with damp cloth. Rinse well.	Rinse out from eyes immediately with plenty of cold water and seek medical advice. Rinse off the skin well and seek medical advice if skin irritation persists.
Acetone, astringent, equipment cleaner, nail enamel thinners, nail enamel remover, solvents, some sterilising agents, surgical spirit, witch hazel	Flammable: vapours catch fire if exposed to flame or ignited by other means.	Do not smoke when dispensing. Ensure bottles are clearly labelled. Use only in a well-ventilated room. Avoid excessive inhalation.	Cool place. Keep sealed. Do not store large quantities together. Always read product labels and follow the advice given.	Small quantities may be poured down the sink and rinsed away. To dispose of large quantities seek advice from your local Environmental Health Officer. Do not flush down toilet or pour into drains.	As above. Move to fresh air immediately if feeling nauseous. Seek medical advice if nausea persists.
Equipment cleaner, some sterilising agents, most nail technology products, brush cleaner, nail glue, eyelash tint	Sensitising: risk of causing acute allergic reaction.	Avoid contact with the skin.	Cool, dry place.	Small quantities can be disposed of normally. For advice on disposing of large quantities, contact the local Environmental Health Officer.	As above. Move to fresh air if feeling nauseous and seek medical advice if nausea persists.
Skin bleach	May cause skin irritation.	Use in well-ventilated area. Wear protective gloves. Avoid inhaling dry powder or contact with eyes and face. Do not use on damaged or sensitive skin.	Cool, dry place, away from sunlight and other sources of heat. Reseal container after use.	Do not incinerate. Use water to dilute and mop up spillages. Dispose of dry powder by washing it down the drain with plenty of water.	As above. If dry powder is inhaled, move to fresh air. If coughing, choking or breathlessness persists for longer than 10–15 minutes, seek medical advice.
Hydrogen peroxide	Irritant to skin and eyes.	Always wear protective gloves. Avoid contact with eyes and face. Do not use on damaged or sensitive skin. Always use non-metallic equipment.	Cool, dry place, away from sunlight and other sources of heat. Store in container supplied and replace cap immediately after use.	Flush down the drain with plenty of water. Do not incinerate or store with easily combustible materials, e.g. paper.	Rinse away from eyes with plenty of water and seek medical advice. Rinse the skin well and seek medical advice.
Gluteraldehyde solution	Can cause allergic reaction by contact or following excessive exposure to vaporised fluid.	Avoid breathing in vapour. Keep off the skin. Wear rubber gloves when handling. Utensils which have been treated should be rinsed with water before using on the skin.	Cool, dry place. Keep in a closed, covered container.	Rinse away down the drain with plenty of water. Empty containers should be rinsed thoroughly with water and treated as household waste.	Rinse eyes continuously for 10–15 minutes. Wash skin and seek medical advice if irritation persists. If headaches and chest discomfort occur, move to fresh air and get medical advice if symptoms persist.
Fine powders: acrylic nail powder, bleaches, loose powder cosmetics, talcum powder, clay mask powders	Irritation caused by inhalation of fine particles.	Take care to control powders when using and mixing them. Avoid creating dust when using them. Do not inhale, even in small quantities. Wear a face mask when dispensing large quantities of powder.	Cool, dry place in a closed container.	Treat as domestic waste unless otherwise instructed by the manufacturer.	Rinse eyes with plenty of water. Wash skin to remove particles inhaled, move to fresh air. If irritation or coughing persists, seek medical advice.

Activity 3.6: Hazardous substances

Working with a colleague, produce a risk-assessment data sheet for one salon treatment of your choice. Imagine that the sheet will be used by your employer for staff training. For each of the products used during the treatment:

1 check the labels on packaging, noting hazard symbols

2 read any health and safety information provided by the manufacturer or supplier

3 consider how the product will be used, for example in a confined space or where there is plenty of ventilation.

Hazardous substances

1 State the four routes by which hazardous substances can enter the body.

2 What is the effect of a caustic substance upon the skin? Give one example of a caustic manicure preparation.

3 Why is special care required when disposing of aerosols?

4 Name three different types of flammable products used in the salon. State the precautions that should be taken when handling flammable products.

5 State the main health risks associated with handling fine powder products.

6 List three ideal conditions for storing beauty products.

Client care

You are responsible for ensuring the health and safety of your clients by taking all possible precautions to avoid injuries and adverse reactions to treatments.

What you must do:

- check that the client is suitable for treatment, with no **contraindications** (see page 53)
- check that equipment, machines and tools are in good working order
- explain treatments clearly to the client beforehand so that they know what to expect
- use correct techniques; never 'skimp' on treatments
- adapt treatments appropriately to suit the needs of individual clients
- keep a check on the client's facial expressions and skin reactions during treatment to ensure that they are comfortable and reacting normally
- always apply skin tests before treatments that require them, and write details of the tests and their results on the client's record card
- keep accurate records of treatments given and note any abnormal reactions or problems
- know the possible **contra-actions** (see page 53) to treatment and how to treat them.

Contraindication

This is a condition that makes a client unsuitable for treatment. The condition may be visible or may be revealed during your discussion with a client. Never treat a client with a contagious skin disease or any other contraindication. If you do, you risk spreading the disease, worsening the condition or harming the client.

Contra-action

A contra-action is the adverse reaction of a client to the treatment. This can sometimes happen even when all of the necessary safety precautions have been taken. You should be able to respond quickly to a contra-action that occurs in the salon. You should also be able to advise a client how to recognise and deal with a contra-action that occurs after they have left the salon.

GOOD PRACTICE

During a consultation, your client may refer to a medical condition or treatment they are receiving or have received recently. If you are unsure about the significance of this information but feel it may be relevant, provide written details of the proposed beauty treatment for your client and ask them to get written permission from their doctor. Do not proceed with the treatment until you have received the doctor's written consent. Keep any correspondence from the doctor safely with the client's records.

Record keeping

Regrettably, we live in a society where people are inclined to sue for all sorts of things. It is very important that you keep written records, including dates, of all the steps you have taken to ensure the suitability of the client for treatment. You should record your client's agreement to the treatment plan, details of any 'tests' given before treatment, the client's reactions to the treatment and any special advice you have given for home care including possible contra-actions. Your written records, countersigned by the client, will provide evidence that proper procedures have been followed.

SELF-CHECKS

Client care

1 Explain the benefit, to a beauty therapist, of professional indemnity insurance.

2 Distinguish between a 'contraindication' and a 'contra-action'.

3 List three possible consequences of giving beauty treatments when there is a contraindication.

4 Why is it important to keep accurate client records?

5 Why might medical approval be required before treating a client? Who is responsible for getting the medical approval?

Treatment hygiene

We spend our lives surrounded by what are commonly known as 'germs'. Some germs are harmless, some are even beneficial, but others present a danger to us because they cause disease.

The germs that cause disease are usually spread by:

- unclean hands
- contaminated tools
- sores and pus
- discharges from the nose and mouth
- shared use of items such as towels and cups
- close contact with infected skin cells
- contaminated blood or tissue fluid.

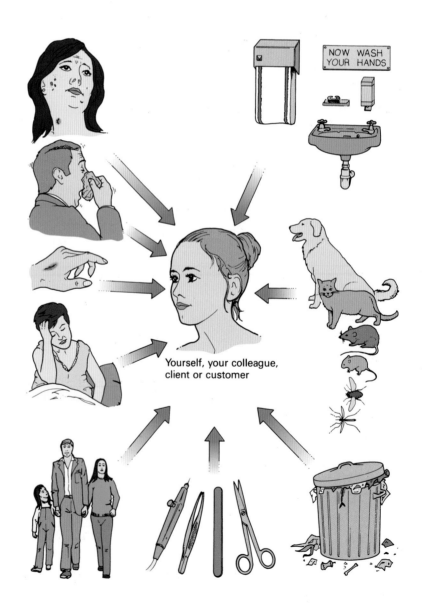

Yourself, your colleague, client or customer

Germs can easily be spread and cause infections

Some diseases are carried in the blood and tissue fluids. Always take adequate precautions to protect yourself during and after treatments which produce spots of blood or tissue fluid on the skin. Wear disposable latex or vinyl gloves whenever possible.

Infection

Infection occurs when the body becomes contaminated, usually with **bacteria**, a **fungus** or **virus**. The reaction to the infection will depend on its cause and the part of the body that is infected. The general signs of infection are inflammation, swelling and pus. Pus is a yellowish substance that forms when the body fights bacteria. It consists of white blood cells, dead and living bacteria and fragments of dead tissue destroyed by the bacteria. Pus is sometimes greenish in colour, depending on the type of bacteria present.

Cross-infection

Cross-infection occurs directly through personal contact or indirectly through contact with an article or implement that has been contaminated. Always work hygienically and do everything you can to avoid the spread of infection.

GOOD PRACTICE

Disposable lip liners, mascara brushes, eyeliner brushes and make-up applicators are becoming more popular in the salon. They are used only once and then disposed of, so there is no risk of cross-infection.

What you must do:
- make sure you can recognise the signs of infection
- avoid any form of contact that might put your client, your colleagues or yourself at risk
- provide a clean gown and towels for each client
- wash your hands regularly, before, during and after treatments
- use only scrupulously clean tools and equipment
- wear disposable gloves when handling waste and during a treatment, when appropriate
- dispose of all materials, including used gloves, in a sealed plastic bag
- put sharp items in containers for disposal
- supervise clients with the application of their own aftercare following treatments that produce spots of blood or tissue fluids on the skin.

REMEMBER

The costs of all 'single-use' items needs to be considered when setting the treatment prices in the salon.

Secondary infection

Secondary infection occurs following injury when the skin is broken and open to infection.

What you must do:
- always practise safe techniques using tools and equipment that are in perfect working order
- look after your hands, keeping the skin soft and pliable; cuts and grazes should be covered with a waterproof dressing

HEALTH
MATTERS

Antiseptics prevent the
growth of bacteria and
infection of wounds.

- if the skin is broken accidentally, clean the area immediately and apply a suitable antiseptic.

Viruses

Viruses are the tiniest germs, yet they are responsible for an enormous range of human diseases. Viruses can only survive in living cells. The following are examples of viral infections:

- common cold – the virus is spread by coughing and sneezing and is carried through the air as a droplet infection
- cold sore – this virus remains dormant in the mucous membranes of the skin and is triggered off by sunlight or general debility. Cold sores are most likely to spread when they are weeping tissue fluid
- warts – there are several types of wart. Verruca plantaris is a wart that occurs commonly on the bottom of the feet and is spread by close contact.

REMEMBER

Dirt and bacteria accumulate in cracks. You must not use tools that are chipped or have a damaged edge as they cannot be cleaned and sterilised effectively. Blunt cutting tools will tear rather than cut, leaving the skin open to infection.

GOOD PRACTICE

If you have symptoms of a cold but are well enough to work, wear a surgical mask over the lower half of your face so that you do not breathe germs over your client.

AIDS (acquired immune deficiency syndrome)

AIDS is caused by a human immuno-deficiency virus (HIV). The virus attacks the body's natural immune system and makes it very vulnerable to other infections, which eventually cause death. Some people are known to be HIV positive, which means that they are carrying the virus without the symptoms of AIDS. HIV carriers are able to pass on the virus to someone else through infected blood or tissue fluid, for example through cuts or broken skin. The virus does not live for long outside the body.

Hepatitis B

Many people feel most threatened by AIDS but, in fact, there is a much higher risk of cross-infection with hepatitis B. This disease of the liver is caused by a virus (HBV), which is transmitted by infected blood and tissue fluids. Hepatitis B is one of the most infectious diseases there is. The virus is very resistant and can survive outside the body. People can be very ill for a long time with a hepatitis B infection. It is a very weakening disease, which can be fatal. Strict hygiene practices are essential to prevent hepatitis B from spreading in the salon.

HEALTH MATTERS

It is important to protect against all diseases that are carried by the blood and tissue fluids. Wear lightweight, disposable gloves when providing treatments that might produce tissue fluid or spots of blood on the skin's surface. Consult your doctor about getting vaccinated against hepatitis B. Vaccination is safe and effective.

Bacteria

Bacteria are tiny and grow from spores that are very productive and highly resistant. They can enter the body by:

- breaks in the skin
- being breathed in
- being taken in with food.

Bacteria are capable of breeding outside the body and can, therefore, be caught easily through personal contact or by touching a contaminated article. The following are examples of bacterial infections of the skin.

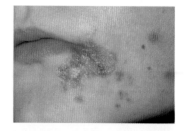

Impetigo
Bacteria enter the body through broken skin and cause blisters that weep and crust over. The condition is highly infectious and can be spread easily by dirty tools.

Impetigo

Boils
Boils occur when bacteria enter the hair follicle through a surface scratch or by close contact with an infected person.

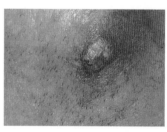

Whitlow
A whitlow can be caused by the bacteria invading the pad of the finger through a break in the skin, for example from a splinter.

Boils

Fungi
Fungi that cause disease are also known as vegetable parasites. This is because, under a microscope, they resemble tiny plants which feed off the waste products of the skin they invade. Some fungi confine themselves to the surface of the skin. Others invade the deeper tissues. Fungal infections are transmitted very easily by personal contact or by touching contaminated articles. The following are examples of fungal infections.

Tinea pedis (athlete's foot)
In this condition, the fungus thrives in the warm, moist environment between the toes and, sometimes, on the bottom of the feet. The condition is picked up easily by direct contact with recently shed infected skin cells.

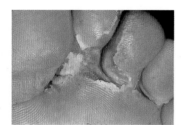

Tinea pedis

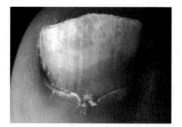

Tinea unguium

Tinea unguium (ringworm of the nail)
This condition may result from contact with the fungus present on other parts of the body. For example, toenails may become infected during an outbreak of athlete's foot, which, if touched, could then spread to the hands.

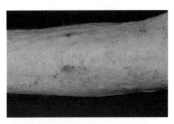

Scabies

Head lice

Animal parasites

Animal parasites are small insects that cause disease by invading the skin and using human blood or protein as a source of nourishment. Diseases caused by animal parasites usually occur as the result of prolonged contact with an infected person. The following are examples of diseases caused by animal parasites.

Scabies

Scabies is caused by tiny mites that burrow through the outside layer of the epidermis and lay their eggs underneath the skin surface. The condition is very itchy and causes a rash and swelling. Characteristic line formations show where the burrows have been formed.

Head lice

Lice are small parasites puncture the skin and suck blood. They lay eggs on the hair close to the scalp. The unhatched eggs are called nits and can be seen as shiny, pearl coloured oval bodies, which cling to the hair shaft.

Sanitisation

The term **sanitisation** refers to any procedures undertaken in the salon to remove dirt and reduce the risk of infection. Specific methods are required to ensure the effective sanitisation of tools, equipment and implements which are used directly on the client during treatment. `

Sterilisation

Sterilisation is the complete destruction of bacteria and their spores. It is very difficult to maintain sterile conditions. Once sterilised items have been exposed to the air they are no longer sterile. Articles that have been cleaned, sterilised and stored hygienically are safe to use on the client.

An autoclave

Autoclave

The most effective method of sterilisation is steaming at high pressure in an autoclave. Steam is produced from a reservoir of water and is contained under pressure at a minimum of 121°C (250°F) for 15 minutes. Thermochromatic indicators change colour when the required temperature has been reached. A stacking facility is usually provided so that articles can be placed at different levels in the autoclave. Sterilisation by autoclave is suitable for stainless steel and glass items. Other items may be suitable, but you should check first that they are made of material which can withstand the process. The very high temperature required to kill spores destroys certain materials in much the same way that over-cooking ruins food.

When autoclaving is not possible, other methods of controlling infection are used. These are less effective and so rely more on recognising infection and avoiding contact with it.

An ultraviolet cabinet

Ultraviolet rays

Ultraviolet rays also sterilise but they have a very low rate of penetration. The rays are emitted from a quartz mercury vapour lamp contained in a cabinet. Ultraviolet radiation sterilises only the surface of objects, so it is suitable only for solid tools such as cuticle nippers. Items have to be turned half-way through the sterilisation process to ensure that all surfaces have been treated with the rays. The generally recommended exposure time is 15 minutes each side. Equipment is often stored in an ultraviolet cabinet until it is required for use.

Chemical sterilants and disinfectants

Concentrated liquid chemical agents are available which have to be diluted for use. Some chemical agents act as sterilants or disinfectants, depending on the strength of their solution and the time during which items are kept in contact with them.

Disinfection

Disinfectants work against bacteria and fungi. They remove contamination but they do not necessarily kill spores. Disinfectants only reduce the number of organisms, but this is usually sufficient for maintaining hygienic conditions. Examples of good chemical disinfectants are listed below.

Gluteraldehyde

A 2 per cent solution is used, which remains active for 14–18 days, after which time it must be discarded. Gluteraldehyde is particularly useful for soaking metal instruments and applicators, but it must be handled with great care (COSHH).

Alcohol

For example, 70 per cent isopropyl alcohol or surgical spirit. Alcohol disinfectants have a very effective bactericidal effect. Alcohol based disinfectants may be used to soak metal instruments and applicators during treatments. The disinfectant used should be discarded after treatment and a fresh solution prepared for the next client.

Quartery ammonium compounds (QUATS)

These are bacteriostatic cleansing agents. They prevent bacteria from spreading but are not effective against very resistant organisms. QUATS are inactivated by soap.

Hypochlorites

These products contain sodium or calcium hypochlorite and are often used for general cleaning purposes because they are relatively cheap. Some are corrosive and should not be used for soaking metal instruments.

Tools should always be washed in warm, soapy water and rinsed well in clean running water and dried with a clean paper towel or tissue before placing them in the disinfectant or sterilising fluid. This ensures the removal of debris, which could act as a barrier. It also prevents contamination of the soaking solution. Tools that have been cleaned and sterilised should be stored in a clean, covered container or in an ultraviolet cabinet.

Activity 3.7: Sanitisation and sterilisation

1 Find out about the cleaning, sterilising and disinfecting methods used in your salon. When you have gathered the information, write up notes on each one, referring specifically to:

(a) the types of equipment and chemical agents used

(b) the salon items each method is used for, including furniture and fittings

(c) instructions for using each method

(d) any special precautions that need to be taken.

2 Besides looking unprofessional, soiled sheets, towels and gowns are also unhygienic. Find out about your salon's laundry arrangements and add the details to your notes. If your salon uses external laundry facilities, estimate the costs of cleaning individual items and the average weekly laundry bill.

Treatment hygiene

1 List four ways of spreading infection in the salon.

2 Describe the general signs of infection.

3 Distinguish between cross-infection and secondary infection.

4 State two precautions that should be taken by the therapist to protect against blood-borne diseases.

5 Why does infection with hepatitis B present a greater risk in the salon than infection with AIDS?

6 Explain the difference between sanitisation and sterilisation.

7 (a) State three items of beauty equipment that may be sterilised effectively in an autoclave.
   (b) Name three items of beauty equipment that are not suitable for sterilising in an autoclave.

8 Give three disadvantages of sterilisation by ultraviolet rays.

9 State three ways of ensuring the effectiveness of disinfectants and sterilising fluids.

Antiseptics

Antiseptics are disinfectants used specifically on the skin. They are particularly effective for treating wounds. Ready-for-use swabs impregnated with 70 per cent isopropyl alcohol are often used for convenience.

Workplace policies

There should be a range of policies in place to ensure that the salon is a safe and healthy place to be for staff, clients and visitors alike. Some of these policies will relate directly to standards of conduct and behaviour. For example:

- Smoking should never be allowed in the salon; besides being unhealthy and smelling unpleasant, many of the substances contained in beauty products are flammable and there is increased risk of fire where there are cigarettes and lighters present.
- Eating should not be allowed in the salon. Separate facilities should be made available for staff to take refreshments, although supplies of fresh drinking water are usually readily available for clients relaxing after hydrotherapy and heat treatments.
- The consumption of alcohol is not normally allowed on salon premises although this might occur, in a limited way, at a social event planned to promote the business. Employees turning up for work under the influence of drink or drugs risk immediate dismissal for gross misconduct. They present an unprofessional image and cannot be trusted to work safely or competently.

Salon security

A salon owner is required by law to ensure adequate security of the business premises. This is particularly important in order to obtain insurance cover in the case of theft from or damage to the property, and also for leasing and mortgaging purposes.

It is virtually impossible to make the salon completely burglar-proof, but steps can be taken to make it more difficult to burgle and to minimise the possible damage once the property has been entered:

- fit locks and/or bolts on all doors and windows, including basements and attics
- install a burglar alarm
- check that glass window panels are intact and that they are not loose; double glazing and window bars give extra security
- fit metal shutters to external doors and windows
- install video cameras.

Strict salon procedures are required to ensure the security of the building both during and outside business hours.

GOOD PRACTICE

It is a good idea, before opening a business, to consult the Crime Prevention Officer at the local police station, and to arrange for a good security firm to inspect the premises and install all necessary safety devices.

REMEMBER

It is not only money that attracts burglars: stock also has a 'street' value. It pays to have a good system of stock control. If your salon is burgled, you will find it easier to list what has been stolen and this will help prompt settlement of insurance claims.

Security outside business hours

REMEMBER

Do not put yourself in danger. If the intruder runs away, report the incident immediately to your supervisor who will contact the police.

GOOD PRACTICE

Details should be written down as soon as possible after an incident. Check the area for damage or theft. It will help the police if you can also provide them with an accurate description of the intruder.

REMEMBER

Every salon has rules regarding the security of money, equipment and stock. Make sure you know the rules and stick to them.

There is obviously a greater risk of burglary when the salon is closed. Particular attention must be paid to locking up at the close of business:

- there should be a minimum number of key holders, with every key accounted for at all times; the police should be given details of key holders in case they need to contact them outside business hours
- a light should be left on all night, preferably at the front of the salon; this may deter a burglar and will help patrolling policemen to keep watch on the premises
- money should not be left in the till overnight; large sums of money should be banked during the day or deposited in the night safe after banking hours
- the till drawer should be left open at night; a thief would try opening it anyway and cause unnecessary damage
- all entrances, lockable cupboards, doors and windows should be checked and the burglar alarm tested before leaving the premises
- external doors should be locked while the internal checks are being carried out.

The person responsible for opening up the salon usually has jobs to do in preparation for the day's business. This person is normally expected to arrive early, before the rest of the staff, which means they are on their own for a short while. During this period:

- the main entrance should remain locked until the opening time of the salon; staff can be let in as they arrive, preferably through an alternative staff entrance
- the burglar alarm should be switched off
- the till and lighting for shop window and display areas should be switched on
- post that has arrived should be put in a safe place for collection
- all internal doors and fire exits should be unlocked to satisfy health and safety regulations.

Security during business hours

It is important to establish the identity of anyone entering the premises and their reason for being there. In most cases, visitors will be attending the salon on legitimate business and will have an appointment card or carry professional identification. Casual callers will expect to be attended to at the reception. If you are suspicious about someone whom you think is not authorised to be in an area of the premises, politely ask for their identity and offer them assistance. If you are still not happy, alert your supervisor or another member of staff.

Stealing by staff and clients

Regrettably, theft by burglary is not the only way in which stealing may take place in the salon. Pilfering by staff and clients (politely known as 'shrinkage') is something that the salon owner must protect against. Pilfering by staff can take the form of 'a hand in the till' or stealing from stock. In the retail industry, stealing by customers or clients is known as shoplifting and refers to the theft of items on display for resale. Shoplifting is not a big problem in beauty salons, but there are obviously risks where items are displayed at reception or in treatment rooms. This type of stealing is much less likely to occur in a salon operating efficient stock control and reception procedures, such as:

- limited staff access to retail, payment and product storage areas
- use of replica 'dummy' stock for 'open' retail displays
- well-lit shelves and display stands that are stocked up neatly
- locked display cabinets for retail products
- electronic cash till
- random checks of stock and money taken through the till.

Security of money

It is worth the salon investing in an electronic cash till for recording and storing payments. The till can be kept locked between uses. Where only one or two named people have the authority to handle cash and have keys for the till, the risk of theft becomes very small.

An electronic till keeps a running total of takings and updated information can be provided instantly for cashing up purposes throughout the day. In this way, discrepancies between the takings and till receipts can be spotted and acted upon quickly.

Stealing by staff and clients

GOOD PRACTICE

It is a good idea to have a system of signing out stock and equipment needed for a treatment and signing it back in when the items are returned to store.

Ideally, money that is cashed up during the working day should be paid straight in to the bank, but this is not always possible. Most banks provide a night safe for depositing money outside business hours. The salon should have a safe for the short-term storage of money and valuables.

It is up to the employer to decide which staff are entrusted with the special combination code that opens the safe, but, clearly, confidentiality is essential in order to provide security.

Security of stock

A good system of stock control monitors the use of consumable and retail products and keeps supplies stored safely in a locked storeroom or cupboard. Usually only one or two people will have keys to the storage areas and they will have responsibility for issuing items to staff and keeping stock records. In this way, general access to stock is limited and the rate of replacement is monitored closely.

Personal property

Staff and clients also need protecting against theft. Ideally, each member of staff should be provided with a lockable cupboard in which to store their personal belongings. If the salon does not provide secure storage facilities for staff, it is best to keep personal possessions in a small purse or wallet, which can be kept safely, nearby, throughout the working day. In larger businesses particularly, leaving handbags and purses on open display in staff rooms or other shared areas is asking for trouble.

The reception should provide secure facilities for storing clients' outer wear and other belongings which cannot be taken into the treatment room. The therapist is responsible for ensuring that the client's handbag and jewellery are kept safely in the treatment area, preferably where they can be seen by the client, or in a locked cupboard. The client's property should not be visible if the treatment area is left unattended.

What you must do:

- keep the amount of money and valuables you take to work to a minimum; this reduces the risk of upset caused by loss or theft
- give your client a small bowl for their jewellery and show them where you are placing it for safe keeping
- show your client the safe place where you are putting their handbag
- do not leave the clients' belongings unattended; if they have to move between different treatment areas of the salon, it may be preferable to place valuable items of jewellery in the safe
- always remember to return your client's jewellery and possessions after a treatment.

An employer would be justified in feeling very angry about losses to the business and personal losses suffered as a result of staff negligence.

Personal safety

Sometimes you may need to work quite late at night. This is not unusual for salons that have extended opening hours. Let your supervisor know when you are leaving. Try and avoid walking on your own after dark. If you need to take public transport, travel with colleagues or friends at night rather than on your own. Keep to well-lit main streets where possible. Carry a personal alarm for extra reassurance.

ACTIVITY

Activity 3.8: Security

Working with a partner or in a small group, decide how effective the security procedures are in your salon. Write a report to your supervisor, making recommendations for improvements where appropriate.

Your report should cover not just the security of the premises: look at how closely the use of salon stock and towels is monitored; also, check the safety of money and retail items on display. How adequate are the facilities available for storing property belonging to clients and staff?

SELF-CHECKS

Security

1   How might a burglar try to gain entry to the salon outside working hours?

2   What security procedures should be carried out at night before leaving the salon?

3   How does a good system of stock control contribute to salon security?

4   Name three ways of ensuring the security of money at reception.

5   Name three ways of ensuring the security of products in:
   (a) the treatment area and
   (b) reception.

6   Give two reasons why it is advisable for the salon to have a safe.

7   Explain the responsibilities for security of:
   (a) the employer and
   (b) the staff.

MULTIPLE CHOICE QUIZ

Health and safety

There may appear to be more than one correct answer. Read each question carefully before making your final decision. Discuss your answers with your colleagues and supervisor, and see if you all agree. If you don't, talk through the issues raised.

1   Bacteria breed:
   (a) only in living cells
   (b) both inside and outside the body
   (c) only outside the body
   (d) only in infected cells.

2   Viruses survive only in:
   (a) warmth and moisture

Health and safety

(b) living cells

(c) contaminated skin

(d) unhygienic conditions.

3 Athlete's foot is caused by:
(a) virus
(b) an animal parasite
(c) a fungus
(d) bacteria.

4 Waste should be disposed of in a sealed container in order to:
(a) keep the trolley tidy
(b) keep the inside of the bin clean
(c) prevent germs from spreading
(d) present a professional image.

5 Strict hygiene procedures are essential in the salon to:
(a) eliminate the risk of cross-infection
(b) protect the clients
(c) protect the staff
(d) eliminate diseases.

6 The therapist's hands should be washed before each treatment so that:
(a) the hands look clean
(b) infection is not spread
(c) surface bacteria are removed
(d) the client feels safe.

7 Smoking is prohibited in the stockroom because of the:
(a) unpleasant smell
(b) hygiene regulations
(c) flammable products
(d) salon's image.

8 A fire blanket is used to:
(a) cover a person who has been injured in a fire
(b) smother a large fire
(c) smother a small fire
(d) cover flammable products during a fire.

9 During a fire, doors should be shut to:
(a) prevent the fire from spreading
(b) prevent the smell from spreading
(c) show that the salon is closed
(d) stop air getting to the fire.

10 A disinfectant used specifically on the skin is called:
(a) an antiseptic
(b) a sanitiser
(c) a steriliser
(d) a bactericide.

11 Staff should be trained in lifting and handling techniques to prevent:
(a) damage to stock
(b) back injuries
(c) insurance claims
(d) accidents in the stockroom.

12 Good ventilation is important in the salon to keep the air:
(a) dry
(b) warm
(c) humid
(d) fresh.

KEY TERMS

You should now understand the following words and phrases. If you do not, go back through the chapter and find out what they mean:

Professional negligence	**Cross-infection**	**Bacteria**
Electric shock	**Secondary infection**	**Fungus**
Risk assessment	**Sanitisation**	**Animal parasite**
Contraindication	**Sterilisation**	**Fire safety**
Contra-action	**Virus**	**Electrical safety**

Chapter 4 Reception
Fulfil salon reception duties

After working through this chapter you will be able to:

- understand the importance of 'reception' to the success of a business
- describe the personal skills and qualities of a good receptionist
- maintain the reception and retail areas
- look after clients and visitors
- deal with enquiries
- deal with problems at reception
- make appointments for salon services
- handle payments from clients.

Before you work through this chapter: Be wise and revise!
Revision topics to help you achieve this unit:

Fulfil salon reception duties

TOPIC	CHAPTER	PAGE
The Sale and Supply of Goods Act 1994	1	13
The **Data Protection Act 1984**	1	14
Professional image	1	16
Communication skills	2	24
Time management	2	31
Lifting and handling	3	40
Salon security	3	61

The reception desk is the control centre for salon operations. Everybody's working day is planned according to the **appointment book**, and then adapted as visitors come and go. Regular clients are welcomed back for treatments. Casual enquirers become new clients. The building up of a successful business starts at the reception, where good first impressions have lasting effects.

First impressions

Think of the last time you sat in a reception area waiting for an appointment. It could have been at the doctor's surgery, the dentist's or maybe the hairdresser's. Can you remember what you did while you were waiting?

- Did you look through the magazines? Were they current and in good condition?
- Did you study other people who were waiting? Did they look comfortable and relaxed?
- Did you watch the receptionist? Was she busy, friendly and attentive?
- Did you read notices on the wall? Were they eye-catching, interesting and well presented?
- Did you keep your eye on the clock? Was the clock right and were people being seen on time?
- Did you examine the decor and furnishings? Were they clean, attractive and well maintained?
- Perhaps you listened in to telephone conversations! Were callers dealt with politely and helpfully?
- Did you study the diplomas and certificates on display? Were you impressed with the qualifications of the staff?

REMEMBER

Waiting time is not wasting time! Clients look and listen while waiting in reception. Good impressions bring the clients back. Good impressions lead to good business!

If your answers to the above questions were 'yes', then you probably felt comfortable with your surroundings and confident that you would receive a good, professional service.

ACTIVITY

Activity 4.1: First impressions

How does your salon's reception stand up to the test? Do you think visitors get a good first impression? Have a good look round. Consider the points covered in this chapter and make notes of your observations. Discuss your findings with colleagues and write up your recommendations for improvements in a memo to your supervisor.

Reception area

The receptionist should arrive at least 15 minutes before the first client of the day. This is to ensure that everything is in its place, and that furniture and equipment is clean and ready for use. Everyone in the salon should know who is allowed at reception and how to behave there. Nothing should be allowed to interfere with the efficiency and professional image of the reception.

REMEMBER

Staff must not be allowed to eat, drink or smoke at reception.

A PRACTICAL GUIDE TO BEAUTY THERAPY

The reception desk

The receptionist is responsible for ensuring adequate supplies of equipment, literature and stationery at reception. Running out of essential items during the working day is inefficient and causes unnecessary delays.

The following items should be readily available at the reception desk:

- appointment book with spare pages
- visitors' book
- appointment cards
- price lists
- promotional leaflets
- pre-treatment/aftercare advice leaflets
- client record cards
- forms, letter paper and envelopes
- pencils, pens, a ruler and eraser
- note/message pad
- calculator
- bill heads/receipt pads
- **petty cash** slips
- gift vouchers
- business cards
- first-aid kit
- credit card payment vouchers
- address and telephone book
- accident/incident report book.

Electronic equipment

The receptionist is responsible for controlling the use and maintenance of electronic equipment kept at reception. The range of equipment available will depend on the size and type of salon. Although some of the equipment is expensive to purchase, the initial investment can usually be justified by the benefits to the business and longer-term savings. At the very least, every salon should have a telephone and an electronic cash register.

Telephone and answering machine

A telephone is essential for any business. For many clients, it is their first contact with the salon. The telephone is the means by which appointments can be made, changed or cancelled quickly, or advice sought and received. It is a good idea for the salon to have a telephone answering machine. This can be used for recording messages outside business hours. These can be dealt with by the receptionist who will play back any messages before the salon opens each morning.

Facsimile transmission service (fax)

A fax transmits black-and-white documents, letters and photographs. The document is fed into a machine and a copy of it is immediately transmitted via a telephone line to a fax machine somewhere else, maybe even in another country. A fax machine is sometimes more convenient than the normal postal service when written information is required quickly.

GOOD PRACTICE

Supplies of stationery and other consumable items should be monitored and reordered before stocks run out.

Reception is the 'hub' of salon operations

REMEMBER

The receptionist is responsible for ensuring that there is enough cash in the till. A '**cash float**' is put in the till each morning to provide change for clients and petty cash if that is not supplied separately. Petty cash is used to pay for small day-to-day purchases such as milk, magazines etc. It is important to keep records of petty cash payments so that they can be accounted for when **cashing up**.

GOOD PRACTICE

If you are working on your own, an answering machine prevents you from being interrupted during a treatment and you are able to ring the caller back later.

Using a computerised salon system

Computer

There are many benefits to the business of having a computer. All sorts of information, such as clients' details, stock records and sales figures, can be stored on a disk. The information can be input and retrieved easily by a trained person. Some manufacturers produce software (programs) specially for use in the salon.

A lot of business information stored on a computer is confidential and may be accessed only by the employer or manager of the salon. Depending on the system purchased, the computer at reception could be used for:

● keeping a database of clients and suppliers

● maintaining records of clients' treatments and purchases

● managing an appointment system

● producing standard letters and price lists

● creating personalised mail shots

● producing promotional literature

● keeping stock records.

GOOD PRACTICE

A **client database** is a form of electronic filing. Information is stored by the computer in an organised way and can be recalled and updated as required. Once you have been trained, it is simple to search out the information you want, and use it or print it out. By keeping a database of all the clients who attend the salon, information is readily available that can be used in a range of ways.

Electronic mail (e-mail)

Businesses that have a computer can arrange to be connected to '**e-mail**'. This is another form of quick communication which allows you to type in a message on a computer screen and then send it to someone else immediately using telecommunication links. The person to whom you have sent the message must also be linked up to e-mail on their computer. The message is stored in their 'mail box' and can be responded to quickly as soon as it is picked up. This form of business communication is very popular.

ACTIVITY

Activity 4.2: Computers

Not all beauty businesses have a computer. If yours does, or if you know of a salon that does, ask if you can have a word with the supervisor about the benefits of a computer to their particular business.

Find out what sort of computer is used and what the staff who use it think about it. Get details of the software packages that are used.

See if there are any plans to replace the computer. If there are, find out why and ask which replacement computer has been chosen. Get details of the staff training involved in computerising a salon.

Electronic cash register

The receptionist is responsible for the security of money in the till and is usually the person who holds the keys. Most salons have an electronic cash till, which records

A computerised till

A PRACTICAL GUIDE TO BEAUTY THERAPY

payments, adds up the bill, issues receipts and keeps money safe. The till may be programmed to provide a lot of other information that is useful to the business.

Electronic funds transfer at point of sale (EFTPOS)

This is an **electronic payment** system which cuts out the need for either cash or a cheque. **Point-of-sale technology** is fast to use and there is very little paperwork. Customers use cards supplied by banks or building societies. In order to offer clients this facility, the salon needs a special terminal through which the client's card is 'swiped'. The receptionist keys in the amount and the information is relayed automatically over communication lines to a central computer. Authorisation for payment comes from the computer, which holds details of the client's account. When authorisation is given, payment is guaranteed. Records of the transaction are issued through the terminal.

A 'swipe' machine for processing card payments

> **REMEMBER**
>
> A mechanical imprinter method of recording payments may be used as 'back-up' in the event of problems with the electronic payment system. This uses special self-carbonating vouchers. The receptionist must ensure that the imprinter is in good working order and that vouchers are available. Being prepared for the unexpected is all part of the job!

Retail displays

The reception is usually the main site in the salon for displaying and promoting retail products – **retail displays**. This is not surprising as every client has to pass through reception at least twice – when they arrive and when they leave! Time spent waiting in reception is time that clients can use to browse through promotional literature and ask advice or take a closer look at products available for purchase. The receptionist is usually the person responsible for keeping the retail area clean and tidy and displaying stock attractively.

What you must do:

- read all of the information about the products you sell; this is so that you can advise and make recommendations to the clients
- inform clients of current promotions: draw the attention of clients to special offers and make sure that promotional material is available and displayed where it will 'catch the eye' of people waiting in reception
- check that shelves are clean, safe and undamaged and strong enough to take the weight of the products on display
- dust the counter, shelves, display cabinets and stock every day; where possible, have regular changes of display
- have samples and testers available; check that they are clean and remove any that are damaged
- display stock attractively; packaging should be displayed with the product
- use 'dummy' stock under bright lighting, this way the colour, texture and fragrance of products will not spoil
- display related products together to encourage multiple purchases
- price the retail products; check that identical products are not priced differently
- if all retail stock is to be displayed, extra space is needed for the fastest-selling lines.

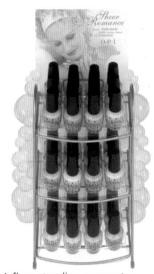

A floor-standing or counter retail display

Handling stock

A lot of money is tied up in stock. The salon loses money on old stock that is sold off cheaply or thrown away. Products approaching their expiry date should be identified at the stock check and steps taken to sell them before it is too late. This may mean offering a special promotion or reducing the price slightly as an incentive to buy. Stock that is not on display is usually kept secure in a locked cupboard or storeroom. The way that stock is stored and handled is important for keeping its value.

What you must do:

- store stock in a cool, dark place
- do not pile boxes too high
- when an order arrives, bring older stock to the front of the shelves and store new stock behind. This method is called FIFO, i.e. first in first out
- take care with flimsy packaging and stack heavier goods on low shelves and not on top of fragile items
- store products correctly so that they do not deteriorate or become damaged; keep fast-moving lines at the front of the shelves and slower-moving ones nearer the back
- carry out regular stock checks to monitor how well different products are selling and to make sure that popular lines are re-ordered before being they are sold out
- store stock in straight lines: this makes counting easier at stock checks
- check price tickets as part of the regular stock checks: old price tickets should be removed before putting on new ones so that a lower price is not disguised
- keep accurate stock records
- do not block aisles or passageways with containers of stock; stock should be kept in a locked cupboard or secure storeroom.

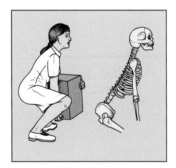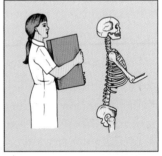

Remember to look after your back when handling stock

REMEMBER

The quality of a product cannot be guaranteed once its expiry date has passed. Stock that has been stored beyond its 'shelf life' has either to be sold off cheaply or disposed of.

ACTIVITY

Activity 4.3: Reception

1 What are the main health and safety issues relating to the reception area? Produce a list, identifying the relevant legislation.
2 List the responsibilities of the receptionist relating to health and safety.

A PRACTICAL GUIDE TO BEAUTY THERAPY

Different colours may be used to record the figures in each column. This is useful if you need to find figures quickly. For example:
Stock = blue
Received stock = green
Orders = black
Sold stock = red

	STOCK LIST			STOCK LIST
1	Dermalesse Cleansing Oil 75ml		21	
2	Dermalesse Cleansing Milk 150ml		22	
3	Dermalesse Cleansing Cream 150ml		23	
4	Dermalesse Exfoliant 100ml		24	
5	Dermalesse Cleansing Milk 100ml		25	
6	Dermalesse Cleansing Cream 300ml		26	
7	Dermalesse Skin Freshener 150ml		27	
8	Dermalesse Skin Tonic 150ml		28	
9	Dermalesse Skin Freshener 300ml		29	
10	Dermalesse Skin Tonic 300ml		30	
11			31	
12			32	
13			33	
14			34	
15			35	
16			36	
17			37	
18			38	
19			39	
20			40	

STOCK BOOK

NO	PRODUCT CODE	PRODUCT	BASE STOCK	DATE: 27/2/04							DATE: 5/3/04						
				Counter stock	Stockroom stock	Total stock (i)	Order	Received	Total stock (ii)	Sold	Counter stock	Stockroom stock	Total stock (i)	Order	Received	Total stock (ii)	Sold
1	00191	Dermalesse Cl. Oil 75ml	10	6	2	8	2	/	8	2	4	2	6	/	2	8	/
2	00192	Dermalesse Cl.Mlk 150ml	10	4	2	6	4	/	6	/	4	2	6	/	4	10	2
3	00193	Dermalesse Cl. Oil 75ml	10	4	2	6	4	/	6	4	2	/	2	4	4	6	1
4	00194	Dermalesse Exfol 100ml	6	4	/	4	2	/	4	1	3	/	3	1	2	5	2
5	00195	Dermalesse Cl.Milk 300ml	5	2	2	4	1	/	4	2	2	/	2	2	1	3	2
6	00196	Dermalesse Cl. Crm 300ml	5	2	/	2	3	/	2	/	2	/	2	/	3	5	1
7	00197	Dermalesse Sk Frsh 150ml	8	4	2	6	2	/	6	4	2	/	2	4	2	4	1
8	00198	Dermalesse Sk Tonic 150ml	8	5	/	5	3	/	5	1	4	/	4	1	3	7	2
9	00199	Dermalesse Sk Frsh 300ml	5	2	1	3	/	2	5	1	3	1	4	1	/	4	2
10	00200	Dermalesse Sk Tonic 300ml	5	3	1	4	1	/	4	3	1	/	1	3	1	2	/
11	00201	Dermalesse Cr Mask 75ml	4	2	1	3	1	/	4	3	1	/	1	3	1	4	2
12	00202	Dermalesse Ampoules	6	3	/	3	3	/	3	2	1	/	1	2	3	4	1
13	00203	Maqui Base Ivory	6	2	3	5	1	1	6	2	3	1	4	2	1	5	/
14	00204	Maqui Base Cream	6	4	/	4	2	/	4	2	2	/	2	2	2	4	1
15	00205	Maqui Base Beige	6	2	/	3	2	1	4	/	3	1	4	/	/	4	2

Accurate stock records are essential for tracking the movement of stock in and out of the business

SELF-CHECKS

Reception

1. State four ways of creating a good first impression at reception.

2. Explain three things that the receptionist needs to do to ensure that reception is ready for business.

3. List six items that should always be available on the reception desk.

4. Why is a 'float' required in the till at the beginning of the day?

5. Name three items of electronic equipment that a receptionist may be responsible for at reception.

6. Give three reasons why security is important at reception.

7. List four ways of promoting retail sales at reception.

8. Give three reasons for carrying out regular stock checks.

9. When are the best times for changing displays and attending to stock?

10. State three ways in which the salon could use a computerised client database.

The receptionist

Not all salons have a full-time receptionist. The duties may be shared by the rest of the staff. Everyone in the salon should be trained in reception skills so that they can confidently take over when needed. It is important that the salon always presents the same professional image at reception.

The receptionist should always look smart, be efficient, and communicate pleasantly and politely with everyone who enters the salon.

Lovely to see you!

The main responsibilities of a receptionist are:

- maintaining the reception and retail areas
- looking after clients and visitors
- handling enquiries
- taking messages
- making appointments
- dealing with problems
- processing payments.

Most of these tasks involve dealing with people either directly or over the telephone. They also include giving, receiving and recording information, which is important for the business to run efficiently.

Interpersonal skills

A good receptionist manages to make every client and potential client feel 'special'. This comes from having good **interpersonal skills**. It is important that everyone, whoever they are and whatever they want, is dealt with in the same, professional way. Remember this particularly when you are tired or very busy and working under pressure.

What you must do:

- be courteous and always show respect: make sure that everybody is treated the same and that your personal feelings do not affect your work
- be sensitive to other people's feelings: avoid saying or doing anything that might offend somebody else, particularly if it involves their race, culture or religion

A PRACTICAL GUIDE TO BEAUTY THERAPY

- never talk about other clients or colleagues: treat everything a client tells you privately as confidential
- show concern for others: always be caring and considerate, giving the right help at the right time.

GOOD PRACTICE

Clients very often have limited knowledge and understanding of what is available in the salon. Sometimes, what they think they want is not always what they need. To find out what the client needs, you must ask the right sorts of questions and listen carefully to the answers.

ACTIVITY

Activity 4.4: The receptionist

1 See how the professionals do it: visit a local salon to obtain details of their treatments and a price list. Pay attention to the interpersonal and communication skills of the person who deals with you. Remember – you could be a prospective client. If you can, visit a few salons and compare the reception you get at each one. Share your findings with your colleagues and supervisor. Summarise your findings in a written report.

2 Working with a partner or in small groups, discuss how a receptionist should use and adapt their interpersonal and communication skills in the following situations:

(a) dealing with a telephone enquiry from a person who has difficulty speaking your language

(b) attending to a deaf client arriving at the salon for treatment

(c) looking after a client in a wheelchair.

SELF-CHECKS

The receptionist

1 State three ways of developing good relationships with clients.

2 List four essential communication skills.

3 Give five examples of problems that might occur in the salon if there is a breakdown in communication.

4 Give examples of three 'closed' and three 'open' questions which a client might be asked at reception.

5 Give three 'messages' that a receptionist should convey using body language.

6 Explain why personal presentation is important for a receptionist.

REMEMBER

Reading, writing, speaking and listening are essential skills for ensuring effective communication in the salon. When communications break down, problems occur. Good communications start at reception.

GOOD PRACTICE

When taking messages, always read back over what you have written. Check that it contains all the relevant information and that it makes sense. This is particularly important when dealing with people over the telephone.

Looking after clients and visitors

Every visitor to the salon should be greeted with a smile and be shown where to wait while the relevant person is informed of their arrival. Visitors such as company representatives or tradespeople doing work on the premises should be asked to sign the visitors' book.

GOOD PRACTICE

Record cards should be kept in strict alphabetical order, using the clients' surnames. Where two or more clients share the same surname, the cards should be filed according to the initial letter of their first name.

REMEMBER

Never leave a client's record card on top of the reception desk where it could be seen by others. The information is private and confidential between client and therapist.

GOOD PRACTICE

In some salons the receptionist prepares a list for each therapist at the beginning of the day, which shows the names of their clients, their expected time of arrival and what they are booked in for. This helps to keep them on schedule. It is kept by the therapist throughout the day and provides a useful, quick reference, particularly if an unexpected client arrives.

REMEMBER

Clients who arrive unexpectedly may be treated provided that there is a therapist available. The receptionist should always check first and then record the client's details in the appointment book.

Dealing with clients

Expected clients who have already made an appointment may show you their appointment card or may have made their appointment on the telephone. Either way, you need to check the client's name, the date, time and treatment against details recorded in the appointment book. You must then look after them until they go for treatment.

What you must do:

- welcome the client and help them with their coat and belongings
- estimate the waiting period and inform the client if this is to be longer or shorter than originally expected
- record the client's arrival at the salon by drawing a diagonal line in pencil across their details in the appointment book
- ensure the comfort and care of the client while they wait, offering magazines and hospitality as appropriate
- when the client has gone through for treatment, draw a diagonal line across the first line to record that they are being attended to
- after treatment, help the client with retail purchases and arrange a convenient time for their next appointment
- help the client with their coat and belongings
- confirm how nice it was to see them and, if possible, accompany them to the door
- keep the client's records up to date and well organised.

ACTIVITY

Activity 4.5: Record cards

1. Work out the order in which the following clients' record cards should appear in the filing system: Sue Mackintosh, Jane McFadden, Helen Makerfield, Elaine McKinlay, Mary Killeen, Elsie MacIntyre, Margaret Killeen, Mary Kenny, Sue McLintock, Sundus Salam. Check your answers with your supervisor.
2. Find out the basic information that is kept on the clients' record cards in your salon. With your supervisor, discuss the importance of keeping this information and the ways in which it may be used.

Dealing with problems

No matter how well you prepare for the clients, problems can still happen.

For example:

- a client may be late for their appointment (the bus was late, the car park was full, an unexpected visitor arrived)
- a client may arrive without an appointment (a regular client who has suddenly been invited out)
- someone could have overbooked (two Mrs Greens may turn up for the same appointment)
- a treatment may take longer than the time allowed so that later appointments start running behind schedule (unexpected complications during a treatment or an extra service provided)
- a member of staff is suddenly absent due to illness (remember to refer this to your supervisor immediately so that bookings can be rescheduled).

If there is a problem with the bookings, keep cool, calm and do not appear flustered! Politely ask the client to take a seat while you explain the situation to your supervisor. An alternative therapist may be suggested, another appointment made or a short wait may be necessary.

It is your job to look after the client until their treatment can start. Use your initiative to make best use of the time. This should include:

- explaining the delay to the client, giving an indication of how long they may have to wait
- offering the client tea, coffee or a soft drink
- offering the client a magazine to read
- informing the client as soon as the therapist is ready and apologising to them for the delay.

ACTIVITY

Activity 4.6: Dealing with problems

Discuss the following problem in a small group and see if you can agree on a solution:

A client arrives 10 minutes late for her manicure appointment and explains, very apologetically, that she has been held up by an unexpected visitor. The appointment book shows that another client is expected with the same therapist in 20 minutes.

Which of the following should you do?

1 Apologise and explain that there is not enough time left for a manicure and ask her to make another appointment.

2 Tell her not to worry; assure her that she can have the manicure and, when the next client arrives, explain that there will be a slight delay.

3 Explain to the client that she can have a manicure but that it will have to be 'cut down' so that it is completed in 20 minutes.

If your answer is 1, do you think that the client should be charged for the treatment she has not had? (After all, you were not able to offer the appointment to someone else.)

If your answer is 2, would it make any difference if the client expected for the later appointment is a regular or new client, visiting the salon for the first time?

If your answer is 3, should the client have the price of the manicure reduced because she has not had the full treatment?

Are there any other possible solutions to this problem?

Making appointments

Details of all appointments should be recorded in the appointment book. Pages should be prepared a few weeks in advance so that courses of treatments can be booked, follow-up appointments made and details of each therapist's availability identified well in advance.

What you must do:

- as appointments are arranged, transfer details to the appointment book in pencil, stating the name of the client, their telephone number (or alternative contact details) and the treatment or service required
- keep the pages neat and tidy: do not 'doodle' or use the appointment book as a note pad

GOOD PRACTICE

Always be positive when negotiating an appointment time with a client. Sometimes clients give the impression of being limited to a particular time when it is possible for them to be more flexible. If their preferred time is not available, always emphasise the times that are or suggest another therapist who might be available.

- make sure that the correct codes and abbreviations are used, and that the start and finish times are made clear
- make out an appointment card for the client, recording details in pen and stating the day, date, time and therapist's name
- check the accuracy of both sets of records and repeat the details back to the client before handing them their appointment card.

Date	Tuesday February 9th			Beauty Box Salon
	Emma	Mel	Nusreen	Joss
8.30	Mrs Ledgard Lash/brow tint			
8.45	953-2417		Mrs Shacklady	
9.00	Mrs Wolf Oil man	Mrs Ledgard Lash/brow tint **C**	Fac/DHF **DNA**	
9.15	943-2136	954-7897	954-1000	
9.30	943-2136	Mrs Smith	Sue Jones	Morning
9.45	Mrs D House	Fac/man	Bridal M/U	Off
10.00				
10.15	Tap/toe	943-9995	942-1892	
10.30	Special	Mrs Gilbert	Mrs Poole	
10.45				
11.00		Gal/facial	steam/facial	
11.15				
11.30	951-2221	950-9930	942-1892	
11.45	Mrs Poole Ped	Mrs Ross s/p lashes		
12.00		948-3626		
12.15	942-1892	Mrs Kelly		Mrs Stewart
12.30			LUNCH	Consultation (F)
12.45	LUNCH	Fac/man		942-3344
13.00				Mrs Gibson Man
13.15		943-9191	Mrs Gordon 1/2 leg wax,	940-7632
13.30	Mrs Cronin Gel/tips	LUNCH	Eyebrow shp 942-8344	
13.45	763-4265			

☐	Available time	⊠	Client has been taken for treatment	☐C	'Last minute' cancellation
◰	Client arrived and is awaiting treatment	DNA	Did not attend – client did not inform, make a note on the record card		

The appointment book provides a 'snapshot' of what is happening in the salon

GOOD PRACTICE

Allow a little extra time in the appointment book for a new client requiring a consultation.

ACTIVITY

Activity 4.7: Recording appointments

Each salon has its own system for recording appointments. It is important that you follow the system used in your salon.

1   Find out the abbreviations used in your salon for recording appointments and the amount of time allocated for each treatment.

2   Make out a chart, preferably on a computer, presenting the information in three columns, i.e. treatment, abbreviation, time. Refer to your chart when making appointments at reception.
(See example on page 79.)

3   Check the next day's page in the appointment book: are there any gaps? If there are, how long are they for and which treatments could be booked in to them?

Here are some examples:

TREATMENT	ABBREVIATION	TIME
Cleanse/make-up	Cl/MU	45 mins
Facial	F	1 hr
Manicure	Man	45 mins
Eyebrow shape	E/B	15 mins

SELF-CHECKS

Making appointments

1 Why should the pages in the appointment book be prepared a few weeks in advance?

2 State two reasons why it is important not to allow too much time in the appointment book for treatments.

3 State two reasons why it is important to allow sufficient time in the appointment book for treatments.

4 Give three details required when recording an appointment in the appointment book.

5 Why should details in the appointment book be recorded in pencil?

Handling enquiries

Although people may call in to the salon to make enquiries, most requests for information will be made over the telephone. Remember that the salon telephone is for business and should not be used for chatty personal calls. Clients who cannot get through may give up and make an appointment somewhere else.

Many enquiries will be about the services offered, their effects, how much they cost, how long they take and the availability of appointments.

Dealing with a telephone enquiry

What you must do:

- keep details of treatments, services, products and price lists available at reception close to the telephone
- know which types of enquiries can be dealt with personally and which need referring to a qualified operator
- ask questions that will help the client to provide the right information in their answer
- take down messages accurately and pass them on, promptly, to the right person
- be able to explain the benefits of the treatments and services available in the salon.

Using the telephone

For many clients the telephone is their first contact with the business. A good receptionist never forgets that calls are from people, each of whom is a prospective client.

Telephone answering techniques

When you answer the telephone at reception, you must sound professional, courteous and friendly.

You should always:

- answer promptly on the second or third ring: this gives both sides time to prepare themselves without the caller becoming impatient
- smile when you pick up the receiver: your voice is you to a caller. Smiles definitely do travel down the telephone!
- let the caller know that they have got through to the salon, give them your name and ask how you can help them. Note the client's name so that you can use it in conversation
- be enthusiastic: enthusiasm is infectious and shows you enjoy being helpful
- listen attentively: it is very off-putting for a caller if they can sense you are being distracted by someone or something else
- repeat back to them any important points discussed and thank them for calling.

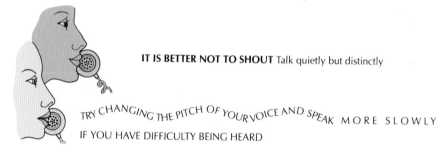

IT IS BETTER NOT TO SHOUT Talk quietly but distinctly

TRY CHANGING THE PITCH OF YOUR VOICE AND SPEAK MORE SLOWLY IF YOU HAVE DIFFICULTY BEING HEARD

Tips for using the telephone

Receiving calls

Here are some reasons why people may call your salon:

- to make, change or cancel an appointment (always repeat the key pieces of information back to your client so that you share the same understanding of what has been agreed)
- to make enquiries about treatments and services offered
- new clients may call to ask for the location of the salon and information on how to get there and where to park
- people may ring up wanting to know if there are any jobs available at the salon, possibly students requesting a work placement (check with your supervisor)
- company representatives may call to check on an order or to make an appointment to discuss products or equipment (you may need to transfer this call to your supervisor or employer)
- someone may make a personal call to a member of staff (check the salon policy about this, as some salons will only allow personal calls to staff in an emergency. You might have to take a message).

ACTIVITY

Activity 4.8: Responding to telephone enquiries

Keep a log of five different telephone enquiries you deal with on reception. Give the name of the caller, the date and time of their call, and the nature of their enquiry. Explain how you dealt with the the call, highlighting any problems and explaining the outcome of the enquiry.

GOOD PRACTICE

If you have to put a call through to another extension, explain to the caller what you are doing and thank them for waiting. If the extension to which you have transferred the call does not answer after six rings, explain to the caller that you can take a message or, if they prefer, you will ask the person concerned to ring back. Take the caller's name and telephone number.

A PRACTICAL GUIDE TO BEAUTY THERAPY

1 Why should the reception telephone not be used for personal calls?

2 Give three techniques that should be used when answering the telephone at reception.

3 Describe four different types of telephone call that may be received at reception.

4 What action should be taken if the person that a caller needs to speak to is not available?

5 How should the receptionist respond to an enquiry left on the salon's telephone answering machine?

REMEMBER

Some messages are confidential. Keep them in a safe place and pass them on to the appropriate person as soon as possible.

Taking messages

When passing on messages, make sure that full and accurate details are written down. Valuable time may be wasted responding to messages if details are missing or unclear. Messages should be written down on a special message or 'memo' pad.

The details should include:

- who the message is for
- who the message is from
- the date and time the message was received
- details of the message
- the telephone number or address of the caller
- the signature of the person taking the message.

```
TELEPHONE MESSAGE

To      Sarah

From    Cath Peel

Date  28.3.04    Time  17.30

Message
Please ring regarding make-up
next Saturday (3 April)
Tel 0161 - 741 - 0491


Message taken by    Janet
```

A completed message slip

Dealing with complaints

Despite everyone's attempts to provide an efficient, personal service, mistakes can sometimes occur. Depending on the circumstances and the mood of the client on the day, some of these can go by more or less unnoticed, while others may result in the client becoming upset and complaining quite openly at reception.

Whatever the cause, it is important to deal with the problem quietly, tactfully and, if possible, away from the rest of the clients.

Here are some tips to help you, but check first with your supervisor to make sure you have authority to deal with a complaint. Your supervisor may wish to handle it.

What you must do:

- keep cool and be pleasant and polite to the client
- ask the client to come with you to a more private area of the salon
- offer the client a seat: a comfortable client is more likely to calm down
- give the client the opportunity to explain to you exactly what the complaint is about
- listen carefully and do not interrupt
- analyse the complaint and ask the client to clarify points that are not clear to you
- do not contradict or argue with the client

GOOD PRACTICE

Do not pretend a mistake has not been made when you know very well that it has. Mistakes on the part of the salon must be acknowledged and rectified as soon as possible.

REMEMBER

Contrary to popular belief, the client is not always right! However, if the situation is handled tactfully, a client will be prepared to accept that they are wrong without feeling embarrassed or offended.

- always show concern and understanding for the client being upset, irrespective of who or what is to blame
- negotiate an acceptable solution: your supervisor may need to be involved by this stage
- do not be tempted to show anger, even if the client is being unreasonable
- explain your answer calmly and confidently, maintaining eye contact
- always apologise for the client being upset or inconvenienced.

ACTIVITY

Activity 4.9: Dealing with complaints

Dealing with complaints is always a good basis for role play!

Working with a partner and, if possible, an observer, create a realistic situation that might occur at reception when a client is unhappy with a service or product received. Have a 'supervisor' on hand in case your client gets out of control! Remember the importance of using the correct body language.

Handling exchanges and refunds

It is usual for the manager to supervise refunds. They will want to find out if the cause of the complaint is due to:

- negligence on the part of the salon: the client may have been given incorrect or incomplete advice. Alternatively, there may have been discrepancies with stock handling or **stock control** procedures
- misunderstandings by the client: sometimes, no matter how much you explain to a client, misunderstandings happen. A product appears not to be working when, in fact, the client is not using it properly
- defective products sold to the salon by a supplier: in this case the terms of the Sale and Supply of Goods Act 1994 apply.

A client requesting a refund should be questioned tactfully. If goods have been returned, they should be examined closely. As always, the client should be dealt with calmly, politely and sympathetically.

A client requesting a refund should be questioned tactfully to determine the cause of the problem

Here is some advice about handling refunds:

- make sure that returned goods are acceptable for a refund or exchange: you are not obliged to compensate for careless breakage or misuse of a product by the client
- sometimes, when a product is returned as faulty, you may suspect that you are not being given entirely truthful information: this can be a difficult situation to handle and you should seek the advice of your supervisor
- the salon will probably have a policy on refunds and exchanges: make sure you know and follow the correct procedures
- if a product that has been returned is faulty, the client is not required by law to produce a receipt: it is obviously reassuring to have evidence that the product was bought from the salon but failure to produce a receipt does not jeopardise the client's rights as a consumer.

The client must feel that they have been dealt with fairly and professionally. A satisfied client will probably come back and, hopefully, recommend you to others. A client who feels humiliated and badly treated is lost for ever.

ACTIVITY

Activity 4.10: Handling refunds

If a product is returned for a refund, you will have to examine it carefully and ask questions before deciding if there are genuine grounds for a refund.

1 Working with a colleague, take each of the following products and, assuming that they were sold in perfect condition, discuss how you would recognise a suspicious situation: a lipstick, eye-shadow palette, eye pencil, block mascara, jar of skin-care cream, nail enamel.

2 Find out how your salon provides refund information through the till and how your manager would deal with a supplier of defective goods.

SELF-CHECKS

Dealing with complaints

1 Why should details of a client's complaint be recorded?

2 State three ways of calming down a client who is upset.

3 Give two reasons for maintaining eye contact with a client who is making a complaint.

4 Describe two pieces of legislation that protect the consumer.

5 Under what circumstances should a client receive a refund?

6 Why should a complaint be dealt with away from reception if possible?

Processing payments

The client's bill will be produced on the electronic cash register or itemised in writing on a bill head. The client should be asked to check the bill before payment is made.

Value added tax (VAT)

Many salons have to charge VAT to the client. This is because their sales of products and services exceed a certain level. The tax is paid back later to the government. Some salons include VAT in their prices. Others total the bill and then add on VAT.

Methods of payment

ACTIVITY

Activity 4.11: VAT

Ask your supervisor for the current rate of VAT. For each of the following treatments work out
(a) how much VAT is payable, and (b) what price the client must pay inclusive of VAT:

- Special facial   £18.50 excl VAT   =
- Manicure   £8.75 excl VAT   =
- Leg wax   £11.00 excl VAT   =

There are various ways in which a client may pay their bill. Make sure you know which methods of payment are acceptable in your salon. These may be:

- cash payments
- payments by cheque
- card payments
- travellers' cheques
- payments in gift vouchers.

The receptionist has to:

- provide an itemised bill for the client
- handle cash payments
- give change from the till
- supervise payments by cheque
- process card payments
- process payments by gift vouchers
- issue receipts.

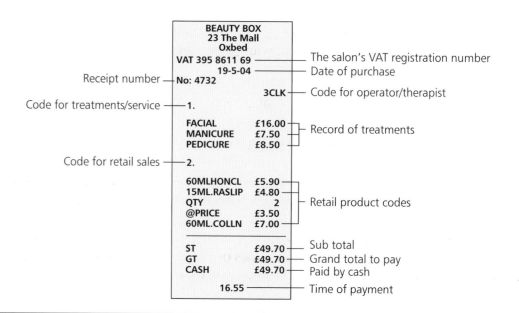

*An itemised till receipt identifies
every detail of the transaction*

Cash payments

Cash tills (cash registers) may be electronic or computerised. All tills have:

- a container for cash or cheques
- a facility for recording the amount taken
- a facility for producing a receipt.

The till may have codes for each type of service and retail product, each operator's name and the method of payment used. The more details that can be provided through the till, the easier and less time-consuming it is to collect information for the business records. The till receipt shown on page 84 is fairly typical.

Always check that you have not taken any foreign money. Many banks will not exchange foreign coins. If there is a shortage of change, tell your supervisor so that the salon does not run out.

You will be trained how to use the till in your salon, but here is the basic procedure for dealing with cash payments:

1 total the bill and inform the client of the cost

2 accept the cash payment and thank the client; check that it is made up of legal currency

3 check the authenticity of bank notes by holding them up to the light: a genuine note will show the watermark and metal strip, which runs through the note, there are also special pens available that show up a forgery when drawn across the note

4 place the money on the till shelf

5 count out the change into your own hand

6 count out the change into the client's hand

7 ask the client to confirm that the change is correct

8 put the payment into the till

9 thank the client and give them their till receipt.

Payment disputes

If you have followed the correct procedures for processing a cash payment there should not be any disputes about the amount of money paid by the client or the amount of change received.

In the unlikely event of a dispute occurring, this is what you should do:

- ask the client how much they think they have overpaid
- politely remind the client of the steps that were taken to ensure that the correct change was given
- explain that when the takings are cashed up at the end of the day the till receipts will be checked against the takings: this will show whether or not there is a surplus in the till
- take the client's telephone number and promise to ring them back to let them know the outcome; if the surplus matches or is more than the amount the client thinks they are owed, the salon is obliged to pay the client.

REMEMBER

Avoid putting cash straight into the till drawer, even if the till automatically works out the amount of change owed. Mistakes can be made that are difficult to deal with once the evidence of payment has gone. This is particularly important when handling notes.

GOOD PRACTICE

If there is a **payment discrepancy** between the takings and the till receipts ('Z reading'), it is worth doing a re-count with another person present just to make sure. If the re-count shows that there is still a discrepancy then the manager must be informed.

GOOD PRACTICE

Never leave the till drawer open after a transaction. The security of money is the responsibility of the receptionist. Leaving the till drawer unattended and insecure is negligent.

Unfortunately, forged bank notes are not always this obvious!

Do not forget to ring the client back as promised. This is good customer relations, even if what you have to say is not what the client wants to hear.

Euro payments

On 1 January 2001, the 12 European countries making up the 'euro-zone' introduced euro notes and coins. This new currency replaced the old national currencies in those countries. Some retail outlets in the United Kingdom are accepting euro payments as well as sterling. However, there is no legal obligation to do so. The countries making up the 'euro- zone' are Austria, Belgium, Finland, France, Germany, Greece, Italy, the Republic of Ireland, Luxembourg, The Netherlands, Portugal and Spain.

Euro notes and coins

ACTIVITY

Activity 4.12: Using the till

1 Have a good look at a till receipt and see if you can explain what the various codes mean relative to the amounts recorded.

2 Ask if you can have a look at the 'Z reading', which is produced by the till during cashing up at the end of the day. The 'Z reading' itemises the total number of transactions that have taken place through the till. What possible reasons can you think of for there being a discrepancy between the amount of money contained in the till and the amount recorded by the 'Z reading'?

A PRACTICAL GUIDE TO BEAUTY THERAPY

Cheque payments

Many clients prefer to pay by cheque. Make sure that the cheque is filled in correctly and that payment is guaranteed by a valid cheque card which covers the amount of the bill.

It is the receptionist's job to ensure that the cheque is made out properly and that the information used is correct. If the correct procedure is not followed, the salon will lose money. What you must do:

- make sure the client has a cheque guarantee card and accept it only if the expiry date (the month and year) has not passed
- check that all of the words and figures are entered correctly on the cheque: the cheque must be made payable to the salon (the salon may have a stamp for this)
- ensure that the value on the cheque does not exceed the cheque guarantee card limit
- if the client has made a mistake, make sure that they initial the correction
- check that the account numbers on the cheque guarantee card and the cheque (the last group of numbers on the bottom right-hand side of the cheque) are the same
- make sure that the client signs the cheque and that the signature on the cheque matches the one on the cheque guarantee card
- write the cheque guarantee card number on the back of the cheque then give the client their card and receipt.

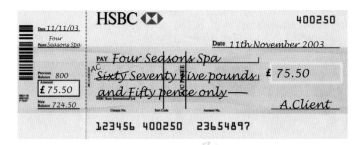

An initialled cheque showing signed correction

Travellers' cheque

Travellers' cheques

If travellers' cheques are to be accepted in your salon, they must be issued in appropriate currency (usually sterling) and accompanied by the client's passport.

Card payments

If your salon accepts card payments, stickers will be displayed at the front door or reception desk indicating which ones may be used. If a client offers to pay by a card that is not accepted in the salon, apologise politely and indicate the methods of payment that may be taken.

Credit cards

Credit cards include MasterCard and Visa. The client presents the card as payment, the credit card company pays the salon and adds the amount to an itemised bill which is sent monthly to the client. A proportion of the bill has to be paid off each month.

The organisation issuing the credit card will give the salon a credit limit ('ceiling'), which is the maximum amount that may be accepted with the card. If the client wishes to use the card to pay a greater amount, this has to be authorised by telephone at the time of the transaction. Some businesses have a policy of requesting telephone authorisation from the issuing credit card company for all purchases over a certain amount.

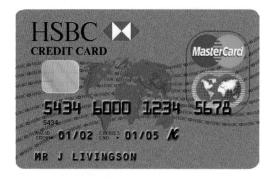

A credit card

Processing credit card payments

Check that the card is genuine and that it has not been stolen:

- the hologram should be clear and distinct
- the date on the card must be valid
- the name and title (Ms, Mrs, Mr etc.) must be appropriate to your client
- the signature on the card must match the name on the front of the card
- the account number must not be one on the credit company's warning list.

Having completed the security checks, you are ready to process the payment. This can be done using an electronic payment system (EFTPOS) or an imprinter.

Electronic payment system

What you must do:

1 check that the terminal display is in 'SALE' mode
2 'swipe' the card through the special terminal
3 when prompted, enter details of the sale using the keypad
4 press ENTER to make the connection with the credit card company
5 wait for confirmation that the card has been cleared and payment authorised
6 the machine will automatically type out a receipt
7 offer the client a pen and ask the client to sign in the space indicated on the receipt
8 check that the client's signature matches the one on the card
9 return the card to the client with their copy of the receipt
10 keep the salon's copy of the receipt safely in the till.

Using an imprinter

If you are a mobile beauty therapist, you will obviously not be able to process electronic payments. However, you may still be able to accept credit card payments by using an imprinter which is lightweight and transportable. Instead of swiping the card through a computerised terminal, special self-carbonating vouchers are filled in and a manual sliding mechanism is used to imprint the card details on the vouchers. Payment is authorised when the credit card company receives a copy of the voucher.

...ist discreetly at reception near the till. If you are presented with a card that is on the list politely excuse yourself, hold on to the card and inform your supervisor who will implement formal procedures.

REMEMBER

Sometimes the card cannot be swiped effectively because the terminal fails to 'read' the magnetic strip on the card. If this happens to you, repeat the swipe, ensuring that the magnetic strip passes over the reader head. If that fails, key the complete card number in to the terminal manually.

GOOD PRACTICE

In most cases a card that fails to 'swipe' is not suspicious, but it is worth checking for signs of tampering. If you are not happy, refer discreetly to your supervisor.

REMEMBER

Always use a ball-point-pen so that the writing can be seen on each of the three copies.

A PRACTICAL GUIDE TO BEAUTY THERAPY

What you must do:

1 complete the voucher by writing in the date, a short description of the service or products for which payment is being made and the amount charged

2 place the card on the imprinter underneath the voucher and press down the handle or slide it across so that the imprinter presses the numbers of the card and the name and address of the business on the voucher

3 ask the client to sign the voucher in ball-point pen

4 check that the client's signature matches the one on the card

5 return the card to the client with the top copy of the voucher as a receipt

6 store the other two copies of the voucher safely in the till: one is kept by the salon for accounting purposes, the other is sent for processing to the credit card company.

Charge cards

This is another type of credit card, for example American Express, which issues charge cards as well as credit cards. Charge cards are paid off in full by the holder each month. (Some charge cards are 'corporate cards' issued by a company for employees to charge business expenses to them, and settled by the company at the end of each month.)

Debit cards

Debit cards include Connect and Switch. Payment is made automatically, using the electronic payment system to transfer money from the client's bank account. Debit cards also serve as cheque guarantee cards.

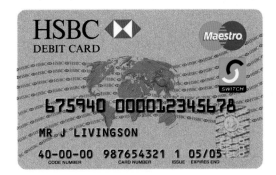

A debit (Switch) card

Gift vouchers

Some salons issue gift vouchers or tokens, which can be purchased as prepayment for treatments or services. Make sure you know how to check that gift vouchers offered for payment in your salon are authentic and valid. Keep details at the till of current special offers and make sure that everyone working on reception knows they are there.

BEAUTY BOX
Salon

• 122 New Road • Hometown • HT4 2OX •
• Tel: 01234 56789 •

This VOUCHER entitles:

to the sum of £

Signed:

Date:

Valid for 6 months from the date of purchase

A gift voucher

Dealing with payments

1 What is the current rate of VAT?

2 When is it 'safe' to accept a cheque payment?

3 How can you tell if a bank note is a forgery?

4 Why should foreign money not be accepted at reception?

5 List three precautions that should be taken to avoid a dispute with a client over their payment.

6 What is the purpose of an imprinter when processing a credit card payment?

7 Give three main functions of an electronic cash till.

8 Why should cash not be put straight into the till following payment?

REMEMBER

Money which is paid after the 'Z' reading has been taken must be included in the next day's figures when cashing up.

BEAUTY BOX SALON
Cashing Up Sheet

Date: *Thursday May 1st*
Opening Float: £25.00

IN		OUT	
CASH			
£50		*Milk*	74p
£20	80.00	*Window clean*	£6.00
£10	50.00		
£5	25.00		327.00
Coins	18.76		
	£173.76		
CHEQUES			
Smith	28.00		
Jones	36.00		
Wray	29.50		
	93.50		
VOUCHERS			
	53.00		
SUB TOTAL			
	320.26		
Payments	6.74		
	327.00		
Minus opening float	25.00		
GRAND TOTAL			
	A 302.00	B Closing float £25.00	

A cashing up sheet

A = The day's takings. This should correspond to the till 'Z' reading.

B = After cashing up, an amount is set aside to be the opening float for the following working day.

The 'Z' reading provides information for the whole of a trading period – usually one day.

Money which is paid after the 'Z' reading has been taken must be included in the next day's figures when cashing up.

BEAUTY BOX
23 The Mall
Oxbed
VAT 395 8911 69
19-2-04
NO 1732
GRAND TOTALS

TOTAL SALES	£302.00
CASH SALES	£173.76
CHEQUE SALES	£93.50
CREDIT SALES	£53.00
DISCOUNT	£00.00
RETURNS	£00.00
FLOAT	£25.00
PAID OUT	£6.74
DRAW BALANCE	£321.74
	2CLK
SALES TRTS	£65.00
SALES RETAIL	£82.00
	2CLK
SALES TRTS	£135.00
SALES RETAIL	£20.00
TOTAL TRTS	£200.00
TOTAL RETAIL	£102.00
CLIENTS = 11	
VOIDS = 0	
TIME 20.15	

The 'Z' reading shows the transactions that have taken place and the total amount taken during the trading period

Cashing up

At the end of the day, all takings are checked, recorded and either secured temporarily in a safe or banked. Cashing up is usually done by a senior member of staff. Alternatively, it may be the receptionist's responsibility, in which case there is usually a second person present.

Cashing up not only confirms the day's takings, it also shows whether the receptionist has handled and recorded payments correctly. A simple sum is done, which produces a total that should balance with the till's 'Z reading'.

The 'Z reading' provides information for the whole of a trading period – usually one day. 'X readings' can be taken periodically during the day to monitor transactions. Following cashing up, some money is 'bagged up' for paying into the bank. An amount is usually kept back for the next day's float.

SELF-CHECKS

Cashing up

1 Give three possible reasons for a discrepancy between the amount of money taken through the till and the amount of money in the till at the end of the day.

2 What action should be taken if there is a discrepancy?

3 Why must receipts for petty cash payments be retained in the till?

4 What is the purpose of an 'X reading'?

5 What is the purpose of a 'Z reading'?

6 Why is cashing up important?

MULTIPLE CHOICE QUIZ

Reception

There may appear to be more than one correct answer. Read each question carefully before making your final decision. Discuss your answers with your colleagues and supervisor, and see if you all agree. If you don't, talk through any issues raised.

1 Petty cash is used to:
   (a) provide change for cash payments
   (b) make small day-to-day purchases for the salon
   (c) make up for cash discrepancies in the till
   (d) make small cash payments.

2 The pages in the appointment book should be made out:
   (a) at the beginning of each month
   (b) one week in advance
   (c) a few weeks in advance
   (d) at the end of each month.

3 If a client arrives at reception while you are speaking on the telephone, you should:
   (a) finish your telephone call and attend to the client
   (b) smile at the client and tell her you will only be a minute

   (c) wave to a colleague to attend to the client
   (d) smile at the client, gesture to a seat and complete your phone call.

4 If a therapist rings in to reception to say that she will not be coming to work because she is ill, you should:
   (a) ring up her clients for the day and cancel their appointments
   (b) move her clients' appointments to another therapist where possible
   (c) inform the manager
   (d) wait and see what happens, hoping the problem will get sorted out as the day goes on.

Reception

5 A client complains of feeling faint while waiting in reception. You should immediately:
   (a) offer the client a cup of tea and tell the manager
   (b) tell the therapist who is due to treat the client
   (c) assist the client to a quiet area of the salon and lie them down with their feet slightly raised
   (d) offer the client a cup of tea and check every now and again how they are feeling.

6 A new client is the only client waiting in reception. She lights a cigarette. The salon has a 'No Smoking' policy and a 'Smoking Prohibited' sign is displayed in reception. You should:
   (a) decide to ignore it because there is no one else in reception
   (b) pretend to cough, hoping this will attract her attention and you can point to the 'No Smoking' sign
   (c) apologise politely, tell her about the 'No Smoking' policy and ask her to put the cigarette out
   (d) apologise politely, tell her about the 'No Smoking' policy and suggest she may like to finish her cigarette outside.

7 A client returns to the salon, saying that she paid her bill with a £20 bank note but realises that she has only been given change for £10. You should immediately:
   (a) give her £10 out of the till
   (b) explain why you think it is unlikely that this has happened
   (c) explain that it would be impossible to make such a mistake
   (d) refer her to the manager.

8 A young client arrives at reception on her own for an ear-piercing treatment. She says her mother made the appointment for her over the telephone. She is 15 years old and there is no evidence of a completed parental consent form. You should:
   (a) allow the treatment to go ahead but give her a consent form for her mother to fill in and return afterwards for the salon records
   (b) allow the treatment to go ahead but give her a consent form and ask her to forge her mother's signature for the salon records
   (c) explain the situation and ask the client if it would be possible for her mother to come to the salon and sign the consent form while she is having her ears pierced
   (d) explain the situation and reschedule the appointment.

You should now understand the following words and phrases. If you do not, go back through the chapter and find out what they mean:

Body language	Cash float	Petty cash
Appointment book	Stock control	Data Protection Act 1984
Client database	Retail displays	E-mail
Interpersonal skills	Payment discrepancy	Cashing up
Electronic payment	Point of sale technology	

Chapter 5 Selling

Promote additional products or services to clients

After working through this chapter you will be able to:

- appreciate the importance to the business of selling
- relate selling to the achievement of performance targets
- know how to promote products and services
- effectively sell products and services
- understand 'link' selling
- give a consultation
- agree a treatment plan
- fill in a client's record card
- understand the law in relation to selling.

Before you work through this chapter: Be wise and revise!
Revision topics to help you achieve this unit:

Promote additional products or services to clients

TOPIC	CHAPTER	PAGE
Professional ethics	1	2
Consumer protection	1	11
Communication skills	2	24
Client care	3	52
Record keeping	3	53
Retail display	4	71
Handling stock	4	72
Handling exchanges and refunds	4	82

Some people worry about 'selling'. They feel that they might be pushing clients into spending money against their will. This is nonsense! Selling should be seen as an extension of the other professional services offered by the salon. Clients trust the recommendations they receive in the salon. They expect, quite rightly, that the products and services on sale there will be of good quality and that they will get the best advice.

Most clients admit quite freely to having wasted money in the past on purchases made elsewhere without proper professional advice

Selling products

A successful beauty therapist who is fully booked with clients can only increase their earning potential by **retail sales**. Retail sales are those which relate to purchases of products sold in the salon. The products may be purchased by clients following a treatment, or by customers who come into the salon solely to get professional advice and buy the products.

GOOD PRACTICE

The more time you spend educating your existing and potential clients about the treatments and products on offer, the more likely it is that they will be interested in trying them. Once they have tried and enjoyed them, the more likely it is that they will come back for more.

REMEMBER

You may be given regular performance targets to reach in relation to the income you generate through treatments and retail sales. These targets are important and contribute to the financial planning of the business.

These days, clients can buy beauty products in all sorts of retail outlets, even supermarkets! When a client has enjoyed the benefits of one of your treatments using products available for purchase in the salon, it does not make sense for them to go and buy different products somewhere else.

Most salons supply 'professional only' retail ranges. This means that the products are only available through approved salons. This gives you an advantage, as the client will not be able to purchase the products from a general retail outlet.

The three important elements of selling are:

- knowing your products
- knowing your customers
- being able to describe the features and benefits of the products and match them to the needs of the customers.

Product knowledge

The first step in successful selling is knowing exactly what it is you are selling! This may sound obvious, but it is surprising how extensive your knowledge needs to be in order to promote across the whole retail range in your salon. It is important to keep up to date, attend any product training courses available to you and take time to read the literature supplied with the products.

You need to be able to:

- describe the product, how it is used and for what purpose
- understand particular *features* of the product, for example any special 'active' ingredients and their effects
- explain the features of the product in such a way that the customer sees the *benefit* to themselves of buying the product.

Knowing your customers

Successful selling is built upon good customer relationships. To be good at what you do, you need to be able to put yourself in the customer's shoes and understand what motivates them. You can then begin to understand them as individuals, and make selling and buying more of a two-way, mutually rewarding problem-solving experience.

What we know generally about customers:

- customers buy for their own reasons. Often, it is for emotional reasons, for how it will make them feel
- customers do not buy products or services. They buy what those products and services will do for them, or the feelings they associate with owning the product or experiencing the service
- customers resent high-pressure sales techniques. A professional low-pressure approach is much more effective.

Successful selling therefore relies on very good communication skills, particularly questioning and listening skills.

The most enjoyable buying decisions are made in relaxed, comfortable surroundings

Creating sales

There are several ways of stimulating the initial interest, which helps in **creating the sale**:

- giving outside talks and demonstrations
- promoting special offers in the salon and in the local press
- maintaining clean and attractive displays of products at reception and in the treatment areas
- sending mail shots using information in your client database
- 'launching' a new treatment or product range, possibly in liaison with the supplier
- providing product and treatment information for clients to read in the reception and relaxation areas
- maintaining clean and attractive display material and point-of-sale information
- giving thorough **client consultations** and detailed home-care advice
- listening to your clients during treatments and recommending other services and products which would benefit them
- using the products yourself and talking from experience.

REMEMBER

The more you understand your customers, the easier the selling process is likely to be.

Promoting new product information at reception

Making the sale

Nothing reassures a customer more than a salesperson who is positive and enthusiastic about a product or service, and confident that the customer will buy it. On the other hand, nothing worries a customer more than a salesperson who sounds doubtful or uncertain.

Here is some advice for **making the sale**. The techniques should be used by everybody who deals with clients in the salon:

- find out exactly what the client needs. This means asking questions and listening carefully to the answers
- use closed questions to get short, straightforward answers (usually yes or no), for example, 'Do you have a regular nail-care routine?', 'Have you ever tried wearing a ridge filler basecoat under your nail enamel?'
- use open questions to invite fuller and more detailed answers, for example, 'How do you normally look after your hands?', 'Can you describe the problem to me?'
- give the client advice: always relate the benefits of the product specifically to the client, for example, 'By using this enriched cuticle cream regularly, you will prevent these splits occurring [indicate them] and your nails will not be as brittle. You will soon notice a great improvement in the appearance of your hands'
- always smile and talk confidently and positively about the product you have chosen; where possible, tell the client about your personal experiences with the product
- explain how the product should be used; if possible, let the client feel, smell or hold the product
- **closing the sale**: look for signals that tell you the client has decided to take your advice and buy the product
- where appropriate, explain the benefits of the different sizes available in the product: these will usually be linked to price
- gain agreement with the client: this is achieved either immediately or after a short period of 'thinking' time. Do not be afraid of silences at this stage. Just keep quiet and wait patiently for the client to make a decision
- use **link selling** to encourage your client to buy complementary products from the same range, for example cleansers and toners, eye creams and eye gels, nail enamels and basecoats
- once you have sold the product, wrap it up and process payment; as you hand over the purchase, check once more that the client understands how to use it
- enter details of the purchase on the **client's record card**.

Complimentary products provide link selling opportunities

REMEMBER

If the client touches, feels and smells the product, then asks the price, the item is practically sold!

REMEMBER

Head nodding in agreement, smiles and friendly eye contact are **positive buying signals**.

GOOD PRACTICE

Be confident when giving the client the price. Hesitation or reluctance to mention the price will give the client the impression that you consider the product too expensive.

REMEMBER

Do not talk yourself out of a sale! Clients will be put off buying if you sound 'pushy'.

REMEMBER

Make sure you read and understand all of the product information so that you can give clients good and reliable advice. If in doubt, ask your supervisor to explain anything you do not understand.

SELF-CHECKS

Selling products

1 Give three reasons why selling skills are important in the salon.

2 Why should your client purchase products from your salon rather than a department store?

3 State three ways of demonstrating confidence in a product when selling it to a client.

4 Why is it a good idea to let the client sample the product before buying?

5 How can you tell when a client is ready to buy a product?

6 What is 'link selling'?

7 Why is sales language so important when describing a product?

8 Name and describe two pieces of consumer protection legislation.

ACTIVITY

Activity 5.1: Selling products

1 Role play a selling situation with a partner. One of you should be the client and the other one the receptionist. If possible, use the salon reception or make a small display of retail products to help set the scene. (Remember the steps to successful selling and practise using open and closed questions. An outside observer may be able to tell you at which point you seemed to have made or lost the sale.)

2 Know your suppliers! When a business deals with only a small number of suppliers, there is usually a special professional relationship with the salon. Get to know the technical representatives who visit your salon. Find out which products each firm supplies, and get details of the service they provide. Get an idea of delivery schedules so that you can give your clients a realistic idea of how long they may have to wait to purchase a product that is out of stock. Write up your findings.

REMEMBER

No two 'noses' are identical. The chemical reaction that occurs between the skin and a perfume means that the same fragrance may not always smell the same on different people.

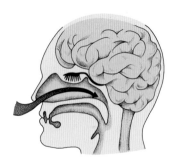

Different smells have different associations through their direct link with the brain

Selling perfumes

Choosing perfume is a very personal matter and should not be rushed. Perfume samples should be allowed to settle on the skin before making a final decision. The true fragrance of a perfume may take up to an hour to develop, so a client should not be expected to judge a perfume by their first impression.

The sense of smell

Smells are picked up by special olfactory nerve cells in the lining of the nose, which connect directly to the brain. Perfumes are volatile (they evaporate) and mix with the air that is breathed in through the nose.

There is a special language used in the perfumery industry to describe fragrances:

TYPE	SOURCES	DESCRIPTION
Floral	single blossoms, e.g. rose, lavender, lily of the valley	light, refreshing, sweet
Citrus	e.g. lemon, orange, lime, bergamot	sharp, fresh, stimulating
Green	pine, cedar blended with mosses, ferns, grasses, flower stems	fresh, woody, crisp, clean, dry, aromatic
Modern	usually contains synthetic oils, which imitate floral, woody and herbal fragrances that are less easy to identify	bright, cheery, cool, clean, fresh
Spicy	cinnamon, cloves, vanilla ginger, exotic flowers	heavy, pungent, sometimes described as 'leathery' in male fragrances
Sweet	very fragrant combinations, e.g. jasmine, gardenia	very sweet, can be overpowering if applied heavily
Oriental	eastern woods and grasses, sandalwood, patchouli	full-bodied, aromatic, heavy, sultry, exotic

The qualities of perfumes are often described to match the 'mood' of the fragrance, for example mysterious, classical, warm, intense, seductive, discreet. This language is used to full effect when marketing a fragrance.

Types of perfumed products

The strength of a perfume refers to the concentration of its base in alcohol or alcohol and water. The natural fragrances are extracted from their sources as oil. The more oil that is contained in a product, the more lingering the fragrance and the more expensive the product.

Two types of raw materials are used to make perfumes:

- natural – these are mainly essential oils obtained from the various parts of plants and flowers
- synthetic – aldehydes, which can be blended quite effectively to imitate natural fragrances.

At one time, the finest perfumes contained ingredients obtained from animal sources, such as ambergris from the sperm whale and musk from musk deer.

These wild animals have become endangered species and the risk of their extinction has prompted strong lobbying by environmental pressure groups. Synthetic alternatives are now widely available.

Perfume

The strongest concentration of a fragrance, perfume is long lasting and contains only a small amount of alcohol. A perfume is the truest version of a fragrance. It should be applied to the pulse points where the warmth of the skin helps to develop its character.

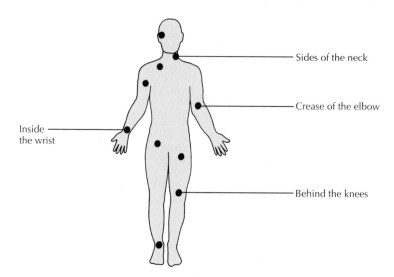

Sides of the neck

Crease of the elbow

Inside the wrist

Behind the knees

Location of pulse points

Eau de parfum

A lighter version of perfume, eau de parfum is suitable for use all over the body.

Eau de toilette/eau de cologne

The most dilute forms of a perfume, probably the most popular strength of fragrance. It is cheaper than perfume and is usually available as a spray or splash-on, which is refreshing to use.

Fragrance notes

A fragrance keeps developing for some time after it has been applied. The true character of the perfume appears only when the alcohol content has evaporated and the other ingredients have settled on the skin.

A fragrance develops in stages called notes:

- top note – the impression made when the bottle is opened and the perfume is first applied
- middle note – the initial top note lingers and gives way to the middle note, which carries the true character and richness of the perfume. This is the best stage of fragrance development. In a good perfume, the middle note lasts for 4–6 hours
- base note – composed of the longest-lasting elements of the perfume, known as fixatives. On their own, the fixatives smell quite unpleasant, but they give permanence and depth to the other components of the perfume.

When only the base note remains, it is time to reapply the perfume.

'Why does this perfume smell different on me?' is not an uncommon question. It can be quite an expensive mistake choosing a new fragrance before testing it properly. The main problem is skin chemistry: if the pH of the skin is not normal, a reaction occurs that affects the development of the fragrance. Perfume lasts longer on an oily skin but tends to turn sweeter. A sharper, more citrus fragrance is usually more suitable.

Other factors that may affect the skin's reaction to a perfume are:

- smoking – apart from the smell of smoke and tobacco clinging to clothing and skin, nicotine can alter skin chemistry and reduce the staying power of perfume
- medication – in particular, the contraceptive pill can affect the skin's reaction to perfume
- menstruation – the perception of smells can change at this time
- climate/environment – warmth makes perfumes evaporate more quickly and speeds up the rate at which the base notes appear
- air pollution – perfume usually needs reapplying more often in a city-centre environment than in the country.

Testing a perfume

It is best not to confuse the perfume testing by sampling more than two products at once. The nose can become over-stimulated, which makes it difficult to distinguish between the different samples.

When helping a client to choose between perfumes, always:

- test the lightest fragrance first
- use a spray – spraying helps the perfume to develop faster and helps the client to choose more quickly
- spray on the wrist, holding the bottle far enough away to avoid dampening the skin
- advise the client to give the alcohol time to evaporate before smelling the fragrance
- instruct the client not to smell the fragrance too closely and to avoid rubbing it into the skin; doing so may eliminate the top notes and interfere with the perfume's development
- perform the second test as soon as the client has made a decision on the first fragrance
- allow time for the client to make a final choice; offer advice only if it is requested.

Fragrance-building

A layering effect can be achieved by using different forms of the same fragrance to produce a build-up effect. **Fragrance-building** actually works out more economically than using only the more concentrated versions of a fragrance.

Link selling

Selling related products from a range is called 'link' selling. When selling a perfume, these could include:

- bath oil
- scented soap
- talcum powder
- deodorant
- shampoo
- body lotion.

REMEMBER

Many perfumes smell sweeter and heavier in tropical conditions. Advise your clients about this if they are going on holiday.

REMEMBER

Applying perfume is a very important part of dressing. Perfume reflects personality, mood and occasion. Women often choose different perfumes for different occasions, for example a light, fresh fragrance for day wear and a 'heavier' aromatic one for evening.

Testing a perfume

GOOD PRACTICE

Once the client has made a decision, use the fragrance on her, but not too close to the face. Spray the perfume outside the triangle which goes from the nose to the shoulders. Be careful not to spray perfume on jewellery, particularly pearls, or on fragile fabrics such as silk or crêpe.

Male fragrances

Male fragrances are usually 'green', 'citrus' or 'spicy'. They contain ingredients that compensate for the 'sweetening' effects of a male skin, which generally tends to be greasier than a female's.

Fragrance-building

There are opportunities for fragrance-building for men by selling a combination of some of the following products:

- after-shave
- foam shave
- shaving soap
- pre-electric shave (for preventing razor burns)
- deodorants
- body and hair shampoo
- talcum powder
- shower gel
- body lotion.

Male fragrance ranges provide good link selling opportunities

Photosensitisation

Perfume ingredients, for example bergamot oil, can make the skin very sensitive to ultraviolet light. The result can be sunburn after only a very short exposure time: sometimes, brown patches appear on the neck where melanin has been produced following photosensitisation of the skin by ingredients in the perfume.

Selling perfumes

1　Why is it better for a perfume to be tested before being purchased?
2　Give two examples of natural ingredients which may be found in each of the following types of fragrance: (a) green, (b) spicy, (c) floral, (d) oriental.
3　Distinguish between a 'perfume' and an 'eau de toilette'.
4　What are the 'notes' of a perfume?
5　What are the correct storage conditions for perfume?
6　Give two reasons why a perfume may smell different on different people.
7　Why should a spray be used when testing a perfume?
8　What is 'fragrance-building'?
9　State two possible contra-actions to perfume.
10　Why should perfume not be worn when lying on a sun bed?

Activity 5.2: Selling perfumes

1　With a partner or a small group of colleagues, visit a perfume department and each test the same two perfumes on the wrists. Wait half an hour and then compare how the fragrances smell on each of you.
2　Try using the language of perfumes to write down a description of the fragrances you have tested. Compare your answers with those of your colleagues.

Selling treatments and services

The most successful salons earn their reputation by providing excellent personal service. A service can only be truly personal when the needs of the individual clients are understood, and treatments and advice are matched to those needs. This is what successful selling is all about.

Assessing the needs of the client

Clients have different reasons for attending a salon for beauty treatment:

- to complete their 'make-over' for a special event
- to keep their hands, skin or body in good condition
- to improve and control the appearance of certain conditions and disorders
- to make them look and feel younger
- to 'spoil' themselves as a special treat
- to 'escape' from the pressures of everyday life
- to boost their confidence and increase their feeling of personal well-being.

There are probably many more reasons. Clients are individuals with different needs and expectations. Once you have managed to find out why the client has come to the salon, you can start planning their treatments. Whatever their reason, it is important for a consultation to take place first. A little extra time should be allowed for this

REMEMBER

Assessing the needs of the client is the most important part of selling.

when making the appointment, alternatively the client may book in for a consultation and then come back at a later date for treatment.

Giving a consultation

Information is obtained at the consultation by asking questions and by examining the area to be treated. Keep eye contact with your client, listen carefully and develop the answers they give you. This way, clients know you are sincerely interested in what they have to say.

The main aims of the consultation are to:

- put the client at ease
- gain the confidence of the client
- establish a good rapport
- find out what the client wants
- determine what the client needs
- ensure the client is suitable for treatment
- discuss the treatment options available
- answer the client's questions
- agree a **treatment plan** with the client
- sell the client appropriate treatments and products.

GOOD PRACTICE

It is important not to rush the consultation. Besides needing enough time to make an accurate assessment of the client, you also need time to talk to your client and build up their trust and confidence in you.

Building trust

Clients are unlikely to understand many of the treatments fully until they have been explained by a professional beauty therapist. They may think they want a particular treatment, but there may be others that are more suitable for them. When recommending a treatment or course of treatments, make sure that the client understands why they are necessary, what costs are involved and any particular conditions required for achieving success with the treatments, for example frequency of appointments, or specific home care.

REMEMBER

The more you explain to the client, the more evidence you provide of your technical knowledge. Clients will have confidence in you and trust your advice.

REMEMBER

The consultation is between you and the client. Any information you are given is confidential and must not be discussed with anyone else. Information contained in computerised client records is covered by the Data Protection Act 1984.

Filling in a record card

During the consultation, you will have to fill in a record card, but try to avoid writing and asking questions at the same time. You must take care to fill in the record card neatly. At some future date, the information you write down may be needed by someone else. It is no good if only you can read your writing!

One side of the card is used for recording the client's personal details and information related to treatment planning. The other side is for recording the dates of the client's visits to the salon with details of the treatments received and retail products purchased.

A PRACTICAL GUIDE TO BEAUTY THERAPY

This side of the record card has the client's personal details. Some of these influence the treatments given and others provide useful practical information.
(i) The initial of the client's surname is printed in the top right-hand corner of the card so that the card can be retrieved quickly from the index storage system.
(ii) The information given here is important for effective communication with the client. It is more polite to ask a client their date of birth rather than their age. Knowing this will help you to assess the condition of the skin and advise the most suitable treatments and home care.
(iii) Details of the client's doctor may be needed in an emergency. It is important to know health and medication details when assessing the skin.
(iv) These details are necessary to make an accurate diagnosis and plan appropriate beauty care.

(i)	BEAUTY BOX SALON		
(ii)	Mr/Mrs/Ms	Address	Tel. no.
	Surname		Home
	Forenames	Date of birth	Work
(iii)	Doctor's name	General state of health	Recent illness/operation
	Doctor's address	Current medication	Allergies
(iv)	Basic skin type	Skin history/treatment	Recommended home care
	Skin tone		
	Skin colour	General comments	Date of consultation
	Muscle tone		Given by
	Problems		Signed
	Contraindications		
	Recommended salon treatments		I have understood and agreed the treatment plan.
			Client signature
			Date

This side of the record card records details of the client's visits to the salon.

(i) This shows the frequency and regularity of the visits/treatments.
(ii) This shows which treatments the client has received, including skin tests.
(iii) Details of the client's reaction to treatments may be recorded; the information may be important to recall for the next visit.
(iv) It is necessary to know which therapist has treated the client. This information may be needed when making a follow-up appointment or when referring to details of the purchases made. This information is used for recommending further purchases.
(v) Client home care may be monitored by referring to details of the purchases made. This information is used for recommending further purchases.

Date	Treatment record	Comments	Initials	Retail purchases
(i)	(ii)	(iii)	(iv)	(v)

A sample record card – front and back

GOOD PRACTICE

If you are giving a consultation for facial treatments, you will spend much of the time seated behind the client, cleansing the face, examining the skin and making notes on the record card. It is best to start off the consultation by sitting in front of the client, with the back of the treatment couch raised so that you can maintain eye contact while you speak. Maintaining eye contact while talking and listening is very important.

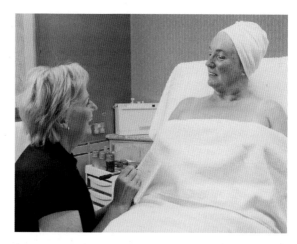

Maintaining eye contact is very important in order to develop trust

Examining the client

Clients are more satisfied when they feel they have been examined thoroughly. Information provided by the examination helps to provide an accurate assessment and more effective treatment plan.

The nature of the examination will depend on the body area concerned. Here are some general guidelines:

- instruct the client about which clothing needs to be removed. A gown should be offered if the client needs to undress down to underwear
- ensure the client is warm and comfortable; areas of the body not being examined should be supported and covered appropriately
- conduct the examination in private, peacefully and avoiding interruptions
- wash and dry your own hands before beginning the examination
- make sure the area to be examined is clean and dry
- examine the skin and nails in good light, preferably through a magnifying lens
- question the client to determine the specific cause of conditions that you come across during the examination
- be pleasant and tactful when asking questions
- write down details of the examination as you go along
- find out details of previous treatments that the client may have had and how successful they were.

Agreeing a treatment plan

When you have completed the examination, there may be other points you wish to discuss with the client before recommending a treatment plan. For example, it is helpful to know how much time the client has available for attending the salon. You may have to amend your treatment plan and consider different options.

By this stage of the consultation you will have assessed your client's needs. Now you must give advice on the treatments and products which are going to be of greatest benefit.

REMEMBER

When you advise the client, you are helping them to make a buying decision; in other words you are selling them the best combination of treatments and products to match their needs.

Remember the basic rules of selling:

- describe the treatments and explain how they work
- relate the benefits specifically to the client
- talk confidently and positively about the treatments
- identify and deal with their concerns and expectations
- state the price confidently
- recognise and respond to buying signals
- do not rush the client into making a decision.

A client who wants to say 'Yes', but acts indecisively may just need final reassurance from you. If you have recognised positive buying signals, let the client know that you agree with their decision and explain why, for example, 'I think that a course of bio-facials will be ideal for you. You will find them very relaxing, the products are beautiful and you will see immediate improvements in your skin.'

Once you have gained agreement with the client, the sale is closed, the consultation has finished and the treatment plan is in place. Your client's signature on the record card will confirm their understanding and agreement with the treatment plan.

REMEMBER

You must ensure that your clients have realistic expectations from their treatments and that they understand how to get the best results from products they purchase for home care. This avoids disappointment later and also helps to develop the clients' confidence in your advice.

SELF-CHECKS

Selling treatments and services

1. Give three main purposes of a client consultation.
2. What information is recorded during the consultation?
3. Give an example of (a) a closed question, and (b) an open question, which might be used during an examination of the client's hands and nails.
4. Give an example of (a) a closed question, and (b) an open question, which might be used during an examination of the client's facial skin.
5. Which particular aspects of the consultation are most likely to give a client confidence in your advice?
6. State three reasons for keeping records of clients' treatments.
7. Give three reasons why a client may be reluctant to commit themselves to a treatment.
8. What are 'positive' buying signals?

Activity 5.3: Selling treatments and services

Working with a partner, role play a consultation with a new client. Imagine that the client has received a gift voucher entitling her to treatments and products from the salon up to a value of £25.00. She has never been to a beauty salon before and has no idea what to expect. She does not really know what she wants, although she has fairly firm ideas of what she does not like about herself.

Enlist the help of a third person to give you feedback on how successful you are. (You will need to sound confident, so brush up on your knowledge of treatments and products before you act through this role play!)

Selling products and services

There may appear to be more than one answer. Read the question carefully before making your final decision. Discuss your answers with your colleagues and supervisor. Talk through issues that are raised.

1 Retail sales are important for the salon because:
   (a) there is a lot of competition
   (b) the business would not make profits without retail sales
   (c) there is a lot of profit on retail sales
   (d) the products cannot be purchased anywhere else.

2 Successful selling is a way of:
   (a) taking advantage of the client
   (b) satisfying the needs of the client
   (c) earning commission
   (d) beating competition.

3 The strongest concentration of a fragrance is available in a:
   (a) perfume
   (b) eau de toilette
   (c) eau de parfum
   (d) eau de cologne.

4 A perfume may smell different on different people because:
   (a) more perfume has been applied
   (b) the perfume has been applied to a different place
   (c) the skin is allergic to the perfume
   (d) the chemistry of the skin is different.

5 The sale is said to be 'closed' when:
   (a) the product has been bought and paid for
   (b) the client has no interest in buying the product
   (c) the client agrees to buy the product
   (d) the client decides not to buy the product.

6 The main purpose of a consultation is to:
   (a) sell the client as many products as possible
   (b) identify the needs of the client and agree an appropriate treatment plan
   (c) identify the needs of the client and sell them as many products as possible
   (d) sell the client as many treatments as possible.

You should now understand the following terms and phrases. If you do not, go back through the chapter and find out what they mean:

Retail sales	Creating the sale	Making the sale
Positive buying signals	Fragrance-building	Closing the sale
Link selling	Client consultations	Client record card
Treatment plan		

Chapter 6 Facial massage and skin care

Improve and maintain facial skin condition

Part 1

Skin analysis, facial anatomy and skin types

After working through this section of the chapter you will be able to:

- use effective communication and consultation techniques
- conduct a skin analysis
- understand the structure and functions of skin
- know the position and actions of the facial, neck and shoulder muscles
- understand the variations in skin characteristics between different client groups
- know the names and position of the bones of the face, neck and shoulder girdle
- know how to recognise different skin types and conditions
- recognise contraindications
- understand how the natural ageing process affects facial skin and muscle tone
- understand how environmental and lifestyle factors affect the condition of the skin
- know the functions of nerves, blood and lymph
- understand the roles of blood and lymph in improving skin and muscle condition.

Before you work through this chapter: Be wise and revise!
Revision topics to help you achieve this unit:

Improve and maintain facial skin condition

TOPIC	CHAPTER	PAGE
Professional image	1	16
Communication skills	2	24
Controlling the salon environment	3	36
Client care	3	52
Treatment hygiene	3	54
Selling treatments and services	5	103

The client's skin and facial features must be assessed accurately so that the best treatments and products can be recommended. A consultation provides the opportunity to examine the skin closely and to ask questions that help build up a clearer picture of the client's needs. Details of the assessment are entered on the client's record card and are used for producing a treatment plan. Chapter 5 on selling provides further details about giving a consultation and more specific information is included in the treatment chapters.

Assessing the client

Your assessment of the client is based on what you see and what you know. By carrying out a facial examination, you will be able to:

● assess the client's skin type: this is important for choosing the correct skin-care preparations and giving the best home-care advice

● recognise minor blemishes and abnormalities: sometimes, the appearance of these may be improved with cosmetic treatments; they certainly will not be made worse by them

● identify contraindications: if these are present, beauty therapy treatment must not be applied to the affected area. This is because there is a risk of spreading infection or making the condition worse. The client may need to be referred for medical advice

● identify specific problems: depending on the client's age, health and previous skin care, there may be conditions present that need particular attention. It may be necessary to adapt the basic salon procedures and to recommend special home-care treatments

● note the client's colouring and facial features: these are particularly important when designing the make-up for a client. Cosmetics are chosen and applied to enhance the client's good points and minimise the bad ones. Sometimes, illusions need to be created to achieve balance. A good knowledge of facial structure is required to do this effectively

● test the elasticity of the skin: skin with poor elasticity forms wrinkles and sags. Clients need advising on the correct way of treating their skin to prevent it from becoming over-stretched. Great care is also needed when choosing and applying professional beauty treatments

GOOD PRACTICE

To test the elasticity of the skin, pinch the skin gently in each of the main facial areas. Skin that is firm with good elasticity will immediately spring back into shape. Skin with poor elasticity has become over-stretched. It will appear crepey and will not recover immediately from the pinch test.

A PRACTICAL GUIDE TO BEAUTY THERAPY

- assess **muscle tone**: the muscles of facial expression produce characteristic lines on the face, which become deeper and permanent with the ageing process. Some of the muscles cause the features to 'sag' when they lose their tone and the contours become less well defined. Beauty treatments help to minimise the effects of reduced muscle tone. The client may be advised how to prevent lines and wrinkles from getting worse.

Examining the face

The examination should start with a general assessment of the skin and then concentrate on specific areas of the face and neck until the whole area has been covered.

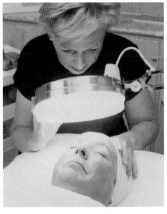

Using an anglepoise lamp to examine the face

Preparing the client

Prepare the client as you would for a facial treatment:

- provide the client with a gown and ask them to undress down to their underwear
- ask the client to remove their earrings and any necklaces, and place them safely in a bowl on your trolley
- assist the client on to the beauty couch and, when they are settled in a comfortable position, cover them with a blanket or large, soft bath sheet
- slip their underwear straps down over shoulders so that the skin of the upper chest and neck can be seen
- place a smaller towel over the front of the client, tucking it into the straps to protect their underwear
- secure the client's hair off their face with a clean headband
- remove all traces of make-up and deep-cleanse, tone and dry the skin.

GOOD PRACTICE

Your assessment actually starts while you are preparing the client. A sensitive caucasian (white) skin will appear pink even after a relatively gentle cleansing treatment. Darker patches will appear on a sensitive black skin.

You are now ready to begin the skin analysis. Put your anglepoise lamp in position and have the client's record card and a pen nearby so that you can make notes as you go along.

Skin analysis

Begin by establishing the basic skin type. Find out about the client's skin history and their general approach to skin care.

Examples of closed questions

- Do you have a skin-care routine?
- Do you protect your skin in the sun?
- Do you ever use soap on your face?
- Do you wear a moisturiser?
- Is your health generally good?
- Have you noticed any changes in your skin recently?
- Does your skin ever react to make-up products?

Examples of open questions

- How do you normally look after your skin?
- What are the main problems you have with your skin?
- Which skin-care products do you use?
- How much make-up do you usually wear?
- Do you go out to work? What sort of environment do you work in?
- What sort of a lifestyle do you have – regular and routine or busy and varied?

When you have made a general assessment, take a more detailed look at the different areas of the face and neck. Continue to question the client carefully at each stage. This will help you to identify the specific causes of conditions that may be present.

The more practice you get, the more confident you will become at carrying out a skin analysis. With experience, you will soon be able to recognise signs and follow them up with the most appropriate questions.

SELF-CHECKS

Assessing the client

1 Give three reasons for examining the skin before giving facial treatments.

2 How should the client be prepared for a skin analysis?

3 How would you expect the skin of a young, healthy client to respond to the 'pinch' test?

4 What is 'caucasian skin'?

5 How can you tell if a black skin is very sensitive?

6 List three conditions that are necessary for ensuring an accurate assessment of the skin.

7 State the main difference between open and closed questions.

8 Give three examples of open questions which could be used during a consultation.

Skin: the facts

Skin covers an area of between 1.2 and 2 m² and accounts for approximately 12 per cent of our total body weight. It moulds to and moves with our body, creating a boundary that separates our insides from the outside world. Constantly in contact with its surroundings, the skin has to be tough enough to withstand both physical and chemical assault, yet sensitive enough to respond to subtle changes in the internal and external environment.

The skin is working all the time, even when we are asleep, helping to protect and regulate body processes which keep us healthy. Healthy skin provides some protection from:

- physical injury
- chemical damage
- damage by infrared (heat) rays and ultraviolet
- invasion by bacteria and other micro-organisms
- sudden temperature changes
- excessive water loss
- penetration by foreign bodies
- **allergens**.

Problems occur if the skin's natural protective functions break down.

Structure and functions of the skin

The skin consists of three layers:

- the **epidermis** forms the outer protective covering of the body
- the **dermis** provides the 'packing' material, which supports all the other structures
- a subcutaneous layer, made up of fatty tissue, cushions the internal organs against shocks, and acts as an insulator and source of energy when required. This fatty layer separates the skin from underlying muscles.

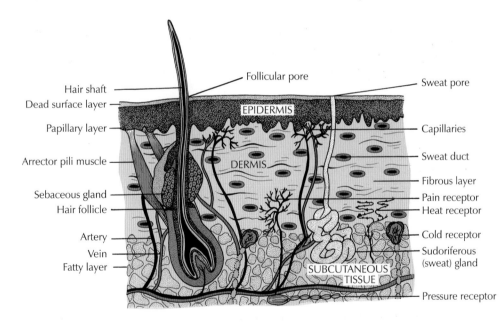

Cross-section through the skin

The skin as a barrier

If harmful organisms or chemicals penetrate the dermis, they get transported round the body by the blood, causing widespread problems. If adequate moisture levels are not maintained within the living layers of the skin, the cells shrivel and die. The epidermis is structured to provide a barrier, which keeps out the bad and keeps in the good.

POSITION	STRUCTURE	FUNCTION
Epidermis: upper portion of skin	Consists of five layers. Cells in bottom layer are living. They reproduce by mitosis (each cell divides into two) and carry on moving upwards through the layers until they eventually die and harden at the surface	Protection
Dermis: lies beneath the epidermis		
Papillary layer: situated at the interface of the dermis with the epidermis	Papillary layer: undulating (wavy) tissue. The waste upward projections are called dermal papillae. They contain blood and lymph capillaries and nerve endings	Papillary layer increases surface area of reproductive cells and provides living layers of epidermis with vessels which supply nourishment and remove cellular waste
Reticular layer: situated beneath papillary layer	Reticular layer: dense and fibrous. Contains the main components of the skin. The protein fibres are produced mainly from fibroblast cells contained in a 'ground substance'	Reticular layer protects and repairs injured tissue. The fibres allow skin to bend and fold over underlying muscle activity: • Collagen: gives skin its strength and and resilience • Elastin: allows the skin to stretch easily but quickly regain its shape • Reticulin: keeps all the other structures in place
Subcutaneous layer: lies beneath the dermis	Fatty layer of skin. Cells called lipocytes produce lipids which are the fat cells from which subcutaneous tissue is formed	Cushions muscles, bones and internal organs against shocks and blows Acts as an insulator and source of energy when required
Sudoriferous glands: situated in the dermis		Eccrine glands help to regulate body temperature by producing sweat which evaporates off the skin's surface and cools it down when it is hot. Eccrine sweat removes some waste materials from the skin and also contributes to the protective acid mantle which coats the surface of the skin
Eccrine glands: present all over the body, being most numerous on the palms of the hands and soles of the feet	Eccrine glands: coiled glands which produce sweat, a watery fluid containing some salt and urea. Sweat passes upwards through a duct and eventually reaches the skin's surface through a sweat pore	
Apocrine glands: found mainly in the armpits, nipples, anal and genital areas	Apocrine glands: fewer in number and larger than eccrine glands. They open up into hair follicles and produce a thicker secretion than eccrine sweat	Apocrine glands are under nervous control and respond to emotional, psychological and sexual stimuli. They are considered a sexual characteristic
Hair follicles: situated in the dermis. Present all over the body except on the palms of the hands and soles of the feet	Formed from a depression of epidermal cells. Sac-like structures which contain hairs. Outer layer of follicle is fibrous and has very good supply of blood and nerves. Innerlayer formed from two layers of cells called the inner and outer root sheath The base of the hair follicle degenerates and rebuilds during the cycle of hair growth and replacement. It contains a dermal papilla which supplies blood to the base of the hair The follicle opens at the skin's surface at a follicular pore	Produce and contain the hairs during their life cycle Help provide nourishment for the hairs

The structure of the skin (continued)

POSITION	STRUCTURE	FUNCTION
Hairs: contained in follicles in the dermis. Present over most areas of the body but do not grow on the lips, palms of the hands or soles of the feet	The length of hair showing above the skin's surface is called the shaft The portion lying in the follicle is called the root The enlarged base of the root surrounding the papilla is called the bulb Hair is made up of the protein keratin. It consists of three layers. The outer layer is made up of scales which overlap upwards and interlock with scales on the follicle lining to keep the hairs in place	Protect against friction and damage from the external environment Hair is a sexual characteristic
Sebaceous glands: situated in the dermis adjacent to hair follicles. They are not present on the palms of the hands or soles of the feet Some glands open directly onto the skin's surface	These lobulated glands produce sebum, a fatty substance containing waxes, fatty acids, cholesterol and dead cells The sebum passes through a duct and up the hair follicle from where it passes onto the skin through a follicular pore	Sebum lubricates skin and hair and combines with sweat to form the protective acid mantle of the skin Sebum also helps to waterproof the skin. It retains natural moisture in the skin and provides some insulation
Arrector pili: muscle which connects the side of the hair follicle with the base of the epidermis	Made up of muscle tissue which contracts in response to sensory stimulation. Contraction of the arrector pili makes the hair stand on end which pulls the surface of the skin up into 'goose bumps'	The action of raising the hairs provides some protection from attack and helps to trap heat next to the skin when the body is cold
Blood vessels: arteries and veins run through the dermis and subcutaneous layer Arteries sub-divide into arterioles. They form a network of capillaries which supply the various components of the skin Veins sub-divide into venules	Arteries carry oxygenated blood. Their walls are muscular and elastic. Blood is pumped around the body in arteries Veins carry deoxygenated blood. Their walls have valves which stop blood from stagnating or flowing backwards Capillaries are very fine vessels made up of a single layer of cells. Some materials can pass in and out through the thin walls of the capillaries The surface blood vessels dilate in response to heat and contract in response to cold	Arteries carry oxygen and nutrients to the skin via the capillaries The veins remove waste products The surface capillaries help to regulate body temperature When the vessels dilate, heat is lost from the body through the skin. When the body is cold, the vessels contract and heat is retained Components of the blood produce clots which prevent further blood loss and infection through broken skin following injury
Nerves: contained in the dermis and subcutaneous tissue. Different types of nerves are distributed according to where they are needed most Special 'sympathetic' nerves supply blood vessels, sweat glands and the arrector pili muscle	Made up of white or grey nerve fibres which terminate in sensory nerve endings. The nerve endings or 'receptors' are specially shaped and positioned to respond to a range of different stimuli: heat, cold, pain, pressure, touch	Nerve stimulation causes a reaction which triggers an appropriate response from the body

REMEMBER

The five layers of the epidermis have no blood vessels running through them and practically no nerve supply. The living cells receive their nourishment from **tissue fluid**, which escapes through the walls of the blood capillaries. The tissue fluid bathes the cells, providing them with nutrients. Waste products are carried away and eventually removed by **lymph**.

The layers of the epidermis

HEALTH MATTERS

The process of cell division that produces new epidermal cells is called mitosis. During mitosis, each cell divides to produce two cells identical to itself.

HEALTH MATTERS

The stratum corneum thickens when exposed to strong sunlight, presenting a further barrier to the penetration of ultraviolet rays. If these rays reach the dermis, they destroy the protein framework of the skin. Sometimes they cause skin cancer. Sunlight is the commonest cause of skin cancer.

REMEMBER

Beauty treatments maintain or improve the appearance of the surface of the epidermis while, at the same time, enhancing its ability to provide a protective barrier.

The epidermis

The outer skin, the epidermis, is made up of a type of body tissue called stratified (layered) squamous (made up of scales) epithelium (covering). An organised production line converts living cells at the base of the epidermis into dead, hardened, compacted layers of protein (**keratin**) on the outer surface.

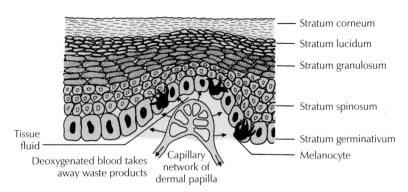

Stratum corneum
Stratum lucidum
Stratum granulosum
Stratum spinosum
Stratum germinativum
Melanocyte

Tissue fluid
Deoxygenated blood takes away waste products
Capillary network of dermal papilla

Stratum germinatum

The stratum germinatum is the 'living' basal layer from which new cells are produced. The deeper cells are pushed up to the surface to replace those which are worn away from the outside. Pigment-producing cells called melanocytes are present in this layer. The cells take their nourishment from tissue fluid originating from blood vessels situated in the deeper (dermis) layer of the skin.

Stratum mucosum (or spinosum)

The stratum mucosum is a living layer which contains prickle cells, so called because tiny outgrowths from the cells give them a prickly appearance. The shape of the cells helps to give this layer rigidity. The 'prickles' help to connect them and provide channels for the passage of nourishing tissue fluid between the cells. Towards the upper part of this layer, the process of keratinisation starts to take place. During this process, living cells containing a nucleus begin to die and flatten out.

Stratum granulosum

The final stages of keratinisation take place in the stratum granulosum and the cells take on a granular appearance. Keratohyalin granules replace the living contents of the cells. By now, the cells have started to become flat and hardened due to the disintegration of their nucleus and loss of fluid.

Stratum lucidum

Known as the clear layer, the cells of the stratum lucidum are dead. They contain no nucleus, are tightly packed and help to provide a barrier to water loss from the deeper layers of the skin. The nails are made up of specialised cells of the stratum lucidum, otherwise this layer is evident only on the palms of the hands and the soles of the feet where the skin is thickest.

Stratum corneum

This outer layer, the stratum corneum, is composed of dead, flat, overlapping, scale-like cells composed mainly of the protein keratin. The cells are tough, horny and tightly packed, providing an effective barrier. They are constantly being rubbed off by friction.

Desquamation

The cells of the epidermis are packed more loosely in the upper layers. This is to prepare them for shedding (**desquamation**), which occurs continuously and helps to remove debris and micro-organisms that might otherwise settle on the skin and cause infections.

Cell growth and renewal

The rate at which new cells are generated by the epidermis depends on the body's available energy:

- regeneration usually occurs during the four hours after midnight when body metabolism has slowed down
- it takes about 200 days for a cell to mature in the epidermis
- the lifetime of the mature cell is 7–20 days
- the replacement time for the stratum corneum is between 32 and 36 days.

The epidermis is never more than 1 mm thick. It is thickest on the palms of the hands and the soles of the feet, where it needs to withstand the friction caused by gripping and walking. It is thinnest on the eyelids, where it must be light and flexible.

Melanin

Melanin is the dark pigment that produces a sun tan. It protects the deeper layers of the skin by absorbing the sun's ultraviolet rays.

The cells that form pigment are called melanocytes. They are spider-shaped with long irregular arms, which reach out from the cell body. The arms of each melanocyte link it with approximately 10 of the surrounding cells. Melanocytes inject pigment granules, melanosomes, into the neighbouring cells, spreading pigment across the skin. Melanocytes make up about 1 per cent of all skin cells.

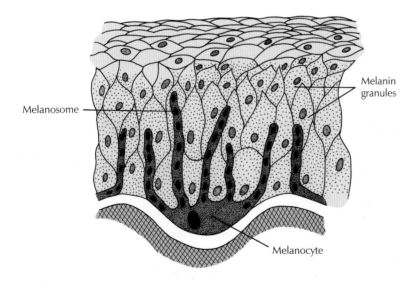

Melanocytes, melanosomes, pigment production

Sebum

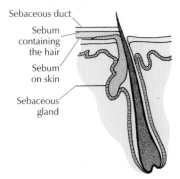

A sebaceous gland; the duct allows a surface coating of sebum on skin and hair

If the epidermis is to be effective as a barrier, it is important that its surface is kept intact – breaks in the skin provide entry to the deeper layers. Sebum is the natural lubricant of the skin, which helps to keep it supple. Made up of fatty substances and the remnants of dead cells, sebum provides a greasy coating, which helps to insulate the skin and prevent natural moisture loss. It also keeps the surface cells compacted and obstructs the passage of substances through the skin. Sebum also helps to block the mouths of hair follicles so that bacteria cannot enter.

Now you will understand why the skin underneath the tips of the fingers and toes goes very soft and wrinkled after soaking in a hot bath. The keratin in the stratum corneum absorbs water and the skin swells above the fatty barrier zone. The patterns created follow the lines of stress in the skin, which also produce our fingerprints.

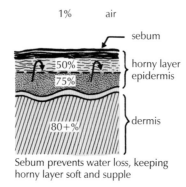

Sebum prevents water loss, keeping horny layer soft and supple

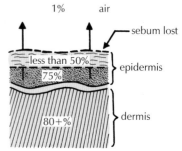

If sebum is lost, water can escape. A dry horny layer is brittle and rough and easily cracked

The distribution of water, and barriers in the skin

The skin as a temperature regulator

The internal systems are so finely balanced that even a slight variation in temperature can affect them. The body is maintained at approximately 36.8 °C (98.6 °F), so that our vital organs can work efficiently. We are all familiar with some of the changes that occur if our body temperature rises above or falls below normal.

In these situations, the body's activity is concentrated on working to restore a normal internal working environment by controlling the amount of heat lost from its surface. Heat is carried around the body by the blood.

We are all familiar with the changes that occur if our body temperature rises above or drops below normal

Thermoreceptors

The skin has an abundance of specialised nerve endings called thermoreceptors, which detect cold and heat. These receptors interact with the hypothalamus, a cluster of nerve cells at the centre of the brain. Changes in blood temperature are detected and the nerve impulses produced stimulate an appropriate response:

- reaction to heat
  a) the superficial blood vessels dilate, allowing more blood to reach the surface so that heat is lost from the body
  b) when the body is hot, the suderiferous glands produce sweat: sweat is composed almost entirely of water, which evaporates from the skin's surface, drawing excess heat out of the body

- reaction to cold
  a) the superficial blood vessels contract, restricting blood flow to the extremities and reducing heat loss
  b) the muscles attached to hair follicles contract, causing the hairs to stand on end, trapping warm air between them.

Heat receptor

Dilation allows more blood to reach the surface so that heat is lost from the body

The reaction of blood vessels to heat

HEALTH MATTERS

There are more receptors in the skin to detect cold than there are to detect warmth. Cold receptors are most abundant in the hands, feet, eyelids, nose and lips. If these areas are not insulated in cold weather, the skin soon becomes dry, chapped and sore.

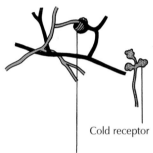

Cold receptor

Special connections (anastomoses) between arteries and veins contract in the cold, restricting blood flow to the extremities and reducing heat loss

The reaction of blood vessels to cold

The high-fibre skin

The protein fibres in the dermis support the skin. They keep all of the various components in place and prevent them from being damaged. They also make the skin tough and help it to change shape over underlying muscle activity. Collectively, the fibres are known as **connective tissue**.

REMEMBER

Sweat glands are larger and more numerous in black skin, with more surface eccrine glands, which keep the body cooler and more comfortable in intense heat. Because black skin allows the body to absorb more heat, the need to sweat to reduce body temperature is far greater.

Collagen fibres

These give the skin its resilience, firmness and strength; the fibres are arranged loosely in the skin and, although not elastic themselves, allow the skin to stretch without tearing. Healthy collagen is flexible and is able to absorb water. Collagen also builds scar tissue to heal skin damaged by cuts and abrasions.

Elastin fibres

These branch out to form a loose network throughout the supporting connective tissue. The fibres are elastic; they stretch easily and return to their former length when tension is removed. Elastin fibres are found everywhere, but they are most numerous on the face and scalp.

Reticulin fibres

These run through and between the other fibres and structures in the dermis, helping to support them and keep them in place.

Black skin has stronger, more stretchy and expandable elastin fibres. This could be why black men and women often make such powerful athletes.

The skin's fibres are contained in a firm jelly called the ground substance, which is rich in nutrients and contains the **fibroblast cells** that produce collagen and elastin. Ageing gradually slows down the production of new cells. The fibres become rigid and inflexible, and less able to perform their functions. In the elderly, the collagen fibres tighten so much that the tiny capillaries become constricted and the supply of blood carrying vital oxygen, moisture and nutrients is gradually cut off.

Free radicals

Free radicals are harmful chemicals that create havoc in the tissues if they are not dealt with. Normally, the activities of these free radicals is counteracted by enzymes produced by the body. However, with age or as a result of an unhealthy lifestyle, the production of these enzymes becomes sluggish, allowing chemicals and other toxic waste to accumulate in the tissues. Changes occur which adversely affect the protein fibres in the skin. The effects are deepening lines, wrinkles, creases, sagging contours and crêpiness.

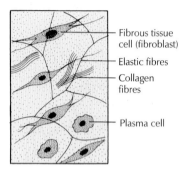

- Fibrous tissue cell (fibroblast)
- Elastic fibres
- Collagen fibres
- Plasma cell

Protein fibres

The following are causes of damage to the skin by free radicals:

- sunlight
- cigarette smoke
- alcohol
- drugs
- petrol fumes
- ozone
- illness
- prolonged stress
- unbalanced diet, consisting largely of sweets, fats and junk food.

Free radicals can damage your skin's health

Skin on the attack

If the living layers of the skin are penetrated or damaged, special cells in the dermis move into action to eliminate the invader and initiate cell repair. The mast cells release **histamine**, a signalling substance, which triggers off a 'pain' reaction and dilates the blood capillaries in the area. The extent of the histamine reaction depends on the nature of the injury.

Histamine reactions

- Itching: caused by stimulation of just a few pain nerve endings. Itching is a symptom of many disorders and is the skin's way of drawing attention to a problem so that appropriate action can be taken. Scratching relieves the irritation of itching, but care should be taken to avoid breaking the skin or infection may occur.

- Erythema: reddening caused by dilation of the blood capillaries in the dermis layer of the skin. The rate of blood flow is increased, which speeds up the removal of irritant or penetrant from the area and the transport of repair materials to clear up the damage.

- Pain: caused by stimulation of a considerable number of pain nerve endings; it is a feature of many skin diseases. A build-up of fluid in the area puts pressure on the nerve endings, which subsides once the infection is cleared or when the irritant is removed.

Strong histamine reaction – pain, swelling, inflammation, pimples, pustules, blisters.

Mild histamine reaction – itching and slight erythema (reddening) of the skin.

- Swelling: the stimulation of blood to an area causes seepage of serum through the capillary walls into the tissues. Serum is the watery component of blood. Localised swelling produces a bubble of the colourless fluid beneath the skin – a blister. More widespread swelling produces a large blister or puffiness of the skin. An increase of fluid in the area helps to dilute the irritant and 'cushion' the deeper layers of the skin from injury.

- Inflammation: the reaction of body tissues to infection or injury. The blood supply to the area is increased, bringing extra white blood cells, which promote healing. The area becomes red, swollen, hot and tender. Any disorder that is an inflammation ends with -itis, for example dermatitis, which is inflammation of the skin.

- Pustule: a raised, inflamed spot on the skin, which contains pus. Pus is a yellowish liquid that forms when the body fights bacteria. It consists of white blood cells, dead and living bacteria, fragments of dead tissue destroyed by bacteria and serum. Pus is sometimes greenish in colour, depending on the type of bacteria present.

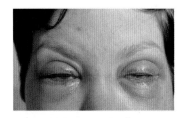

Histamine reaction: itchy, swollen eyes

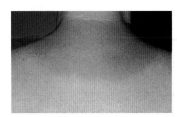

Histamine reaction: sunburn

Protection from disease

Infections occur when the skin becomes broken and invaded, or when the acid mantle that coats the skin surface breaks down. Made up of sebum, sweat and keratin, this mantle creates a slightly acid coating to the skin, which supports the least harmful bacteria but keeps them fairly inactive.

The life on skin

The skin provides a home for many different types of organisms, including bacteria, which coexist quite happily. They actually help the skin to stay healthy by taking up space which might otherwise be invaded by more harmful organisms. Different types of organisms thrive in different conditions. Those that survive on the greasy centre panel of the face would not be found on the much drier skin of the forearm. Everyone has their own collection of bacteria and other organisms which are as distinct to a microbiologist as fingerprints are to a detective. Bacteria occupy most of the skin's surface. They are acquired at birth, multiply rapidly and remain for life.

When the skin is slightly acid, the resident organisms consume anything nutritious on its surface. By removing all traces of 'food', these large populations make it difficult for new organisms to become established.

pH of the skin

The relative acidity of the skin is referred to as the pH. The pH scale ranges from 0 to 14 with 7 being neutral. The lower the number, the more acidic and the higher the number the more alkaline. Skin has a pH that is lower than 7 and is therefore acidic.

Some average pH values are:

- facial skin   5.4–6.2
- forehead, backs, limbs   5
- armpits, groin, toes   6–7

These values vary according to a person's age, sex and state of health. White skins tend to be more acidic than black skins. Men have a more acidic skin surface than women.

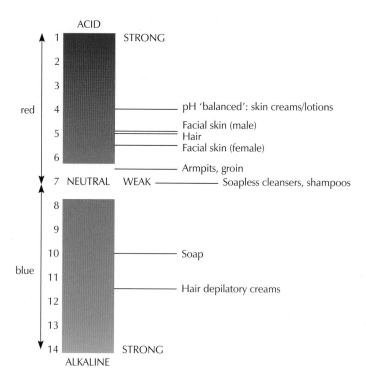

ACID

STRONG

pH 'balanced': skin creams/lotions

Facial skin (male)
Hair
Facial skin (female)

Armpits, groin

7 NEUTRAL   WEAK ——————— Soapless cleansers, shampoos

Soap

Hair depilatory creams

STRONG

ALKALINE

Some average pH values

SELF-CHECKS

The skin

1   What is the main function of the epidermis?

2   Name the three types of protein fibres in the skin. In which layer of the skin are they found?

3   Name two functions of the fatty layer of skin.

4   a) Name two differences between apocrine and eccrine sweat glands. b) Give two functions of eccrine sweat glands.

5   List three areas of the body that do not grow hair.

6   What is sebum? List three functions of sebum.

7   a) What are 'free radicals'? b) Give four ways of preventing damage to the skin by free radicals.

8   a) What is histamine? b) Why does the body produce histamine? c) What are the signs of a histamine reaction?

9   Why is it important to maintain the pH balance of the skin?

10   Why does fair skin appear pink when it is warm?

Activity 6.1: The skin

1 Make a large copy of the diagram of a section through the skin. Use different colours to identify the various parts and then try to label them without looking at the book. No cheating!

2 Five of the following statements are true and five are false. Decide which is which and then write down an explanation for each of your answers.

(a) The epidermis is dead.

(b) Black skin has twice as many melanocytes as white skin.

(c) The dermis contains more water than the epidermis.

(d) A healthy skin is slightly acid.

(e) Sweating is bad for you.

(f) Healthy skin is free from bacteria.

(g) The pores are spaces between loose skin cells.

(h) Sebum helps to protect the skin from sunburn.

(i) The skin is nourished by blood.

(j) Ageing slows down the rate of skin cell replacement.

3 Explain, briefly, what is happening in the skin when the following reactions occur:

(a) itching

(b) erythema

(c) pain

(d) swelling

(e) inflammation

(f) pustule

Bone structure

Facial contours are determined by the relative sizes, shapes and positions of the facial bones, together with the muscles and fatty tissue that lie over them.

The skull provides the basic framework of the head and consists of 22 bones in all:

- Cranium (8): extends over the front, top, back and sides of the head. The bones of the cranium are thin and slightly curved. They surround and protect the brain and meet at fixed joints called sutures.

- Facial (14): contribute to the structure of the face and help shape the openings containing the eyes, nose and mouth. Seven of the bones are situated more deeply in the facial cavities and do not contribute to facial contour.

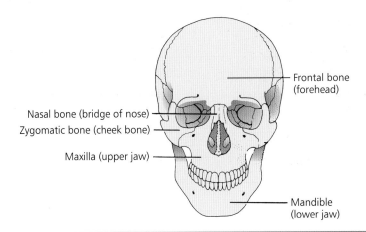

Frontal bone (forehead)

Nasal bone (bridge of nose)

Zygomatic bone (cheek bone)

Maxilla (upper jaw)

Mandible (lower jaw)

Bones that give contour to the face

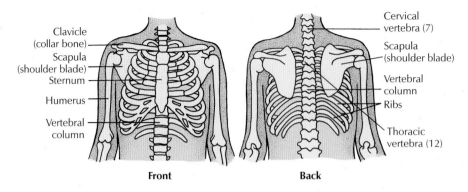

Clavicle (collar bone)
Scapula (shoulder blade)
Sternum
Humerus
Vertebral column

Cervical vertebra (7)
Scapula (shoulder blade)
Vertebral column
Ribs
Thoracic vertebra (12)

Front   Back

Bones of the neck, chest and shoulders

REMEMBER

The bone structure usually becomes more prominent with age, when fat is lost from the face and the skin becomes less well supported.

REMEMBER

There are ethnic variations in bone structure. For example, oriental people have less prominent zygomatic bones, which give them flatter facial features than other races.

The mandible is the only movable bone in the skull. It moves at hinge joints and is used for chewing and talking.

Bones of the head

LOCATION	NAME	NO.	POSITION
Skull	Occipital	1	Back of skull
	Frontal	1	Forehead
	Parietal	2	Sides and top of skull
	Temporal	2	Sides of skull under parietals
	Sphenoid	1	Base of skull
	Ethmoid	1	Eye socket and nasal cavities
Face	Zygomatic	2	Cheekbones
	Mandible	1	Lower jaw
	Maxillae	2	Upper jaw
	Nasal	2	Bridge of nose
	Vomer	1	Between nasal passages
	Turbinate	2	Nasal cavity
	Lacrimal	2	Eye socket
	Palatine	2	Nasal cavities and roof of mouth
Neck	Cervical vertebrae	7	Upper spine
Shoulder girdle	Clavicle	2	Collar bone
	Scapula	2	Shoulder blades
	Humerus	2	Upper arm
Chest	Sternum	1	Breast bone

A PRACTICAL GUIDE TO BEAUTY THERAPY

Bone structure

1 Name the bones that form a) the forehead, b) the cheek bones, and c) the lower jaw.

2 What are 'sutures' and where are they found?

3 Name the bones in the neck at the top of the spine.

4 What is the main difference between the mandible and the other bones of the skull?

5 Why do our facial contours change as we get older?

6 How does knowledge of the client's bone structure influence beauty therapy treatments?

Muscles of the head, face, neck, chest and shoulders

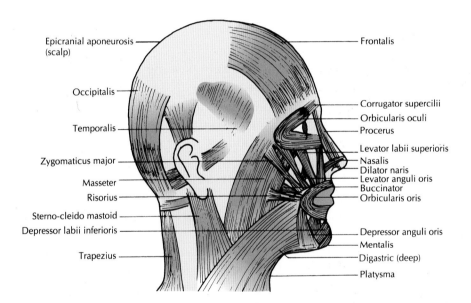

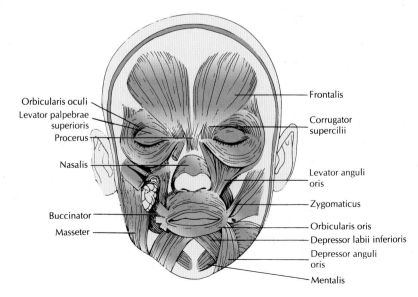

Muscles of the face and neck

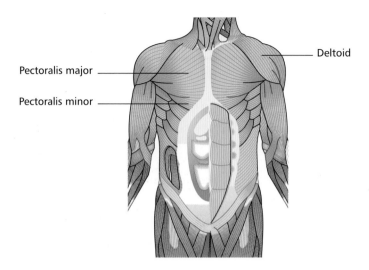

Pectoralis major

Deltoid

Pectoralis minor

Muscles of the chest and shoulders

All muscles are made up of bundles of tiny fibres. The fibres of most muscles lie parallel to one another, but special muscles called sphincters have fibres that surround openings. When sphincter muscles contract, the openings close up.

Muscle movement

Muscles have an origin at one end and an insertion at the other. When a muscle contracts, movement takes place at the insertion:

- Some of the facial muscles insert into the skin so when the muscle contracts, the attached skin moves with the muscle, across the direction of the **muscle fibres**. This is how facial expressions are produced.
- When the muscle inserts into bone, there is movement at a joint, for example the masseter muscle inserts into the mandible (lower jaw bone) and raises the jaw.

Muscle tone

Muscles with good tone remain in a state of tension even when they are relaxed. This helps to keep the contours firm and well defined. Muscles in poor tone become slack. When this happens the contours drop and the appearance of the face changes.

Wrinkles and expression lines

When facial muscles contract, the skin to which they are attached falls into wrinkles and folds, which form across the direction of the underlying muscle fibres. Where muscles interact with one another, the lines produced join together to form a curve. Skin that has good elasticity returns to normal once the muscle relaxes. Skin that has lost its elasticity develops permanent expression lines and wrinkles. This happens as a natural consequence of the ageing process, but can occur prematurely if the fibrous proteins in the skin become damaged.

Location and action of the muscles of the face and neck

AREA	NAME OF MUSCLE	LOCATION	ACTION
Forehead	Frontalis (1)	Front portion of the occipito-frontalis muscle which covers the upper part of the cranium	Lifts the eyebrows causing the skin of the forehead to form horizontal creases
	Corrugator (1)	Interlaces with the frontalis muscle and is positioned below the inner corners of the eyebrows	Draws the eyebrows together producing vertical wrinkles between the brows, as in frowning
	Procerus (1)	Lies over the nasal bone and inserts into the skin of the brow and forehead between the eyebrows	Depresses the wider part of the eyebrows producing horizontal wrinkles over the bridge of the nose
Eyes	Orbicularis oculi	Sphincter muscles which surround the eye. Extend over the temporal regions and downwards over the upper cheeks	Close the eye. A strong contraction produces wrinkles which fan out from the outer corner of the eye (crow's-feet) and beneath the eye
	Levator palpebrae (2)	Upper eyelid	Raises the upper eyelids
Nose	Dilator naris (2)	Sides of nostrils	Expand the nostrils
	Nasalis (1)	Over front of nose	Compresses nose, causing it to wrinkle
Mouth	Orbicularis oris (1)	Sphincter muscle which surrounds the mouth and forms most of the lips	Produces a small opening, as in whistling, and closes the mouth
	Levator labii superioris (2)	Run upwards from the upper lips	Lift the upper lip and assist in opening the mouth
	Depressor labii inferioris (2)	Run downwards from the lower lip	Draw down the lower lip and assist in opening the mouth
	Levator anguli oris (2)	Run upwards from the corners of the mouth	Lift the corners of the mouth
	Depressor anguli oris (triangularis) (2)	Run downwards from the corners of the mouth	Draw the corners of the mouth downwards
	Mentalis (1)	Lies over the chin and inserts into the lower border of orbicularis oris	Lifts the skin of the chin and turns the lower lip outwards
	Digastric (1)	A deep muscle located underneath the chin	Moves the bones involved in swallowing. The digastric is responsible for a 'double chin' condition
Cheeks	Buccinator (2)	Form the greater part of the cheek. The fibres cross the cheek and enter the lips, blending with orbicularis oris	Puff out the cheeks and help to increase the pressure in forced blowing. The muscles maintain tension in the cheek and are used to keep food between the teeth in chewing
	Risorius (2)	Placed horizontally in the cheeks, the muscles join with the corners of the mouth	Pull the corners of the mouth out sideways, as in smiling and grinning
	Zygomaticus (2)	Situated in the middle face, the muscles run downwards to the corners of the mouth	Pull the corners of the mouth upwards and sideways
Sides of the face	Temporalis (2)	Run down the sides of the face to the mandible	Aid mastication (chewing) by raising the mandible and closing the mouth
	Masseter (2)	Powerful muscles which run downwards and backwards to the angle of the mandible	Lift the mandible and exert pressure on the teeth when eating. The masseters are responsible for jowls which develop if the muscles lose their tone
Neck	Platysma (1)	A weak, superficial muscle which arises from the upper part of the chest and shoulders and covers the neck. The upper fibres pass over the mandible and blend with the muscles around the mouth.	Depresses the jaw and lower lip causing the skin of the neck to wrinkle (necklace lines)
	Trapezius (1)	A large, flat triangular muscle which covers the back and sides of the neck and the upper part of the back	Assists with movements of the shoulders and upper arm. Tension causes the fibres in the upper back to harden or develop nodules
	Sterno-cleido mastoid (2)	Powerful muscles which run down each side of the neck towards the collar bone.	Flex the neck and rotate the head on one side. When used together, the muscles bow the head forward
Chest and shoulders	Pectoralis major (2)	Covers upper chest	Draws the arm forwards and rotates it towards the middle of the body
	Pectoralis minor (2)	Underneath pectoralis major	Draws shoulder downwards and forwards
	Deltoid (2)	Thick, triangular muscle that caps the shoulder	Moves the arm away from the body and draws it backwards and forwards

Nerves

A nerve is made up of a bundle of nerve fibres. Some fibres are called sensory fibres and send impulses to the brain. Others are known as motor fibres. These carry impulses from the brain to a muscle or gland. When a muscle receives impulses from a **motor nerve**, a movement is produced. A nerve may consist wholly of sensory fibres (**sensory nerve**), or wholly of motor fibres (motor nerve), or some of each (mixed nerve).

Sensory nerve endings are situated in the skin and give us the sensation of touch: we can distinguish heat, cold and pain, as well as differences between light and deep pressure.

Motor nerve endings supply the muscles that produce facial expressions and move the eyes, neck and lower jaw.

Nerves of the face and neck

Nerves arising from the brain are called cranial nerves. There are 12 pairs of cranial nerves, some of which are sensory, some motor and some mixed. The main cranial nerves supplying the face and neck are the trigeminal, facial and accessory nerves.

5th cranial (trigeminal) nerve
This has three main branches:

- ophthalmic branch, which is sensory and supplies the upper part of the orbital cavity and also the skin of the nose, forehead and scalp
- maxillary branch, which is sensory and supplies the upper teeth, part of the nose and cheek and part of the eye orbit
- mandibular branch, which is motor and supplies the lower teeth, lower jaw and the muscles of mastication (chewing).

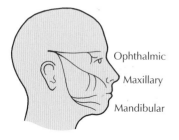

Ophthalmic

Maxillary

Mandibular

5th cranial nerve

A PRACTICAL GUIDE TO BEAUTY THERAPY

7th cranial (facial) nerve

This is responsible for facial expressions and branches to various muscles:

- temporal branch supplies the muscles of the forehead and eyebrows
- zygomatic branch supplies the muscles of the eyes and nose
- buccal branch supplies the muscles of the cheeks, upper lip and sides of the face
- mandibular branch supplies the muscles of the lower lip and chin
- cervical branch supplies the platysma muscle of the neck.

The 11th cranial (accessory) nerve is a motor nerve, which supplies the sternomastoid and trapezius muscles.

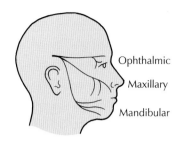

7th cranial nerve

SELF-CHECKS

Nerves of the face and neck

1 State two differences between a 'motor' and a 'sensory' nerve.

2 Name the three cranial nerves that supply the face and neck.

3 Which nerve supplies the muscles of facial expression?

4 Which nerve supplies the temporalis muscle?

5 Which types of sensory nerve endings are affected during a massage?

Blood supply

Blood carries food, oxygen and water to the body's tissues and takes up their waste products for excretion by the kidneys, lungs and skin. The heart is the pump, which drives the blood through the circulation. Blood circulates around the body in different types of blood vessels.

Blood vessels

Arteries
Arteries carry oxygenated blood (red) from the heart to the tissues. Large arteries are elastic and pulsate with the heart beat. They drive the blood on through the system. Arteries sub-divide into arterioles.

Veins
Veins carry deoxygenated blood (is bluish in colour) from the tissues to the heart. Thinner than arteries, they have valves to keep the blood flowing in the right direction. Veins sub-divide into venules.

Capillaries
The walls of these tiny vessels are thin and porous. They consist only of a single layer of cells. Capillaries join arterioles with venules. The gaps between the blood capillaries and the cells contain tissue fluid. The interchange of nutrients and waste products takes place through this tissue fluid.

REMEMBER

The superficial capillaries dilate to regulate body temperature. This turns the skin pink. Capillaries that have been over-stimulated become damaged. They remain permanently dilated or broken and appear as a network of fine, red lines underneath the skin.

Tissue fluid

Fluid leaks out of the capillary walls and bathes the tissues. The nutrients contained in the fluid penetrate the walls of the cells. Waste products leave through the walls of the cells, and enter the tissue fluid before passing into the capillary network and then on to a large vein.

Although some of the tissue fluid containing waste products returns to the blood capillaries, much of it is collected up by a second set of vessels that form the lymphatic system.

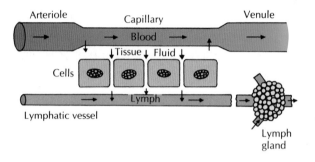

Tissue fluid exchange

Blood supply to the face and neck

The external carotid artery is the main vessel supplying blood to the upper part of the neck and face. It sub-divides into branches, which supply different areas. These include the following arteries and veins.

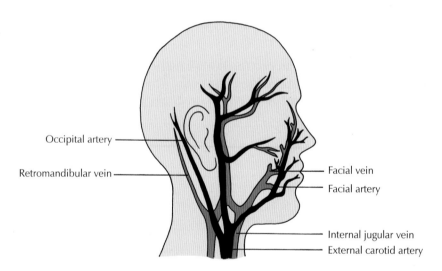

The main blood vessels supplying the head and neck

Facial artery

The facial artery lies between the superficial and deeper muscles, and supplies the upper and lower lips and facial muscles.

Occipital artery

The occipital artery supplies the upper part of the neck and the back of the scalp.

Superficial temporal artery

The superficial temporal artery supplies the face by its transverse facial branch.

A PRACTICAL GUIDE TO BEAUTY THERAPY

Internal jugular vein

This vein is the main vessel draining blood from the face and neck. Blood is supplied to it by smaller veins, which drain different areas. These include:

- the facial vein, which drains the front of the scalp and the superficial structures of the face
- the retromandibular vein, which drains the face below the jaw and the back of the scalp.

Lymphatic vessels

Lymphatic vessels are present in the tissue spaces as blind-ended tubes, which remove proteins and surplus fluid from the tissue spaces. In this way, swelling is prevented. The vessels contain lymph, a fluid made up of cells (mainly lymphocytes) and plasma (a watery fluid containing some proteins). Lymphocytes are special cells that fight off infection.

The lymphatic vessels create a network through the tissue spaces in very close proximity to the blood vessels.

Lymphatic glands or nodes are found at intervals along the path of these vessels. The lymph nodes 'filter' foreign bodies and quickly produce lymphocytes to deal with them. When there is a severe infection, this activity causes the glands to swell. Eventually, the large lymphatic vessels empty their contents back into the blood circulation.

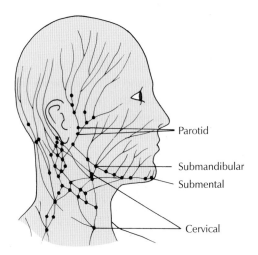

Lymphatic circulation

Parotid

Submandibular

Submental

Cervical

Lymph drainage

Lymph from the left side of the head and neck eventually passes through the thoracic duct and empties into the left subclavian vein.

Lymph from the right side of the head and neck eventually passes through the right lymphatic duct and empties in to the right subclavian vein.

Direction of lymph drainage

chin	→	submental nodes
middle part of face and cheeks	→	submandibular nodes
sides of cheeks and forehead	→	parotid nodes

Diseases and disorders of the skin

Disorders of pigmentation

Pigmentation disorders are caused by irregularities in melanin production and can usually be concealed quite effectively with cosmetic camouflage. The following disorders do not contraindicate beauty therapy treatments.

Melanoderma

Melanoderma is a general term for patchy pigmentation of the face. It usually describes an increase in melanin, caused by applying a cosmetic or perfume, which contains a light-sensitising ingredient. This means that the area of skin to which the product is applied becomes extra sensitive to ultraviolet. Bergamot oil, used in the perfumery industry, is one such ingredient. Some drugs have a similar effect.

Freckles (ephelides)

Freckles are tiny, flat, irregular patches of pigment, which occur commonly on the face, arms and legs of fair-skinned people, particularly those with blond or red hair. Instead of being distributed evenly throughout the skin, the melanin appears in small clumps.

Freckles become more noticeable on exposure to strong sunlight. They often increase in size and join up to form larger pigmented patches. The skin between freckles contains little or no melanin, so burns easily in the sun.

Lentigines

Lentigines are larger and more distinct than freckles. They are sometimes slightly raised from the skin's surface, but not as much as a pigmented mole. Lentigines do not darken or increase in number on exposure to sunlight.

Chloasma

Chloasma is a smooth, irregularly shaped patch of brown pigmentation, which occurs when there is increased production of the melanocyte-stimulating hormone (MSH). A chloasma often appears on the face during pregnancy and the condition is especially marked on the temples. A similar reaction occurs as a side-effect of taking the contraceptive pill, in which case the neck and mouth may also be affected. The discoloration usually disappears once the balance of hormone levels is restored.

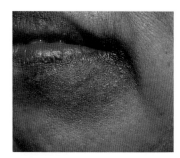

Chloasma

Vitiligo (leukoderma)

In vitiligo, small patches of skin appear white due to the destruction of melanocytes in the basal cells of the epidermis. Sometimes, the patches converge to create larger ones. Vitiligo is most noticeable on dark-skinned people. The white patches burn easily in the sun, in contrast with the surrounding skin which tans normally.

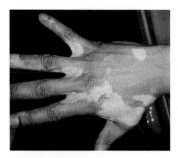

Vitiligo on black skin

Albinism

People with albinism have no melanin at all; consequently their skin and hair are white, and their eyes are pink. Albinos have to take extreme care when out in the sun due to the increased risk of damage to their skin and eyes from the effects of ultraviolet rays.

Skin blockages

The pores are openings in the skin which allow sebum and sweat to flow freely onto its surface. Obstruction of the pores may occur through increased glandular activity or when a barrier is created over the pore opening. This causes sebum or sweat or both to build up and become trapped rather than dispersed over the skin's surface.

Blocked pores

This term usually describes a build-up of sebum in the openings of hair follicles as a result of excessive sebum production. Over a period of time the pores become stretched. The blockages need releasing to prevent an accumulation of sebum further down the follicle. Special pore-cleansing treatments may be given as part of a salon facial.

Sebaceous cyst (steatoma or wen)

A cyst forms when sebum retained behind a very small, tight pore collects in the duct of the gland and then in the gland itself, which stretches and forms a swelling under the skin. The swelling may appear as a small nodule or may grow to be the size of a small egg. If a small cyst is squeezed, the released contents have a very characteristic rancid smell which is produced by the bacteria present.

REMEMBER

Skin blockages are unlikely to occur if a good, regular skin-care routine is followed.

GOOD PRACTICE

Warming the skin beforehand helps to soften and loosen skin blockages, reducing the risk of skin damage when they are removed. This may be done with a steamer or warm towels.

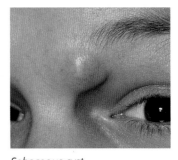

Sebaceous cyst

Comedones

Comedones (blackheads)

Comedones occur when sebum becomes trapped in a hair follicle. Cells from the epidermal lining of the upper follicle mix with the sebum, forming a hardened plug at the surface. The characteristic black tip of the comedone is due to oxidation in air of the exposed sebum and, also, melanin contained in the deposited skin cells. The sebum beneath the blackhead is pale and has a soft, 'cheesy' consistency. Comedones may be removed after the skin has been cleansed and softened. Care should be taken during their removal to prevent damaging and infecting the skin.

> **REMEMBER**
>
> Comedones occur commonly on greasy skin. Their effects on the walls of the follicle, the sebaceous duct and the gland itself depend on the amount of sebum being produced and the length of time the pore remains blocked. Comedones become inflamed when they are a symptom of acne.

Milia

Milia (whiteheads)

Milia appear as small, solid, white pearly nodules and are formed when a fine cuticle of skin grows over the mouth of the hair follicle, obstructing the passage of sebum onto the surface of the skin. Milia often occur around the eyes and above the cheekbones of people with dry skin. They can be exposed and removed from the follicle with a sterilised needle, but great care is required to minimise skin damage and prevent infection.

Miliaria rubra (prickly heat)

Prickly heat is most likely to occur in very hot, humid weather and particularly affects fair-skinned people visiting the tropics. The increased amount of sweat produced by the body is not able to evaporate and, instead, the skin becomes soggy. Keratin plugs form in the tiny sweat pores, blocking the further flow of sweat up to the skin's surface. When sweating occurs, the blocked sweat duct ruptures forming a vesicle, which is like a small blister, within the epidermal layers. Small hard lumps called papules appear on the skin's surface, accompanied by intense itching. Treatment consists of cooling the body and keeping the skin dry.

> **REMEMBER**
>
> Haemangioma contraindicate stimulating beauty treatments, but they are not affected adversely by those treatments that have a cooling, soothing effect.

Haemangioma

Haemangioma is a condition caused by permanent dilation or damage of the superficial blood vessels. They can usually be camouflaged successfully with make-up.

Dilated capillaries

Dilated capillaries result from a gradual loss of elasticity in the walls of the blood vessels. The capillaries fail to contract back after stimulation and remain permanently dilated, making the skin a pronounced pinkish-red colour. The cheeks and nose are the areas most affected, but people with extremely fine skin may have a more widespread condition.

> **REMEMBER**
>
> Dilated capillaries usually appear after many years of exposure to weather conditions, harsh rubbing of the face when washing and general lack of protection by the skin. Internal stimulants such as alcohol, spicy foods and very hot drinks can also be a factor. People with dry, sensitive skin are most likely to have dilated capillaries.

A PRACTICAL GUIDE TO BEAUTY THERAPY

Split capillaries

Sometimes the walls of the vessels weaken so much that they rupture and blood leaks out into the surrounding tissues. The individual capillaries can be seen quite distinctly and usually respond well to treatment with diathermy by a trained electrologist. This treatment cauterises (seals by heat) the blood vessels, cutting off the flow of blood.

Spider naevus (stellate haemangioma)

'Spider' accurately describes the appearance of this condition, where fine capillary 'legs' radiate out from the 'body', which is a central dilated vessel. Spider naevi occur most often on the upper part of the face and cheeks, particularly in pregnancy when oestrogen levels are raised. They respond well to treatment with diathermy.

Port wine stain

A port wine stain is a bright purple, irregularly-shaped, flat birthmark, which may be quite small or may cover extensive areas of the body. The colour is thought to be due to blood capillaries that have been damaged by pressure upon them in the womb before birth. A port wine stain grows with the body. It does not generally fade and may cause particular distress if located prominently on the face. Cosmetic camouflage usually has very successful results.

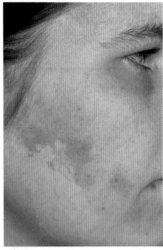

A port wine stain on the face

Tumours of the skin

A tumour is formed by an overgrowth of cells. Almost every type of cell in the epidermis and dermis is capable of benign or malignant overgrowth. Tumours are lumpy and, even when they cannot be seen, they can be felt underneath the surface of the skin.

Benign (non-cancerous) tumours

Benign tumours do not contraindicate beauty therapy treatments, but special care is needed to avoid over-stimulation and disturbance of the skin cells in the area. Many benign tumours appear at birth or shortly afterwards and are referred to as birthmarks. The majority of these tumours remain harmless, but some may undergo changes later in life and so are potentially dangerous.

Malignant (cancerous) tumours

These definitely contraindicate beauty therapy treatments. If you suspect that a client has a malignant growth, tactfully recommend a prompt visit to their doctor. Malignant tumours appear more commonly in old age but can develop as the result of changes in an existing tumour.

HEALTH MATTERS

Over-exposure to strong sunlight is a major cause of skin cancer. The incidence of skin cancer is increasing, particularly in young people with fair skins. It is possible to develop skin cancer later in life as a result of being badly burned by the sun just once when younger. People with fair skins, particularly those who are prone to moles, should stay out of strong sun or keep their skin covered up.

Moles

Moles vary in size and may be raised or flat, pigmented or a normal skin colour. Their surface can be smooth or rough, hairy or hairless. Moles are usually harmless. They have a very good blood supply and the individual vessels can often be seen quite prominently in the smooth, raised, skin-coloured type.

Pigmented moles are not usually present at birth but develop over the years of childhood and, sometimes, even later. They are caused by an overgrowth of melanocytes in the basal layer of the epidermis at its junction with the dermis. As time goes by, the cells drop into the dermis and become permanently lodged there. The majority of pigmented moles are harmless, but some may become malignant, particularly if they are over-exposed to strong sunlight.

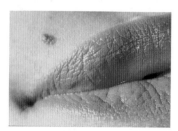

A flat, pigmented mole

Skin tags

Skin tags are tiny, loose, painless growths of skin, which sometimes develop on the eyelids and sides of neck. They usually appear in middle age, are quite harmless and should be left alone. If skin tags are annoying because they catch on clothing or jewellery, they can be surgically removed under anaesthetic by a doctor or cauterised by a trained electrologist.

Hyperkeratosis

Hyperkeratosis is a rare disorder in which layers of horny overgrowth produce grossly thickened skin with deep ridging. The presence of hyperkeratosis can restrict beauty therapy treatment.

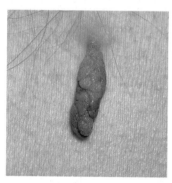

A skin tag

Skin cancers

You are sometimes in a position to see a skin condition which is normally out of view for your client or may be dismissed as insignificant. If the early signs of skin cancer are recognised and followed up promptly with a visit to the doctor, medical treatment by radiation, excision or chemotherapy is usually very successful.

Malignant melanoma

This deeply pigmented mole is life threatening if not recognised and treated promptly. The most dangerous type of mole is smooth, slightly raised, very dark brown, bluish-black or greyish and measures less than 2 cm across. Some melanomas develop on areas of previously healthy skin not normally exposed to sun.

Rodent ulcer (basal cell epithelioma)

This malignant tumour starts off as a slow-growing pearly nodule, often at the site of a previous skin injury. As the nodule enlarges, the centre ulcerates and refuses to heal. The centre becomes depressed and the rolled edges become translucent, revealing many, tiny blood vessels. Rodent ulcers do not disappear. If left untreated, they may invade underlying bone.

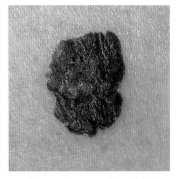

A malignant melanoma

Squamous cell epithelioma

This tumour is also malignant and arises from the prickle cell layer of the epidermis. It is hard and warty, and eventually develops a heaped up, cauliflower-like appearance. The tumour is very slow growing and medical treatment is usually very successful if the condition is diagnosed before it spreads.

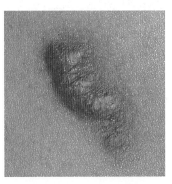

A rodent ulcer

Scars

Scars are formed from replacement tissue during the healing of a wound. Depending on the type and extent of skin damage, the scar may be raised and shiny (hypertrophic), rough and pitted (ice-pick) or fibrous and lumpy (keloid). Alternatively, a scar may show as loss of skin tissue. When the protein fibres in the dermis are damaged by a cut, burn, injury or disease, they knit together differently as the skin tries to repair itself. The deeper and more extensive the injury, the more fibres are affected and the thicker and lumpier the resulting scar is . Scars do not usually grow hair or have skin sensations.

A keloid scar

Healing of scars

Scars heal at different rates on different people. You should take care to avoid giving beauty therapy treatments over a scar that has not completely healed. The general signs of healing are:

- the scar is not painful
- the scar is sealed and dry
- there is no inflammation.

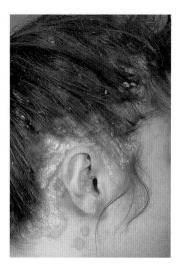

Psoriasis on the scalp

GOOD PRACTICE

Do not give stimulating beauty therapy treatments to skin that is troubled by psoriasis. If the condition is present in a very mild form, the client may have basic skin-care and make-up treatments.

Skin disorders

The following conditions are not infectious, but they may contraindicate beauty therapy. The decision to go ahead with treatment depends on the severity of the condition. Occasionally the symptoms flare up, making the skin particularly sensitive and unsuitable for treatment. Sometimes secondary infection may be present, which would also contraindicate beauty treatment.

Psoriasis

In this condition there is an abnormally rapid rate of cell turnover in the epidermis. It may take only four days for new cells to reach the stratum corneum. When the cells reach the surface, they clump together producing round or oval, dull, red plaques of different sizes, covered in silvery scales. The skin feels very rough and, if the scales are removed, tiny spots of bleeding occur.

Psoriasis is an inherited condition. It occurs on areas of skin that do not have much underlying flesh, such as the limbs, elbows and knees. The scalp and face are sometimes affected. The symptoms flare up prominently in the teens and twenties and then later in life, in the fifties and sixties. They seem to be more severe as a result of shock, stress or illness, but often fade away as quickly as they appear. The specific cause of psoriasis is not known.

HEALTH MATTERS

Make sure that the plaques of psoriasis are not disturbed during treatment or bleeding may occur and the skin will be open to infection.

Acne vulgaris

This is the most common of all skin disorders and affects the face, shoulders, upper back and chest. The main symptoms of acne are:

- greasy skin
- blackheads
- whiteheads
- papules
- pustules
- inflammation.

Acne vulgaris on the male face

GOOD PRACTICE

A client who is being treated medically for a skin disorder should get the written consent of their doctor before having beauty therapy. The consent letter should be kept safely with the client's record card.

Acne usually appears at puberty when the body starts producing more sex hormones. It takes some time for the correct balance of hormones to be achieved. When an excessive amount of male hormones (androgens) are produced, the sebaceous glands become over-active and the skin appears very shiny. This condition of excess greasiness is called seborrhoea.

How acne develops

Bacteria that are present in the hair follicle break down the sebum and fatty acids are released, which irritate the wall of the follicle. The epidermal lining thickens, narrowing the upper end and opening of the follicle so that sebum builds up further down. When the follicle pore becomes completely enclosed with hardened skin cells, a whitehead results. When the pore becomes blocked with hardened sebum, a blackhead (comedone) is formed.

Papules develop as the follicle and sebaceous gland swell with trapped sebum. Sometimes the contents of the follicle escape into the surrounding dermis, causing inflammation and pustules. In cases of severe acne, inflamed, painful cysts occur, which often heal leaving permanent scarring and pitting of the skin.

Medical treatment of acne

Acne cannot be cured but it can be controlled. The medical treatment varies depending on the severity of the condition but usually includes degreasing, medicated skin care and antibiotics. The condition may last for between eight and 12 years. It is usually most severe in females of about 17 and males of about 19. After these ages, the acne gradually improves and usually disappears completely by the age of 25.

Beauty treatments and acne

A client with mild acne may be given facial treatments in the salon as long as there are no inflamed pustules present. Salon treatments should concentrate on gentle degreasing of the skin and careful releasing of skin blockages. Skin with mild acne should be warmed gently and softened before blockages are removed.

Home treatment of acne

Many people believe that, because acne usually appears on greasy skin, very strong drying agents should be used to degrease the skin. This is wrong. Products with a strong detergent or degreasing action irritate the skin, causing it to harden and thicken over the mouths of hair follicles. This makes the removal of skin blockages difficult and increases the formation of whiteheads and blackheads.

Secondary infection occurs if bacteria invade through breaks in the skin. This may be caused by picking spots and squeezing blackheads. Warn your client of the risks and always take care yourself when treating acne in the salon.

Rosacea

Rosacea usually affects people over the age of 30, some of whom may have been troubled previously by acne vulgaris. The skin appears very flushed over the nose, cheeks and forehead. A characteristic butterfly shape is produced by the blood vessels, which are dilated in these areas. The increase in skin temperature stimulates the production of sebum, making it appear greasy. Open pores, papules and pustules are often present in rosacea, but blackheads are not a feature. In severe cases, the sebaceous glands may become so enlarged that the skin appears very coarse and lumpy.

Causes of rosacea

Rosacea often begins as occasional flushing in response to stimulants such as:

- hot foods and drinks
- spicy food
- strong coffee
- alcohol
- exposure to cold, wind and sun.

GOOD PRACTICE

You should not apply any stimulating facial treatments to a client troubled by rosacea. Handle the skin very carefully and keep it cool. Inflamed pustules contraindicate beauty therapy.

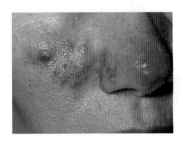

Rosacea

Chronic flushing may be brought on by stress, hormonal disturbance or permanently damaged blood vessels. There may be long periods of remission. Medical treatment consists of antibiotics and, sometimes, tranquillisers for anxiety to help reduce facial flushing.

GOOD PRACTICE

You should not apply any stimulating facial treatments to a client troubled by rosacea. Handle the skin very carefully and keep it cool. Inflamed pustules contraindicate beauty therapy.

Viral infections

Viruses spread very quickly and are quite resistant to medical treatment. Very often, the original viral infection is made worse by a secondary infection caused by bacteria entering through broken or damaged skin.

Warts

Warts are small, solid growths of skin tissue. The virus invades the stratum germinatum of the epidermis and causes abnormal keratinisation. There are different types of wart. The warts that affect the face and neck are:

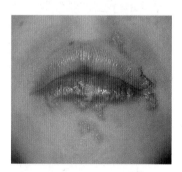

Seborrheic warts

- plane warts – very small, smooth and skin-coloured or light brown, these occur on the face in clusters and sometimes disappear spontaneously without treatment
- seborrheic warts – these start to appear at middle age and begin as a brown thickening of the skin, which grows to approximately 3–25 mm across, darkens and develops a rough, greasy surface
- filiform warts – these appear on the face, neck and eyelids as thin strips of skin up to 3 mm in length with a hard tip. Filiform warts may occur singly or in clusters.

HEALTH MATTERS

Most warts eventually disappear spontaneously without treatment, but special pastes and paints are available, which must be used carefully. Persistent warts may be treated medically.

Cold sore (herpes simplex)

This condition usually recurs at the same site of the face, either the lips, cheeks or side of the nose. The virus lies dormant in sensory nerve cells and is activated by stimuli such as a bad cold, menstruation, sunburn, infection or general debility. The onset is usually sudden: tingling, burning and itching may be felt for a few hours before blisters appear.

The skin may become infected with bacteria, causing pain. Crusts form, which take approximately 10–14 days to heal. Application of a spirit-based lotion helps to dry out the condition and prevent secondary infection of the skin.

Cold sore (herpes simplex)

HEALTH MATTERS

The blisters contain the cold sore virus. A cold sore is most infectious when the blisters have formed and shortly afterwards, when they break and weep.

A PRACTICAL GUIDE TO BEAUTY THERAPY

Shingles (herpes zoster)

Shingles is a very painful condition which produces a rash and blisters along the path of a sensory nerve. Scales form after a week and the rash disappears after two or three weeks, leaving some scarring. Pain may persevere for quite a long time after the skin symptoms have disappeared.

Bacterial infections

Although some bacteria survive quite happily on the skin without causing problems, there are others that are harmful and can cause disease. These are known as pathogenic bacteria. A doctor will usually prescribe antibiotics to help clear up a bacterial infection of the skin.

Boil (furuncle)

This is a local pocket of infection which starts around the base of a hair follicle. The follicle and surrounding skin cells are killed by bacteria and form pus. The amount of pus keeps increasing until, eventually, it bursts through the skin and escapes. Sometimes, several follicles in an area are infected, producing a carbuncle. This causes an extensive pustular infection with several heads that burst.

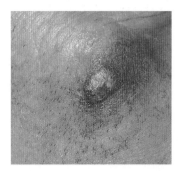

A boil (furuncle)

Boils are most likely to occur on hairy areas prone to friction, for example the neck. They are often brought on by general debility and over-tiredness when the body's resistance is low. A heating poultice may help to draw out the infection. If the boil is persistent and very painful it may be lanced by a doctor, who will probably also prescribe oral antibiotics.

Impetigo

A highly contagious skin infection, impetigo is particularly common in children but can be caught easily by adults. The nose and mouth are the areas of the face most frequently affected. Impetigo starts off as a red spot. This becomes a blister, which quickly breaks down and discharges, causing yellow crusts to develop. The crusts spread and other spots then develop near the earlier infection. Oral antibiotics, prescribed by a doctor, help to speed up recovery. The sores may be treated by bathing with an antiseptic solution or applying an antibiotic ointment.

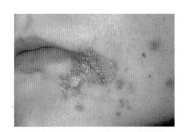

Impetigo

Conjunctivitis

This infection affects the very thin skin that covers the white of the eye and the inner surface of the eyelids. Conjunctivitis is the commonest cause of red, itchy and sticky eyes. Although the main cause is bacterial, the condition can be provoked by a virus or irritants such as a foreign body, tobacco smoke or eye cosmetics. Sometimes it may be an indication of an allergy.

Conjunctivitis

HEALTH MATTERS

Infections of the skin around the eyes are usually caused by the spread of bacteria from the nose and mouth. Cross-infection should be avoided by washing the hands after touching the face, and not sharing face cloths and towels with other people.

Stye

This is a small boil in the glands at the root of the eyelashes. It is a common, unsightly and uncomfortable condition, but can usually be treated without medical help. A stye begins as painful swelling and redness of the eyelid. After a few days, pus forms and discharges from the swelling on to the margin of the eyelid. The regular application of hot compresses helps to bring the stye to a head and speed up the recovery process. If the stye has not burst after three days, a doctor may recommend the use of an antibiotic ointment.

Fungal infections

Fungi live off the waste products of the skin and some invade the deeper tissues, causing **fungal infections**. A doctor may prescribe anti-fungal cream and a course of antibiotics.

Ringworm (tinea corporis)

Ringworm is a highly contagious condition. The fungus lives on the dead horny outer layer of skin and is usually found on warm, moist areas of the body. Red pimples appear and spread at the edges, producing red rings with a clearing of normal skin colour in the centre. Scales and pustules usually develop over the rings. Ringworm can spread to the face from other infected areas of the body, such as the feet and head. Domestic animals and cattle are a source of the infection.

Infestations of the skin

Infestations such as scabies and pediculosis are disorders involving invasion of the skin by tiny animal parasites that live off human blood. They are highly contagious. Secondary infection often occurs as a result of breaking the skin through scratching.

Scabies

Commonly known as 'the itch', scabies is caused by a female mite, sarcoptes scabiei, which becomes fertilised on the skin surface and then burrows into the skin to lay its eggs. The eggs hatch after four days and the mature mite appears on the skin surface 10 days later. Characteristic greyish ridges track the routes of the burrows in the skin. Itchy pimples appear as an allergic reaction to the mite, the eggs and larvae. These become more uncomfortable at night when the body is warm. Persistent scratching produces inflammation and coarsening of the skin.

Ringworm

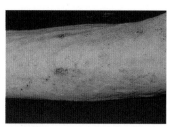

Scabies

HEALTH MATTERS

Scabies appears most commonly between the fingers, the insides of the wrist, the palms of the hands and the soles of the feet. Treatment is medical and consists of applying a preparation to kill the parasites followed by an anti-bacterial cream.

Pediculosis

Pediculosis is a skin irritation caused by a tiny insect parasite, the head louse, which invades the scalp and lays its eggs (nits), which become attached to the hairs. The nits are a characteristic silvery grey colour. There is intense itching at the site of the infestation and blisters and sores invariably appear as a result of scratching. Towels and bedding which have been in contact with pediculosis should be disinfected before being laundered.

Allergies

An allergic reaction occurs when the body tissues react abnormally to a substance with which they have been brought into contact. The contact may be external (by touch) or internal (by inhaling, eating or drinking). Asthma, hay fever, eczema and urticaria are all due to allergies. Allergies can develop 'overnight'. A person may have been exposed to a substance or used a product for years without any previous problems.

Allergic reaction

There are millions of tiny cells scattered throughout the tissue linings of the body called mast cells. They produce and store chemicals including histamine. Histamine is responsible for producing the symptoms of tissue damage. The mast cells also carry special antibodies, which react with certain substances and trigger off an allergic reaction.

When the offending substance (antigen) penetrates the body, a chemical reaction occurs between the antigen and the antibody, and histamine is released into the surrounding tissues. The reaction that occurs depends on the tissues affected:

- eyes – watering of the eyes, irritation and swelling of the eyelids
- nose – irritation, sneezing, runny nose, nasal blockage
- lungs – wheezing, breathlessness, tightness of the chest
- intestine – stomach pains, diarrhoea
- skin – irritation, itching, inflammation, swelling, rash, blisters.

Allergies affecting the skin

Some substances, particularly if they are similar in their chemical composition, are more likely than others to provoke an allergic reaction in people who are hypersensitive. All products containing the offending substance will cause an allergic response, even if the substance is present only in tiny amounts. An allergic reaction of the skin may be local or more widespread, depending on whether the skin has been irritated or sensitised by the offending substance.

Primary irritation

This results from the direct action of the irritant upon the skin and occurs when the substance contacted is exceptionally harsh or concentrated, or when there is repeated contact with an irritant substance which gradually breaks down the skin's natural protective mechanisms. Primary irritation causes inflammation and itchiness of the skin. The condition is called contact dermatitis and usually shows up quite quickly on the area of skin to which the substance has been applied.

Examples of common irritants are:

- detergents
- disinfectants
- solvents
- bleach.

Contact allergic dermatitis

Allergic dermatitis

Depending on the concentration of the substance, how promptly remedial action is taken and how sensitive the skin is, the symptoms may develop into contact allergic dermatitis. When this happens, the live skin cells become damaged and release histamine. This causes fluid to collect in the tissues, the skin swells and blisters appear, which eventually burst, weep and then scab over. The symptoms may take up to 48 hours to appear.

Some common causes of contact allergic dermatitis are:

- armpits – perfumes, antiperspirants, deodorants
- trunk – nickel fastenings and elastic on underwear
- head and neck – cosmetics, hair sprays, plants
- hands – washing powders, dyes, flowers, rings, bracelets, watch straps, gloves
- feet – dyes and chemicals in leather shoes and boots.

It is obviously very important to avoid using any product that contains a substance known to harm the skin. The cause of a dermatitis reaction may be determined quite easily because the reaction is fairly immediate. However, an allergic reaction involving sensitisation is delayed and it is usually more difficult to isolate the cause.

Sensitisation

Sensitisation is the 'true' allergic reaction and involves a delayed response. On first contact with the offending substance there is no obvious reaction, but the skin becomes sensitised. It recognises the substance as alien and produces special antibodies which wait in readiness for the next time contact is made. Subsequently, the symptoms of dermatitis occur at the site of contact with the substance.

Urticaria

Certain foods can produce allergic symptoms of the skin. Dairy produce and wheat-based products sometimes cause an eczema reaction. Strawberries, lobster and shellfish are often the cause of urticaria (nettle rash or hives). In this condition there is intense irritation of the skin. Swollen areas of pale skin occur surrounded by red weals. The weals may appear anywhere on the body and vary in size from a tiny pimple to a large patch, several centimetres across. They last for 8–24 hours and fade without trace. Urticaria can also be caused by an allergy to certain drugs (for example aspirin, penicillin), flowers or an insect sting.

Contraindications to facial treatments

Beauty therapy treatments are designed to improve the appearance and condition of the skin, and to help control minor skin problems. They should never be applied to areas of skin that are sore, damaged or infected, or where there is a risk of the skin reacting adversely to treatment.

Failure to recognise or respond to a contraindication could result in:

- cross-infection – an infectious disease could spread to other areas of the face and, also, to other clients or salon staff
- prolonging the condition – disturbing infected or damaged skin could interfere with the natural healing process
- worsening of the condition – stimulating treatments could put further strain on damaged blood vessels and also speed up the rate of abnormal activity of diseased skin cells.

The general contraindications to facial treatments are:

- undiagnosed lumps, bumps and swellings
- cuts and abrasions
- any infectious skin condition
- recent scar tissue (less than six months old)
- severe sunburn
- allergic reaction
- malignant tumour.

SELF-CHECKS

Diseases and disorders of the skin

1 State two ways in which a good skin-care routine helps to prevent blocked pores.

2 What special care is required by clients who have vitiligo?

3 How do capillaries become permanently dilated?

4 What are milia and how are they formed?

5 State three early signs of skin cancer.

6 Why is the texture of a scar different from the surrounding skin?

7 Describe the appearance of psoriasis, identifying the main sites of the body in which it appears.

8 Explain the cause and appearance of acne.

9 Name and describe two viral infections affecting the skin of the face.

10 Name and describe one bacterial infection of the skin.

11 Explain the difference between 'primary irritation' and 'sensitisation'.

12 What is an antigen?

ACTIVITY

Activity 6.2: Diseases and disorders of the skin

Visit your library or study centre and find a dermatology book that contains information about the diseases and disorders described in this chapter. Make notes of any additional information you find which helps to increase your knowledge and understanding of these conditions.

Basic skin types

Skin is usually described as being balanced (normal), dry, greasy or combination. In addition, it may be sensitive, dehydrated, mature, congested, blemished or infected.

Balanced skin

Balanced skin is exactly what it says it is: it has a good balance of oil and moisture secretions, which keep the skin soft, supple and flexible. Desquamation and cell generation take place at the same rate, so that there is an even replacement of the surface layers. This helps to keep the skin smooth and clear. The pores are small, the texture fine and even, and the colour healthy. The skin feels slightly warm to touch due to its good blood supply. A balanced skin rarely develops spots and blemishes and, when it does, it usually heals well.

HEALTH MATTERS

Hundreds of thousands of dead, surface skin cells are sloughed off each day by desquamation, taking with them dust and other debris that has settled on the skin. As the cells fall away, they are replaced by newer cells from underneath. This cycle of cell development and replacement helps to keep the skin healthy.

Dry skin

Dry skin has a matt, uneven texture. This is because there is not enough sebum to lubricate the surface cells and keep them compacted together. In the absence of a greasy coating, natural moisture becomes lost from the upper layers. The surface cells curl up and flake. The skin lacks suppleness and often feels tight. Dry skin is usually thin and fine with no visible pores. It forms lines and wrinkles prematurely, particularly around the eyes. Commonly dilated capillaries appear on the nose and cheeks.

HEALTH MATTERS

Dilated capillaries result from a gradual loss of elasticity in the walls of the blood vessels. Instead of contracting back after stimulation, the superficial capillaries remain permanently dilated. White skin with dilated capillaries appears pink or red. Black skin is less likely to show dilated capillaries because the surface layers are thicker. If they are present, they appear as a darker shade of the skin colour.

Causes of dry skin
Hormone imbalance
A dry skin occurs naturally when there is an imbalance of male and female sex hormones circulating in the blood. Androgens are the male sex hormones, responsible for activating the sebaceous glands. Oestrogens are the female sex hormones. A higher-than-normal level of oestrogen in the blood holds back the production of sebum.

HEALTH MATTERS

Oestrogen has water-attracting properties, which influence the amount of moisture held in the skin. If the amount of oestrogen circulating in the body is reduced, so is the amount of moisture that is available for the skin.

Incorrect skin care
Using harsh products strips the skin of its natural surface lubricant. If the body does not produce enough sebum to replace it quickly, then the surface of the skin becomes dry, parched and irritated. Harsh products include lotions containing alcohol, alkalis, detergents and abrasives.

Central heating and air conditioning
These create a dry environment which takes water from wherever it can. Plants and skin lose moisture with similar effects. Skin becomes parched and dehydrated if it is not protected adequately against central heating and air conditioning.

Extremes of temperature
When the weather is very hot or very cold the air is usually dry. Unless the skin is protected well, it gives up its moisture in the same way as if it is exposed to central heating. The production of sebum slows down when skin is exposed to cold windy weather, so there is less protection from moisture loss.

Over-exposure to sunlight
The sun's rays overheat and dehydrate the tissues. The effects occur not only in the surface layers, but also deeper in the dermis. Sensible sunbathing consists of building up exposure times, keeping sensitive areas of skin covered and wearing a suitable sunscreen. If these precautions are not taken, the skin suffers considerable damage.

Prolonged illness
During periods of ill health, blood and lymph are diverted away from the surface tissues towards the diseased areas of the body. This reduces the amount of fluid circulating in the epidermis (top layer of skin), which leads to surface dehydration. Illnesses producing a high body temperature dehydrate the skin. Some medicines, for example antibiotics, can cause the skin to become dry.

Crash dieting
Water intake is reduced considerably with 'crash dieting'. This results in the body drawing on its reservoir of moisture in the skin to maintain its essential water balance. Anorexia nervosa is a serious diet-related disease where little or no food is eaten. The production of sex hormones stops, causing changes in the body which include dehydration and thinning of the skin.

Smoking

Smoking dilates the surface blood capillaries. This raises the temperature of the skin and causes dryness in the skin of people who smoke heavily. The chemical toxins produced by smoking damage the protein fibres in the skin. They also interfere with the way in which the fibres hold moisture in the skin.

Excess alcohol

Drinking too much alcohol raises the blood pressure and, over a prolonged period, causes permanent damage to blood vessels. Chemical toxins build up in the body, making the protein fibres harden and lose their water-binding properties. Dehydration is a short-term side-effect of excessive alcohol intake. The body responds to high concentrations of chemicals in the blood by drawing water from the skin in to the circulation.

Medication

Some prescribed drugs, for example antibiotics, can cause short-term dryness of the skin. Once the course of drugs has been finished, the condition of the skin improves.

Greasy skin

Greasy skin produces more sebum than is needed to give the normal amount of lubrication and protection. Consequently, its surface appears shiny, thick, coarse, dull and often grimy. A build-up of sebum in the ducts and hair follicles stretches the pores, which become enlarged. Depending on how the skin is cared for, the pores may be open or blocked. Open pores provide a route for bacteria, which cause spots and infections. Blocked pores often result in comedones (blackheads).

REMEMBER

Skin that produces excess sebum can still become dehydrated if it is not treated correctly.

The thicker coating of sebum on the skin delays the rate at which desquamation takes place. Instead of being shed evenly, the surface cells remain 'stuck down', attracting more dust and grime. Meanwhile, new cells continue to be produced in the epidermis so that the overall thickness of the skin increases. This, together with the extra fatty content of the epidermis, gives the skin a dull, sallow (yellowish) appearance.

Causes of greasy skin
Hormone imbalance
A greasy skin occurs naturally when the balance of androgens is higher than normal. Greasy skin commonly occurs at puberty before the balance of sex hormones has settled down.

Ethnicity (race)
Grease absorbs ultraviolet light. People who are natives of countries with hot, sunny climates produce more sebum to help screen the skin against the damaging effects of the ultraviolet in sunlight.

Combination skin

Any combination of skin types may exist on the face where different areas show different physical characteristics. The most common combination consists of normal-to-dry skin over the cheeks and sides of the face, with a greasier T-zone down the centre panel. There are more sebaceous glands present on the centre panel of the face and they are situated nearer the skin surface.

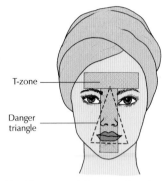

The T-zone and danger triangle

Sensitive skin

All healthy skins are sensitive, but this term is used in beauty therapy to describe a condition where the skin is hypersensitive, i.e. it 'over' reacts to even the mildest stimulus. The skin flushes very easily, causing redness which may appear in patches or as a clearly defined network of dilated capillaries. Skin that has been neglected over a number of years may have permanently dilated capillaries which are more pronounced when the blood supply is stimulated.

Dry skin types are most likely to be sensitive. This is not surprising as they lack the protection normally given by sebum. Other types of skin can also be sensitive, however, particularly if the stimulus is an ingredient of a cosmetic or skin-care preparation.

Dehydrated skin

'Dehydrated' means lacking in moisture. The skin looks dull and parched, and may feel tight and itchy. Dry skin is dehydrated, but any skin type may suffer temporary dehydration if it is not properly protected and cared for.

Mature skin

Mature skin has lost the firmness and suppleness of youth. It is lined and crêpey, with some loss of underlying muscle tone. Skin normally ages very gradually and is described as mature once the changes brought about by ageing have become established.

Congested skin

Congestion can often be felt as well as seen. The pores become blocked and waste accumulates beneath the upper layers of skin. The texture feels coarse and lumpy. Whiteheads and blackheads may be present. The skin becomes congested when sebum and sweat are prevented from flowing freely onto the surface. If the skin's surface is not kept soft and supple, the upper layers of the epidermis harden over the pores, preventing the flow of sebum and sweat.

Causes of congestion

- Inadequate cleansing of the skin: stale make-up and other matter builds up in the mouths of the hair follicles and the sweat pores.
- A humid atmosphere: sweat does not evaporate readily and this creates a build-up in the ducts which carry sweat from the glands to the surface of the body.
- Very fatty skin-care products can also clog up the pores.
- Illness: toxins and waste matter build up in the skin.

Blemished skin

Any irregularity in the colour or texture of the skin is called a blemish. A blemish may be permanent (for example a pigmented birthmark) or temporary (for example a pustule).

Blemishes must be identified correctly before recommending treatment. Most of them are harmless, many improve with beauty therapy, but there are others that must not be treated in the salon.

Infected skin

The appearance of infected skin depends on the nature of the infection. Bacteria, fungi and viruses affect the skin in different ways and each infection has its own distinctive characteristics. Inflammation, swelling, irritation or pain, discoloration or pus are all general signs of infection.

Male skin

It would be quite wrong to suggest that there is a 'male' skin type. There are just as many variations in the types and chacteristics of male skin as with female skin. However, due mainly to the hormonal differences between men and women, there are certain generalisations that can be made. Testosterone, the hormone produced by the male glands, gives men a thicker epidermis, approximately 2 mm compared with 1.5 mm in a woman. Their skin tends to be tougher, more elastic and less sensitive than female skin. It is also more acidic and has a more efficient supply of blood and sebum. This means it tends to 'age' better than a woman's skin, remaining softer and firmer.

Of course, men's skins are just as exposed, if not more, to environmental and lifestyle conditions which affect their skin. Pollution, stress, alcohol, smoking and an unhealthy diet all take their toll. Additionally, for most men, their daily shaving routine increases the risk of skin rashes, infections and ingrowing hairs, which not only affect their appearance but can also be very uncomfortable.

Basic skin types

1. Why does a balanced skin rarely develop spots?
2. Why does our skin tend to get drier as we get older?
3. Give three possible causes of congested skin.
4. Where is the 'danger triangle' and why is it so called?
5. Why is the 'T-zone' greasy in a combination skin?
6. Give two reasons why a greasy skin appears sallow.
7. Describe the characteristics of a 'sensitive' skin.
8. Explain how 'crow's-feet' are formed.
9. Why is smoking bad for the skin?
10. List three general signs of skin infection.
11. State two differences between male and female skin.

Activity 6.3: Basic skin types

Good product knowledge is essential for choosing and recommending the best skin-care products for your clients. You must know all about the range of products available in your salon.

Design a treatment chart for each of the basic skin types: balanced (normal), dry, greasy, combination and sensitive, which explains briefly, but clearly, the characteristics of the skin type and the home use of recommended retail products available in the salon. Do not forget to include special treatment preparations, for example for the eyes and neck.

Use a computer to design your charts and illustrate them with details of the salon and a suitable logo. If you are pleased with the results, you can have copies made to give to your clients after their consultation.

Ethnic skin types

The most obvious physical distinction that can be made between people of different racial origins is that of skin colour. The variety of colours is enormous, ranging from palest cream to darkest blue-black. Although we inherit our skin colour from our parents, its basic shade and tone results from years of evolution and adaptation to climatic conditions. In people native to hot sunny climates, the colour of the skin, together with variations in its thickness and structure, provide extra protection against damage from ultraviolet and the heating effects of sun on the body.

African-Caribbean skin

Asian skin

Caucasian skin

Oriental skin

REMEMBER

In black skins, fat and blood have virtually no influence on skin colour due to the density of melanin pigment. The paler the skin, the more significant the contribution of blood and fat.

Skin colour

The colour of skin depends on the degree of absorption and reflection of light from its surface. When light hits the skin, the epidermis absorbs some of it and reflects the rest. The reflected light is converted into a colour sensation. The colour produced is a combination of three main factors:

- melanin – the natural pigment produced by special cells in the epidermis. Melanin absorbs ultraviolet and is a protective mechanism against sun damage. This is why the skin will normally produce melanin pigment to tan when exposed to the sun. The intensity of UV absorption is relative to the amount and type of melanin present in the skin: eumelanin, which is dark brown/black; pheomelanin, which is yellowish red

- fat – fatty material in the skin frequently has the fat-soluble vitamin carotene dissolved in it. Carotene is taken into the body in the diet and is contained in green vegetables and carrots. It has a yellowish colour and people who follow a vegetarian diet often have sallow skin because of this

- blood – the influence of the blood on skin colour depends on the thickness of the epidermis and whether the vessels are dilated or contracted. The superficial capillaries add pink to the overall skin colour. Oxygenated red blood cells contain a red pigment, oxygenated haemoglobin. Deoxygenated blood appears bluish.

HEALTH MATTERS

People with fair skin run the greatest risk of severe sunburn, premature ageing and skin cancer. It is very important to know the best ways to protect the skin in hot sun if there is not enough melanin present to give natural protection. Sunlight is not the only threat to fair skins, which need additional protection in all extreme weather conditions.

Black skin — 5%, 25%, 70%
White skin — 15%, 60%, 25%

☐ % UV rays reflected from the skin's surface

▨ % UV rays absorbed by the epidermis

▧ % UV rays absorbed by the dermis

Percentage of UV light reflection and absorption by black and white skin

REMEMBER

The melanocytes in dark skins are always in an active state, unlike those in fair skin, which need stimulating into activity.

How melanin is produced

The natural skin colour relies on a constant process of melanin production. Melanocytes, present in the germinating layer of the epidermis, inject coloured granules, melanosomes, into adjacent keratinocytes. These cells then carry melanin upwards through the layers of the epidermis to produce a dense layer of pigment. Sometimes, the transfer of melanin into the keratinocytes is blocked. When this happens, no colour is produced.

The shade of the skin is determined by the size, maturity and distribution of the pigment granules:

- size – melanosomes are larger in dark skin than in fair skin
- maturity – the melanosomes go through various stages of development before reaching maturity. Only fully matured cells transfer melanin with them into the keratinocytes. In dark skin, all the melanosomes produced reach maturity. In fair skin, not all the melanosomes reach this state
- distribution – the epidermis of dark skins is more densely packed with melanin than fair skins.

Developing a suntan

The production of extra melanin in the skin involves chemical processes, which take between 36 and 48 hours following initial exposure to sunlight. In fair people, it takes considerably longer to produce enough melanin to protect the skin.

This is not always appreciated by holidaymakers anxious to make a start on developing their tans as soon as they reach their sunny destination. All too often, the sore pinkness of sunburn during the first few days of a holiday is mistaken for the initial stages of suntan development. This is not the case!

People with active melanocytes in their skin develop a tan much more readily than those whose melanocytes are inactive. Increased intensities of ultraviolet develop the colour of the melanin and speed up the rate at which the pigment-bearing cells travel up to the surface of the skin. People with inactive melanocytes burn in the sun if their skin is not well protected.

Ultraviolet rays

The sun gives out heat, light and other rays which travel towards the earth. Most of the harmful rays are absorbed by the atmosphere. The ones that reach earth are made up of visible light (white light or daylight), infrared (produces heat) and ultraviolet. It is the ultraviolet that produces a suntan.

Ultraviolet is made up of rays of different wavelengths:

- UVA – these rays have a long wave length and work on melanin granules already contained in the upper epidermis. They produce a rapid tan in people who tan easily. UVA rays speed up the ageing processes of the skin. They damage the protein fibres which make the skin firm and supple. Sometimes they cause allergies. UVA rays are thought to enhance the effects of UVB.
- UVB – these rays have a medium wavelength and are strong enough to penetrate cells, making them produce more melanin. They also cause thickening of the epidermis. The tan produced by UVB rays takes longer to appear than with UVA; the melanin-producing cells have to be stimulated into activity before working their way up through the layers of epidermis. However, the resulting tan lasts much longer.
- UVC – these rays have the shortest wavelength and 'cut off' before they reach the earth. They do not reach the skin. UVC rays are very destructive. They are often used in sterilisation procedures because they destroy living cells. When the ozone layer is intact, it acts as a barrier to UVC rays.

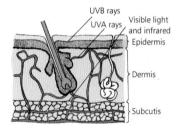

Penetration levels of UV rays through the skin

The ozone layer is a layer of ozone gas which exists high up in the atmosphere, about 20 miles away from the earth's surface. The ozone layer prevents much of the ultraviolet produced by the sun from reaching earth. Other gases, such as those produced by aerosols, rise up and replace or break down some of the ozone. This makes the layer a less effective barrier to the sun's rays.

The natives of countries with a relatively mild climate do not need the same amount of protection as those living in regions with extreme climatic conditions. As a result, fairer skins are usually thinner, with fewer active sebaceous glands. Unfortunately this means that there is very little natural protection for people with fair skins who move to or take holidays in hot, sunny countries.

A thicker epidermis with a generous coating of sebum helps to screen out UV rays. As dark skins absorb more heat than pale skins, the larger and more numerous sweat glands of a person with black skin help to keep them cooler and more comfortable in intense heat.

The characteristic 'muddy' tone of a Latin complexion, while not always deeply coloured, usually has sufficient melanin present in its epidermis to enable the skin to tan quickly without burning in hot sun.

Which tanning type are you?

TYPE	FEATURES	ADVICE
Easy tanner	Skin quite fair but sallow; goes red at first then tans very easily The melanocytes are active: exposure to strong sunlight speeds up the rate at which they produce melanin	Remember that there is a risk of burning on initial exposure to strong sunlight. Don't rush into prolonged sunbathing sessions without proper protection. Build up exposure times and wear a suitable sunscreen. Reapply it regularly. Remember that areas of the body which are usually covered will need extra protection from the sun. Always apply after-sun skin care to compensate for moisture loss
Faster tanner	There is already a lot of melanin developed in the skin, so it can tan very quickly; the fast tanner very rarely suffers sunburn	There is always a slight risk of burning at first if sensible precautions are not taken. Avoid over-exposure. Protect the skin with a suitable sunscreen and reapply it regularly. Always apply after-sun skin care
Slow tanner	Skin quite fair. Very little developed melanin in the skin. Melanocytes need activating by UVB to stimulate melanin production. Skin goes red very easily but tans eventually. Initial impatience invariably leads to burning which prolongs the overall time required to develop a healthy-looking tan. Freckles may increase in size and join up to produce larger, brown patches	Build up exposure times gradually. Avoid sunbathing when the sun is at its hottest (usually between midday and 2 p.m.). Use a suitable sunscreen and reapply it regularly, particularly before and after going in the sea. Use after-sun products to soothe the skin and keep it moisturised
No hoper!	Very pale skin which does not contain enough active melanocytes to produce a tan. The skin burns very easily. Sometimes small clusters of melanin appear as freckles and the skin burns in between them	Accept that you are not going to get a tan and be sensible about protecting your skin in the sun. Wear loose light clothing, a good sunscreen (preferably a total sun-block) and a big hat. Stay in the shade as much as possible. Congratulate yourself on how well you are nursing your collagen through prolonged youth by keeping it away from harmful ultraviolet!

SKIN TYPE	ORIGIN	COLOUR	OTHER FEATURES
White: Caucasian	Britain Scandinavia E/W Europe N America S Australia Canada New Zealand	Basic colour pale buff. Relatively small amount of melanin present. Some skins appear pinkish while others have a yellowish (sallow) tone	Hair usually red, blonde, 'mousey' or brunette Eyes usually grey, green or blue Prone to freckles (especially redheads) Skin comparatively thin, translucent and fragile Fewer and less active sebaceous glands Very limited natural defence to sunlight Greatest risk of severe sunburn, premature ageing and skin cancer (redheads with freckles most at risk)
Oriental/ Light Asian	China Japan Middle East	More melanin present. Skin basically creamy coloured with tendency to yellow and olive tones	Skin very rarely shows blemishes and defies normal symptoms of ageing Oriental skin particularly remains trouble free with sparse facial and body hair Sebaceous glands less active Scars are more likely to occur and hyper-pigment, causing unevenness, troughs, pits and hollows on the skin surface
Mediterranean/ Latin	Italy Spain Greece Portugal Yugoslavia S America Central America	Sallow skin with some reddish pigment. Far more melanin present which obscures the colour of blood vessels	Skin tends to have generous coating of sebum and additional fatty tissue Although oily, rarely suffers from spots, blackheads or acne Quite tough, and ages later than fairer skins Tans easily and deeply without burning Tendency to excessive hair
Dark Asian	Pakistan India Sri Lanka Malaysia	Very dark skin colours, deeply pigmented with melanin which do not reveal the blood capillaries	Smooth and supple with minimal wrinkling Ageing symptoms do not usually start until well after 40. Protein fibres degenerate much more slowly Sweat glands larger and more numerous. The sweat gives a sheen which is often mistaken for oiliness
Afro-Caribbean/ African	West Indies Africa	Black	Sebum fattier, sebaceous glands larger, more numerous and closer to skin surface, open pores. Thick, tough skin which desquamates easily and forms keloid scars when damaged

Examining black skin

Some aspects of the skin analysis are difficult on black skin because of the amount of pigment present. A more accurate assessment can be made if the examination is carried out under a Wood's light. This is an inspection lamp which produces deep ultraviolet rays. It makes different types of skin fluoresce (glow) characteristically in different colours and intensities.

The Wood's light

SKIN TYPE	COLOUR OF FLUORESCENCE
Balanced skin	purplish-blue
Dry skin	weak violet
Greasy skin	coral pink
Hydrated skin	strong violet
Thick stratum corneum	strong white
Thin stratum corneum	purple
Build-up of dead skin cells	silvery white
Increased pigmentation	brown

Black skin generally ages at a much slower rate than white skin. This is mainly due to the extra protection provided by melanin, which not only screens out UV but also absorbs free radicals. Free radicals are chemicals produced in the body which cause the degenerative effects of ageing upon the skin.

1   There is greater risk of hyperpigmentation in black skin. This is because of the increased distribution of melanin pigment. Following any skin injury, for example a burn, cut, scar or inflammation, black skin develops patches of pigmentation.

2   Any erythema or sensitivity shows up as a darkened area rather than the pink or red which would appear on white skin.

3   In mature black skin, irregular pigmentation can be a particular problem. Over-abrasion of the skin, including the use of strong soaps and alcohol-based lotions, can also result in pigmentation problems.

4   Inflammatory disorders such as eczema and dermatitis may result in pityriasis alba (light patches and scales) or lichenification (clusters of dark papules joining to form thickened plaques).

5   There can be a sudden, unexplained loss of pigmentation due to the depletion of melanocyte cells. Vitiligo can occur after a severe burn or physical injury.

6   Sweat glands are larger and more numerous in black skin. The duct opens at the surface into a longer and more noticeable pore.

7   Heat is absorbed more readily in black skin but it is lost more quickly because of increased sweating.

8   The sebaceous glands are larger and more numerous in black skin. There is one sebaceous gland for every seven sweat glands. The pores created by the sebaceous ducts are larger than the pores on white skin. Despite this, black skin is not oilier and does not suffer from acne more often than white skin.

9   Because black skin has more and larger sebaceous glands, light is easily reflected from the skin's surface. This can give the effect of shiny (greasy) skin when, in fact, black skin is often dehydrated and prone to flakiness.

10   Black skin is usually thicker than white skin and is prone to congestion and comedones.

11   In black skins, one-tenth of sebaceous glands open directly on to the surface of the skin. Extraction work to clear blockages is an obvious need for black skin, but this must be done gently to avoid inflammation.

12   The increased thickness of the stratum corneum can cause dehydration, which leads to increased skin shedding. This can create an 'ashen' effect as the loose cells build up on the skin.

13   Black skin develops 'keloid' scarring when healing after injury. Keloid scars are thick and lumpy, and often extend beyond the borders of the wound.

14   The hair follicles in black skin are curved, which can cause problems with ingrowing hairs after a depilatory waxing treatment.

Ethnic skin types

1. List three factors that contribute to the colour of skin.

2. State four differences between black and caucasian skin.

3. Compare the effects upon the skin of UVA and UVB rays.

4. How does a Wood's light work?

5. State three characteristics of an oriental skin type.

6. What advice should be given to a fair-skinned client who is about to go on holiday in a hot, sunny climate?

7. Why must the ozone layer be preserved?

8. Why do pale skins usually appear more sensitive than darker skins?

9. What is the main difference between a skin that tans easily and a skin that tends to burn in the sun?

10. What is responsible for the 'sheen' characteristically associated with Asian skins?

Male with clean, glowing skin

Characteristics of skin by facial area

The diagram divides the face and neck into areas that have particular characteristics because of their structure. It is important to include all of these areas in your facial examination.

Female with clean, glowing skin

Area 1 The forehead

The skin of the forehead contains very little fat and fits closely to the broad, flattish frontal bone underneath. There are numerous sebaceous glands present and the area is contained in the greasy T-zone of a typical combination skin.

COMMON CHARACTERISTICS	POSSIBLE CAUSES
Pimples, pustules and blackheads	greasy/combination skin greasy hair worn with a fringe
Horizontal creases	ageing (loss of muscle tone)
Deep vertical creases between the eyebrows	ageing prolonged eye strain stress

Area 2 The eyes

The area surrounding the eyes consists of two movable skin folds, the upper and lower eyelids. The skin of the eyelids is very thin and does not usually contain fat. There are very few sebaceous glands so the skin easily becomes dehydrated and develops lines, wrinkles and crêpiness before any other part of the face.

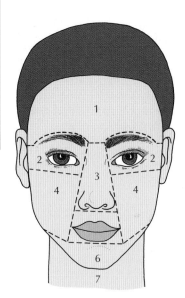

Facial areas

The skin underneath the eyes becomes even thinner with ageing and the blood supply network shows through as a reddish blue colour. Glands can also be seen as tiny, skin-coloured lumps.

COMMON CHARACTERISTICS	POSSIBLE CAUSES
Dark circles beneath the eyes	Heredity, racial characteristic, tiredness, ill-health, excessive exposure to sunlight, sallow complexion
Swelling/puffiness	Tiredness, hay fever, sinus problems, catarrh, heavy or greasy creams
'Bags' under the eyes	Ageing, over-stretching the skin
Milia (whiteheads)	Dry skin
Split capillaries	Constant rubbing
Crow's feet	Ageing, dry skin, smoking, prolonged exposure to sunlight, prolonged eye strain
Skin tags (tiny, fibrous growths)	Ageing
Xanthomas (buff coloured 'fatty' lesions)	Ageing, diabetes, high-fat diet

HEALTH MATTERS

'Bags' under the eyes are a result of the ageing process. The contour of the eye area changes where the lower eyelid meets the upper cheek. Ageing causes a rift to develop between the two as the skin loses its support. Eventually, a broad, thin-skinned, semi-circular 'bag' develops below the eye, causing a deeply shadowed groove.

Area 3 The nose

The nose is the most prominent of the facial features and varies in width and shape between individuals and different races. Only the upper part of the nose is made up of bone; the main part of it is cartilage, which is soft and flexible.

The skin of the nose is abundantly supplied with sebaceous glands, which are larger than normal and situated near the surface. The nose is contained in the T-zone of a typical combination skin and generally has a tendency towards greasiness.

COMMON CHARACTERISTICS	POSSIBLE CAUSES
Open pores, blocked pores, spots and blackheads	Greasy/combination skin, inadequate cleansing or make-up removal
Split capillaries	Friction from glasses, a heavy cold, exposure to extreme heat, persistent rubbing

HEALTH MATTERS

The prominence of the nose exposes it even more to the effects of sunlight and harsh winds. If adequate protection is not worn, the capillaries in the skin dilate and often rupture, leaving a permanently red nose.

Area 4 The cheeks

The skin of the cheeks is smooth, firm and 'plump' in youth, but gradually, through the ageing process, the cheeks lose their full contour and the underlying bone structure becomes more prominent. This is due to the loss of moisture, fat and support from the deeper layers.

COMMON CHARACTERISTICS	POSSIBLE CAUSES
Dilated capillaries	Dry sensitive skin, exposure to extreme heat, inadequate protection in harsh weather, harsh rubbing, alcohol, spicy foods, hot drinks
Milia	Dry skin
Naso-labial folds (nose-to-mouth lines)	Ageing, loss of muscle tone, rapid weight loss e.g. after illness or strict dieting.

Area 5 The mouth

The shape of the mouth becomes slightly smaller and less well defined with age. The gums shrink slightly, pulling the corners of the mouth inwards. Lines develop across the fibres of the underlying muscle. The deeper these lines get, the more difficult lipstick application becomes.

COMMON CHARACTERISTICS	POSSIBLE CAUSES
Lines around the mouth	Ageing and loss of muscle tone, tension, smoking
Deep creases at corners of mouth	Ageing, loss of muscle tone, loss of skin elasticity, ill-fitting dentures
Excess hair growth above upper lip	Ageing (menopause), racial characteristic, medical condition e.g. hormonal drugs e.g. steroids

Area 6 The chin and jaw

The front part of the chin is contained in the T-zone and tends to be more greasy than other areas of the face. The horizontal crease in the chin becomes particularly congested if it is not cleansed properly.

COMMON CHARACTERISTICS	POSSIBLE CAUSES
Open pores, blocked pores, spots and blackheads	Greasy/combination skin
Dropped contours (jowls)	Ageing and loss of muscle tone, loss of skin elasticity
Double chin	Ageing and loss of muscle tone, loss of skin elasticity, bad posture

Area 7 The neck

The neck is often neglected in a skin-care routine. Consequently, it often looks sallow and sluggish compared with the rest of the face. The skin of the neck is attached fairly loosely to the underlying structures. It lacks bony support and has a relatively small amount of fat, which means that it can be pulled and stretched quite easily.

The neck is the first area to lose fat and this will be noticeable in people who have lost a lot of weight through illness or strict dieting. Gradual loss of fat from the neck also occurs during the ageing process. There are very few sebaceous glands in the skin of the neck, so dryness and crêpiness are common problems.

COMMON CHARACTERISTICS	POSSIBLE CAUSES
Crêpey neck	Ageing and loss of skin elasticity, sun damage, dry skin, illness, 'crash' dieting
Skin tags	Ageing
Blotchiness, discolouration	Ageing, sun damage, perfume
'Necklace' lines	Ageing, loss of muscle tone

HEALTH MATTERS

A patch of brown pigmentation is sometimes evident on each side of the neck when perfume containing a photosensitising ingredient (something that reacts with the sun) has been applied directly to the skin from the bottle.

REMEMBER

If you come across something you are not sure about during the examination, ask your supervisor for assistance.

SELF-CHECKS

Characteristics of skin by facial area

1 Give two possible causes of deep, vertical lines between the eyebrows.

2 Why should only lightweight skin-care products be used in the eye area?

3 Give three reasons why dilated capillaries appear commonly on the cheeks?

4 Give two reasons for excess hair growth above the upper lip.

5 List five effects of ageing upon facial appearance.

6 Give two causes of a crêpey neck.

7 State three causes of premature signs of ageing of the skin.

8 Why should perfume not be worn in the sun?

Activity 6.4: Examining the face and neck

Practise examining the skin through an illuminated magnifier. You will need to reposition the lamp for examining different areas, making sure that it does not touch the client or get in the way of your assessment. Do not be afraid to gently move your client's head if it helps you to get a better view through the magnifier.

Examine as many different types of 'clients' as you can, perhaps starting with one or two of your colleagues. Make sure their skin is clean and then go through the full consultation procedure, using closed and open questioning techniques. Fill in a record card for each of your clients and keep additional notes to show your supervisor when they check your results.

MULTIPLE CHOICE QUIZ

Examining the face and neck

Ask your supervisor to check your answers.

1 The main function of the epidermis is:
   (a) insulation
   (b) absorption
   (c) regulation
   (d) protection.

2 The dermis is a:
   (a) fatty layer
   (b) fibrous layer
   (c) dead layer
   (d) barrier layer.

3 The arrector pili is a:
   (a) muscle
   (b) blood vessel
   (c) nerve ending
   (d) hair follicle.

4 Sweat is produced by the:
   (a) suderiferous glands
   (b) sebaceous glands
   (c) blood supply
   (d) hormones.

5 Connective tissue is made up of:
   (a) fat cells
   (b) epidermal cells
   (c) keratin
   (d) protein fibres.

6 Fat cells are stored in the:
   (a) subcutaneous layer
   (b) epidermis
   (c) dermis
   (d) papillary layer.

7 The sensations of touch, pain, hot and cold are transmitted by:
   (a) capillaries
   (b) muscles
   (c) collagen
   (d) nerves.

8 The dermal papillae contain:
   (a) sebaceous glands
   (b) hair follicles
   (c) blood capillaries
   (d) fatty tissue.

9 The protein found in the epidermis is:
   (a) melanin
   (b) keratin
   (c) reticulin
   (d) elastin.

10 Collagen fibres are:
   (a) waterproof
   (b) elastic
   (c) sensitive
   (d) strong.

11 Comedones occur commonly on:
   (a) dry skin
   (b) black skin
   (c) greasy skin
   (d) caucasian skin.

Examining the face and neck

12 Pale skins appear more sensitive than darker skins because:
(a) the colour of the underlying blood supply shows up more clearly on pale skin
(b) pale skins are more allergic than dark skins
(c) changes in skin colour show up more clearly on pale skin
(d) darker skins are not sensitive.

13 The neck is one of the first areas to show signs of ageing because:
(a) it burns easily in the sun
(b) there are very few sebaceous glands in the neck
(c) the neck muscles are not strong
(d) the skin of the neck is thin.

14 Dark shadows under the eyes may be caused by:
(a) tiredness
(b) tension
(c) melanin
(d) poor diet.

15 A double chin is caused by:
(a) obesity
(b) loss of muscle tone
(c) sudden weight loss
(d) hormone imbalance.

KEY TERMS

You should now understand the following words and phrases. If you do not, go back through the chapter and find out what they mean:

Connective tissue	**Fibroblast cells**	**Muscle tone**
Free radicals	**Histamine**	**Epidermis**
Allergen	**Dermis**	**Keratin**
Desquamation	**Muscle fibres**	**Tissue fluid**
Motor nerve	**Melanin**	**Sensory nerve**
Haemangioma	**Lymph**	**Fungal infections**
Bacterial infections	**Viral infections**	

Improve and maintain facial skin condition

Part 2

Salon treatments and home care

After working through this section of the chapter you will be able to:

- treat a range of skin types and conditions
- know about the range and uses of products available for facial treatments
- know about different types of specialist skin products and how to apply them
- apply and adapt facial massage techniques to suit skin types and conditions
- understand the effects of different products and treatments on the skin
- recommend skin-care products for home use
- state the benefits of facial massage and other skin-care treatments
- carry out a basic facial treatment.

Before you work through this chapter: Be wise and revise!
Revision topics to help you achieve this unit:

Improve and maintain facial skin condition

TOPIC	CHAPTER	PAGE
Health and Safety at Work Act 1974	1	5
Sale and Supply of Goods Act 1994	1	13
Data Protection Act 1984	1	14
Cosmetic Products (Safety) Regulations 1989	1	14
Professional image	1	16
Communication skills	2	24

Controlling the salon environment	3	36
Client care	3	52
Treatment hygiene	3	54
Selling products	5	94
Selling treatments and services	5	103
Agreeing a treatment plan	5	107
Examining the face	6	111
Contraindications to facial treatments	6	145
Basic skin types	6	146
Male skin	6	150
Ethnic variations in skin type	6	151
Characteristics of skin by facial area	6	157

There was a time when salon facials were considered to be luxury treatments, enjoyed only by wealthy women with a lot of time on their hands. This idea is now very out of date. Regular facials have become an important part of the routine and lifestyle of many people. They know that the salon provides a complete service of professional treatments and retail products backed up with support and advice about all aspects of skin care. This is reflected in the way that beauty salons now offer their services. They have become more 'accessible'. Evening and Sunday openings are not unusual and most salons offer a good range of affordable treatments.

Skin care

A beautiful skin is a healthy skin. Good skin care, practised routinely, helps to keep the skin healthy by:

- keeping the outer surface clean, soft and pliable
- maintaining adequate moisture levels
- ensuring a healthy blood supply to living cells and tissues
- helping the skin to resist infection and infestation
- providing protection from external damage.

The main aim of skin care is to create or maintain a balanced skin. A balanced skin is a healthy skin. The therapist can use a wide range of treatments and products to help 'balance' any skin type and improve or control skin problems, but, ultimately, the clients must understand what they have to do to keep their skin healthy.

Advice for home care

The following advice is intended for all clients, whatever skin type they may have:

1   Eat a balanced diet. This should include plenty of fresh vegetables, fruit and fibre. Foods containing vitamins A, B and C are particularly important for healthy skin. So are proteins and the essential fatty acids.

(a) Good sources of vitamin A: milk, eggs, butter, margarine, fish liver oils (e.g. cod, halibut).

(b) Good sources of vitamin B: cereals, pulses, meat, milk, wholemeal flour, leafy vegetables.

(c) Good sources of vitamin C: fresh fruit, particularly blackcurrants, strawberries, oranges, lemons and grapefruit, fresh vegetables, particularly sprouts, cauliflower, cabbage, tomatoes and potatoes.

(d) Good sources of protein: meat, fish, milk, eggs, beans, peas and lentils (pulses), edible seeds, nuts and fruit containing oil.

(e) Good sources of essential fatty acids: polyunsaturated vegetable and nut oils, soft margarines.

2   Drink plenty of water. This helps to maintain a healthy water balance in the body and speeds up the elimination of waste and toxins which can affect the skin.

3   Get enough sleep. Remember that the rate of skin cell repair and replacement increases when we are asleep. Tiredness and exhaustion deprive the skin of the energy it needs to recover and regenerate.

4   Protect the skin. A balanced skin can easily become dry if it is not protected from the weather, extremes of temperature, central heating, sunlight, pollution and cosmetics. Wear a moisturiser to create a barrier between the skin and outside elements. Whenever possible, avoid exposing the skin to strong sunlight; otherwise use a suitable ultraviolet screening product.

5   Exercise regularly. Apart from stimulating the flow of blood and supply of oxygen to the body tissues, regular exercise speeds up cell division and helps to build collagen. Keeping the body fit minimises stress and its effects upon the skin.

6   Keep the skin clean. Do not allow dirt and grime to build up, which could block the pores and irritate the skin.

7   Avoid harsh treatment. Do not pull or stretch the skin. Be gentle when washing the face and using skin-care products. Remember that blood vessels are very near the surface of the skin and can become damaged quite easily. Avoid using perfumed products on facial skin or those with an alcohol or alkaline base, which are very degreasing.

8   Do not smoke. Besides being extremely hazardous to general health, smoking produces gases (mainly carbon monoxide and nitrogen oxide) which are carried round the body in the bloodstream in preference to oxygen. As a consequence the cells do not receive enough nourishment. The skin suffers oxygen starvation. Other chemicals produced in the body by smoking interfere with the protein fibres in the skin and deplete the body of vitamin C, which is essential for healthy skin.

9   Control alcohol intake. Alcohol raises the blood pressure and causes the blood capillaries to dilate. Over a period of time this can cause the walls of the capillaries to rupture and become permanently damaged. In the short term, excessive alcohol intake produces chemicals in the body which dehydrate the skin. In the longer term puffiness, coarsening of the skin texture, deepening of lines and wrinkles, and chronic redness of the skin occur.

10   Monitor the skin. A balanced skin becomes drier with age as the body processes slow down. Keep a look out for early signs of changes in the skin so that cosmetic skin care can be adapted at the right time.

GOOD PRACTICE

Professional skin care starts with a preliminary consultation, when the client is questioned and examined closely before deciding on the best course of action. Once the treatment plan has been agreed, the therapist and client are clear about their own responsibilities for looking after the skin and dealing with any problems that may be present.

REMEMBER

Giving advice to clients and monitoring their home care is all part of the professional service.

Selling skin-care products

A good home care routine is essential for looking after the skin in between salon treatments. Remember, when selling skin care, you should describe the features of the products and explain their benefits to the client.

Features

Features include the main ingredients and their effects, plus any other special characteristics of the product, for example:

- fragrance free
- biodegradable packaging
- not tested on animals
- double concentrated, so more economical
- contains plant extracts.

Benefits

These must relate to the client's particular needs, for example:

- particular skin problems
- lifestyle
- ease of use
- reason for buying
- personal preferences.

Advert for female skin-care products

Selecting skin-care products

The first step towards good skin care is choosing the right products. It is important for a salon to research the market well before deciding upon which range or ranges to carry. Price is not always the most important factor. A salon that offers a range of specialised facial treatments will need different types of products for both salon use and retail sale. Specialist skin-care ranges provide for every type of skin and include preparations for treating specific skin problems.

Male skin-care products

Activity 6.5: Skin-care products

1 Collect information about all of the skin-care products available in your salon:

   a) read the packages and labels to discover their main ingredients
   b) learn about their specific uses and effects
   c) note the advice given regarding application and removal of the products
   d) make sure you know the different sizes available in retail lines and their selling prices.

2 Referring to your product information, write out a list of the features and benefits of each of the items in your salon's retail range. Try learning what you have written so that you are well prepared for your next sale!

Cleansers

Cleansing products

Cleansing is the first and most important stage of any skin-care routine. It prevents a build-up of waste products and surface matter which would otherwise congest and irritate the skin:

- if dirt and grime accumulate on the skin, they prevent efficient desquamation and block up the pores

- make-up that is left on the skin becomes stale, irritates the surface of the skin and blemishes appear

- over the course of the day, the skin's secretions attract dust, parasites and pollution from the atmosphere; these create further congestion which must be dealt with promptly to prevent skin problems.

Cleansing also ensures the effectiveness of any skin-care treatments applied afterwards.

Most cleansers are a basic oil and water emulsion with the addition of perfume and, sometimes, a detergent. Products that contain a higher proportion of oil than water (water-in-oil emulsions, or w/o) have a heavier, creamier texture. Those with a higher water content (oil-in-water emulsions, or o/w) are lighter and more fluid.

REMEMBER

Skin-care products and beauty treatments will not be effective if there is a barrier created by make-up or other surface matter. 'Active' skin treatments rely on the absorption of substances through the hair follicles and between the cells of the epidermis. If these channels are blocked, there is no way through.

Cleansers are available as:

- cleansing creams
- cleansing milks
- cleansing lotions
- make-up removers
- 'wash off' cleansers.

The choice of cleansing products for a client depends upon the type and sensitivity of their skin, the amount and type of make-up worn and their preferred method of use.

Cleansing creams

The mineral oil in a cleansing cream dissolves grease and oil-based products on the skin. A wax, such as beeswax or paraffin wax, is often added to give the cream a stiffer texture. The water content cools the skin and makes the cream easier to spread.

Some cleansing creams have a more fluid consistency which is lighter than a traditional cream but 'richer' than a cleansing milk. These are often promoted as 'make-up removers' and most of them are suitable for removing both facial and eye make-up.

Uses

Cleansing creams are particularly good for removing make-up and for cleansing balanced, dry and mature skin types. This is because:

- they melt quickly when applied to the skin and penetrate the pores, dissolving stale make-up and grime
- they are not absorbed by the skin, so provide a good medium for deep-cleanse massage movements.

Cleansing creams are applied to the face and neck with the pads of the fingers, using gentle, upward circular movements.

Cleansing milks

These have a similar formulation to creams, but with a much higher proportion of water and a little detergent added. Cleansing milks are not always as efficient as creams for dissolving make-up, but they do have the following benefits:

- the detergent and water content of cleansing milks emulsifies grease on the skin so that it can be removed effectively, together with any dust or other debris adhering to it
- because they are water-based, cleansing milks are easier to wipe off the skin than creams
- some cleansing milks can be worked up into a lather with water to wash the face
- cleansing milks with a higher oil content will effectively remove a light make-up.

GOOD PRACTICE

Always remove make-up from the eyes and lips separately before treating the other facial areas. This is to prevent spreading deeply pigmented products around the face.

REMEMBER

Whichever cleansing product is used, it should leave the skin looking and feeling clean, cool and fresh. The skin should feel soft to the touch and not 'tight' or irritated.

REMEMBER

The warmth of the skin 'melts' oil-based and wax-based products, providing slip for the massage. This means that the movements can be performed without dragging or stretching the skin. This is particularly important when treating dry, sensitive and mature skins.

REMEMBER

An **emulsifying agent** is an ingredient that allows oil and water to mix together instead of separating. Borax is an emulsifying agent which is often contained in skin creams to stabilise the mixture.

A PRACTICAL GUIDE TO BEAUTY THERAPY

Uses

Clients often prefer the lighter texture of cleansing milks. Their detergent action makes them particularly suitable for younger, greasier skins. Clients with a tendency to dryness or who have mature skin should only use cleansing milks with a high oil content. Cleansing milk is either applied directly to the skin with clean, damp cotton wool pads stroked firmly but gently over the face and neck in upward and outward movements, or it is applied with clean fingers in small, gentle circular movements, working well into the creases of the skin.

Make-up removers

There are different types of products available for removing make-up:

- make-up removers with a high oil content, which are suitable for removing all types of make-up
- others have special formulations which make them suitable for removing 'stubborn' eye make-up, in particular waterproof mascara.

Uses

Whereas a therapist may use make-up remover at the initial stage of a facial, for preparing the skin for further cleansing and deep-cleansing treatments, clients often want a 'convenience' product, which is quick and easy to use and will fulfil the requirements of the whole of their cleansing routine.

All-purpose make-up removers

Creams and lightweight w/o emulsions remove all types of make-up:

- oil-based make-up removers liquefy easily on the skin and dissolve pigments and other make-up ingredients without causing irritation
- some make-up removers are supplied as lotions and rely on their detergent effect for removing cosmetics. The action of these products can leave the skin feeling dry and they are generally not as efficient at removing make-up.

Eye make-up removers

Available as oils, lotions and gels, eye make-up removers break down the strong pigments and basic ingredients in eye cosmetics so that they can be removed easily from the skin, eyelashes and eyebrows:

- eye make-up remover pads are lint pads soaked in mineral oil, which are particularly convenient for home use
- oil-based eye make-up removers are usually more efficient and gentler on the skin than non-oily eye make-up removers.

Cleansing lotions

These are solutions of detergents in water. Some cleansing lotions contain oil, but only in very small amounts. Some cleansing lotions contain antibacterial ingredients (for example hexachlorophene) to help a greasy, blemished, problem skin.

Uses

Cleansing lotions are primarily for home use. They are quick and easy to use, being wiped over the skin with damp cotton wool pads. Their degreasing action makes them particularly useful for younger, blemished skins and for clients with a greasy skin or greasy T-zone. Cleansing lotions are not suitable for clients with balanced, dry, or mature skins.

'Wash-off' cleansers (facial washes)

Some clients do not feel that their skin is clean unless they have washed their face. You need to consider this when recommending a suitable home care routine. Traditional 'soap and water' washing is not suitable for the face, but a wide range of products are available which can be used with water. These provide the benefits of washing without the drawbacks.

Uses

Each facial wash product has instructions for use and identifies the skin types for which it is suitable. Clients with dry, mature or sensitive skin should only use a product specially formulated for their skin type.

GOOD PRACTICE

Some professional deep-cleanse routines involve the use of a gentle, soapless lathering cleanser after the removal of skin blockages. The product is applied all over the face and neck with a damp complexion brush. Small, circular movements are used to work the product up into a creamy textured lather, which penetrates the pores. The skin looks and feels beautifully clean afterwards and also benefits from the mild, stimulating effects of the brush massage.

Retail 'wash off' cleansers are available in a variety of forms including bars, gels and milks.

Cleansing bars

These look and feel like bars of soap, but are actually compressed blocks of cleansing cream containing a soapless detergent. The benefits of cleansing bars are:

- they lather up with water and feel the same as soap, but without any of the undesirable after-effects
- they are usually alkaline-free and have a pH that helps to preserve the natural acid mantle of the skin.

Male skin-care ranges often include a cleansing bar. They particularly suit male clients who have not yet mastered a skin-care routine.

Cleansing gels

Cleansing gels are quick and easy to use and are often promoted as being suitable for all skin types, including sensitive skins. Cleansing gels are applied to damp skin and a light foam is created as the hands 'wash' the face.

A PRACTICAL GUIDE TO BEAUTY THERAPY

Cleansing milks

Some cleansing milks can also be applied to damp skin and used as a facial wash. A mild lather is created when the product is combined with water and the skin is left feeling clean, soft and cool.

What is wrong with soap?

Soap is a strong detergent with an alkaline **pH**. It strips the skin of grease, thereby removing its protective coating.

People with greasy skin are more likely than others to be able to wash their face with soap and water without suffering any ill-effects. The skin stabilises itself quite quickly once the sebaceous glands have produced enough sebum to restore the acid mantle. However, people with a normal (balanced) or dry skin run the risk of dehydrating the skin, causing it to become parched, flaky, tight, sore and inflamed.

SELF-CHECKS

Cleansers

1 (a) Explain why cleansing is so important.
   (b) List three features of a good cleansing product.

2 What does w/o emulsion mean? Name one example of a cleansing product that is a w/o emulsion.

3 (a) Why is a detergent contained in a cleanser?
   (b) State one type of cleansing product that contains a detergent.

4 (a) Give two advantages of using an 'oily' eye make-up remover.
   (b) Name the type of oil that is usually contained in an eye make-up remover.

5 Why might a client prefer to use a non-oily eye make-up remover?

6 (a) Give three reasons why a client should be advised against using soap for cleansing the face.
   (b) Give two preferable alternatives to soap.

Exfoliants

To exfoliate means to peel off in scales or layers. All types of skin benefit from the weekly use of exfoliating products to brighten up the complexion and refine the skin texture. Regular use of an **exfoliant** prevents the build-up of dead cells so that skin is kept smooth.

Uses

Exfoliants help to reverse some of the damage caused by too much sun, general neglect and the ageing process. Dryness, uneven pigmentation and premature wrinkles are all helped by regular exfoliating treatments. Special skin treatments are more effective when applied after using an exfoliant.

Some exfoliants achieve their effects by gentle abrasion, others through the chemical or physical effects of their ingredients.

Facial scrubs

These products are basically cleansing milks or cleansing creams containing 'grains', such as finely ground olive stones, nuts, oatmeal or tiny synthetic micro-beads. Facial scrubs combine a detergent cleansing action with gentle abrasion.

Uses

Facial scrubs are usually applied to damp skin and massaged over the face with upward and outward movements (omitting the eye area). When massaged over the skin, they loosen dead cells and other surface debris. These are then rinsed off the skin with clean, warm water, leaving the skin clean, soft and smooth. Facial scrubs are recommended particularly for greasy skin. Their abrasive action helps to loosen surface blockages and stimulate the blood supply, improving skin colour.

Exfoliating masks

These are usually cream-based masks containing clay for absorbency and natural, biological ingredients to help slough off skin cells and prevent skin irritation.

Uses

Exfoliating masks are suitable for most skin types, even dry, mature and sensitive skins, which require gentle exfoliation. As the clay in the mask dries out, it contracts slightly, absorbing dead skin cells. A gentle rotary massage, performed with the pads of the fingers, loosens the clay, taking the dead skin cells with it. Any remaining mask is rinsed off the skin with clean, warm water.

Fruit acid peels

These are available as lotions or masks and contain alpha hydroxy acids (**AHAs**). AHAs are **fruit acids** derived from natural sources such as citrus fruits, bilberries and sugar cane. They gently soften and remove dead skin cells, making the skin look smoother, brighter and softer.

Uses

The fruit acids dissolve dead, surface skin cells and stimulate the blood supply. They soften the appearance of fine lines and help to fade skin discoloration. The products are available as lotions and masks to suit most skin types. They are particularly recommended for dry, mature skin.

Exfoliants

1 List four beneficial effects of exfoliating treatments.

2 How does exfoliating the skin help to prepare it for other beauty treatments?

3 Give three characteristic signs of ageing which are improved by regular exfoliation.

4 State two precautions that should be taken when using a facial scrub.

5 What are AHAs and why are they contained in exfoliating products?

6 What advice should be given to a client before giving an AHA treatment?

Toners

Toners cool and refresh the skin. Stronger toners contain alcohol, which helps to dissolve grease and complete the cleansing process. They have an **astringent** effect, which tightens the skin temporarily and makes the pores appear smaller. Milder toners contain little or no alcohol and, therefore, have a much gentler effect on the skin. All toners contain water and a **humectant** such as glycerine, which attracts water. The humectant in a toner helps to keep moisture in the upper layers by holding back its evaporation.

Uses

Toners are applied to the skin with damp cotton wool pads, stroked firmly but gently over the face and neck. Toners help to restore the acid balance of the skin after washing or cleansing and are wiped over the skin between different stages of a facial treatment. The strength of a toning lotion depends on the amount of alcohol it contains:

- skin tonics contain 20–60 per cent alcohol
- skin bracers and fresheners contain 0–20 per cent alcohol.

Skin tonics

These are strong toners. In addition to alcohol, they contain other powerful astringent ingredients, such as witch hazel or alum.

- Skin tonics dissolve grease and have an antibacterial effect on the skin.
- When the alcohol evaporates off the skin, the superficial blood vessels contract and the skin feels cold.

Uses

Skin tonics that contain more than 25 per cent alcohol are only suitable for greasy skin. Serious dehydration is likely to occur if a skin tonic containing more than 50 per cent alcohol is used.

REMEMBER

Stronger toning lotions are required for removing the greasy film remaining on the skin after facial cleansing or massage. Milder toning lotions should be used for applying directly to clean skin when there is no greasy barrier present.

Greasy	25%–50%
Balanced	10%–25%
Dry	0%–20%
Sensitive	0%–10%

Recommended percentage alcohol content in toning lotions for different skin types

Skin bracers and fresheners

The lower concentration of alcohol in these products makes them less efficient at removing grease. The basic ingredient of bracers is often a flower water such as rose or orange blossom:

- bracers containing up to 20 per cent alcohol do not usually dry out the skin any more than water would
- fresheners containing 0–10 per cent alcohol often have soothing ingredients added, such as azulene, camomile and allantoin.

Uses

Skin bracers containing alcohol may remove a light film of grease, but those with no alcohol will remove only water-soluble substances from the skin.

SELF-CHECKS

Toners

1 How should the skin feel after toner has been applied?

2 What are the effects on the skin of using a toner which is too strong?

3 State the main difference between a skin tonic and a skin bracer.

4 Give two benefits of using a toner in between different stages of a facial treatment.

5 Why is water not always a suitable toner?

Moisturisers

REMEMBER

Moisturisers are often referred to as 'day' creams. This is to distinguish them from 'night' creams, which are also moisturisers, but with a richer formulation that makes them less suitable for day wear.

The most important ingredient of a moisturiser is water, but if water is splashed onto the skin, it will not stay there. Moisturisers are basically oil and water emulsions which contain a humectant, for example glycerine or sorbitol, which attracts water and helps 'fix' it in the upper layers of the skin. Moisturisers are often marketed as 'after-shave balms' for male clients.

HEALTH MATTERS

Moisture that is lost from the skin needs replacing quickly so that the surface is kept soft and smooth. The living cells in the deeper layers need water so that they will not shrivel and die.

REMEMBER

Moisturisers sometimes contain UVA and UVB sunscreens, which help protect the skin from the damaging effects of sunlight. These may be tinted, providing an alternative to foundation.

The combination of oil and water in a moisturiser protects the skin by:

- providing a barrier between the skin and the external environment
- softening the skin so that it can move comfortably, without cracking over underlying muscular movements
- preventing loss of natural moisture from the deeper layers of skin.

Moisturiser should be worn under make-up to:

- even out skin texture and provide a smooth base for foundation
- keep the make-up looking nicer for longer by fixing it on to the skin
- act as a barrier between the skin and make-up so that cleansing is made easier
- help prevent the penetration of pigmented products into the pores.

A PRACTICAL GUIDE TO BEAUTY THERAPY

Moisturising creams

Creams contain approximately 60 per cent water. Their relatively high proportion of oil or wax prevents natural moisture escaping from the deeper layers of skin.

Uses

Moisturising creams are recommended particularly for people with dry skin who benefit from the **emollient** (softening) effects of the oil and waxes contained in the moisturiser. A cream moisturiser should be worn when the surrounding atmosphere is dry and there is an increased risk of natural moisture loss, for example in central heating and extremes of hot and cold weather.

Moisturising milks

Milks have a more fluid consistency because of their higher water content (at least 85 per cent). Apart from increasing the amount of moisture in the upper layers of skin, they attract water from the atmosphere.

Uses

Moisturising milks have a lighter texture than creams and soak quickly into the upper layers of a parched dry skin. They are sometimes preferred by clients who do not want a greasy film left on the skin.

Night creams

Often described as 'nourishing' creams, these products are basically rich moisturisers. They soften, balance and refine skin texture, and help to combat the effects of dehydration and ageing on the skin. Some 'anti-wrinkle' creams claim to improve the elasticity of the skin. Collagen and elastin are sometimes contained in anti-wrinkle creams. It is unlikely that they have any effect on the natural fibrous proteins of the skin, but, being humectants, they are useful moisturising ingredients.

REMEMBER

A dry atmosphere will take up water from wherever it can. Moisturiser must be replaced frequently to compensate for this. If the water content of the moisturiser evaporates, dry air will then draw natural moisture out of the skin.

GOOD PRACTICE

Clients who come for facials should be encouraged to use special products for evening care which maintain the benefits of their salon treatments. An evening skin-care routine does not need a lot of time. A few minutes before going to bed is all that is required for removing make-up, cleansing and toning the skin, and applying a special treatment cream. This can become a most relaxing part of the day, particularly if the client has time to perform a few gentle massage movements when applying the cream.

HEALTH MATTERS

Lanolin, which is extracted from sheep's wool, is sometimes used as a softening ingredient contained in skin creams. It is also a known allergen. The cosmetics products regulations require that products containing lanolin identify this on their labels.

SELF-CHECKS

Moisturisers

1 (a) Why do moisturisers contain a humectant?
   (b) Give one example of a humectant that is often contained in a moisturiser.

2 How does a lack of natural moisture affect a) the superficial skin cells, b) the cells in the deeper layers of skin?

3 Why is it important to keep the skin soft?

4 Give three reasons for wearing a moisturiser under make-up.

5 List three factors that influence the choice of moisturiser for a client.

6 State two benefits of an evening skin-care routine.

Face masks

A face mask

A wide range of ready-mixed face masks is available for retail sale. These should be used weekly by the client as part of their regular skin-care routine.

More specialist products are available for professional use. These are divided into two basic types: setting and non-setting face masks.

Setting masks

These are applied to the face and neck in a thin layer and allowed to dry out on the skin. The effects of the masks depend on their ingredients and the length of time they are left on the skin. There are three types of setting mask:

- clay masks
- peel-off masks
- thermal masks.

Clay masks

These contain natural earth ingredients, which absorb surface matter and draw out impurities; they leave the skin feeling very clean and fresh and some of them help to nourish the skin by stimulating its blood supply. Others contain soothing ingredients.

Uses

A variety of clays and other mineral ingredients are mixed with distilled water, witch hazel or rose water to produce a creamy textured paste which is painted on the skin and allowed to dry. As the moisture evaporates, the mask contracts and tightens the skin beneath. Impurities are drawn to the surface. The clay content absorbs grease, sweat and loose skin cells. Depending on its ingredients, a clay mask may have a stimulating effect, which leaves the skin slightly pink, or a soothing effect, which cools the skin and reduces high colouring.

A client may have a recipe made up which contains the ingredients best suited to their skin. This gives the treatment a personal touch that clients appreciate. Sometimes different masks may be mixed to treat different areas of the face.

REMEMBER

If the client has a very sensitive or mature skin, a vegetable oil can be substituted for water to produce a non-setting clay mask. Use an oil that is not too expensive and does not smell unpleasant. Arachis (peanut) oil is ideal.

HEALTH MATTERS

Arachis oil should be avoided if there is a history of peanut allergy.

Know your ingredients

Kaolin White (China) clay	Has a 'drawing' effect which is deep cleansing and is useful for bringing spots and skin blockages to a head. Used for congested, greasy skin.
Fuller's Earth Greyish-green clay	Very absorbent and deep cleansing. Has a strong stimulating effect on the circulation, so not suitable for more sensitive skins. Used for greasy, congested skin.
Magnesium carbonate Fine, white powder	Mildly astringent. A gentle refining mask which tightens the pores and softens the skin. Used for open pores on balanced (normal) skin. Can be mixed with calamine for drier, more sensitive skins.
Calamine Pale, pink powder	Mildly astringent. Contains zinc carbonate which soothes the skin and calms down high colouring. Used for sensitive skin.
Sulphur Light, yellow powder	Has a drying action which is useful for healing individual blemishes such as pustules and papules on a greasy skin.

The clays should be mixed with a suitable lubricant, depending on skin type

Greasy	witch hazel
Balanced	distilled water or rose water
Dry	rose water or vegetable oil
Sensitive	vegetable oil

Peel-off masks

These are based on waxes, gelling agents, latex or plastic resins, which are applied wet but dry out on the skin. They have a milder effect than clay-based masks because they are not absorbent.

Uses

A peel-off mask forms an occlusive covering. This means that it totally encloses or 'seals' the skin, intensifying the penetration of active substances that may have been applied beforehand. Sealing the skin also prevents the loss of natural lubrication. Moisture levels increase in the upper layers, 'plumping out' the superficial skin cells and leaving the skin feeling soft and smooth.

Peel-off mask applied to the face on pre-cut shapes

Depending on their ingredients, peel-off masks can either stimulate or soothe the skin:

- Gel masks containing ingredients such as collagen and seaweed products are mildly astringent and cool the skin. They have soothing, calming, moisturising and tightening effects, which reduce the appearance of fine lines and wrinkles. Gel masks are particularly suitable for mature, sensitive skins.

- Latex and plastic masks tighten the skin temporarily. Some of them lower skin temperature and feel very cool on the skin. Others stimulate the blood supply, causing the skin to go pink. Latex and plastic masks are particularly suitable for dry and mature skins.

- Paraffin wax masks retain their heat and warm the skin. This promotes sweating, which deep cleanses and softens the skin. Paraffin wax masks stimulate the blood supply, causing the skin to go slightly pink. They are suitable for balanced and dry skins. They are not suitable for very sensitive skins.

Thermal masks

These masks contain mineral ingredients that are mixed to a paste and applied to the skin over a special skin cream. After a few minutes the paste begins to harden and a chemical reaction occurs between the ingredients, which creates heat and warms the surface tissues. The heat disperses after 20 minutes, after which time the mask becomes rigid and can be eased away from the skin.

Uses

This mask has powerful deep-cleansing, tightening and stimulating effects. The heat produced encourages absorption of the cream applied underneath. Clients with a nervous disposition or who have sensitive skin are not suitable for treatment.

Non-setting masks

These consist of ready-prepared cream masks and warm oil masks:

- Cream masks are quick and easy to apply. They have a cooling, refreshing,

GOOD PRACTICE

Warm oils penetrate more readily on a warm skin. An infrared lamp may be used during the treatment to keep oil, which has been applied to the face on gauze, at a comfortable temperature. The oil that remains on the skin after treatment is used to perform a facial massage.

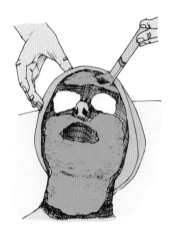

Biological mask applied over gauze

Natural plant ingredients

REMEMBER

Always read the instructions before mixing and applying face masks. Manufacturers know the most effective ways of using their products.

softening effect upon the skin and can be used to helping to specific skin problems. There are cream masks available for all skin types.

- Vegetable oils such as arachis, olive and almond are particularly beneficial when they are absorbed by the upper layers of skin. Warm oil mask treatments are beneficial for balanced, dry and mature skins. They are not suitable for clients with very sensitive skin who have dilated capillaries or general high colouring.

Biological masks

These products have a gentle but effective action on the skin. They are based on natural 'active' ingredients, such as flower, plant, herbal and vegetable extracts. Available as creams, gels or emulsions, they form a light film on the skin, which becomes firm and dry but does not tighten.

Uses

The biologically active ingredients have different effects on the skin depending on their source. The following is a very general guide.

- Soft fruits: correct the pH balance of a dry skin and increase its moisture level.
- Plants: stimulate the circulation and increase cell metabolism.
- Herbs and vegetables: tone, stimulate, balance and regenerate a problem skin.
- Marine products: hydrate and stabilise the skin.

SELF-CHECKS

Face masks

1 How do clay face masks achieve their cleansing effect?

2 Suggest a suitable clay mask treatment for a client with a typical combination skin and mild acne. Identify and explain your choice of ingredients.

3 Name two possible ingredients of gel masks.

4 Describe three different types of face mask suitable for a client with mature skin and explain the specific benefits of each.

5 (a) What is the purpose of applying a skin cream before giving a thermal mask treatment?
   (b) State two contraindications to applying a thermal mask.

Activity: 6.6 Promoting retail sales

Find out which skin-care products sell particularly well in your salon. Think of ways the salon could promote the sales of slower-moving lines. Send your ideas in a memo to your supervisor.

Specialist skin products

The basic skin-care programme can be enhanced by using specialist products for treating specific conditions, or different areas of the face, or for using on particular occasions.

Ampoules

Ampoules are hermetically sealed glass or plastic phials, which keep their ingredients fresh and 'active'. The ingredients are contained in serums made up of biologically active concentrates. Once an ampoule is opened, the serum must be used up to prevent the **active ingredients** from deteriorating.

Active ingredients are those that cause a response from one or more of the body's systems. This may show as a physical response to treatment where the skin looks and feels different. Ingredients that are not active include water. Water is the main ingredient in many skin-care products. It does not have any active properties itself but it is a perfect carrier of other substances that do have active properties.

Uses

Ampoules are often applied as intensive treatments over a prescribed period, usually 7–28 days. Others may be used regularly, once or twice a week, to complement the regular skin care given with other products from the range. Ampoules are most effective when used after a skin-peeling treatment when they can be absorbed more effectively by the skin. The 'active' ingredients in serums are selected according to the type and condition of skin.

A very wide range of biological ingredients are used in skin-care products. You must become familiar with the ones contained in your salon's skin-care range. Here are some examples and their uses:

- horse chestnut, camphor, sage *for* greasy skin with open pores
- juniper, lemongrass, tea tree, birch, nettle *for* acned skin
- collagen, elastin, patchouli, rosewood *for* dry skin showing fine lines and signs of premature ageing
- aloe vera, sandalwood, camomile, lavender *for* mature, dehydrated, sensitive skin
- eucalyptus, lavender *for* highly coloured, vascular skin.

REMEMBER

The active ingredients contained in skin-care products are most effective during the hours of sleep, when the skin is most receptive. This is the busiest time for cell repair and renewal, when the body does not require its energy supplies for more demanding activities.

Eye care

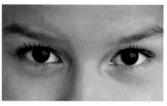

Bright, beautiful eyes

The skin around the eyes is very thin and does not contain many sebaceous glands. It is attached very loosely to the underlying muscles and lacks the fatty supporting tissue which is present in other areas of the face. As a result, the skin in the eye area is the first to show signs of ageing. Dryness, crêpiness and wrinkles appear prematurely if the skin is not cared for properly. Most professional skin-care ranges have special products for the eyes which are also available for retail.

Eye creams

These are basically moisturising creams that contain lightweight fatty materials so that they do not drag and stretch the skin. Very fine oil-in-water emulsions are absorbed easily by the skin and create a good base for eye make-up. Richer water-in-oil emulsions are greasier and are applied at night time.

Uses

Eye creams used regularly help to soften the skin and prevent the formation of lines and wrinkles around the eyes. The more lightweight products may be used during the day and at night; they are suitable for all skin types. Richer eye creams are particularly beneficial for dry or mature skins. They are massaged gently into the skin at night time and the excess is blotted off before going to bed.

Eye gels

These are basically astringents thickened with an ingredient such as methyl cellulose. They work by cooling, soothing, firming and tightening the skin. Witch hazel is an astringent often used in eye gels. Other ingredients that may be included are plant and herbal extracts, collagen, camomile, cornflower and azulene.

Uses

The astringent effect of eye gels makes them very useful for revitalising tired eyes and reducing the effects of fine lines, puffiness and slackness of the skin. They can be applied at any time of day and most can be worn under make-up.

Eye lotions

These are similar to eye gels but do not contain a thickening ingredient. Eye lotions contain ingredients such as witch hazel, cucumber and camomile, which are cooling, refreshing and mildly astringent.

Uses

The lotion is usually applied on cotton wool as an eye compress to cool, soothe, tighten and refresh tired eyes. Pads moistened with eye lotion may be applied during a facial to aid relaxation when the face mask has been applied.

REMEMBER

Products are available for treating both the eyes and lips. These may be promoted as eye and lip contour creams or eye and lip 'balms'. They are fine-textured products that protect and soften the skin, and are designed to reduce the appearance of fine lines around the eyes and mouth.

REMEMBER

When giving home care advice, make sure your client knows the correct way of applying and removing creams from around the eyes.

REMEMBER

It is important to avoid overloading the eye area with greasy cream at night. The body heats up during sleep, causing a rich cream to melt and invade the eye area. The cream blocks the tear ducts so that fluid is retained and the eyes appear puffy the next morning.

Neck care

Many people only start paying attention to their neck when it starts to show signs of ageing. The skin on the neck is thicker than the skin around the eyes, but otherwise they have a similar structure and share the same problems.

Neck creams are very 'rich' formulations, which may contain moisturising ingredients, for example collagen, and other ingredients such as plant extracts for softening, tightening and stimulating the skin.

Uses
Neck creams should be used regularly by clients over the age of 25 to help soften, tighten and brighten the skin, and to aid cellular renewal. The cream should be massaged in lightly with the pads of the fingers before going to bed.

Lip care

The skin of the lips does not contain melanin and therefore there is little protection against the effects of sunlight. The lips can soon become dry, chapped and sore if they are not adequately protected. Lip balms and lip creams are available which combine softening and moisturising ingredients to prevent the lips from becoming chapped.

Uses
Lip creams may be included in the regular skin-care routine if the skin is prone to dryness. As well as softening the lips, they help reduce the appearance of fine lines around the mouth. Lip creams provide a good base for lip cosmetics. Lip balms are usually provided as 'sticks'. They are formed from a high-melting-point, hardened fat, which provides a relatively thick protective coating for the lips, preventing skin dehydration.

Sun care

In the UK, melanoma affects twice as many women as men. Fifty per cent of all melanoma in women are seen on the lower leg, whereas for men, the most common site is the back. In elderly people, the most common site of melanoma is the face.

The damaging effects of the sun's rays upon the skin are well known. Despite this, there are many people who feel more confident and attractive when they have a suntan. It is essential to advise your client about a sensible approach to sunbathing and to recommend the appropriate skin-care products.

Specialist sun-care retail range

HEALTH MATTERS

The incidence of skin cancer is increasing. Since the early 1990s, cases in America, Australia and Scandinavia have doubled. In Scotland, during the same period, there was an 80 per cent increase in the number of patients suffering from malignant melanoma. Research into the environment has shown that there will be a sustained annual 10 per cent decrease in ozone, leading to an increase of over 300,000 cases of non-melanoma skin cancers each year.

REMEMBER

Fair skins are more at risk in the sun than dark skins, but all skins need protecting from the ravaging effects of UV.

REMEMBER

The salt in sea water intensifies the effects of the sun. Burning is a serious threat if the skin is not protected when swimming or relaxing in the sea.

Sunscreens

These are a basic skin cream, milk or oil formulation containing a chemical sunscreen ingredient. The greasier the product, the more effective is the sun screening effect. Moisturising ingredients help prevent the skin from drying out.

Uses

Sunscreens filter out harmful UVA and UVB rays so that they do not penetrate and damage the deeper layers of the skin. They are smoothed over the skin before exposure to sun and are replaced regularly, particularly before and after swimming.

HEALTH MATTERS

UVB rays are responsible for sunburn. They penetrate to the lower epidermis and damage living cells. UVB rays are known to be a major cause of skin cancer. UVA rays penetrate the epidermis and damage collagen and elastin fibres. They cause premature ageing of the skin.

Sun protection factor

The effectiveness of a sunscreen product is measured by its **sun protection factor** (SPF). The SPF number is identified on the product and usually falls within the range 2–30. It indicates how much longer than normal a person wearing the sunscreen may stay out in the sun before getting burned (see the table below). SPF numbers relate only to UVB rays. They do not indicate the amount of protection provided against long UVA rays, which cause premature ageing of the skin.

HEALTH MATTERS

High-factor sunscreens slow down the tanning process and this is better for the skin. However, as a result of this, many people stay out longer in the sun and end up damaging their skin anyway!

SKIN TYPE	SPF	EFFECT
Person with skin which tans easily but tends to get sore during initial stages of sunbathing	Uses SPF 2	May stay out in the sun up to twice as long before burning
Fair-skinned person who normally goes pink after 15 minutes	Uses SPF 10	Skin will take 10 times longer (150 minutes) before it burns
Person with pale skin which burns very easily, particularly over bony areas	Uses SPF 25+	This is a total sun block which gives complete protection if applied regularly

Star rating

The amount of protection provided against UVA rays is indicated by a 1–4 'star' rating scale. Three stars *** means that a product will give three-quarters of the protection from UVA compared with UVB. A rating of two stars ** means that a product will give half (i.e. 2/4) of the protection against UVA compared with UVB.

After-sun

These are moisturisers that contain an astringent such as zinc carbonate to cool the skin and an ingredient such as calamine to soothe.

HEALTH MATTERS

Some salons advertise their products as a means of developing a protective tan before going on holiday. Sunbeds create a tan through UVA. Such a tan only has a protection factor of 2, which means that it does not protect against burning.

Uses

After-sun lotions prevent the skin from drying out and peeling. They make the skin feel more comfortable after sunbathing and prolong the effects of a tan.

Self-tanning

The active ingredient is a harmless coal-tar derivative called dihydroxyacetone. This chemical reacts with the keratin in the skin and then gradually oxidises to produce a yellowish brown colour.

Uses

Self-tanning products are available as creams, gels, mousses and sprays and are particularly useful for fair-skinned people who want to look tanned without being exposed to the sun. They can be used to even out patchy skin colouring and to top up a natural tan which has started to fade. This type of fake tan lasts for a few days and fades as the surface skin cells desquamate.

REMEMBER

The effects of a self-tanning cream will be more natural if it is applied after using an exfoliant. This will ensure that the skin texture is smooth and even. Care should be taken to wash the cream off the hands immediately after application so that the palms do not turn orange!

SELF-CHECKS

Specialist skin-care products

1 What are the benefits of applying skin-care products at night?

2 Why should excess cream be removed from around the eyes before going to bed?

3 State two main differences between an eye cream and an eye gel.

4 Why does the neck require special skin care?

5 Name three active ingredients contained in skin-care products and explain their effects.

6 Why is water contained in most skin-care products?

7 What advice should be given to a client regarding the application and removal of skin-care products around the eyes?

8 Why should a client be advised to purchase a lip balm when going on holiday?

9 What is the significance of the SPF number on a sunscreen product?

10 What does the star rating of a sunscreen product indicate?

Caring for black skin

It would be very wrong to generalise about the treatment of black skins. Many of the blemishes and abnormalities which are obvious on a white skin become much harder to diagnose when they are obscured by skin colour. The Wood's light (see page 155) is an invaluable aid to analysing black skin. Very careful questioning of the client is required to ensure the best recommendations for skin care.

HEALTH MATTERS

Black skin has more sweat and sebaceous glands than white skin, but this very often leads to an assumption that all black skins are greasy. Black skins do tend to be shiny, but this is a normal characteristic. Some black skins are greasy, of course, but not all of them. A wrong assumption can result in the use of products that are too harsh and may irritate the skin and cause more problems.

Black skin

Skin-care products

Cleansing is probably the most important part of the skin-care programme. Black skin is thick and desquamates more than white skin. Dead cells build up on the skin surface, attracting dust and grime from the atmosphere. Skin that is not cleansed thoroughly morning and evening looks dull. It develops skin blockages and an uneven texture.

Cleansers

Cleansing milks are usually preferred for the deep cleanse. These are particularly beneficial when combined with a brush cleanse. The friction of the brush helps to loosen the accumulated surface matter and improve the texture of the skin.

Toners

Mild tonics or flower waters are more suitable than stronger preparations. Alcohol may act as an irritant on black skin.

Exfoliants

These should be used at least once or twice a week to control the effects of desquamation. Greasy skins benefit from the abrasive effects of a facial scrub; otherwise peeling creams may be used.

Moisturising

Oil-in-water emulsions, which have a matt finish, are preferable to greasy creams, which leave a shine.

Night creams

Clients with black skin do not need to worry so much about the use of rich, 'anti-ageing' skin-care preparations. Their skin has very strong protein fibres which keep wrinkles and crêpiness at bay usually until they are well into their late fifties. Night care should concentrate on the prevention of moisture loss and the use of creams for the eyes and neck, where the skin is thinner and less protected.

Biological skin-care preparations containing plant extracts have a stimulating effect and help to refine skin texture.

Face masks

These should be used weekly as part of a regular skin-care routine. Clay-based face masks are particularly beneficial due to their absorbent and astringent effects. Great care must be taken to remove all traces of the clay so that a fine film is not left on the skin and in the pores.

Clynol

SELF-CHECKS

Caring for black skin

1 Name three common skin problems affecting clients with black skin.

2 Why is the regular use of an exfoliant particularly beneficial for clients with black skin?

3 What special care is required when giving a clay mask treatment to a client with black skin?

4 Why does black skin generally stay 'younger' for longer?

5 Recommend a suitable cleanser, toner and moisturiser for a client with black skin.

A PRACTICAL GUIDE TO BEAUTY THERAPY

Professional facial treatments

With such an extensive range of skin-care products available, a new client may wonder why they need come for professional facial treatments! The answers are simple – apart being able to enjoy the benefits of a pleasant and relaxing salon environment, the client will be treated by a trained therapist who has:

- specialist knowledge, which is necessary for correctly diagnosing and advising on skin problems
- technical knowledge of the treatments and products available so that reliable advice can be given
- professional skills, which ensure that each client gets maximum benefits from the treatments
- the use of professional tools and equipment, which make treatments more effective and, sometimes, more comfortable for a client
- the knowledge and skills to treat the skin safely and hygienically
- the ability to monitor a client's progress and adapt the treatments when necessary
- the confidence of having a professional qualification
- up-to-date information about new treatments and products.

Salon facials allow the client to benefit from specialist treatments and equipment which would otherwise be unavailable to them. They also provide the opportunity for discussing progress with home care and receiving qualified advice on other beauty problems.

Facials – how often?

The frequency of facials depends on the individual client and the condition of their skin. If the skin has been neglected or has an established condition requiring treatment, facials may be needed twice a week at the beginning. Once the client's skin has become balanced, a full facial may be recommended every 28 days – similar to the rate of skin renewal.

Preparing for a facial

As usual, the area must be well organised to avoid wasting time during the treatment. Consult the client's record card for details of previous treatments and products used. Get a new record card to fill in for a client who has not already had a consultation. Make sure you have a range of products available so that you can adapt the treatment to suit the client.

Preparing the treatment area

A facial is always given with the client lying down, or in a semi-reclining position, and the therapist works from behind. This helps to promote total relaxation, which is important for the success of the treatment. Other ways of creating a relaxing atmosphere include making sure that:

- there is no unnecessary noise
- the room is warm and there are no draughts
- the lighting is subdued (the illuminated magnifier will be used for close work)
- there are pillows and bedding for the client's comfort (the client may need extra support under the neck, back and knees)
- everything needed is readily available to avoid interrupting the treatment.

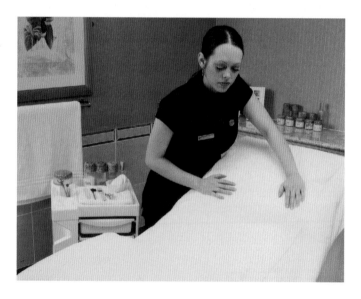

Preparing the treatment area

Preparing the trolley

The trolley should be clean, tidy and well stocked. The products should be arranged in a logical order so that you can go straight to them without searching.

You will need:

- a selection of skin-care products
- a jar of prepared sterilising fluid
- a comedone extractor
- clean spatulas
- cotton buds
- cotton wool pads
- tissues

A PRACTICAL GUIDE TO BEAUTY THERAPY

- four bowls – for waste, for client's jewellery, for cotton wool and for mixing/removing face mask
- one headband
- one hand towel
- one mask brush
- two mask sponges
- a record card and pen
- a hand mirror.

You may also need face towels, a complexion brush, a facial steamer, a mechanical brush cleansing unit and tweezers.

Preparing the client

The client should not wear any clothes that are tight or may restrict access to areas of the body included in the facial. The fewer clothes that are worn, the more comfortable and relaxed the client is likely to be.

1   Having settled the client comfortably on the couch, ensure that their shoulders are free from straps and that earrings and necklaces are removed.

2   Allow the clients to choose between keeping their arms inside or outside the bedding and place a towel over the chest, tucked into underwear straps if they are being worn.

3   Adjust the height of the couch (and your stool if you prefer to be seated) so that both you and the client are comfortable.

4   Raise the client's head slightly to take the strain off their neck and to prevent dizziness when they get up after treatment.

Now you are ready to begin, but first, remember:

- wash your hands immediately before and during the treatment as required
- always use a clean spatula for removing cream from its container
- transfer cream to the client from the back of your hand
- pour runny creams into the palm of your hand before using them
- put tops back on bottles and jars immediately to prevent their contents from becoming spoiled or spilled.

SELF-CHECKS

Facial treatments

1   List five advantages of being treated by a professional beauty therapist.

2   What advice should be given to a client with contact lenses when booking them in for a facial?

3   Give four ways of helping a client to relax during a facial treatment.

4   Why should the client's head be raised slightly during a facial treatment?

5   List four hygiene precautions that should be taken when applying skin-care products.

6   How often should facials be recommended?

Cleansing the skin

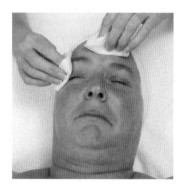

Cleansing the eye area

Even if the client claims not to be wearing make-up, always give a superficial cleanse. This will help you to make an accurate assessment of the skin. It will also help the other skin treatments to be more effective by removing make-up and other surface debris.

Superficial cleanse

Always treat the eyes and lips first before moving to the larger areas of the face and neck. This is more hygienic and prevents spreading heavily pigmented make-up products over the face.

1 Instruct the client to keep their eyes closed.
   (a) Apply a small amount of cleansing milk or eye make-up remover to the eyelids. Spread the cleanser over the upper eyelids with small, gentle, rotary massage movements. Use the pads of the 'ring' fingers and avoid applying pressure over the eye.
   (b) Alternatively, apply the cleanser directly to the eyelids on damp cotton wool pads, supporting the skin at the temples and ensuring cleanser does not penetrate the eye.

2 Stroke a little cleanser underneath the eyes, working towards the nose. Ensure that cleanser does not penetrate the eyes.

3 Use damp cotton wool pads to wipe away cleanser from around the eyes. Treat one eye at a time. Stroke outwards over the upper eyelid and then keep the skin supported while cleaning underneath with a second pad.

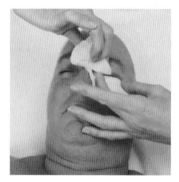

Dissolving and removing mascara

4 For removing mascara, place damp cotton wool pads beneath the lashes and dissolve mascara with a suitable eye make-up remover. A tipped orange stick or cotton bud is useful for getting to the base of the lashes.

5 Remove make-up from the lips with small, rotary massage movements, and wipe away cleanser and dissolved make-up with a damp cotton wool pad.

6 Apply the appropriate cleansing product to the neck and main facial areas, omitting the eyes and lips.

7 Use gentle upward stroking and rotary massage movements to spread the cleanser and work it well into the skin creases (for example above the chin and at the sides of the nose), where grease and make-up tend to build up.

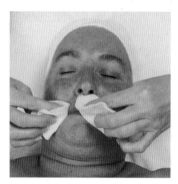

Cleansing the lips

8 Remove the cleanser with firm upward and outward movements, using damp cotton wool pads.

9 Wipe over the skin with a mild toner (low alcohol content) on damp cotton wool pads. This should remove the greasy film remaining after the cleanse without disturbing the skin's surface.

10 Blot any excess moisture on the skin. Split a tissue into single ply and create a hole in the centre for placing over the nose. Lay the tissue over the face and gently press it against the skin. Gradually roll the tissue down the face and onto the neck.

Deep cleanse

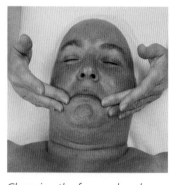

Cleansing the face and neck

Once the type and condition of the skin has been assessed, choose a suitable deep-cleansing product and apply it to the face and neck.

The deep cleanse involves the use of special massage movements which:

- are relaxing
- stimulate the flow of blood and Lymph through the skin
- assist the penetration of cleanser into the hair follicles, dissolving make-up or dirt that has penetrated them
- help soften and loosen surface blockages
- aid desquamation (shedding of surface cells).

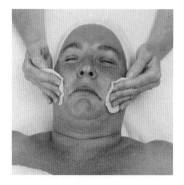

Removing cleanser with damp cotton wool pads

REMEMBER

The ring fingers exert the least pressure. They are the best ones to use when working over the very thin and delicate skin around the eyes.

GOOD PRACTICE

Use an oily eye make-up remover to remove stubborn waterproof mascara.

REMEMBER

The cleansing products work by either dissolving grease or by using a detergent action, which suspends dirt and make-up so that they can be wiped off the skin.

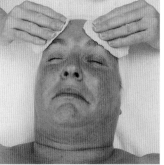

Applying toner

REMEMBER

Effective cleansing has taken place only when the tissues or cotton wool pads used for removing the cleanser appear clean when wiped over the face.

GOOD PRACTICE

Repeat the superficial cleanse if heavy make-up is being worn.

REMEMBER

Be gentle and use the right products: if you are heavy-handed or use products that are too strong, the skin will be over-stimulated and will not show its normal characteristics for the skin analysis.

Blotting the face with a tissue

Procedure for deep cleanse

The following sequence ensures that all areas of the face and neck are cleansed thoroughly, and that the movements flow smoothly into one another so that a relaxing rhythm is maintained.

Whichever procedure you use, make sure that:

- your hands are clean, smooth and relaxed. Stiff hands put extra pressure on the face, which is less comfortable for the client
- the movements are adapted to the size and shape of the area being treated, for example over the cheeks and forehead
- pressure is reduced when working over bony areas and sensitive skin.

REMEMBER

Do not worry if the deep cleanse procedure you learn is different from the one described here. As with most beauty therapy treatments, there are different correct ways of giving the treatment.

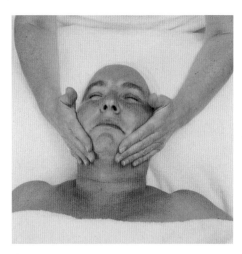

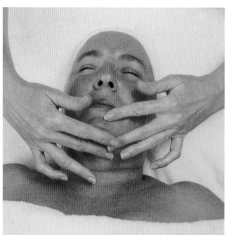

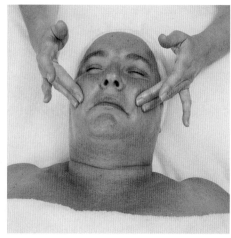

1 *With hands resting on jawline, stroke them towards the angles of the jaw, then down the sides of the neck and firmly upwards from the base, avoiding pressure over the trachea (wind pipe); repeat six times*

2 *Slide hands up over the chin and work into the crease with the index fingers, one after another, sliding them back under the chin to repeat the movements; repeat six times for each hand*

3 *Perform small circular movements with the pads of the fingers, covering the cheeks from the corners of the mouth to the sides of the nose and carrying on up to the temples. Slide hands back gently to the corners of the mouth to repeat the movements (six times)*

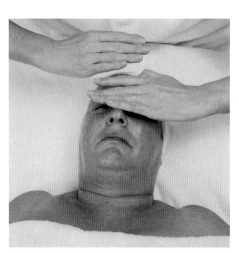

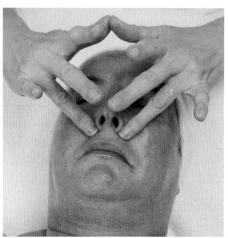

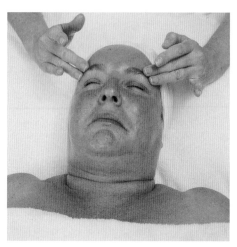

4 *Slide hands from the temples to the centre of the forehead and, keeping the fingers straight but relaxed, stroke them down the nose, one after another, six times for each hand*

5 *Use the pads of the ring fingers to work thoroughly, upwards and downwards, into the creases at the sides of the nose; repeat six times in each direction*

6 *Slide the hands back up the sides of the nose. Stroke out over the eyebrows and then inwards, underneath the eyes, producing a big circular movement; repeat six times*

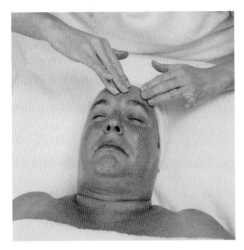

7 *Perform circular movements over the forehead with the pads of the fingers. Work across from temple to temple, one hand following the other, so that the forehead is covered (six times), finishing in the centre*

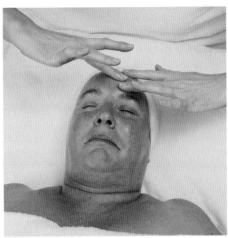

8 *Still using the pads of the fingers, work from temple to temple across the forehead, with small interlocking zigzag movements. Cover the forehead six times, finishing in the centre*

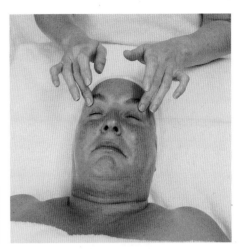

9 *Stroke the ring fingers out over the eyebrows and then inwards underneath. As a circle is completed, gently perform three very light lifting movements beneath the brow, starting with the index finger. The ring finger should then be correctly positioned to repeat the whole movement*

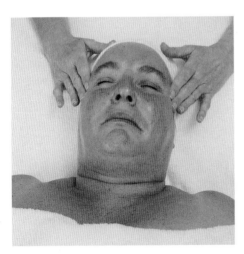

10 *Finally, slide the fingers up the sides of the nose, over the forehead and apply a little pressure at the temples to let your client know the routine has finished*

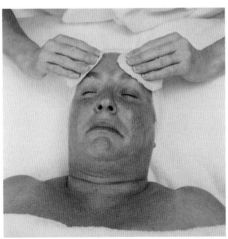

11 *Complete removal of cleansing product with skin toner*

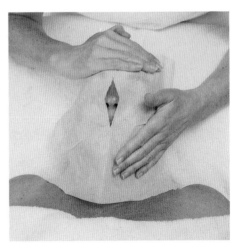

12 *Blot the skin with a tissue*

After the deep cleanse

Remove all traces of cleanser and wipe over the skin with a suitable toning lotion. Blot the skin dry and check that there is no grease remaining in the skin creases, eyebrows, eyelashes and hairline.

You should always use damp cotton wool pads to remove creams and lotions from skin that is dry, sensitive, mature or particularly fine, for example the eyes and lips. These are more gentle than tissues but are less efficient for absorbing oil-based preparations. A toner must be used afterwards; this should contain just enough alcohol to remove the greasy film without stripping the skin of its natural sebum.

Removing skin blockages

The deep-cleansing procedure helps to soften comedones (blackheads) and excess sebum which has collected in the pores. Warming and softening the skin with hot towels, hot damp cotton wool pads, or by steaming also makes it easier to remove blockages without damaging the surrounding skin.

Preparing a hot towel

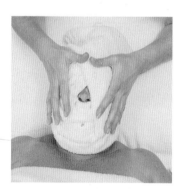

Applying a hot towel

To prepare a hot face towel, fold it once down its length and then once across its width. Place the folded edge over the side of a sink and run the hot water tap until the water is very hot. Soak the folded half of the towel in hot water, turn off the tap and then roll up the towel from the wet end towards the dry end. Squeeze the towel out firmly and then open it up over your hands before folding it over the client's face, pressing gently over the skin and moulding the towel to the facial contours. This procedure may be repeated if required. The skin feels beautifully clean afterwards.

Using a facial steamer

Using a facial steamer

Steaming is done for 3–20 minutes, depending on the type and condition of the skin, and keeps the skin warm so that sebum is softened not only at the surface, but also deeper down the hair follicles.

Adjust the distance of the steam outlet from the face according to skin type

Dry, mature skin	40 cm (15 in)
Balanced skin	30 cm (12 in)
Greasy skin	20 cm (10 in)

Most facial steamers are designed so that the steam can be produced on its own or combined with ozone to help heal greasy, blemished skin. Ozone is drying and has an antibacterial effect.

Benefits of steaming

Ozone is not necessary for loosening skin blockages. Steaming alone benefits the skin by:

- warming and softening sebaceous blockages
- dilating the pores, making it easier to release their contents
- stimulating the sweat and sebaceous glands
- softening and hydrating the skin
- increasing the rate of blood and lymph flow through the skin
- increasing desquamation.

After warming the skin, the face should be blotted with a tissue. The loosened blockages may then be removed gently and hygienically.

Removing comedones (blackheads)

It is important to avoid bruising or damaging the skin when removing comedones.

1   The pads of the fingers may be used, as long as they are clean and covered with a soft facial tissue or soft, fine towel. The area around the blockage may rolled and squeezed between the fingers so that the contents are forced gently out of the follicle without breaking the skin. A clean tissue takes up the waste.

2   A 'looped' comedone extractor is used to apply light pressure around the blocked pore to ease out the contents. Blockages may be treated individually or the extractor may be stroked along a crease in the skin to remove accumulated matter.

3   Following comedone removal, the skin may be either brush cleansed, exfoliated or wiped over with a mild antiseptic to prevent infection through the open pore.

4   The comedone extractor is washed, rinsed, dried and sterilised ready for the next treatment.

Brush cleansing

This may be done after removing skin blockages using a gentle, soapless lathering cleanser and a soft complexion brush. The dampened brush is used in small circular movements over the face and neck to distribute the cleanser and work it into the pores. Treatment continues for approximately three to five minutes depending on skin type.

Mechanical brush cleansing

This piece of electrically powered equipment has a variety of applicator heads which may be used as alternatives or in addition to manual cleansing and massage treatments.

> **REMEMBER**
> Pressure should not be applied with the brush. Strokes should be directed upwards and outwards to avoid dragging and stretching the skin.

Treatment with a mechanical brush system is adapted by using different applicator heads, and by varying the speed and directional controls:

- sponge head – used dampened with a soapless, lathering cleanser
- soft brush heads – available in a range of shapes and sizes for deep cleansing, exfoliating and massaging different facial and body areas
- bristle brush head – particularly good for using on male clients to deep cleanse, exfoliate and stimulate strong, firm skin
- pumice head – used as a peeling stone for exfoliating and refining a coarse skin texture.

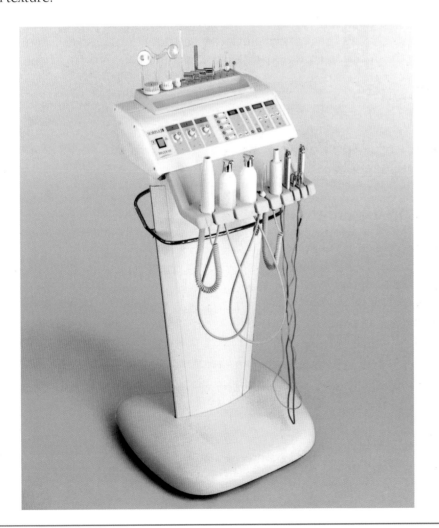

> **REMEMBER**
> Pressure should not be applied with the brush. Strokes should be directed upwards and outwards to avoid dragging and stretching the skin.

Mechanical brush-cleansing equipment

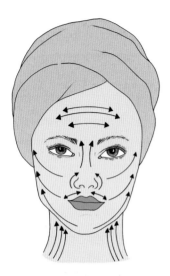

Direction of strokes for brush cleansing

Contraindications to mechanical brush cleansing are:

- broken skin
- infected skin
- dilated capillaries
- very loose skin
- inflamed or irritated skin
- very sensitive skin.

The cleanser is removed from the face with clean warm water and facial sponges, and the skin is blotted in readiness for the next stage of treatment.

Exfoliating

Exfoliation should occur after the deep cleanse and before the massage to ensure maximum benefits from later treatments in the facial routine:

- younger cells are exposed, improving the appearance of the skin
- skin preparations are absorbed more easily
- the blood supply is stimulated, bringing oxygen and nutrients to the skin cells and improving skin colour.

There are many different types of exfoliating products, each designed to be used in a particular way. Always check the manufacturer's instructions on application and removal of the exfoliant, and afterwards wipe over the skin with a mild skin bracer.

REMEMBER

One of the best compliments your client can pay you is falling asleep while you are giving them a massage. You can't get much more relaxed than that!

SELF-CHECKS

Cleansing

1 List five beneficial effects of a deep-cleansing massage.

2 What special care is required when removing cleanser from the face of a client with dry, mature skin?

3 Why should skin blockages be softened before removal?

4 What are the benefits of using a facial steamer for softening skin blockages?

5 State six safety precautions that should be taken when using a facial steamer.

6 Why is using a looped comedone extractor preferable to using the fingers when removing skin blockages?

7 Give four contraindications to mechanical brush cleansing.

8 What should the skin look like and how should it feel after a deep-cleanse treatment?

Facial massage

Effective massage requires extreme sensitivity and an expert touch. The cream, powder or oil used to perform the massage provides 'slip' so that movements flow smoothly, without causing discomfort. Active ingredients contained in massage creams and massage oils help to improve the appearance and texture of the skin. Powder may be used in preference to an oil-based product for massaging a greasy skin.

The main benefits of facial massage are that it:

- increases the supply of oxygen and nutrients to skin and muscles
- stimulates removal of waste products from the tissues
- improves cellular activity
- relieves tension and fatigue
- improves the texture of the skin
- promotes total relaxation.

Classifications of massage movements

There are many different types of massage movements and routines used for treating the face. Many skin-care companies develop specific techniques for facial massage which complement their products.

The combination of movements used depends on the main reason for the massage (for example lymphatic drainage, relaxation), the condition of the skin and underlying tissues, and client preference.

- Superficial massage movements with slight pressure soothe nerve endings and promote relaxation.
- Stronger pressure movements stimulate the venous and lymphatic circulation, encouraging both drainage and elimination of waste from the tissues.
- Deep, static movements and pressure influence muscle tone.

Effleurage

Effleurage describes the light, even, stroking movements that prepare the tissues for deeper massage and link up other movements in the facial sequence. The pressure of effleurage strokes may be increased over less bony areas.

The effects of effleurage are:

- relaxation from lightly applied effleurage movements
- increased desquamation and loosening of surface adhesions
- stimulation of blood supply through superficial circulation, causing a slight increase in skin temperature.

Petrissage

Petrissage describes compression (pressure) movements using either the whole of the palmar surface of the hand or just the pads of the thumbs and fingers. Kneading, knuckling, rolling and pinching are examples of petrissage movements which may be included in a facial sequence. Small, deep petrissage movements are more stimulating than larger, more superficial ones.

The effects of petrissage are:

- an increase in the rate at which blood and lymph flow through the area: this is due to the rhythmical filling and emptying of vessels and ducts which occurs with petrissage. Oxygen and nutrients are supplied to the cells and waste products are removed
- the skin appears smooth, clear and refreshed as a result of desquamation
- muscle fibres become relaxed and their tone is improved.

HEALTH MATTERS

The trapezius muscle covers the upper back and shoulders, and the back and sides of the neck. The muscle becomes hard and develops **tension nodules**, which can be felt along the upper fibres of the back in clients who are over-tired or stressed. Thumb kneading to the trapezius helps to loosen the knotted muscle fibres and release the build-up of toxins. This breaks up the tension nodules and increases the supply of blood to the muscle.

Tapotement

Tapotement describes percussion movements, for example tapping and slapping, which are performed lightly and briskly without compressing the skin.

The effects of tapotement are:

- stimulation of the superficial nerve endings causing temporary toning and tightening of the skin
- improved blood flow resulting from alternate constriction and relaxation of the blood vessels
- removal of static lymph from tissues, for example from beneath the chin in a client with sluggish circulation.

Vibrations

These are quite difficult movements to perform. The muscles of the lower arms and hands are rapidly contracted and relaxed so that a mild shaking or trembling movement is produced by the fingers or thumbs. The vibrations run through a nerve centre or along a nerve path. There is very little surface stimulation.

The effects of vibrations are:

- relaxation
- gentle stimulation of the deeper skin layers
- relief from fatigue and muscular pain.

Sequence of facial massage

The following massage sequence takes approximately 20 minutes. It combines variations of each of the basic massage movements to produce a treatment which stimulates the tissues but also relaxes the client.

A PRACTICAL GUIDE TO BEAUTY THERAPY

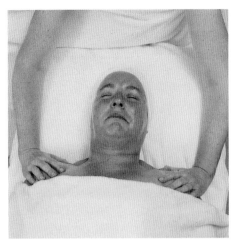

1 *Hands relaxed in starting position*

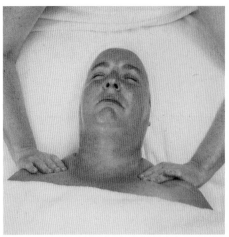

2 *Effleurage to shoulders*

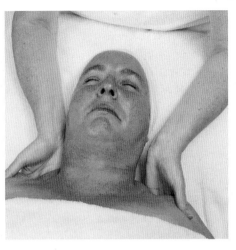

3 *Thumb kneading shoulders*

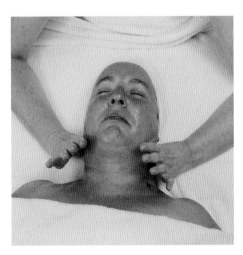

4 *Thumb stroking up neck to occipital cavity*

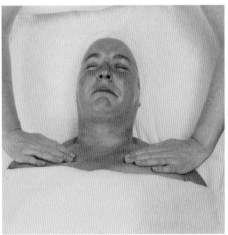

5 *Link effleurage over upper chest*

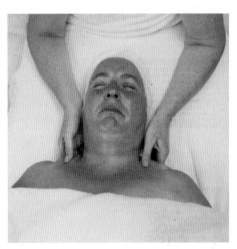

6 *Finger kneading shoulders*

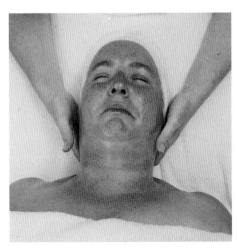

7 *Light vibrations, occipital cavity*

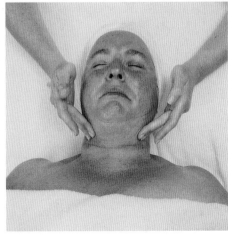

8 *Finger kneading neck*

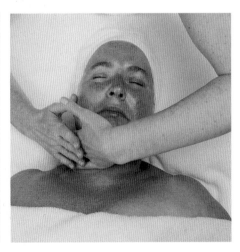

9 *Firm, reinforced effleurage to neck*

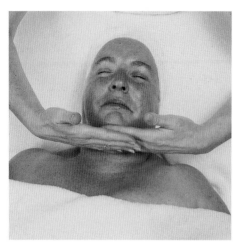

10 *Link effleurage to other side of neck*

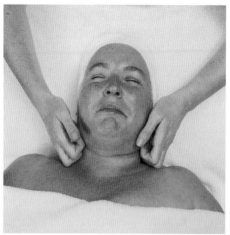

11 *Knuckling to neck*

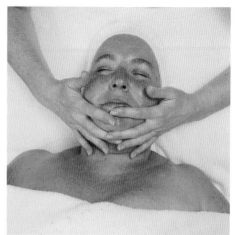

12 *Chin brace*

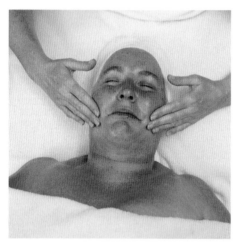

13 *Link effleurage*

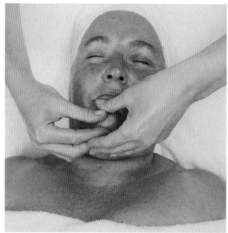

14 *Thumb kneading above chin and lower jaw*

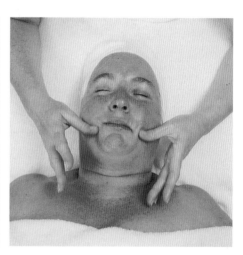

15 *Swift flick ups to corners of mouth (1)*

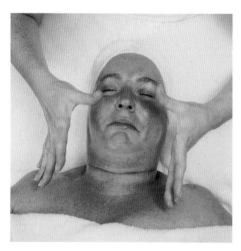

16 *Swift flick ups to corners of mouth (2)*

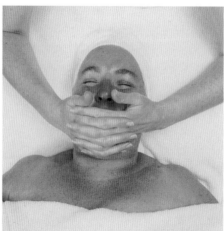

17 *Full face brace (1)*

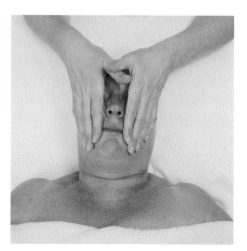

18 *Full face brace (2)*

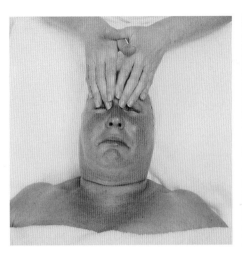

19 *Full face brace (3)*

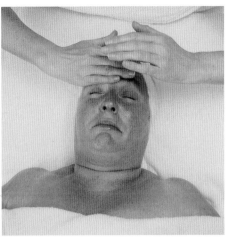

20 *Upward stroking eyebrow lift*

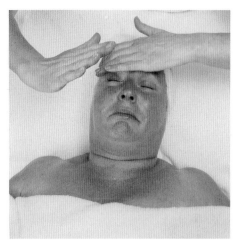

21 *Repeat movement*

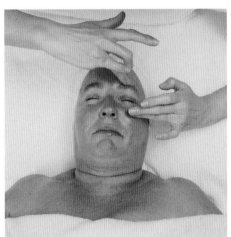

22 *Stroking the temples*

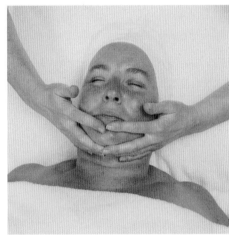

23 *Half face brace*

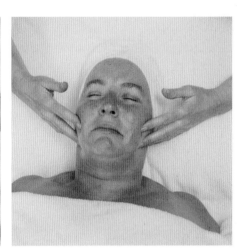

24 *Repeat movement*

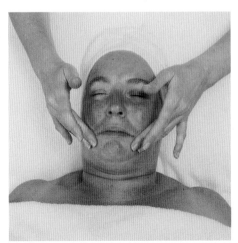

25 *Finger kneading chin, mouth, nose, temples*

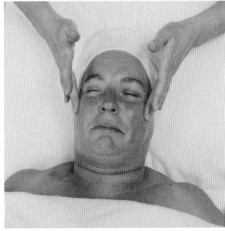

26 *Link effleurage*

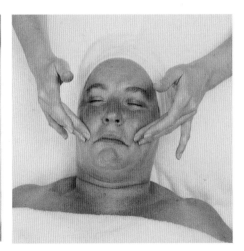

27 *Repeat movement*

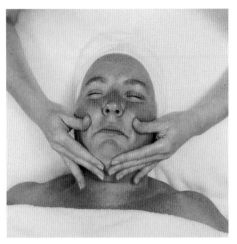

28 *Thumb kneading to cheeks*

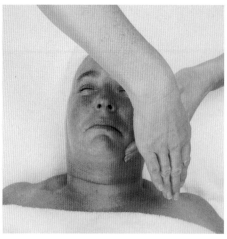

29 *Tapotement beneath chin and mandible*

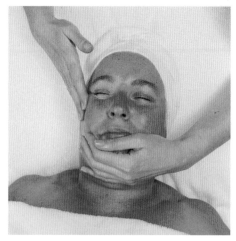

30 *Lifting masseter alternatively each side*

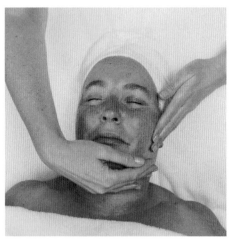

31 *Other side*

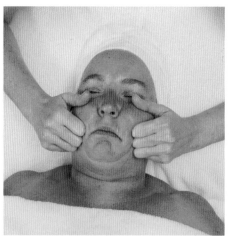

32 *Rolling cheeks*

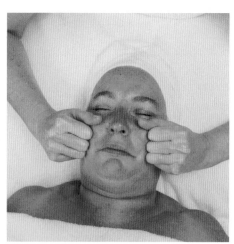

33 *Pinching cheeks*

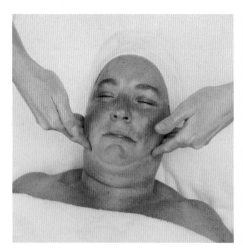

34 *Lifting mandible*

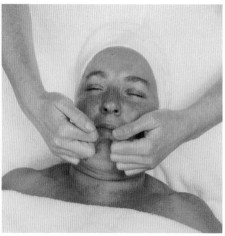

35 *Knuckling above jawline*

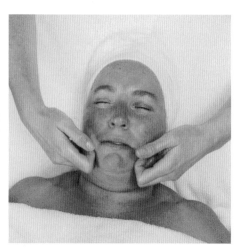

36 *Knuckling below jawline*

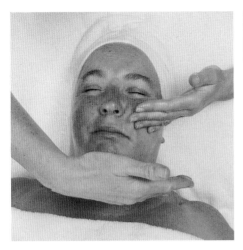

37 *Lifting tapotement to cheeks*

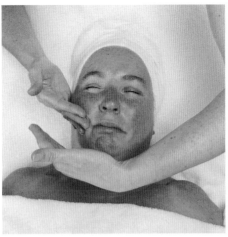

38 *Repeat movement*

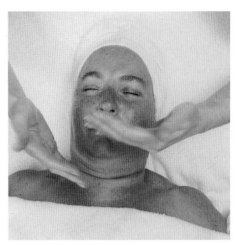

39 *Repeat movement*

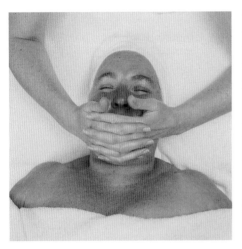

40 *Full face brace (1)*

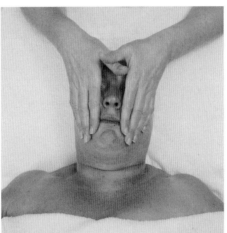

41 *Full face brace (2)*

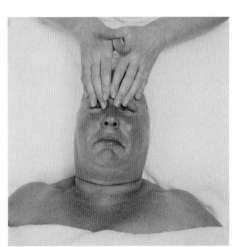

42 *Full face brace (3)*

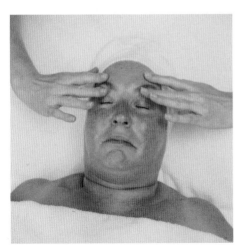

43 *Scissor movement to eyebrows*

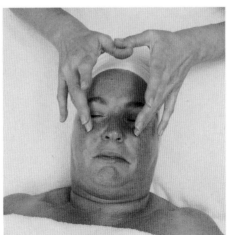

44 *Stroking inwards beneath eyes*

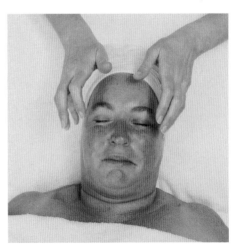

45 *Light tapotement around the eyes*

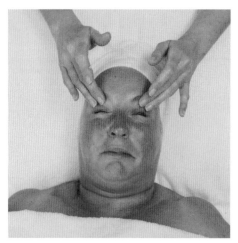
46 *Stroking around the eyes*

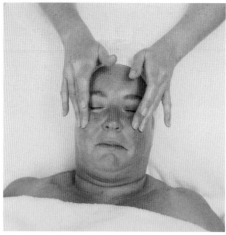
47 *Repeat movement*

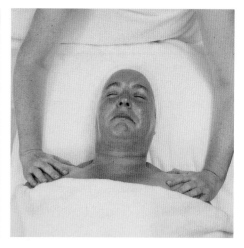
48 *Effleurage to shoulders*

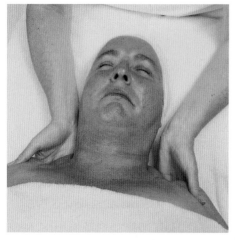
49 *Effleurage to upper back*

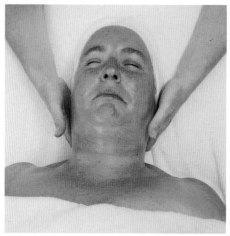
50 *Light vibrations, occipital activity*

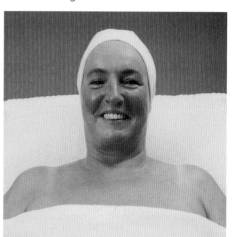
51 *Skin glowing after facial massage*

SELF-CHECKS

Facial massage

1. Explain three ways in which you could ensure the relaxation of the client during a facial massage.

2. Compare the effects of superficial and deep effleurage massage movements.

3. What are tension nodules and how do they benefit from massage?

4. Give two contraindications to tapotement massage movements.

5. Name two types of petrissage movements used during a facial massage.

6. Give two different types of massage medium that may be used to treat a client with greasy skin.

7. State two benefits of using a cream for massaging a client with dry skin.

8. For which type of skin is oil a suitable massage medium? Recommend a suitable oil for massaging the face.

9. Which types of massage movements are the most suitable and how should they be adapted for working over a) dilated capillaries, b) a double chin, c) a crêpey neck, and d) the eye area.

10. Why would it not be advisable for a bride to have a full facial on the day of her wedding?

A PRACTICAL GUIDE TO BEAUTY THERAPY

By this stage of the treatment, the skin should feel slightly warm and appear clean, smooth and refreshed. Any excess cream or oil should be removed with tissues, damp sponges or damp cotton wool. The skin should then be toned and blotted dry in preparation for the face mask. Talc may be applied to the upper back and shoulders to absorb any grease remaining on the skin after the massage.

> **REMEMBER**
>
> The skin looks its best two to three days after a facial. This is because the stimulating effects of the massage continue for up to 48 hours after the treatment. During this time, the skin throws off waste and toxins, which may cause blotchiness and minor blemishes. The client should be warned in advance that these reactions are likely to occur and that they are due to the deep-cleansing effects of the treatment. A soothing lotion will help to calm down any unwanted redness.

Applying a face mask

Information will be provided by the manufacturer regarding the mixing, application and removal of specialist face masks. Make sure you have a good knowledge of the products used in your salon and follow the manufacturer's instructions. Below are general guidelines to follow when applying a face mask.

Preparation

1   Tuck a facial tissue under the edge of the headband to prevent it from becoming soiled.
2   Decide upon the basic mask ingredients required. These may be different for treating different areas of the face and neck.
3   Prepare the mask ingredients according to the manufacturer's instructions.
4   Explain to the client:
    (a) which mask you are using
    (b) what it is going to do
    (c) how it will feel when applied
    (d) the normal skin reaction to the mask
    (e) how long it will be left on the skin.

> **REMEMBER**
>
> Do not use your mask brush for mixing a clay-based mask. If you do, clay will collect at the base of the bristles. This can damage the brush and produce an uneven mask application.

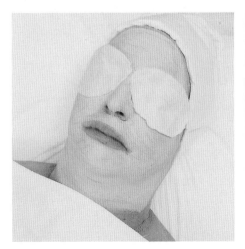

Mask applied, eye pads in place

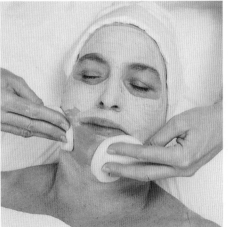

Removing the mask with damp sponges

Filling in the record card and planning the next treatment

GOOD PRACTICE

As a general rule, do not apply the mask very thickly. The effects of the treatment occur where the skin is in contact with the mask, so building it up thickly is both uneconomical and a waste of time. However, when applying a peel-off mask, you must ensure that there is a thick enough border to enable the mask to be peeled off the skin easily.

GOOD PRACTICE

The resting period during the mask treatment is very important for continuing the relaxing effects of the massage. Make sure the client is kept warm and is not disturbed during the treatment.

REMEMBER

Clay that has not been removed from the skin dries and forms a fine film. This is particularly noticeable on black skins. Keep wiping over the skin with clean, damp sponges until you are sure that every trace of mask has been removed.

REMEMBER

When selling skin-care products, make sure the client knows how to apply and remove the products safely and effectively.

Application

1 Apply the mixture neatly, quickly and methodically with a mask brush, ensuring even coverage of the face and neck, but avoiding the area immediately around the eyes and mouth.

2 Apply the mask to the centre panel first if this area is being treated separately from the rest of the face.

3 Make sure the mask is applied up to the hairline and right down to the base of the neck.

4 When application is complete, apply cool, soothing eye pads and lift the front towel up over the client's shoulders.

5 Start timing the face mask. Most masks are left on the skin for between 10 and 20 minutes. Setting masks will start drying out with the heat of the skin and the surrounding environment. While this is beneficial for greasy skins, which benefit from the maximum drawing effects of a setting mask, for drier and more sensitive skins this may be too long.

Removal

1 Discard the eye pads and explain to the client what you are going to do.

2 Use clean, warm, damp sponges to soften the hardened mask before wiping it away with firm upward movements.

3 Repeat the removal procedures until you are satisfied that all traces of the mask have been removed, in particular from around the hairline, eyebrows and nostrils.

4 Finally, tone and blot the skin, and continue to the next stage of the treatment.

Contra-actions

If the client experiences an abnormal, uncomfortable skin reaction, for example itching or burning, remove the mask immediately, wipe over the skin with witch hazel to cool it and apply a soothing lotion. Similarly, if the skin appears inflamed after removing the mask, take steps to calm the skin down and enter details of the skin reaction on the client's record card. Next time, use a different mask on the client.

SELF-CHECKS

Applying a face mask

1 List three factors that influence the choice of face mask for a client.

2 Which areas of the face are not usually treated with a face mask?

3 For how long should a face mask be left on the face?

4 What action should be taken if a client complains of a 'burning' skin sensation while the face mask is applied?

5 How should the skin look after a calamine face mask has been applied?

6 How should the skin feel after a gel face mask?

7 What is the possible cause of erythema following an oil mask treatment?

8 How should a face mask brush be cleaned and sanitised after use?

Activity 6.8: Selling skin care

A facial treatment provides the ideal opportunity for promoting and advising on purchases for home care. It makes sense for the client to be using products that complement those used in their salon treatments.

1 Have a look at some of the record cards at your salon that have been completed for facial clients:

    (a) read the information given about the client's skin and see what recommendations have been made for their skin care

    (b) note the combinations of products that are used for salon treatments and home care.

2 With a colleague, discuss all the different ways in which you could promote retail sales during a facial treatment. Write a list and share your ideas with your colleagues and supervisor. Set yourself a target of selling at least one skin-care product to each of the next six clients you treat. Good luck!

REMEMBER

Heavy make-up is not suitable immediately after a facial treatment. Foundation tends to change colour and go blotchy. Clients should be warned of this when making their appointment.

Completing a facial treatment

Clients who arrive at the salon wearing make-up sometimes expect to be wearing it when they leave. Others prefer the feeling of clean, fresh skin, which may be spoiled if make-up is applied. If possible, avoid applying make-up after a facial. The client will benefit from having just a little moisturiser applied for protection. A light covering of translucent face powder, eye make-up and lipstick may be applied if the client feels uncomfortable about not wearing make-up.

The last few minutes of the treatment should be spent discussing what has been achieved during the facial and agreeing details of the client's next visit to the salon. This is also the time to give home care advice and to check if your client needs to purchase any retail products.

Enter final details of treatments and purchases on the client's record card and assist with arranging their next appointment.

Activity 6.9: Improving facial skin conditions

You must be able to show that you are able to improve skin conditions by using the correct skin care and facial massage techniques.

1 Provide a full facial treatment for each of the following:

    (a) a mature client with dry skin and the typical characteristics of ageing

    (b) a younger client with greasy skin, possibly troubled with acne

    (c) a client with a combination skin.

2 For each of your clients, keep:

    (a) copies of client record cards and treatment plans

    (b) any notes you make about your clients and details of their treatments including any problems and what you did about them

    (c) written comments from your clients on how they found the treatments

    (d) 'before' and 'after' photographs showing the improvements in your clients' skin conditions.

GOOD PRACTICE

When the treatment has finished, check that the client is happy with the results and then raise the head of the couch slowly to an upright position. If the client gets up too quickly, there will be a sudden rush of blood away from the head, causing dizziness.

Facial massage and skin care

Work your way through these questions and discuss your answers with a colleague. Sometimes there may appear to be more than one right answer, in which case decide which one is the most important. Check with your supervisor if there is anything you are not sure about.

1 Smoking is bad for the skin because it:
(a) reduces the amount of oxygen available to skin cells
(b) blocks the pores
(c) produces carbon dioxide
(d) discolours the skin.

2 For selling purposes, the benefits of a product relate to:
(a) the cost of the product
(b) the size of the product
(c) the reason for buying
(d) the features of a product.

3 A w/o emulsion contains:
(a) more water than oil
(b) more oil than water
(c) a balance of oil and water
(d) less oil than water.

4 Non-oily make-up remover has:
(a) an astringent effect
(b) a detergent effect
(c) an emollient effect
(d) an emulsifying effect.

5 Glycerine may be contained in a toner because it is an:
(a) astringent
(b) emollient
(c) detergent
(d) humectant.

6 The active ingredients in skin-care products are most effective when applied:
(a) first thing in the morning
(b) last thing at night
(c) before a face mask
(d) after a face mask.

7 Kneading movements are a type of:
(a) vibration
(b) effleurage
(c) tapotement
(d) petrissage.

8 The massage sequence begins and ends with effleurage movements because they are:
(a) flowing
(b) stimulating
(c) warming
(d) relaxing.

9 All face masks have a:
(a) cleansing effect
(b) tightening effect
(c) soothing effect
(d) stimulating effect.

10 A clay mask suitable for treating greasy, blemished skin contains:
(a) calamine and sulphur
(b) magnesium and sulphur
(c) Fuller's Earth and kaolin
(d) Fuller's Earth and calamine.

KEY TERMS

You should now understand the following words and phrases. If you do not, go back through the chapter and find out what they mean:

pH	**Emulsifying agent**	**Astringent**
Exfoliant	**Emollient**	**Humectant**
Ampoules	**Active ingredients**	**AHAs (fruit acids)**
Sun protection factor	**Effleurage**	**Petrissage**
Tapotement	**Tension nodules**	

Chapter 7 Eyebrow and eyelash treatments

Enhance the appearance of eyebrows and lashes

After working through this chapter you will be able to:

- explain the benefits of eyebrow and eyelash treatments
- apply the treatments safely, hygienically and effectively
- carry out a skin test for eyelash tint and respond appropriately to the results
- recommend the appropriate eyebrow shape for a client
- describe the contra-actions to eyebrow and eyelash treatments
- give appropriate home care advice.

Before you work through this chapter: Be wise and revise!
Revision topics to help you achieve this unit:

Enhance the appearance of eyebrows and lashes

TOPIC	CHAPTER	PAGE
Healthy and Safety at Work Act 1974	1	5
COSHH Regulations 1988	1	9
Public liability insurance	1	10
Sale and Supply of Goods Act 1994	1	13
Communication skills	2	24
Client care	3	52
Treatment hygiene	3	54
Selling treatments and services	5	103

Because the eyes are the focal point of the face, any treatment that enhances them makes an immediate, significant impact. Eyebrow shaping and tinting treatments are very popular in the salon. They take a short time, use only small amounts of products and can be given separately or together with other facial treatments if required.

Eyelash and eyebrow tinting

Well-defined eyebrows and eyelashes emphasise the eyes and define their shape. They also help to balance facial features. Tinting the hairs makes them appear darker and thicker. The colour fades gradually with exposure to sunlight and the loss and replacement of tinted hairs.

The advantages of tinting the eyelashes and eyebrows are:

- the eyes and facial features are enhanced, even without make-up
- the effects are very natural
- less time is required for applying make-up
- the colour is waterproof and does not smudge or streak.

It is not only fair-haired clients who benefit from eyelash and eyebrow tinting treatments. The colour intensities of the darker tints emphasise the lashes and help to create a more defined eyebrow shape on people with darker hair. Eyelash and eyebrow tinting treatments are often the preferable alternative to mascara and eyebrow cosmetics and should be recommended to clients who:

- wear glasses or contact lenses
- are allergic to or prefer not to wear mascara
- have difficulty applying make-up
- feel they do not to have time to apply eye make-up
- have had their hair tinted a darker colour
- are due to go on holiday
- participate regularly in active sports
- work or live in a hot environment.

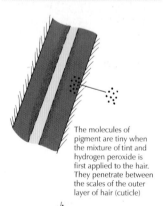

How tinting works

A small amount of **eyelash tint** is mixed with hydrogen **peroxide** and the mixture is then applied to the hairs. During the development time, some of the dye penetrates the hairs and becomes oxidised. The dye molecules enlarge and become trapped inside the hairs, which are then permanently coloured. The effects of tinting generally last for up to six weeks.

Hydrogen peroxide

Hydrogen peroxide is an oxidising agent. This means that when it is mixed with tint, oxygen is released. This activates the tint chemically and the colour starts to develop. An **oxidation** reaction takes place. A relatively weak strength of hydrogen peroxide (3 per cent or 10 vol) is used for mixing with eyelash tint. This is because of the sensitivity of the eye area. Anything stronger could irritate or 'burn' the skin if brought into contact. In the salon, hydrogen peroxide is usually referred to as 'peroxide'.

Hydrogen peroxide will not work if it has 'gone off' and lost its strength (and its oxygen). This will happen if it is not stored properly and it is left exposed to air.

You must always:

- keep the container closed tightly

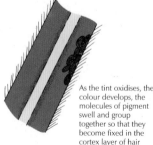

The molecules of pigment are tiny when the mixture of tint and hydrogen peroxide is first applied to the hair. They penetrate between the scales of the outer layer of hair (cuticle)

As the tint oxidises, the colour develops, the molecules of pigment swell and group together so that they become fixed in the cortex layer of hair

Oxidation reaction

- replace the lid immediately after use
- measure out the exact amount of hydrogen peroxide you need; never pour any excess back into the bottle
- mix the tint with the hydrogen peroxide immediately before use, not some time beforehand
- store hydrogen peroxide in a cool, dark place.

Choosing a tint

The products used for tinting eyelashes and eyebrows usually come as creams or gels in basic colours of black, brown, grey and blue. These colours may be mixed to provide variations in tone. The choice of colour is a matter of personal preference and is based on:

- the client's overall skin and hair colouring
- the colours and type of eye make-up (if any) that is normally worn
- the age of the client.

General guidelines are as follows.

General guidelines for hair and tint colours

HAIR COLOUR	TINT COLOUR
Fair	Brown
Red	Brown
Dark	Black
Grey	Grey

GOOD PRACTICE

Always read the manufacturer's instructions before mixing eyelash tint. Make sure you use the right amount and strength of hydrogen peroxide mixed with the correct quantity of tint. Always use a non-metallic dish for mixing the tint. Hydrogen peroxide reacts with metal, releasing its oxygen immediately and causing ineffective processing of the tint.

Skin test

Eyelash tints contain vegetable dyes and relatively safe chemical dyes such as toluenediamine. The chemical reaction that takes place between these dyes and hydrogen peroxide can cause an unpleasant allergic reaction in some people.
The reaction may occur immediately on contact or within a few hours afterwards.
You must carry out a **skin test** 24–48 hours before the scheduled tinting appointment to make sure your client is not allergic to the tint. A skin test is also known as a 'patch' test.

To perform a skin test you will need:

- surgical spirit or an astringent to cleanse the skin
- cotton wool
- a clean cotton bud
- a small, non-metallic dish
- a small amount of the desired tint mixed with two drops of 3 per cent (10 vol) hydrogen peroxide.

REMEMBER
Hydrogen peroxide must be stored and handled with care. This is a requirement of the COSHH regulations.

REMEMBER
As clients grow more mature, they lose a lot of natural colour from their hair, lashes and brows. Brown or grey tints are preferable to black for producing softer, more natural effects.

REMEMBER
You must never use hairdressing products for tinting the eyebrows and eyelashes. Hair dyes contain strong chemicals such as 'para' dyes, which are not suitable for using in the eye area. Much stronger hydrogen peroxide is used for developing hairdressing tinting products.

HEALTH MATTERS
Body chemistry can change overnight and allergies develop just as quickly. A client who has been having tinting treatments for years without any trouble must still have a skin test. This protects both the client and the salon.

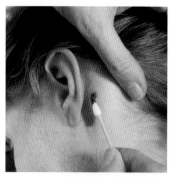

Patch testing for eyelash tinting

The procedure is as follows:

1   Wash and dry your own hands.

2   Cleanse and dry an area of skin behind the ear or in the crease of the elbow, whichever site the client prefers.

3   Apply the prepared tint to the cleansed skin. The test patch should be no larger than a very small coin.

4   Leave the tint to develop on the skin for five minutes.

5   Remove excess tint with cotton wool and advise the client to wash off the stain after 48 hours or sooner if there is a **positive skin test reaction**.

Reactions to skin test

Positive reaction

Inflammation, irritation and swelling of the skin in the test area, which may not show up until the next day. In severe cases, the client may feel quite unwell. The client is allergic to the tint and, therefore, is not suitable for eyelash or eyebrow tinting treatments.

Advice to client with positive reaction

● Wash off the stain and apply a soothing cream or lotion such as one containing calamine or witch hazel.

● Contact the salon as soon as possible to inform the therapist or receptionist about the skin reaction.

Negative reaction

A **negative skin test reaction** means that there is no change in the skin. The client is suitable for treatment. Check that there are no other contraindications and proceed with treatment.

Contraindications to eyelash and eyebrow tinting

Any infection or disorder causing sensitivity of the eyes and surrounding skin is a contra-indication to eyelash and eyebrow tinting, for example:

Conjunctivitis

● inflammation

● swelling

● **conjunctivitis**

● stye

● tired, watery eyes

● eczema or psoriasis in the eye area

● undiagnosed lumps

● cuts and abrasions

● allergy to eye cosmetics

● positive reaction to skin test.

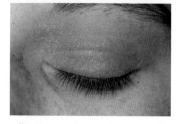

Allergic reaction to eye cosmetics

Eyelash tinting

Eyelash tinting treatments usually take approximately 20 minutes. It is helpful if the client is not wearing a lot of eye make-up when they arrive for their appointment. This helps to cut down the amount of time required for cleansing the eye area and reduces any risk of skin irritation or sensitivity of the eyes before applying the eyelash tint.

Preparing for treatment

All equipment and materials should be prepared on the trolley before the client arrives. These include:

- a protective headband
- a towel or cape for protecting the client's upper clothing
- a hand towel for yourself
- a small, non-metallic (usually glass) dish or plastic palette for mixing the tint
- a clean spatula and orange sticks
- a disposable or clean, sanitised applicator brush
- a hand mirror
- a record card and pen
- a covered container for waste
- cotton wool and tissues
- a clean eye bath and a small container of distilled water (for bathing the eye in an emergency)
- preformed eyeshields
- eyelash tint in a selection of colours
- 3 per cent (10 vol) hydrogen peroxide
- eye make-up remover, cleanser and toner
- barrier cream or petroleum jelly
- skin stain remover.

Preparing the client

1   Help the client into a comfortable, semi-reclining position, and protect their hair and clothing with a headband and towel.
2   Wash and dry your own hands.
3   Cleanse, tone and dry the eye area, ensuring that all make-up and grease is removed from the eyelashes.
4   Use a cotton bud soaked in make-up remover to get rid of traces of make-up 'trapped' at the base of the lashes.
5   Check the eyes and surrounding skin, ensuring that there are no contra-indications.
6   Protect the skin above and underneath the eyes with a barrier cream or petroleum jelly. Take care not to get any of the product on the lashes.
7   Secure eye shields comfortably beneath lower lashes.

REMEMBER

When making an appointment for eyelash tinting, advise the client to wear only a little or no eye make-up when they come for treatment.

GOOD PRACTICE

It is a good idea to store hydrogen peroxide in a dark-coloured 'dropper' bottle for use during an eyelash tinting treatment. This helps to prevent the hydrogen peroxide from losing its strength and measures out an accurate amount of peroxide when mixing the tint.

GOOD PRACTICE

Contact lenses must not be worn by the client during an eyelash tinting treatment. The client should be advised beforehand to bring in some soaking solution and a container for their lenses so that they can be kept safely on the trolley during treatment.

REMEMBER

Take care not to irritate the eyes before an eyelash tinting treatment or they may be too sensitive for you to carry on. Use a special eye make-up remover which will dissolve and remove mascara quickly and gently.

GOOD PRACTICE

When applying barrier cream above the upper lashes, gently lift the skin from underneath the eyebrows with your fingers. This will release the fold of skin at the base of the lashes, ensuring thorough coverage of the skin with barrier cream.

GOOD PRACTICE

Do not mix the tint until you are ready to use it, otherwise the colour will start developing before the mixture is applied to the hairs. Once the peroxide has given up all its oxygen, the colour will not develop any more.

GOOD PRACTICE

Lift the skin of the eyelids gently from below the eyebrows so that tint can be applied right down to the base of the lashes. Include the shorter hairs which grow near the inside corners of the eyes.

Barrier cream

Barrier cream prevents the tint from staining the surrounding skin and spoiling the effect of the treatment. However, it also prevents tints from penetrating the hairs if it touches them.

Use an orange stick tipped with cotton wool or a cotton bud to apply barrier cream to the skin above the eyes.

When applying barrier cream below the eyes, either:

- stroke it directly on to the skin with a brush or tipped orange stick and position the eyeshields on top, close to the base of the lashes, or
- coat the underneath surface of the eyeshields with barrier cream and slide them into position.

Applying the tint

Precautions should be taken to ensure that neither the tint nor applicator penetrates the eye. There should not be any problems provided that:

- the tint is applied carefully
- the lashes are not overloaded with tint
- the client's eyes are kept still
- the client's eyes do not start watering.

The procedure is as follows:

1 Prepare the tinting mixture according to the manufacturer's instructions (usually three or four drops of peroxide to 5 mm of tint).
2 Ask the client to look upwards, away from the applicator; cover the lower lashes with tint.
3 Instruct the client to gently close their eyes; apply tint downwards over the upper lashes.
4 Cover the eyes with slightly dampened cotton wool pads. This will help to keep the client's eyes closed and trap in warmth, which aids the development of the tint. A client who prefers not to wear eye pads will need leaving a little longer for the tint to develop.
5 Note the time and allow between 10 and 15 minutes for the tint to process, according to the manufacturer's instructions. The colour should be checked at intervals and tint reapplied if necessary.
6 At the end of the development time, hold the eye shields and cotton wool pads together and remove them firmly in one, swift action, enclosing any excess tint. Remove any remaining tint with damp cotton wool pads. Continue to wipe downwards over the lashes and inwards towards the nose until no more tint appears on the clean cotton wool pads.
7 Ask the client to open their eyes; check that there is no tint remaining at the base of the lower lashes. If there is, remove it with clean, damp cotton wool pads stroked underneath the eyes towards the nose.
8 Finally, wipe over the area with skin tonic to remove all traces of barrier cream.
9 Offer the client a hand mirror and seek their approval of the final result.
10 Enter details of the treatment on the client's record card.

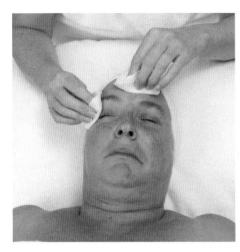

1 *Ensuring lashes are clean and free from make-up*

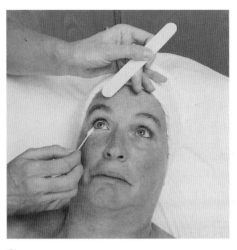

2 *Applying barrier cream*

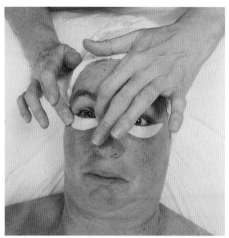

3 *Securing eye shields*

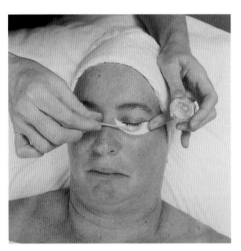

4 *Applying the tint*

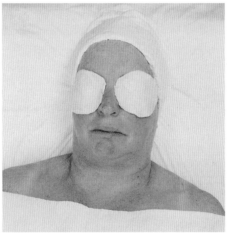

5 *Processing time*

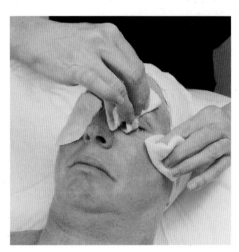

6 *Removing tint*

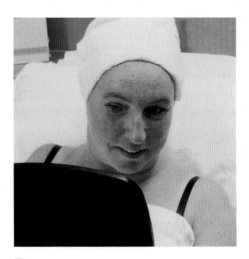

7 *Checking the results*

Contra-actions

If the client complains of uncomfortable prickling or the eyes begin to water:

- remove the tint immediately using damp cotton wool pads
- rinse the eyes using the clean eye bath and distilled water
- apply damp cotton wool pads soaked in witch hazel to cool and soothe the eye area.

Do not proceed with tinting until the eyes have calmed down and, only then if you are sure that the client is suitable for treatment.

Eyebrow tinting

The development time for tinting the brows is much shorter than for the lashes, usually between one and three minutes. Care must be taken to prevent the brows from becoming too dark as this creates a 'hard' effect which is particularly unattractive on older clients.

1 Prepare the treatment area and the client in the same way as for eyelash tinting.
2 Use a clean eyebrow brush to separate and lift the eyebrow hairs from the skin.
3 Apply barrier cream or petroleum jelly around the eyebrows, as close to the hairs as possible.
4 Apply the tint mixture to the eyebrows with a fine brush or orange stick tipped with cotton wool, working gradually from the outer and underneath hairs towards the centre.
5 After one minute, remove a little tint from the inner corners of the eyebrows and check how the colour is developing. Apply more tint and repeat colour checks at one-minute intervals until the desired effect has been achieved.
6 Remove the tint with clean, damp cotton wool pads.
7 Wipe over the area with skin tonic to remove all traces of barrier cream.

A PRACTICAL GUIDE TO BEAUTY THERAPY

Assessing results

A successful tinting treatment produces the required colour changes to the lashes or brows without staining the skin. Even the shortest lashes should be coloured evenly from their base. Blond 'roots' after an eyelash tinting treatment show that not enough care was taken. The skin fold of the eyelid was probably not lifted away from the base of the hairs when applying the tint.

The tint will not have coloured the lashes or brows successfully if:

- there was grease, make-up or barrier cream left on the hairs
- old tint was used
- the hydrogen peroxide had lost its strength
- the tint and peroxide were mixed incorrectly
- the tint was removed too early.

GOOD PRACTICE

If you wish to colour and shape the eyebrows in the same treatment, tint the hairs first and then use the tweezers. This prevents over-stimulating the skin before applying the tint.

SELF-CHECKS

Eyelash and eyebrow tinting

1 When would be particularly good times of the year to promote eyelash and eyebrow tinting treatments?

2 State three specific benefits of eyelash tinting for a client who wears contact lenses.

3 Explain briefly how the hairs become coloured by eyelash tint.

4 How long do the effects of eyelash tinting last?

5 State three questions which you should ask a client before tinting their eyelashes for the first time.

6 State two reasons for performing a skin test before tinting treatments.

7 Why should details of the skin test be written on the client's record card?

8 Describe a positive reaction to a skin test.

9 List five contraindications to eyelash and eyebrow tinting.

10 Give three possible causes of a client's eyes watering during an eyelash tinting treatment.

REMEMBER

Do not shape the eyebrows if there is any skin or eye irritation following the tinting treatment.

ACTIVITY

Activity 7.1: Costing eyelash and eyebrow tinting treatments

It is important not to make up too much tinting mixture as any excess cannot be used and has to be thrown away. Wasting products is wasting money.

1 Work out the approximate number of treatments which should be provided by one tube of eyelash tint. Work out the cost of tint used for each treatment based on the wholesale price (do not forget VAT).

2 Work out the costs of all the other materials and items used during an eyelash tinting treatment and add these to the cost of the tint that was used.

3 Assuming that the cost of the therapist is £5.20 per hour, work out the profit made on an eyelash tinting treatment which is priced at £8.50 in the salon.

GOOD PRACTICE

The action of plucking the eyebrows stimulates the blood supply to the hair follicles, making the skin pink and sometimes red if the hairs that have been removed are particularly coarse. This reddening of the skin is called erythema. The erythema is temporary but, while it is there, the skin is more sensitive than usual. Do not provide a full eyebrow shaping treatment immediately before any other stimulating eye treatment or before a special make-up, where the redness would spoil the effect.

Activity 7.2: Eyelash and eyebrow treatments

Decide which colour or colours of eyelash tint you would recommend for tinting the eyelashes and eyebrows of each of the following clients:

1 Young client with fair skin and natural ash blond hair.

2 Middle-aged client, a natural redhead with quite a few white hairs.

3 Naturally blond client, with tinted auburn hair.

4 Client in mid twenties with dark brown hair.

Check your answers with your supervisor.

Manual tweezers

Eyebrow shaping

Shaping the brows emphasises the eyes and helps give character to the face. The most popular method of shaping is by plucking with tweezers. **Automatic tweezers** are used to remove the bulk of excess hairs growing beneath the eyebrows. **Manual tweezers** create the final shape. The brows can also be shaped using warm wax. This is covered in Chapter 9 on Depilatory Waxing.

A full eyebrow shaping treatment takes approximately 15 minutes. Eyebrow shaping can be provided on its own or combined with other treatments. A follow-up eyebrow trim takes five minutes.

1 Thin, arched

The eyebrow hairs grow in skin that lies over the base of the frontal bone at the upper part of the eye socket. The thicker hairs, which make up the general shape of the brows, protect the bony prominence. Finer hairs grow further down towards the eye socket. These fine hairs are more obvious in darker people. They tend to give a 'heavy' appearance to the brows, which can dominate the upper eye area. In fair people, these hairs are less obvious but they spoil the effect of eye make-up.

2 Thick, arched

By removing excess hair, the skin becomes smoother and more suitable for make-up. Eye-shadows can be blended in more evenly, producing a softer, more professional finish.

Choosing an eyebrow shape

3 Thick, angular

Eyebrow shapes come in and out of fashion as often as make-up fashions change. For younger clients, fashion may be the only influence on their choice of eyebrow shape.

4 Thin, angular

An eyebrow shape should be chosen which:

- suits the client's face
- emphasises their eyes
- suits the natural growth of their eyebrows
- complements or corrects their natural eyebrow shape
- does not expose any skin imperfections (for example, scarring)
- is suitable for the age of the client.

5 Thin, straight

6 Thick, straight

Different eyebrow shapes

A PRACTICAL GUIDE TO BEAUTY THERAPY

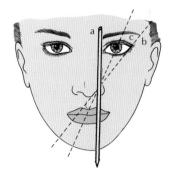

Measuring for eyebrow shaping

Here are some guidelines to help you measure up for an eyebrow shaping treatment.

1   Position a clean orange stick vertically at the side of the nose so that it crosses the brow. You will need to remove any hairs growing in area (a).

2   Swivel the orange stick round so that it crosses the brow in line with the outer corner of the eye. Eyebrow hairs growing in area (b) will have to be removed.

3   Reposition the orange stick, still at the side of the nose but so that it crosses the brow on a line that passes through the centre of the eye. The hairs in area (c) should be removed to produce the highest point of the eyebrow arch.

Creating effects

The natural shape, thickness, hair growth and spacing of the eyebrows determine what can be achieved by plucking. The basic guidelines may need adapting for dealing with particular problems. Sometimes a little eyebrow make-up is needed afterwards to achieve the final effect.

Close-set eyes

Eyes that are less than one eye's width apart need the illusion of extra space created between them. This can be helped by plucking between the eyebrows, slightly increasing the distance between them and by extending the length of the brows beyond the normal guideline.

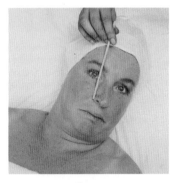

Inner corner of eye

Eyes too wide apart

Eyes that are more than one eye's width apart need to look closer together. This can be achieved by reducing the distance between the eyebrows and finishing the shape slightly inside the normal guideline.

Eyebrows that meet

Eyebrows that meet in the middle produce a frowning effect. The hairs should be cleared from above the bridge of the nose to draw the brows apart.

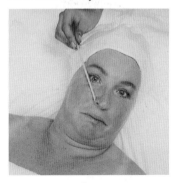

Outer corner of eye

'Droopy' eyebrows

Eyebrows that grow too far down at the sides make the eyes look sad or tired. Shorten the brows so that they do not extend beyond the outer corners of the eyes.

Thick, untidy eyebrows

The brows look heavy and the eyes lack definition. Clear excess hair from above the eye socket and create an arch. This 'opens up' the eye, emphasising the eye shape and surrounding bone structure.

Excessive eyebrow hairs on mature skin

Excess hairs emphasise the effects of loose skin and slack muscle tone in the eye area. Clear the excess hairs and create an arch at the outer edges of the brows to give a more youthful 'lift' to the eye area. Do not make the brows too thin.

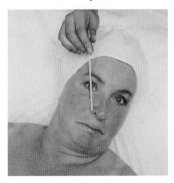

Centre of eye

Face shapes

The shape and thickness of the eyebrows can be adapted to help balance the facial features.

Gently tapered arched brows enhance an oval face

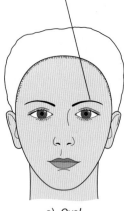

a) *Oval*

Eyebrows quite thick at inner edge, tapering to a high angular arch to draw attention away from fullness of face and help create illusion of extra length

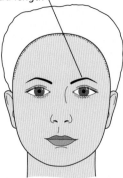

b) *Round*

Smooth tapering arch softens effect of an angular face shape

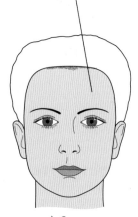

c) *Square*

Tapered eyebrows, not too thin, help enhance deeper and wider upper part of face without drawing attention to widest points of the head

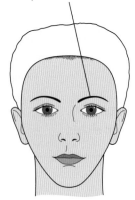

d) *Heart-shaped*

Well-defined angular arch helps to create balance with widest part of face

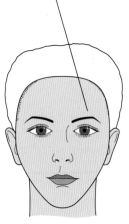

e) *Diamond-shaped*

Brows of medium thickness kept almost straight help to divide length of face and draw attention across its width

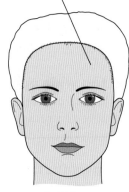

f) *Oblong*

Angular brows with high arch at outer corners help to widen the forehead and provide balance with heavier bone structure in lower part of face

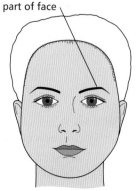

g) *Pear-shaped*

Face shapes and eyebrow techniques

A PRACTICAL GUIDE TO BEAUTY THERAPY

Round

Eyebrows that are quite thick at the inner edge and taper off into a high angular arch draw attention away from the fullness of the face and help create an illusion of extra length.

Square

A smooth tapering arch is best to soften the effects of an angular face shape. Do not make the brows too thin or they will be 'lost' on a face with heavy bone structure.

Heart-shaped

An arched brow that is not too thin will help balance the deeper and wider upper part of the face without drawing attention to the highest points of the forehead.

Diamond-shaped

A well-defined angular arch helps to square off the forehead and balance it with the widest part of the face.

Oblong

The brows should be of medium thickness and taper off slightly. They should be kept almost straight to divide the length of the face and draw attention across its width.

Pear-shaped

Angular brows with a fairly high arch at the outer corners help to widen the forehead and balance it with the heavier bone structure of the lower part of the face.

Preparing for eyebrow shaping

Make sure your trolley is prepared before the client arrives. You will need:

- a headband and towel for the client
- a towel for yourself
- a jar of sterilising fluid containing automatic and manual tweezers and scissors
- a covered bowl containing clean cotton wool pads
- tissues
- a covered bowl for waste
- eye make-up remover, cleansing lotion, toner, surgical spirit, witch hazel and a soothing antiseptic cream
- an eyebrow pencil
- a hand mirror
- a record card and pen.

Depending on the practice in your salon, you may also need a facial steamer for warming the skin and relaxing the hair follicles prior to tweezing.

GOOD PRACTICE

Make sure you will be working in good light. This will help you to produce good results and will reduce the risk of you nipping the skin with tweezers. A magnifying lamp should be used which will show up even the finest hairs.

REMEMBER

Tweezers that have been cleaned, sterilised and stored hygienically are ready for use at a moment's notice.

Preparing the client

Many clients come to the salon for eyebrow shaping treatments because they find the treatment too uncomfortable to do for themselves. A thick growth of dark, strong eyebrow hairs can be particularly painful to remove if the skin and hairs are not prepared properly.

The procedure is as follows:

1 Help the client into a comfortable position on the beauty couch.

2 Secure their hair off the face with a headband and cover their upper clothing with a towel.

3 Wash and dry your hands.

4 Remove all make-up from the eyebrow area and wipe over with toner to remove any traces of grease.

5 Using the magnifying lamp, check the area for contraindications:
(a) diseases and disorders of the skin
(b) cuts and abrasions
(c) lumps and swellings
(d) recent scar tissue
(e) hypersensitive skin
(f) sensitive or infected eyes.

6 If it is safe to proceed with treatment, brush the eyebrows upwards to separate the hairs and then brush them into their natural shape.

7 Assess the client's preferences relative to the natural growth and shape of the eyebrows and give appropriate advice. Agree a treatment plan.

8 Warm the brow area by using a facial steamer or by applying either a warm damp towel or warm, damp cotton wool pads.

Shaping the eyebrows

Plucking begins above the bridge of the nose where the skin is less sensitive. The eyebrows are then worked on alternately, removing a few hairs at a time until the bulk of excess hairs has been removed. Automatic tweezers make plucking much more comfortable, because they can be used very quickly and this counteracts the discomfort caused by pulling out hairs more slowly, one at a time. Manual tweezers achieve the final eyebrow shape.

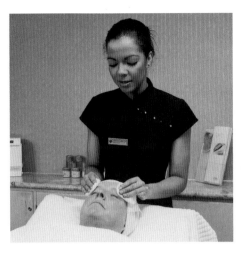

1 *Eyebrows cleansed and examined before treatment*

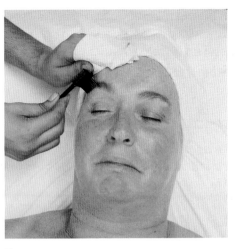

2 *Separating the eyebrow hairs*

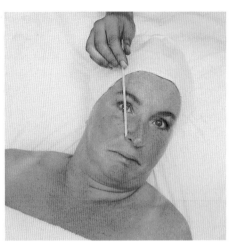

3 *Measuring eyebrows with orange stick*

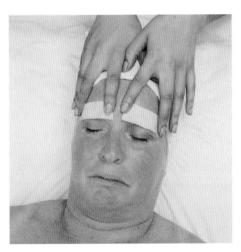

4 *Warming the area*

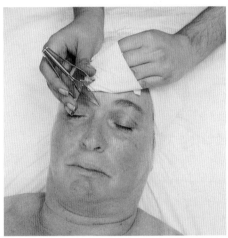

5 *Commencing treatment above the bridge of the nose*

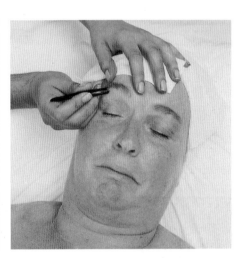

6 *Creating the 'arch' of the eyebrow*

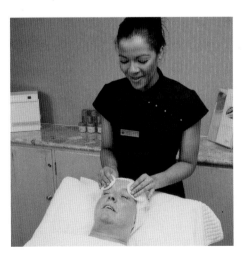

7 *Soothing the skin after tweezing*

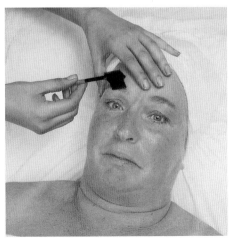

8 *Brushing the eyebrows into shape*

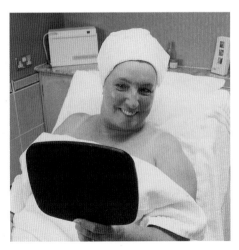

9 *Seeking the client's approval*

Use the following techniques to ensure a comfortable, safe and effective eyebrow shaping treatment:

- *keep the skin taut*: use your index finger and middle finger to stretch the skin in the area being treated. This helps to deaden the nerve endings, it also makes the hairs stand on end so that they are easier to grip; there is less chance of nipping the skin
- *pluck hairs out in the direction of growth*: hairs will be removed cleanly from the follicle; they will not break off at the surface of the skin
- *apply warm pads throughout the treatment*: keeping the area warm soothes the nerve endings and makes the treatment more comfortable particularly when plucking coarse hairs.
- *work as quickly as safety allows*: it does not matter if the automatic tweezers do not pluck out a hair every time, so long as the whole area is cleared within a reasonable time
- *monitor the skin*: check for signs of skin sensitivity and do not continue if there is an extreme reaction to the treatment
- *brush brows into shape regularly*: keep an eye on how the treatment is progressing, particularly when doing detailed work with the manual tweezers. Make sure the brows are shaped evenly and at the same level
- *remove plucked hairs*: do not leave loose hairs on the skin, but transfer them to a clean tissue or cotton wool pad
- *keep tweezers clean*: during the treatment, wipe over the ends of the tweezers regularly with surgical spirit. This removes any adhering hairs and skin cells and keeps the tweezers disinfected.

Completing the treatment

The treatment is not finished until you know the client is pleased with the results:

- wipe over the brows with witch hazel to soothe the skin and reduce redness
- brush the eyebrows into shape
- lift the head of the beauty couch so that the client's head is raised
- offer the client a hand mirror to examine the eyebrows
- finally, seek the approval of the client.

If any adjustment is needed, the brow area will have to be warmed again before using tweezers. If the client is satisfied with the treatment, apply some soothing antiseptic cream to prevent the skin from becoming infected.

Advice for home care

If adequate precautions have been taken, any slight erythema will disappear quickly after eyebrow shaping and the skin will soon return to normal. A more sensitive reaction to the treatment may take longer to calm down. The client should be advised to apply soothing antiseptic cream regularly and to refrain from applying make-up to the area while the skin is still pink.

REMEMBER

Details of the treatment and any retail sales should be entered on the client's record card.

REMEMBER

The tweezers will need turning half-way through the sterilising period to make sure that all sides are treated with the UV rays.

HEALTH MATTERS

Good hygiene is essential when shaping the brows. Empty hair follicles provide a route for bacteria to enter the skin.

After treatment

It is important to clear up immediately after treatment so that the next client can be attended to promptly:

- dispose of waste and return soiled towels and linen to the laundry
- wash the tweezers and eyebrow brush in detergent and rinse thoroughly under clean, running water
- immerse the brush in a suitable disinfectant and then place it in an ultraviolet cabinet
- wipe over the tweezers with surgical spirit and place them in the ultraviolet cabinet.

GOOD PRACTICE

If your tweezers become damaged, they are of no use to you.

- When storing automatic tweezers, always release their hinges and oil their joints regularly to ensure a smooth action.
- Keep the tips of the tweezers protected and do not use them for any other purpose: if the tips of tweezers become scratched, they will collect germs.

SELF-CHECKS

Eyebrow shaping

1 Why are automatic tweezers preferable to manual tweezers for removing the bulk of eyebrow hairs?

2 What hygiene precautions should be taken before, during and following an eyebrow shaping treatment?

3 What steps should be taken to ensure the comfort of the client during eyebrow shaping?

4 Why is the treated area wiped over with witch hazel after eyebrow shaping?

5 State three factors that influence the choice of eyebrow shape for a client.

6 How often should a client return to the salon for an eyebrow shaping treatment?

7 State the difference between eyebrow shaping and an eyebrow trim. Indicate the length of appointment that should be made for each treatment.

8 Explain the basic guidelines to follow when measuring up for an eyebrow shape.

9 Describe a contra-action to eyebrow shaping and give the appropriate home care advice.

10 Why might a facial steamer be used during an eyebrow shaping treatment?

Eyelash perming

Eyelash perming treatments arrived in the UK after they became popular in the US and also in the Far East where Asian lashes tend to be very straight. Initially, many beauty therapists were concerned about the safety aspects of using perm products so near the eyes, but many salons in the UK have now successfully introduced eyelash perming in their businesses, proving that safe, effective eyelash perming treatments have arrived!

Eyelash perming treatments are given individually or are combined with other facial treatments. During eyelash perming, the lashes are stretched and curled over rods, curlers or rollers and 'fixed' into their new shape using chemical products. The lashes remain curled even when they are wet. The effect is very attractive, with the eyes taking on a more youthful appearance. Some clients consider eyelash perming to be the natural-looking alternative to mascara and less damaging for the eyelashes than regular use of eyelash curlers. The effects of eyelash perming last up to eight weeks depending on the stage of the hair growth cycle.

GOOD PRACTICE

Before carrying out an eyelash perming treatment it is essential to have a consultation with the client so that you can discuss what they require and what is achievable.

HEALTH MATTERS

A skin test should be carried out 24–48 hours before the scheduled appointment. Apply a small quantity of the perm products which are to be used. A positive reaction to the test includes itching, redness and swelling, indicating that the client is contraindicated to treatment. See page 211 for the skin test procedure.

Effects of eyelash perming

During the eyelash perming process the structure of the eyelash hairs is broken down by the perming lotion or gel. The hairs are then stretched into their new shape over flexible rods, rollers or curlers and their new structure is 'fixed' with a **neutraliser**, otherwise known as an oxidising agent or fixative.

Eyelash perming enhances the lashes and makes them appear longer. This makes the eyes look larger and gives them more definition. The treatment is recommended for:

- clients who wear contact lenses or glasses
- mature clients with sagging eyelids
- clients who prefer not to wear mascara
- clients going on holiday or participating in active sports
- clients living or working in a hot environment
- clients who have short, straight lashes
- special occasions.

Contraindications

The eyelashes should not be permed if any of the following conditions are present:

- inflammation or swelling
- an eye infection
- eczema in the area of the eyelash hairs
- psoriasis in the eye area
- any cuts or abrasions in the area
- conjunctivitis or watery eyes
- allergy to eye cosmetics
- dry, flaking skin on or around the eyelids.

Preparing for eyelash perming

Make sure your trolley is prepared before the client arrives. You will need:

- a protective headband
- a towel or cape to protect the client's upper clothing
- a hand towel for yourself
- non-oily eye make-up remover and toner
- a special water-soluble adhesive
- **eyelash perm lotion** or gel
- eyelash perm 'neutraliser' (oxidising agent, fixative)
- eyelash nourishing lotion
- a selection of small, medium and large **eyelash perm rods** (rollers, curlers)
- witch hazel
- lint-free cotton wool pads, eye shields
- tissues
- a clean wooden spatula and orange sticks
- cotton buds
- a covered container for waste
- a hand mirror
- a record card and pen
- a clean eye bath and a small container of distilled water (for bathing the eyes in an emergency).

HEALTH MATTERS

The products used for perming eyelashes are milder versions of those used for perming hair. They are chemically based so great care is required using them as the eye area is particularly sensitive. The products usually come as lotions or gels. Always follow the manufacturer's instructions when storing and using eyelash perming products, and remember the importance of the COSHH regulations. Check the manufacturer's recommendations regarding follow-up treatments such as eyelash tinting.

Preparing the client

Before the treatment, explain exactly what you are going to do and what products you are going to use. Some perming lotions have quite a strong smell. Warn your client about this and reassure them that the products are quite mild.

1 Help the client into a comfortable, semi-reclining position and protect their hair and clothing with a headband and towel.
2 Wash and dry your own hands.
3 Cleanse the eye area, ensuring that all make-up is removed from the eyelashes.
4 Use a cotton bud soaked in make-up remover to get rid of traces of make-up trapped at the base of the lashes.
5 Tone and dry the area to remove all traces of grease.
6 Check the eyes and surrounding skin, ensuring that there are no contraindications.
7 Position damp cotton wool pads or eye shields beneath the lower lashes.

GOOD PRACTICE

It is advisable for a client who wears contact lenses to remove them before having their eyelashes permed. This will be more comfortable for them and, in the unlikely event of an accident, their contact lenses will not be damaged.

Perming the eyelashes

Before you begin, assess the size of rods, rollers or curlers required. Use the natural length of the lashes, how straight they are, and their thickness and texture as a guide. The smallest rods are used for shorter lashes or if a tighter curl is required. The larger rods produce a looser curl.

Prepare both sets of eyelashes following stages 1–3 below, then proceed with the perming process from stage 4.

1 Apply a small amount of the special water-soluble adhesive to the main body of the rod. This will help to keep both the lashes and the rod in place.
2 Position the rod along the upper lashes, bending it to fit neatly to the contour of the eyelid.
3 Separate and wrap the lashes evenly around the rods, with no kinks or strays. Check that no lashes are caught underneath the rod.

A PRACTICAL GUIDE TO BEAUTY THERAPY

 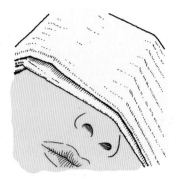

4   Using a cotton bud, carefully apply a small amount of the perm lotion to the lashes, ensuring even coverage.

5   Cover the eyelids while the perm solution is developing and check on progress after five minutes. Refer to the manufacturer's instructions for minimum and maximum processing times.

6   Apply neutralising lotion to the lashes in the same way as the perming lotion and leave to develop for the recommended time.

7   Remove all chemicals from the lashes using damp cotton wool followed by a nourishing lotion to help condition the lashes.

8   Raise the head of the treatment couch gently and provide the client with a hand mirror to approve the final result. The lashes should look natural, gently curved and not curled too tightly.

9   Enter details of the treatment on the client's record card.

Before   *After*

Contra-actions

Some clients find it difficult to keep still with their eyes closed for any length of time. This can be a problem during eyelash perming because it is important that the perming products do not get in the client's eyes. Explain to the client the importance of keeping their eyes closed and warning you if they need to open them.

If the client complains of an uncomfortable prickling or stinging sensation, or if their eyes start to water:

- remove the perming products immediately using damp cotton wool pads
- rinse the client's eyes using the clean eye bath and distilled water
- apply damp cotton wool pads soaked in witch hazel to cool and soothe the eye area.

Other potential problems which may occur through incorrect treatment techniques are:

- dry, brittle eyelashes: chemical products left on too long, nourishing lotion not applied afterwards
- broken eyelashes: chemicals left on too long
- patchy loss of eyelashes: over processing
- lashes pointing in different directions: inadequate attention to separating and spreading lashes evenly over the rod
- fish-hook lashes: incorrect wrapping of lashes over the rod, rod size too small and kinking the tips of the lashes during winding
- unevenly curled eyelashes: incorrect positioning of rod, patchy application of perm lotion, uneven tension on lashes when spreading over rod
- lashes too curly: size of rod too small
- no change in the appearance of the lashes: size of rod too large, perm lotion and/or neutraliser not left on for long enough, inadequate cleansing of the lashes beforehand creating a barrier to the products.

SELF-CHECKS

Eyelash perming

1 How long do the effects of an eyelash perming treatment last?

2 Why is a skin test required before perming the eyelashes?

3 State the specific effects on eyelash hairs of: a) perming lotion; b) neutraliser.

4 List five contraindications to eyelash perming.

5 Give two alternative names for the rods used in an eyelash perming treatment.

6 Give two alternative names for the neutraliser used during an eyelash perming treatment.

7 State three precautions which should be taken during an eyelash perming treatment to ensure a successful result.

8 Give four different reasons why clients may want to have their eyelashes permed.

Activity 7.3: Eyebrow and eyelash treatments

Make copies of completed record cards and treatment plans for eyebrow and eyelash treatments you have given in the salon. Keep these in your assessment portfolio, together with any work logs, witness testimonies, photographs or comment sheets you have received in relation to the treatments and to your customer care. Ask the permission of your clients before copying their record cards and treatment plans. Explain why you need them.

MULTIPLE CHOICE QUIZ

Eyebrows and eyelash treatments

Work through the following questions either on your own or with a colleague. Check your answers with your supervisor.

1 Eyelash tint colours the hairs by a process of:
(a) pigmentation
(b) hydration
(c) oxidation
(d) reduction.

2 Hydrogen peroxide must be handled carefully because it is:
(a) poisonous
(b) an irritant
(c) a gas
(d) an allergen.

3 The strength of hydrogen peroxide, which is usually mixed with eyelash tint, is:
(a) 10 vol
(b) 20 vol
(c) 30 vol
(d) 40 vol.

4 A skin test for eyelash tint is given:
(a) immediately before treatment
(b) up to one week before treatment
(c) when the client arrives for treatment
(d) 24–48 hours before treatment.

5 A positive reaction to a skin test means that:
(a) the client may have an eyelash tinting treatment
(b) care must be taken when giving an eyelash tinting treatment
(c) the client must not have an eyelash tinting treatment
(d) the client may need another skin test.

6 The eyebrow area is warmed before tweezing to:
(a) relax the client
(b) relax the hair follicles
(c) soften the skin
(d) soothe the pain.

7 Eyebrow shaping should commence:
(a) beneath the arch of the brow
(b) above the brow
(c) at the thickest part of the brow
(d) above the bridge of the nose.

8 The main advantage of automatic tweezers is that they are:
(a) quick
(b) hygienic
(c) painless
(d) efficient.

Eyebrows and eyelash treatments

9 The effect of a neutraliser during eyelash perming is to:
   (a) change the structure of the lash hairs
   (b) break down the structure of the lash hairs
   (c) fix the new structure of the lash hairs
   (d) fix the lash hairs to the rods.

10 The tightness of curl produced by perming the lashes depends upon:
   (a) the size of the rods
   (b) the length of the rods
   (c) the processing time of the perm lotion
   (d) the processing time of the neutraliser.

KEY TERMS

You should now understand the following words and phrases. If you do not, go back through the chapter and find out what they mean:

Eyelash tint	**Skin test**	**Conjunctivitis**
Automatic tweezers	**Negative skin test reaction**	**Eyelash perm lotion**
Peroxide	**Positive skin test reaction**	**Neutraliser**
Manual tweezers	**Oxidation**	**Eyelash perm rods**

Chapter 8 Make-up

Provide make-up treatment

After working through this chapter you will be able to:

- appreciate the different types of make-up products available and how to use them
- match and apply make-up products to different skin types and conditions
- understand about the effects of lighting on make-up
- plan and apply make-up for different occasions
- disguise minor imperfections using make-up
- apply false eyelashes
- advise clients about their make-up
- recognise contra-actions and contraindications to make-up.

Before you work through this chapter: Be wise and revise!
Revision topics to help you achieve this unit:

Provide make-up treatment

The salon may offer a wide range of services to promote make-up treatments. Some of these present exciting challenges for the creative beauty therapist who is interested in developing specialist make-up skills. All clients appreciate a professional make-up treatment, even if they have never worn make-up before. Once they have seen the possibilities, they want to be able to achieve the same effects themselves. This is good for both the treatment and retail sides of the business.

Make-up services

The range of make-up services offered by a salon depends very much on the nature of the business and the expertise of the staff who are employed there. Here are some ways in which you could use your make-up skills:

- basic day make-up
- make-up for evening and special occasions
- make-up lessons
- weddings
- photographic work
- demonstrations
- fashion shows
- remedial camouflage.

Make-up is very much about the individual, how they see themselves and how they would like to see themselves. What one person feels happy and confident with might be totally inappropriate for someone else. It is important to listen to your client and get as much information as possible before designing and applying the make-up.

Light, natural day make-up

Glamour evening make-up

Bridal make-up

Male fashion model

GOOD PRACTICE

Talk through your own and the client's ideas before agreeing the treatment plan.
Be sensitive to their preferences and opinions when giving advice.

'What one person feels happy and confident with might be totally inappropriate for someone else!'

Basic day make-up

Clients generally prefer their **day make-up** to be more natural looking. Lightweight products in subtle shades are used to enhance the client's natural colouring and emphasise their best features. Products are carefully blended to avoid hard demarcation lines which show up very clearly in natural daylight.

Make-up after a facial

Ideally, the skin should be left clean and free from make-up after a facial. A little moisturiser is all that is required. However, some clients prefer to have make-up applied, particularly if they are not going straight home after treatment. If possible, limit this to tinted moisturiser and a light application of loose face powder, eye make-up and lipstick.

REMEMBER

Some of the effects of a full facial continue once the treatment has finished. A stimulating massage speeds up the rate at which waste products are removed from the deeper layers of the skin and this can temporarily upset the acid balance. The skin may react with **foundation**, turning it an orange colour. The foundation may also go blotchy, making it difficult to achieve a smooth finish. The skin has usually calmed down and is at its best 48 hours after a facial.

Make-up for evening and special occasions

Whatever the event, if the client wants to look special, then the event is special. Some special occasions take place outside, where the make-up has to look good in natural daylight. Others take place inside, in the evening, and the effects of **artificial lighting** have to be considered. Colours and techniques must be adapted to suit the occasion.

Effects of lighting on make-up

Natural daylight is pure white light. Although it is produced by the sun, daylight does not just fall on the face from above. It is reflected onto the face from any light-coloured surface it hits, including walls and floors. Unlike artificial light, natural daylight shows up the true colours and textures of make-up.

REMEMBER

Make-up colours tested and chosen in the wrong lighting can lead to expensive mistakes. Many of your clients will have discovered this in the past with products purchased from a shop or store. Retail display cabinets should be fitted with 'day light' (warm white fluorescent) lighting for testing colours; if this is not available, the products should be tested by the nearest source of natural daylight.

REMEMBER
Colours look stronger in daylight than in artificial light and this affects the choice of make-up products.

REMEMBER
Daylight is the cruellest form of light for showing up imperfections; this includes less-than-perfect make-up applications!

Artificial light

The effects of artificial lighting on make-up depend on the source and type of lighting:

- Filament lamps contained in standard light bulbs produce a yellowish light, which dulls the effect of blue-toned colours and makes red tones appear darker. The bright glare produced from a light bulb is usually softened with a lamp shade, which reduces the amount of light given out and directs it downwards, creating sharp shadows.
- Fluorescent lamps are contained in tubes: white tubes give out a harsh bluish-white light, which takes the warmth out of make-up colours. Fluorescent tubes are usually covered with diffusers, which soften the light and disperse it so that very little shadow is created.
- The light produced from warm white fluorescent tubes is closest in colour to natural daylight and is the best type of artificial lighting for matching up make-up colours.

As a general rule, **evening make-up** requires warmer shades of foundation and stronger make-up colours for contouring the face, and defining the eyes and mouth. Exciting colour combinations, high gloss and pearlised products and false eyelashes may be used to help to achieve the desired effect. The special occasion make-up must complement the outfit and accessories that will probably have been bought especially for the event.

Make-up lessons

Most clients are more aware of their bad points than their good points. It is not until they have had their make-up applied by a professional that they realise how attractive they really are. A make-up lesson should focus on the client's good points and help build up their confidence.

Most lessons begin with creating a make-up for day wear, which is then adapted for evening. The lessons take place with the client positioned comfortably in front of a large mirror so that they can watch the demonstration of techniques on their own face and then copy them under the expert instruction of the therapist.

The client takes part in the facial analysis and the relevance of structure and colour is explained at each stage. Particular emphasis is placed on:

- *preparing the skin for make-up*: advising on the importance of a clean 'canvas' and recommending the most appropriate cleanser, toner and under-make-up base
- *choosing and applying the cosmetics*: matching the colour, texture and types of products to the client's features and the effects required
- handling the skin correctly to avoid stretching or over-stimulating the skin
- supporting the hand, keeping control of the applicator to ensure a good finish when making up the eyes and lips
- *applying make-up effectively and hygienically*: matching client's abilities with the types of products and applicators used, and stressing the importance of keeping them clean

Giving a make-up lesson

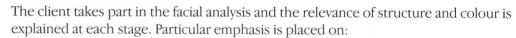

A natural, daytime look which can be adapted for a 'glamour' look for evening

- *keeping the make-up looking fresh*: touching up with pressed powder, using a fine mineral spray or damp cotton wool and reapplying lipstick throughout the day
- *removing make-up*: choosing and applying cosmetic cleansers and basic skin-care products.

Contents of a make-up bag

Record keeping

At the end of the lesson, a completed make-up chart is provided for the client which gives details of the products used and how they should be applied.

MAKE-UP RECORD CARD

Surname:		Date of Birth:		
First Names:				
Address:		Client requirements:		
Tel no:				
Date of Consultation:		Consultant:		

	Colour:	ADVICE	AM	PM
Skin	Type:	Under make-up base		
		Colour correction		
	Problems:	Foundation		
		Powder		
Bone Structure	Face shape:	Blusher		
	Problems:	Highlighter		
		Shader		
Eyes	Colour: Shape/size:	Eye shadow		
	Problems:	Eye liner		
		Mascara		
		Eyebrow pencil		
Lips	Shape/size:	Lip pencil		
	Problems:	Lipstick		

Make-up record card

Weddings

There are enough things that can go wrong on a wedding day without the bride's make-up being one of them! Many brides prefer to have their make-up applied professionally so that they can be confident of looking their best on this special day.

Of course, not all weddings are white. They do not necessarily take place in a church and the bride can be any age between 16 and 90 or beyond! It is, therefore, impossible to generalise on specific wedding make-up techniques: the make-up must, as usual, be adapted to suit the individual.

> **REMEMBER**
>
> Spring is traditionally the wedding season and this is a particularly good time for promoting special offers for brides.

> **REMEMBER**
>
> False tanning or sunbed treatments may be recommended if the dress has a low back or scooped neckline which reveals paler areas of the body.

Preliminary consultation

A preliminary consultation with the bride is essential. Apart from providing important information, this will give you an opportunity to get to know your client better and gain her confidence.

> **REMEMBER**
>
> Some brides prefer to have the make-up applied in the relative calm of the beauty salon. Others may request that you treat them at home: in this case, there will be an extra charge for the time that you are not available at the salon.

> **REMEMBER**
>
> Nail extensions and 'French' manicure effects are very popular with brides, particularly those whose natural nails are in poor condition. Every wedding album contains a close-up photograph of the new bride's wedding ring in place after the ceremony!

You will need to find out:

- *The date and time of the wedding*: this will help you to schedule pre-wedding appointments for carrying out a facial assessment, applying beauty therapy treatments and practising the make-up. The final make-up appointment will have to be scheduled within the overall wedding preparations and enough time must be allowed for the bride to be able to relax and enjoy the treatment. Ideally the make-up should be applied just before the hair is dressed and the wedding gown is put on.

- *Details of the wedding dress*: the design, colour and material of the dress will influence the make-up design. Make-up colours will look stronger contrasting with a pale, traditional wedding gown than with a more colourful outfit. The make-up effect will have to be softer for lightweight materials than for heavier or embossed fabrics. It is helpful if you can see a sample of the wedding dress material and, also, that of the bridesmaid's dresses. These will help to co-ordinate the colour scheme for the make-up.

- *Hair style and head-dress*: the bride's choice of head-dress may require her hair to be styled in a way that affects the appearance of her face and the balance of her features. **Corrective make-up** work may be necessary to compensate for this.

- *Flowers*: lipstick and nail enamel colours must tone in with the colour scheme of the bouquet and any other flowers that are being carried or worn.

- *The client's experience with make-up*: all brides want to look beautiful on their wedding day, but they also want to feel comfortable with how they look. Importantly, they want to be recognised! A wedding day is not the right time to go for dramatic change. The bride must feel confident that the make-up is enhancing the way she likes to look.

- *After-wedding arrangements*: make-up applied in the morning may be expected to survive not only the marriage ceremony and formal reception, but also an evening party when the bride may be meeting some of the guests for the first time. Your client will need advice on keeping her make-up refreshed throughout the celebrations. She will be photographed throughout the events and will need to reapply her lipstick regularly to maintain colour balance.

GOOD PRACTICE

Recommend that the bride keep a compact of pressed powder available for touching up make-up during the day. Face powder helps to absorb excess grease and reset the foundation. This is important for reducing the effects of shiny skin on the photographs.

REMEMBER

The make-up contributes greatly to the image of the bride captured for the wedding album on photographs and possibly also on video. Make-up that is applied well will look good in close-up and will withstand the discerning eye of the camera lens.

ACTIVITY

Activity 8.2: Wedding package

Ask your supervisor which of the following tasks should be completed using a computer:

1. Create a promotional leaflet for a wedding treatment 'package' which could be offered by your salon for a Spring Bride campaign. When designing the package, think about which treatments would benefit the clients before the wedding day and which services should be provided on the day.

2. Prepare a schedule that you would work to for preparing and providing your services at the bride's home on the wedding day. Assume that your salon is about half-an-hour's drive away from the bride's house, the journey from the bride's home to the church will take about 20 minutes and her wedding is due to take place at 3 p.m.

3. Work out the price of your wedding package for the bride above, showing your costings. Remember, it will cost more for the bride to be treated at her home rather than at the salon. Explain how you will allow for that in the price and reflect it in your costings.

Photographic make-up

If you enjoy photographic make-up, you may get the opportunity to work with a local studio or fashion photographer. You will be fascinated by the range of effects that a photographer can create by adjusting camera angles and lighting schemes, and by using special lenses. Here are some points for you to consider when applying make-up for photographs:

- photographic lighting can get very hot and the make-up may begin to melt, particularly during a long sitting; do not apply a heavy make-up and keep the skin as cool as possible during application

- grease on the face produces an unattractive shine and emphasises creases and open pores; do not use a greasy under-make-up base, avoid using cream-textured products and reapply loose translucent face powder throughout the make-up procedure to achieve a matt finish

- pearlised make-up products can look attractive on photographs because they reflect light, but they can cause glare. They are most effective when kept to a minimum and contrasted with matt-finish products

- the camera will pick up patches of discoloration and natural shadows created by skin folds; you will need to even out the skin colour and lighten areas such as under the eyes and the creases at the sides of the nostrils and above the chin before you apply the foundation

- photographic lighting wipes out the natural highlights and shadows created by facial contour; you will have to use **highlighting** and **shading** techniques to define the bone structure and balance the features. The foundation colour should be as light as possible to enhance the effects of the **contour cosmetics**

- hard lines are emphasised on camera; all make-up products must be blended well, ensuring that there are no hard demarcation lines. This is particularly important when applying contour cosmetics and blending foundation under the jawline and into the hairline.

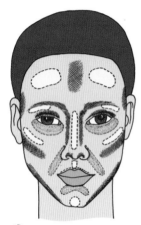

◯ = Highlighter

● = Shader

◓ = Very pale foundation

Specialised contouring techniques for photographic work

Demonstrations

Make-up demonstrations are an excellent way of attracting new clients to the business. They have great interest value because they are visually entertaining and the effects are immediate. Local community groups are usually very pleased to schedule demonstration evenings in their social calendar and these provide good opportunities for promoting the salon and its services.

GOOD PRACTICE

If the demonstration is being carried out in a hall or large room with a high ceiling, sound will not carry well. You may need to use a microphone. Practise with it beforehand and check that it is working properly.

GOOD PRACTICE

Always take plenty of the salon's price lists and any other leaflets or promotional material with you to a demonstration. Make sure you understand enough about the full range of treatments to be able to explain their benefits and give general advice.

Planning a make-up demonstration

A good make-up demonstration needs organising well. Here is some advice to help you with the planning:

- *Find out as much about your audience as possible*: you will need to know approximately how many people will be attending and their age range; this is useful for preparing your talk and selecting the most appropriate products.

- *Try to visit the venue beforehand*: once you have seen the room you will have a better idea about the lighting and acoustics. You may wish to liaise with the organisers about seating arrangements, organising a display area and accessing facilities.

- *Find out when the demonstration is due to finish*: you may have to vacate the premises by a certain time and you will need to plan your demonstration accordingly, allowing extra time for answering questions from the audience.

- *Make a list beforehand of everything you need to take*: the demonstration may be taking place at the end of a working day. If you plan well, you can use the interval before the event to have a break and freshen yourself up for the evening. This is much better than rushing about at the last minute.

- *Pack your products and equipment neatly and in logical order*: make-up display stands are useful for transporting, as they provide a good range of colours and minimise the number of small individual items that you need to take. Make sure that drawers are sealed before you leave so that they do not get damaged in transit.

- *Try to use as many unbreakable containers as possible for carrying cleansers, toners and moisturisers*: take prepared pads of cotton wool in a plastic bowl with a sealed lid and provide disposal bags for waste. You may need to take a container of water if the room does not have a supply of running water.

- *Plan to arrive at the venue at least half an hour before the demonstration is due to start*: you will need to set up the area and prepare your equipment in peace. It is more difficult to do this once the audience starts to arrive, as your display will probably attract a lot of attention and you may be distracted by having to answer questions.

Preparing for a make-up demonstration

Giving the demonstration

Your first demonstration will probably be quite a nerve-racking experience! Don't worry, the time passes very quickly once you have started and you will probably be surprised to discover how knowledgeable you are. Confidence grows with experience and each demonstration is good practice for the next one. Here are some guidelines to help you through your first demonstration:

- *Starting proceedings*: begin on time, smile and welcome the guests. Make sure that everyone knows your name (and the names of any of your colleagues) and which salon you represent. If anyone looks puzzled, describe the location of the salon.

- *Inviting a volunteer from the audience*: you will need a model to work on. If you have a choice, do not select the youngest and most attractive person who applies their own make-up well. Choose someone who will look significantly different at the end of the demonstration. This will have a greater impact on the audience.

- *Instructing on skin care and make-up*: at each stage of the demonstration explain about the products you are using and the best way of applying and removing them. Tell the audience what you intend to do and how you are going to do it. When you have finished, invite them to confirm that you have done it!

- *Keeping the audience interested*: make sure you do not block the view of the audience when applying the make-up. Involve the audience in what you are doing. Invite them to help you choose colours and then explain your final choice.

- *Maintaining the flow*: if you are providing the commentary and someone else is demonstrating the make-up, do not read a prepared speech. Reading shows a lack of confidence and encourages you to talk to the floor; your voice will become 'lost' and will not be heard by most of the audience. If necessary, use small prompt cards in the order of the talk. These will have key words written on them as a quick reminder of where you should be up to.

- *Seeking approval*: invite the audience to acknowledge how lovely your model looks before you show her the final effect. The approval of other people will give her the confidence to accept her new look.

- *Finishing the demonstration*: ask the audience to join you in thanking the model and, if possible, offer her a small gift. This could be a lipstick or a gift voucher for the salon. Invite the audience to have a closer look at the finished make-up and to ask questions.

ACTIVITY

Activity 8.3: Demonstrations

You can pick up lots of useful tips by watching experienced demonstrators at work.

1 Find an opportunity to go and watch a professional demonstration. This could be in the cosmetic department of a large store or at a professional beauty exhibition. If a more senior member of staff in your salon is due to give an outside demonstration, ask if you can go and watch. Make notes on things that seem to work really well.

2 Find out which are the most common problems experienced by people applying their own make-up. Talk to friends, colleagues and clients. Prepare some good advice and make-up tips for your next make-up demonstration.

3 Give a demonstration! Prepare an evaluation questionnaire on computer beforehand to get feedback from your audience about how it went. Discuss with your supervisor the design of the questionnaire and the responses you get .

A PRACTICAL GUIDE TO BEAUTY THERAPY

Fashion shows

It makes good sense for local businesses to support each other and attract extra customers to the area. Fashion shows are a very effective way of involving different businesses in a joint promotional event. Besides sharing the work and costs of putting on the show, they also share the success and publicity, which will create new business.

Make-up for the catwalk

The techniques used for evening, special occasion and photographic make-up are adapted for the catwalk or stage. The strong, artificial lighting that floods the stage drains a lot of colour out of the make-up and this has to be compensated for with warmer shades of foundation and bolder colours for eyes and lips.

Stage lighting produces a lot of heat, particularly if spotlights are used. Do not apply the make-up thickly: it will make the face perspire even more and the foundation will melt. If this happens, there is a risk of the clothes becoming damaged during costume changes.

The catwalk

REMEMBER

The make-up will be less obvious to people sitting near the back of a large hall or theatre, so extra definition is required when contouring the face and making up the eyes, eyebrows and lips. A greater contrast between highlighters and shaders is required.

GOOD PRACTICE

Look after your models during the show. Help them to keep cool so that the make-up is not spoiled. Use a fine water spray over the face or press over the make-up with damp cotton wool pads. Reapply face powder to keep the surface of the make-up dry.

Remedial camouflage

Special training is required for learning remedial camouflage techniques. The work is concerned mainly with concealing disfiguring birthmarks, pigment disorders and bad scarring resulting from skin injury or plastic surgery. The clients for remedial camouflage are often very embarrassed by their skin problem, and include men and children who have to be taught how to apply the make-up for themselves. Remedial camouflage is often carried out by a qualified therapist in a hospital out-patients department. It is also offered privately, which is preferred by clients who are reluctant to visit a beauty salon with their problem.

Make-up products

The products used for remedial camouflage are different from the standard ones. They contain very dense pigments in a light textured base so that they can even out the skin colour in an area without creating too much of a contrast with the texture of surrounding skin. The make-up is designed to be resilient and some of the products are waterproof.

Different colours may have to be mixed to match a skin tone and this may mean adding yellow, green, black or white pigments from the range. Clients need to be able to mix and adapt make-up colours to allow for changes in their skin, for example when they develop a tan in the summer.

Preparing for make-up

The make-up area must be well organised before the client arrives. A wide range of cosmetics should be available, providing a good selection of colours.

The following are standard requirements for a make-up treatment:

- clean head-band, hair clips, cape or gown, and tissues for protecting the client's hair and clothing
- selection of clean cosmetic sponges, make-up brushes, disposable applicators and an eyebrow brush
- a pair of manual tweezers in a small jar of prepared sterilising fluid
- spatulas, orange sticks and a make-up palette
- cotton wool pads, soft facial tissues and cotton buds
- client record card and make-up chart
- hand mirror
- two small bowls (one for the client's jewellery and one for water if required)
- pencil sharpener
- skin-care preparations: eye make-up remover, cleansers, toner and bracer, moisturiser, under-make-up base
- facial cosmetics: colour-corrective products, concealers, a selection of foundations, blushers, shaders, highlighters and loose face powder

REMEMBER

Manual tweezers may be needed during a make-up treatment to remove a stray eyebrow hair or to use while attaching false eyelashes. A full eyebrow shaping treatment should not be given immediately before applying make-up. This is because of the increased sensitivity of the area after tweezing and the likelihood of a resulting erythema spoiling the effect of the make-up.

- eye cosmetics: a selection of matt and pearlised eye-shadows, eyeliners, eye pencils, mascaras, eyebrow pencils and eyebrow shadow
- lip cosmetics: a selection of lip pencils, lipsticks and lip gloss
- eyelash curlers
- fine water spray.

GOOD PRACTICE

With experience, you will learn which products and colours are the most popular. Monitor stock levels of these items and make sure you always have some available for retail sales.

GOOD PRACTICE

A display of colour always attracts attention. When preparing your make-up area, arrange the products attractively so that they catch the eye. This helps to promote interest in the products and increase retail sales.

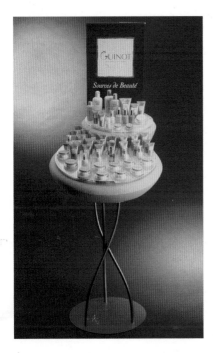

A make-up product display stand

REMEMBER

You will have to analyse your client's bone structure and facial features. This can only be done accurately if the client is upright with the face relaxed. The client's features may look different if they are lying down.

HEALTH MATTERS

Contact lens wearers should be offered the choice of either taking out their lenses or keeping them in during treatment. Some people find even the slightest pressure on their eyelids when wearing contact lenses very uncomfortable. Clients with less sensitive eyes may choose to keep their lenses in place during the treatment. This helps to prevent particles entering the eyes and becoming trapped beneath the contact lenses when they are replaced.

Preparing the client

A client who is comfortable will relax and enjoy the treatment. Ensure the comfort of your client by:

- asking them to loosen or remove restrictive clothing before placing protection around their neck
- removing their earrings, neck chains and any other jewellery which could get caught or pulled during make-up application
- securing their hair off the face using a head-band and clips if necessary
- helping the client into a comfortable, upright position with their head well supported: this is to prevent them straining their neck
- advising them to remove contact lenses if their eyes are sensitive.

Assessing the client

Once the client is prepared and settled, the face should be cleansed, toned and dried so that an accurate assessment can take place. This involves asking the client questions and analysing the face in good lighting. Note the information provided on the client's record card so that it can contribute to the treatment plan.

Here are some questions to help get useful information from your clients:

- How much make-up do you normally wear?
- Which do you think are your best features?
- Which of your features are you less happy with?
- Do you have any favourite make-up colours?
- Are there any colours you do not really like wearing?
- Is this make-up for a special occasion?
- What colour scheme will you be wearing?
- Is there a special 'look' you would like me to create?
- Do you have any allergies to make-up?

Make sure that light is falling directly on the client's face so that you can make an accurate visual assessment. You will need to assess:

- the type, colour, tone and texture of the skin, including the neck
- details of any skin blemishes or skin problems
- muscle tone, lines and wrinkles
- bone structure, facial contours and face shape
- balance of facial features
- colour and shape of the eyes and eyebrows
- lip shape and colour and condition of the teeth.

Once you have completed your assessment, you will be able to make recommendations and agree a treatment plan with your client.

HEALTH MATTERS

It is a good idea for the salon to carry a **hypo-allergenic make-up** range for clients who have previously reacted adversely to standard make-up products. Hypo-allergenic products contain less perfume and fewer pigments and preservatives, so there is less risk of them causing an adverse reaction.

ACTIVITY

Activity 8.4: Preparing for make-up

1 Your assessor will not always be available to see how you handle a make-up consultation. Your clients are probably the best people to do that anyway! Design an evaluation sheet for a number of your make-up clients to fill in after their treatments. Give them the opportunity to comment on:
   (a) the presentation of yourself and your work area
   (b) your attention to hygiene and safety
   (c) your communication skills
   (d) your care for their comfort and well-being
   (e) the thoroughness of your facial analysis
   (f) the resulting treatment plan.

   There is a lot to cover, but try and make the form as simple as possible. If you can, produce the form on a computer. It will look much more professional.

2 Decide, with your supervisor, how many forms you need to have completed and when they are returned, produce a summary of the responses. The way you collect the information depends very much on the design of your form and how you have asked the questions.

3 At your next meeting with your supervisor, discuss the results and talk through any issues raised.

Make-up procedure

Most make-up treatments will take place with the client seated in front of a mirror or lying comfortably on a beauty couch with their head raised. Light should be falling directly onto the face without casting shadows.

Order of work

Here is a summary of the make-up procedure. It applies to any make-up treatment and is adapted to the requirements of the service being provided. Further details on the choice and application of make-up products is included later in this chapter.

1 Apply under-make-up base

A light moisturiser should be worn under make-up to:

- even out skin texture and provide a smooth base for foundation
- keep the make-up looking nice for longer by fixing it on the skin
- act as a barrier between the skin and make-up so that cleansing is made easier
- help prevent the penetration of pigmented products into the pores.

Gel products are available which set matt and can be applied to greasy skin as an alternative to moisturiser. These help prevent the underlying grease from shining through the make-up.

2 Apply concealer and foundation

Patch test the foundation first if you are not sure about the colour. If the foundation goes darker, apply a lighter one.

Apply foundation with a clean damp sponge or clean fingers and blend outwards from the centre of the face. This helps to prevent the build-up of make-up in the hairline.

REMEMBER

Tinted moisturisers are available as an alternative to pigmented foundation for clients with clear skin who do not want or need a heavier foundation.

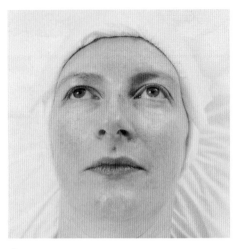

1 *Skin clean, under-make-up base applied*

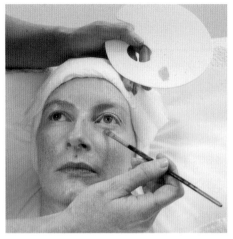

2 *Applying concealer*

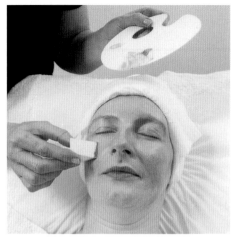

3 *Applying foundation*

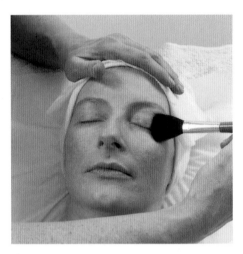

4 *Applying face powder*

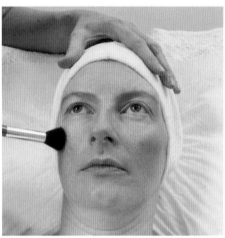

5 *Brushing off excess powder*

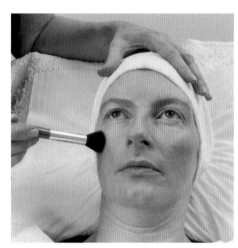

6 *Applying blusher*

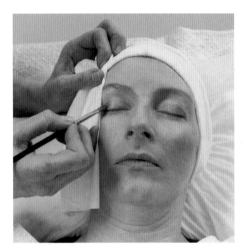

7 *Applying eyeshadows*

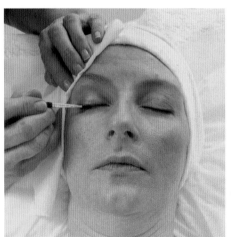

8 *Applying eyeliner*

9 *Applying mascara to upper eyelashes*

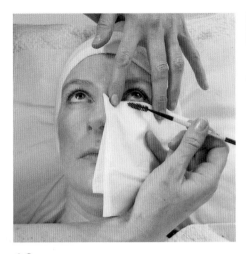

10 *Applying mascara to lower eyelashes*

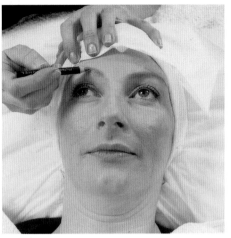

11 *Applying eyebrow pencil*

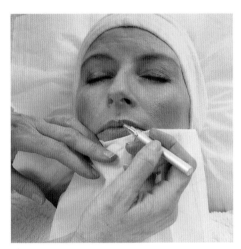

12 *Applying lip liner – creating the 'bow'*

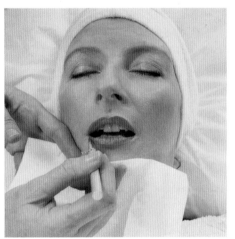

13 *Applying lip liner – outlining the mouth*

14 *Blotting lipstick after filling in*

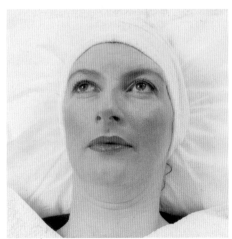

15 *Lip gloss applied*

3 Apply face powder and contour cosmetics

Oil-based products, which are not pearlised, need setting with loose face powder. Press the powder into the make-up with clean pads of cotton wool. Cover the whole of the face, eyelids and lips. Remove excess powder by brushing upwards and then down the face.

4 Apply eye cosmetics

Apply the products to both eyes in the following order:

a) eyeshadows to the upper and lower lids, eye sockets and brow bone areas
b) eyeliner (softened with a further eyeshadow application if required)
c) mascara
d) eyebrow pencil or eyebrow shadow (comb or brush the eyebrows first).

Keep a check on the balance of the eye make-up as you work through the procedure.

5 Apply lip cosmetics

Outline the mouth with lip pencil or lipstick, making corrections to the lip shape if necessary. Fill in the outline with colour and blot with tissue; apply a second coat of lipstick and finish off with a coat of lip gloss if required.

6 Make final checks

Remove head-band if worn and make final check of blending around hairline. Check the overall balance of colour and symmetry of the make-up application and rectify if necessary. 'Set' the make-up with a fine water spray if a less matt finish is required.

7 Seek approval from the client

Offer the client a hand mirror for closer inspection; ask if they are pleased with the make-up and make any adjustments requested.

8 Fill in make-up chart

Provide the client with a chart and talk through the make-up procedure, referring to the products used; interest the client in retail purchases.

9 Fill in record card

Enter details of treatments and purchases; ask the client to sign the record card.

10 Assist client

Ensure all personal belongings are returned and accompany the client to reception to make retail purchases and process payment.

Tidy up!

GOOD PRACTICE

As soon as your client has left, wipe over make-up containers and return to storage; wash and disinfect tools and equipment. Ensure the treatment area is prepared hygienically, ready for the next client.

Hygiene precautions

The main sources of infection during a make-up treatment could be:

- infected skin
- dirty tools and equipment
- contaminated make-up products.

A high standard of personal and treatment hygiene protects against the risk of infection and builds client confidence.

Personal hygiene

Personal hygiene is important to protect both the therapist and the client:

- wash your hands immediately before the treatment and regularly throughout
- cover any broken skin on your own hands with a clean plaster
- wear a clean overall and protective apron
- make sure your hair is clean and styled so that it will not fall over your client's face during the make-up procedure
- long nails are not suitable when applying make-up; neither is the wearing of nail enamel.

HEALTH MATTERS

The longer your nails the more likely it is that germs will accumulate underneath them. It is unacceptable to have long nails when treating the face. Your nails should not extend beyond your fingertips. Do not wear nail enamel, which could cause an allergic reaction if brought into contact with your client's skin.

Treatment hygiene

Always ensure professional standards when giving make-up treatments:

- check for **contraindications to make-up** before proceeding with treatment
- secure the client's hair off their face when applying the make-up
- do not apply make-up over infected skin
- use only clean tools and equipment
- maintain a clean and tidy working area
- remove creams from pots and jars with a clean spatula, not your fingers
- where possible, transfer products to a clean make-up palette before applying them to the face
- replace lids and caps on make-up containers immediately after use
- protect the applied make-up with a clean tissue when supporting your hand on the face
- dispose of waste immediately in an appropriate container.

HEALTH MATTERS

Do not proceed with the make-up treatment if any of the following contraindications are present: skin infection, for example impetigo, cold sore, ringworm; eye infections, for example styes or conjunctivitis; rash, inflammation, swelling, cuts, abrasions, allergic skin reaction, scar tissue that has not yet healed.

Tools and equipment

It is important to prevent make-up palettes and applicators from becoming contaminated. Do this by cleaning and disinfecting them after use and storing them hygienically between treatments. Disposable make-up applicators are available which can be thrown away immediately after use. This cuts out the need and cost for cleaning and disinfecting brushes.

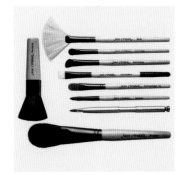

Selection of make-up brushes and applicators

GOOD PRACTICE

Always have a good supply of clean make-up sponges and brushes available. Sponges soon start to crumble when used and cleaned regularly. Brushes need cleaning after each treatment and cannot be re-used until the fibres have dried.

REMEMBER

Using disposable applicators increases the cost of providing make-up treatments and this must be reflected in the price charged to the client.

Cleaning

This is done with hot, soapy water. Liquid detergent should be worked well into the fibres of brushes and sponges, before rinsing them thoroughly under clean, running water. Make-up palettes may need scrubbing gently with a brush before rinsing.

Disinfecting

Sponges and brushes are more difficult to disinfect than solid items of equipment:

- *sponges*: soak these in a solution of hypochlorite for at least an hour and then rinse them thoroughly in clean water
- *brushes*: give the fibres a final cleaning with alcohol or a solution of suitable disinfectant before allowing them to dry
- *make-up palettes*: wipe over with a suitable disinfectant.

Product hygiene

There is very little risk of make-up products becoming contaminated if normal hygiene procedures are followed during the treatment and if containers are kept clean and in good condition.

Particular care must be taken to avoid contaminating products that are normally applied directly to the face:

- *foundations*: transfer the required amount to a palette or your clean hand, depending on the consistency of the product. Remove creams from their container with a clean spatula, not your fingers
- *cosmetic sticks*: transfer a small amount of the stick to a clean spatula or orange stick before applying it to the skin
- *loose powder*: either a) take up the amount of powder required on a clean cotton wool pad, tap off the excess into the palm of your hand and then work from the supply of powder in your hand, or b) transfer powder with a spatula to a clean tissue in the palm of your hand
- *pressed powders*: keep a good supply of clean make-up brushes available to avoid contaminating blushers and eyeshadows
- *cosmetic pencils*: sharpen pencils before using them in order to expose a clean surface
- *mascaras*: automatic mascaras cause a particular problem because the brushes are designed to be fitted back into the tube container after use; overcome this by using a disposable spiral brush or a block mascara with a flat brush which can be cleaned and disinfected in the normal way
- do not use make-up from containers that are cracked or have broken lids
- replace the lids and caps on make-up containers immediately after use.

GOOD PRACTICE

Throwing away a half-used container is a waste of make-up and a waste of the money that was paid for it.

Hygiene and safety

1 List three ways of ensuring the comfort of the client when preparing for make-up.

2 Why might a client prefer to remove their contact lenses before a make-up treatment?

3 State the three main sources of infection during a make-up treatment.

4 List five hygiene precautions which should be taken during a make-up treatment.

5 Describe how make-up brushes and sponges should be cleaned and stored after use.

6 Why should broken make-up containers be discarded?

7 What is the cause of a cosmetic sponge starting to smell?

8 Why are long nails not suitable when providing make-up treatment?

9 Why should nail enamel not be worn when providing make-up treatment?

10 What are the legal implications of taking inadequate hygiene precautions during a make-up treatment?

Choosing and using make-up products

Cosmetics are not selected purely on the basis of colour. When it comes to making the best choice for a client, the textures of products and their contents make some more suitable than others. The colours used to create the make-up should enhance the client's colouring and co-ordinate with the clothes and accessories that are being worn. They should also be suitable for achieving the overall purpose of the make-up.

Colour correction

The uses and effects of **colour correction** are based on the **complementary colour theory**. Lightweight pigmented creams are available which are applied before the tinted foundation to correct skin tone:

- green counteracts redness in areas of high colouring, for example the cheeks and nose
- pink/lilac brightens a sallow complexion.

Colour-correction creams spread easily and are used to give general coverage. They are not suitable for masking major blemishes however.

GOOD PRACTICE

- Apply the colour-correction product with a clean cosmetic sponge or your hands.
- Restrict the use of green cream to the pink or red areas of the face (you could make your client look quite ill otherwise!).
- Do not disturb the green cream when applying the rest of the make-up: stipple the foundation over the corrective cream to prevent the green from spreading.

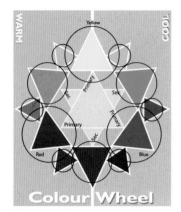

A colour wheel

Understanding colour

The colour wheel shows the relationship of colours that make up the colour spectrum and how they interact.

- The large circles show the three *primary* colours: red, yellow and blue. Primary colours cannot be created by mixing other colours.
- The middle-sized circles show the *secondary* colours, which are created by mixing two adjacent primaries, e.g. red + yellow = orange; blue + yellow = green. The secondary colour is midway between two primaries.
- The small circles show the *tertiary* colours created by mixing a primary colour with one of its secondaries, e.g. red + orange = red–orange; blue + green = blue–green.

Colours that occur next to each other on the colour wheel are referred to as 'harmonious' because they share the same base colour, for example yellow–orange, orange and red–orange are harmonious because they have orange in common.

Every colour can be described by its hue, tone and intensity.

Hue	The name of the colour, for example red, yellow. The variety of 'hues' increases all the time by varying the amount of primary colour. Moving round the wheel, in any direction, each colour is a gradual change from its adjacent colour.
Tone	The lightness or darkness of a colour. Colours are made darker by adding black to them to create 'shades'. Colours are made lighter by adding white to produce 'tints'.
Intensity	Colours with a strong intensity are described as 'vivid'. Colours with a weak intensity are described as 'dull', meaning subtle rather than dreary.

The colours on the right of the wheel (above) range from yellow–green to blue–violet and are known as 'cool' colours. They have a leaning towards blue.

The colours on the left of the colour wheel range from yellow–orange to red–violet and are known as 'warm' colours. They have a leaning towards red.

Complementary colour theory

Colours that are opposite each other on the colour wheel are known as complementary colours. Each primary has a complementary secondary colour and vice versa:

- orange is the complementary colour of blue
- green is the complementary of colour red
- violet is the complementary of colour yellow.

Complementary colours together: orange and blue; green and red; violet and yellow

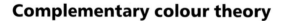

The complementary colour theory is applied extensively for creating make-up effects, including colour correction.

When they are put next to one another, complementary colours are very striking, for example orange and blue, green and red, violet and yellow.

When mixed together, the colours have a neutralising effect on each other so that the effect is duller.

Camouflage creams

These combine very dense pigments in a cream base, which completely covers all blemishes, including dark shadows under the eyes, thread veins, pigmentation marks, red birthmarks and other skin problems. They are set with a special fixing powder which is waterproof and will not rub off. Camouflage creams are produced in a range of basic colours and tints which can be blended to produce a perfect match with the skin.

Concealers

Available as cover sticks and creams, concealers mask minor, isolated skin blemishes, shadows under the eyes, spots and thread veins. They are produced in fair, medium and dark shades to blend in with tinted foundation.

Applying concealer

ACTIVITY

Activity 8.5: Colour-matching black skin

Matching black skin tones can sometimes be difficult because of the colour limitations of standard make-up ranges. Learn to mix and match products to create the effect that is best for your client. Record details of what you have used successfully for reference next time. Practise mixing and matching products to camouflage:

1 areas of skin lacking colour (hypopigmentation)

2 areas of skin with increased pigmentation (hyperpigmentation)

3 areas of skin with small, brown/black papules (dermatosis papulosa nigra).

Applying foundation

Foundation

Foundation is probably the most important product choice. The foundation provides the backdrop to the make-up. The depth and tone of the foundation colour influences the effects of all the other products that are applied. Foundation is applied to:

- enhance or improve the natural skin colour
- provide a smooth, even finish
- conceal minor blemishes
- protect the skin.

Choosing a foundation colour

The main considerations when choosing a foundation colour are the natural skin colour and hair colour. When we are born, the colours of our skin and hair are determined and, because they are natural, they are considered to be the best for us. However, we are not always satisfied with what we have got and our 'natural' look can be the last thing we want!

GOOD PRACTICE

When applying make-up to a client for the first time, always test the foundation first on the forehead or above the angle of the jaw. Some people whose skin has a slightly higher or lower pH (acidity) than normal will cause the foundation colour to go darker with an orange tone. You will need to choose a paler and 'cooler' shade of foundation to compensate for this.

Ideally, the foundation colour should match the facial skin, but this rule does not always work when the hair has been dyed a different colour or when some colour-corrective work is necessary to 'lift' the complexion or create a special effect.

Skin colours

Skin can be described as pale, medium or dark with neutral, pink, yellow, red or blue–tones. The tones are created by pigment present in the epidermis, blood circulating in the superficial blood vessels and fat contained in the skin. Skin with yellow tones is referred to as sallow or olive.

Simple rules can be followed to help choose a foundation colour for any shade of skin. Foundation colours should be chosen to:

- match or add warmth to neutral skin tones (golden, honey and tan shades)
- neutralise pink or red skin tones (beige and olive shades)
- brighten yellow or blue skin tones (rose, golden and bronze shades).

Hair colours

Hair colours range from the lightest pastel blonde, through brown to darkest blue-black. The tones of hair are usually described as ash, which is 'cold' and neutral, golden, which is yellowish, and red, which is warm.

The colour of the foundation should compensate for cold and warm tones in the hair so that there is a contrast, which adds interest to the make-up.

Cosmetic manufacturers create commercially acceptable names to describe make-up colours. The foundation colours recommended in the following table are descriptive.

GOOD PRACTICE

Sometimes clients with black skin have patchy pigmentation that is difficult to conceal with standard make-up products. A foundation with good coverage should be used, in a colour which is half-way between the lightest and darkest shade of the face.

Choosing foundation colours

| SKIN COLOUR | HAIR COLOURS | | | | | | |
| | BLONDE | | | BROWN | | | BLACK |
	ASH	GOLDEN	STRAWBERRY	ASH	GOLDEN	RED	BLUE
Pale Neutral	Light warm beige Honey beige	Creamy beige Natural beige	Creamy beige Honey beige	Light warm beige Honey beige	Natural beige	Ivory Creamy beige	Ivory Creamy beige
Sallow	Light rose beige Light warm beige	Natural beige	Natural beige Honey	Light rose beige Light warm beige	Natural beige Honey	Natural beige Light warm beige	Light rose beige
Pink	Honey beige	Natural beige	Natural beige	Natural beige	Natural beige	Natural beige	Natural beige
Medium Neutral	Honey Warm beige Rose beige	Natural beige Light tan	Creamy beige Natural beige Honey	Rose beige Warm beige Light golden	Honey beige Light tan Natural beige	Honey beige Light tan	Creamy beige Honey beige
Olive	Warm beige Light tan	Rose beige Light bronze	Natural beige Light tan	Warm beige Rose beige	Rose beige Light bronze	Light tan Warm beige	Rose beige Warm beige
Pink	Honey beige	Natural beige	Natural beige	Warm beige	Olive/beige	Olive/beige	Natural beige
Dark Olive				Bronze beige Golden tan	Bronze beige Medium tan	Warm beige Golden tan	Bronze beige Golden tan
Light brown Bronze beige				Clear golden	Light bronze Clear tan	Light bronze Clear tan	Dark warm beige Clear golden
Dark brown Dark golden				Clear bronze	Golden tan Dark tan	Clear bronze	Dark golden Clear bronze
Ebony/ Blue–black				Dark golden Clear bronze	Clear bronze Dark tan	Clear dark tan Dark golden	Bronze Dark golden

Types of foundation

Most foundations are an emulsion of oil and water, with pigments and other ingredients added to change the texture and effect of the product. Foundations are available in the following forms:

- cream
- liquid (including medicated)
- gel
- cake/compact.

Cream

Wax, powder and a humectant such as glycerol are added to the basic emulsion. Cream foundations blend easily on the skin because they are oil-based. They give medium coverage because of their powder content. Most cream foundations require setting with loose powder, although all-in-one creams are available which contain a greater proportion of powder and leave a matt finish.

Alabaster

Ivory

Honey

Caramel

Foundation colours from Virgin Vie

Cream foundations are suitable for the following skin types:

- normal
- dry
- dry parts of a combination skin
- mature.

Liquid

These are a thinner version of a cream foundation and contain a higher proportion of water. They give light-to-medium coverage. Sometimes the oil is replaced by alcohol, which evaporates, leaving powder and pigments on the skin. They are also available as mousses.

Liquid foundations provide colour without being too heavy. They are suitable for the following skin types:

- *oil-based*: normal, dry, mature
- *water-based*: combination, greasy
- *alcohol-based*: greasy, acned.

Gel

Sometimes the client may not want or need the covering properties of a standard foundation. A gel product will provide a thin translucent film of colour, which looks quite natural. Gels that produce a tanned effect are very popular during the summer and some contain sunscreens. The jelly-like consistency is produced by adding an ingredient such as gum tragacanth to a liquid foundation formulation. Gel foundations provide sheer, non-greasy coverage and are suitable for:

- tanned skin
- black, unblemished skin
- smooth, clear skin requiring a natural effect.

Cake/compact

This type of foundation is popular for home use because of its convenient compact form. Most cake foundations are compressed creams with extra powder added for good cover. More solid cake foundations, which consist mainly of powder and a binding agent such as wax or gum, are available. Cake foundations are usually applied with a damp sponge. They can be applied as thinly or thickly as required with the sponge and by adjusting the amount of water used.

Cake foundations give medium to heavy coverage and are suitable for:

- normal skin
- combination skin
- blotchy, blemished, discoloured or scarred skin
- dry skin (cream based)
- mature skin (cream based)
- greasy skin (powder based).

A PRACTICAL GUIDE TO BEAUTY THERAPY

Tips for applying foundation

- Apply foundation with clean hands or a clean cosmetic sponge: make-up wedges or flat brushes help to blend foundation over awkward areas such as around the nose and the eyes.
- Work quickly when applying foundation; if you don't, the make-up will streak where freshly applied foundation meets make-up that has already started to dry and set on the skin.
- Blend foundation outwards from the centre of the face towards the hairline; this helps to prevent a build-up of make-up in the hairline.
- Cover the eyelids and lips with foundation; this will provide a good base for the eye and lip make-up so that it adheres better.
- Blend foundation in well beneath the jawline or down the neck if that is more suitable; avoid applying foundation where it could rub off on clothing.
- Mix a little moisturiser with foundation under the eyes and over the neck if the skin is crêpey: this will thin out the foundation a little so that it does not show up the creases.
- Check the application afterwards; make sure that foundation has not built up in the eyebrows, hairline, in the naso-labial folds and the crease above the chin.
- Check for demarcation lines; the foundation should provide smooth, even coverage of the face, which blends in subtly with the skin.

GOOD PRACTICE

Foundations will deteriorate if they are not stored properly:

- keep them in a cool place, away from sunlight
- clean round the tops of tubes and bottles before replacing the lids
- always finish off one tube or jar of foundation before opening another one of the same colour
- throw away all empty containers.

When applying foundation:

- do not 'over work' the foundation; if you do it will start to streak
- do not be heavy-handed; this will disturb the make-up application and irritate the skin.

SELF-CHECKS

Foundations

1 Give three factors that are important to consider when choosing a foundation for a client.

2 What is the cause of a foundation product changing colour on the skin?

3 Suggest a suitable foundation product for each of the following: a) a young client with mild acne; b) a 50-year-old client with dry skin and dilated capillaries on the cheeks; c) a 25-year-old client with combination skin.

4 Why should foundation be applied to the lips and eyelids?

5 Describe a suitable foundation colour for each of the following: a) a client with pale, sallow skin and red hair; b) a client with medium, neutral skin and ash brown hair; c) a client with dark brown skin and black hair.

6 Give three advantages of using make-up sponges to apply foundation.

7 State three ways of avoiding a demarcation line when applying foundation.

8 Why should foundation be applied quickly?

9 State two possible reasons for a foundation product 'separating' in the bottle.

10 Give two hygiene precautions which should be taken when applying foundation.

Face powder

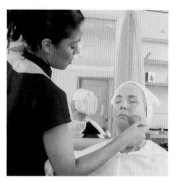

Applying face powder

Most cream-based make-up products that have been applied to the skin are set with powder. Loose powder is used for all professional make-up applications. Pressed powder is supplied for retail purchase.

The purpose of face powder is to:
- 'fix' the foundation
- reduce shine
- absorb grease
- give a smooth, matt finish
- protect the skin
- help conceal minor blemishes.

Loose powder

'Heavy' powders contain a high proportion of kaolin and chalk, and an ingredient such as titanium dioxide for giving extra cover; they are often pigmented to complement a foundation shade and provide good cover.

'Fine' powders are based on talc or mica. Most fine powders are translucent, allowing the colour of the skin or foundation to show through.

Chalk, starch and powdered silk are often added to powders to give the skin an attractive, smooth finish. Some powders contain finely ground metallic particles, which create a pearlised effect suitable for high fashion and evening wear.

Pressed powder

Pressed powder is produced in a block which fits into a compact. A binding agent, usually gum or wax, holds the particles of powder together. Pressed powder is very useful for touching up make-up during the day, but it is not used in the salon for two reasons:
- it is not fine enough to produce an even finish over freshly applied foundation
- it is not as hygienic to use as loose powder.

Choosing a face powder

Translucent powders are the most popular as they are fine and allow the foundation colour to show through. However, there are times when more dense coverage is required, for example when concealing discoloration or blemishes. In these cases, a powder should be chosen that matches the shade of the foundation.

A PRACTICAL GUIDE TO BEAUTY THERAPY

Contour cosmetics

These consist of blushers, highlighters and shaders, which are similar to foundations and face powders but with different pigments added. The pressed powder types are the most popular. Liquid, cream and gel products are more difficult to control and mistakes with stronger colours are not easily rectified. Good-quality powder products

GOOD PRACTICE

It is better to build up your application of blusher rather than risk applying too much to begin with. The only way of removing blusher is by wiping it off with clean cotton wool and this disturbs the underlying make-up.

have a creamy texture, which means they blend easily and produce an attractive, smooth finish.

Blushers add warmth to the make-up and help define facial contour; they are produced in a wide range of colours from palest pink to deep burgundy. The paler colours 'soften' the features. The brighter ones accentuate them. Blushers balance the make-up once the eye and lip cosmetics have been applied.

Shaders contain brown pigments, which produce colours ranging from medium beige to dark brown. Shaders are applied to create artificial shadows which define bone structure, or to reduce the effects of excess width or length.

Highlighters are very pale colours; they reflect light and, depending on how they are applied, emphasise features and create the illusion of extra width or length. Pearlised products are even more effective as highlighters because of their light-reflective qualities.

Blushers

There is an extensive range of blushers, which is why this type of product is so versatile. The palest silvery pinks may be used as highlighters; the corals, peaches and reds add warmth; and the deep tawny colours and bronzes are often effective as shaders.

When choosing blusher for a natural look, the colour should complement the foundation shade, and harmonise with hair colouring and clothing.

The colour of the blusher often looks quite different once it has been applied to the face. The effect created depends on the shade of the foundation or natural skin colour to which the blusher has been applied.

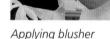

Applying blusher

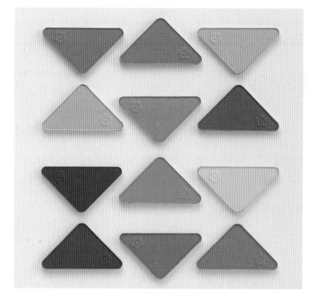

Blusher colours

REMEMBER

Black skins need strong colours of blusher. Blue-toned reds and deep pinks are ideal for applying over golden and bronze foundation shades. Orangey-red blushers are more effective on very dark blue–black skins.

Cool colours

Cool colours have quite a lot of blue pigment in them. They include the purplish and vivid pinks and some reds and bronze shades. Applied to a pale, neutral base, the blue tones in cool colours become emphasised and the overall effect is 'cold'. This may sometimes be the effect that is required when applying a high fashion or special effect make-up.

Applied to a darker, 'warmer' base, the blue tone of the blusher becomes neutralised by orange tones in the foundation and the effect is no longer cold.

Warm colours

These contain more red and yellow pigments, and include coral pinks, peaches, rusts and orangey-reds. When applied to a pale, neutral base, red and orange tones in the blusher become emphasised and the overall effect is very 'warm'. The effect can look quite natural if the blusher is a pale colour and more dramatic if it is vibrant.

When a very warm blusher colour is applied over a darker, warm-toned foundation, the make-up can become too orange or red. The result does not look as natural as when using a 'cooler' shade of blusher.

Highlighters and shaders

For highlighters and shaders to be effective, they should be significantly lighter or darker than the foundation colour without looking theatrical:

- white, ivory and pale cream highlighters produce more subtle effects on a pale skin than they do on darker skins
- when applying highlighter over a darker foundation, the colour chosen should have the same tone as the base colour. For example, very pale peach is effective as a highlighter over warm colours of foundation; very pale pink looks good over rose-toned shades
- beige is dark enough to be used as a shader over a pale base
- a darker foundation needs a deeper colour of shader.

The colour density of powder highlighters and shaders makes them more suitable for evening wear, photographic and young, fashion make-up. Subtle effects for day wear can be achieved by using different colours of foundation. These should be in the same tone as the base colour. The highlighter should be two shades lighter than the foundation, while the shader should be two shades darker.

REMEMBER

Tips for applying contour cosmetics

- Use very soft, round-ended brushes to apply contour cosmetics; square-ended brushes often produce a demarcation line, which is difficult to blend in with the surrounding make-up.
- Apply liquid and cream blushers with a rolling action of the fingers or a small sponge to prevent spreading the colour too far.
- Tap excess powder blusher off the brush on to a clean tissue before applying it to the face.
- Use upward movements when blending blusher along the cheekbones; this prevents you applying colour too far down the face and losing the desired effect.
- Regularly check that you are achieving a balanced effect when applying contour cosmetics.
- Keep contouring effects subtle for day wear when clients require a more natural look.

SELF-CHECKS

Contour cosmetics

1 What is the main difference between blushers, highlighters and shaders?

2 Why is special care required when applying contour cosmetics for day wear?

3 Name three factors that should be considered when choosing the colour of blusher for a client.

4 Suggest a suitable shade of blusher for each of the following: a) a mature client with tanned skin and grey hair; b) a young client with pale skin and ash blonde hair; c) a client with light brown skin and dark hair.

5 Why should blusher not be applied too near the eyes of a middle-aged client?

6 How should the use of contour cosmetics be adapted for a photographic or catwalk make-up?

7 Why should powder blushers be applied after the face powder?

8 State two contraindications to blusher.

Corrective make-up

There are basic guidelines that can be followed when deciding where to place blusher, shader and highlighter. These use the oval face as the perfect face and assess all other face shapes according to where they fall inside or outside the perfect oval. The other basic face shapes are round, square, heart, diamond, oblong and pear. In reality, very few people have faces that fall strictly into one category and 'fashionable' face shapes come and go, depending on who is enjoying the most glamorous media coverage at the time!

Make sure your client has realistic expectations about what can be achieved with corrective make-up. Particularly for day wear, you are very limited in what you can achieve. For more dramatic fashion make-up and photographic work, there is far more scope because you can use stronger-coloured products and lighting or camera 'tricks' to your advantage.

Face shaping

Using the 'perfect oval' theory, here are some guidelines for you to follow. In time, you will develop an 'eye' for where the products should go.

Corrective make-up

FACE SHAPE	AIM OF CORRECTIVE WORK	TECHNIQUE
Oval	To accentuate the bone structure and balance contours of the face	Blusher blended upwards along the cheekbones towards the temples. Shader applied below the cheekbones, highlighter above.
Round	To create the illusion of length down the centre of the face. To reduce width from the sides of the face and the temples	Highlighter blended subtly in a narrow strip down the centre of face. Blusher applied high on cheekbones up towards the temples. Shader blended on lower half of face over the angles of the lower jaw and over temples.
Square	To soften the jaw line and reduce width from the forehead and lower half of the face	Blend shader over the angles of the lower jaw and sides of the forehead. Apply blusher to the fullness of the cheeks or, alternatively, upwards from under the cheekbones towards the temples.
Heart-shaped	To reduce the width of the forehead and widen the lower half of face	Apply shader to the sides of the forehead and temples. Highlight the angles of the lower jaw. Apply blusher to the fullness of the cheeks or, alternatively, from under the cheekbones up towards the temples.
Diamond-shaped	To reduce the illusion of length. To widen the forehead and lower half of the face. To create the illusion of fullness to the centre of the face	Apply shader to tip of chin and narrowest part of forehead. Apply highlighter to sides of temples and lower jaw. Apply blusher to the fullness of the cheeks.
Oblong	To reduce the illusion of length. To create fullness and extra width	Apply shader to the hairline and point of the chin. Highlight the angles of the lower jaw and temples. Blend blusher to the fullness of the cheeks or along the cheekbone out towards the ears.
Pear-shaped	To create width to the forehead. To reduce the lower-half width of the face. To emphasise cheekbones	Apply highlighter to the sides of the forehead. Apply shader to the sides of the chin and angles of the lower jaw. Apply blusher to the fullness of the cheeks or, alternatively, along the cheekbones towards the temples.

Gently tapered arched
brows enhance an oval face

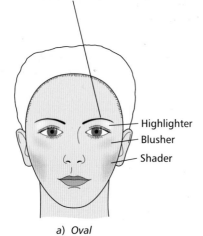

Highlighter
Blusher
Shader

a) *Oval*

Eyebrows quite thick at inner edge,
tapering to a high angular arch to
draw attention away from fullness
of face and help create illusion of
extra length

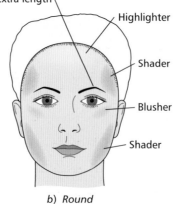

Highlighter
Shader
Blusher
Shader

b) *Round*

Smooth tapering arch softens
effect of an angular face shape

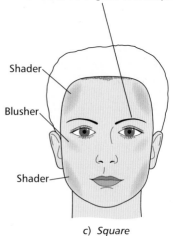

Shader
Blusher
Shader

c) *Square*

Tapered eyebrows, not too thin, help
enhance deeper and wider upper part
of face without drawing attention to
widest points of the head

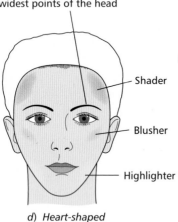

Shader
Blusher
Highlighter

d) *Heart-shaped*

Well-defined angular arch helps to create
balance with widest part of face

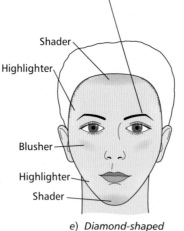

Shader
Highlighter
Blusher
Highlighter
Shader

e) *Diamond-shaped*

Brows of medium thickness kept
almost straight help to divide
length of face and draw attention
across its width

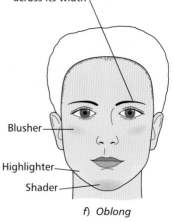

Blusher
Highlighter
Shader

f) *Oblong*

Angular brows with high arch at
outer corners help to widen the
forehead and provide balance with
heavier bone structure in lower
part of face

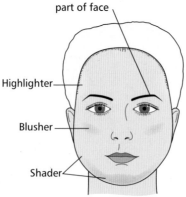

Highlighter
Blusher
Shader

g) *Pear-shaped*

Corrective face make-up

Corrective make-up for the nose

Blusher is never applied to the nose for corrective purposes. Shader and highlighter are used with discretion. Application must be very accurate and blended in well. If the products are spread too far, they may emphasise a problem rather than disguise it.

PROBLEM	TECHNIQUE
Nose too broad	Apply shader to each side of the nose
Nose too short	Apply highlighter in a narrow strip down the centre of the nose from the bridge to the tip
Nose too long	Apply shader to the tip of the nose
Bridge of nose too wide	Apply shader either side of the bridge of the nose
Bridge of nose too narrow	Apply highlighter either side of the bridge of the nose
Bump on the nose	Apply shader to the prominence of the bump
Crooked nose	Apply shader over areas that need 'straightening'

Corrective make-up for the chin and jaw line

Highlighter and shaders may be used to balance the effects of bone structure or reduced muscle tone around the lower jaw.

PROBLEM	TECHNIQUE
Double chin	Apply shader to the fullest area of the double chin, ensuring you blend it in well with the surrounding make-up
'Heavy' jaw line	Apply shader to each of the two angles of the jaw to break up the jaw line. Apply highlighter in a narrow strip down the centre of the chin
Protruding chin	Apply shader over the prominence of the chin
Receding chin	Apply highlighter over the centre of the chin
Dropped contours	Apply shader to the 'jowls' created by slack muscles over the angles of the jaw

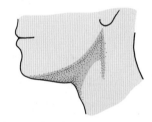

Jaw contouring

Eye cosmetics

The eyes are usually the main focus of the make-up. This is not surprising as they are the most expressive feature of our face. There is virtually no limit to the effects that can be achieved with the extensive range of eye make-up products and colours available.

Eyeshadows

Eyeshadows are used to emphasise the eyes and to co-ordinate the colour of the make-up with clothing. They are available as powders, creams, gels and soft pencils.

Powders

Powder eyeshadows have a talc base mixed with oil to give a creamy texture. They are available as loose powders or in pressed powder form. The pressed powders are easier to control. Ingredients such as bismuth oxychloride or mica produce a frosted or pearlised effect. Fine particles of gold leaf, aluminium or bronze may be included to produce a metallic effect.

Applying eyeshadow

Creams

Cream eyeshadows contain wax, oil and pigments. They are the least popular type of eyeshadow as they tend to 'melt' on the skin and settle in the creases of skin on the eyelids.

Gels

Gel shadows have a similar composition to gel foundations but with different pigments added. They produce a translucent wash of colour, which is effective on young clients wanting a more natural look.

Pencils

Eyeshadow pencils have a basic formulation of oils and waxes with pigments added. They are soft enough to be blended in like an eyeshadow if a hard line is not required. Eye pencils are popular for retail because clients find them easy to apply.

Eyeshadow colours

Different eyeshadow colours achieve different effects, depending on how and where they are applied. The client will often express a preference for a particular eyeshadow colour; this may need contrasting with other colours and using different shades to create the best effects:

- dark, muted colours, for example charcoal, brown, olive and plum, are used for defining eye contour and producing a sophisticated look. They are particularly effective on clients who have dark hair colouring and dark eyes. Applied carefully, with a fine brush, they can also be used to produce subtle eye-lining effects on people with fairer colouring, particularly more mature clients

- pastel colours, for example pale blue, light aqua, pale green and peach, produce very soft effects, particularly when applied to people with blonde or grey hair. They emphasise the colour of the eyes when applied in the same tone

- very pale colours, for example white, pearl and cream, have highlighting effects when contrasted with darker eyeshadows. They are applied to emphasise the arch of the brow and to help make the eyes appear bigger

- soft, muted shades, for example grey, beige, sage and mauve, produce more subtle effects than the 'purer' eyeshadow colours. They are used when a more natural effect is required
- bright colours, for example blue, green, yellow, violet and red, are fun to use in young fashion or glamour make-up if the client has the confidence to wear them, but they can look very hard and unattractive on more mature or sophisticated clients. Some bright colours are suitable to be worn as eyeliners where they complement the eyeshadow scheme.

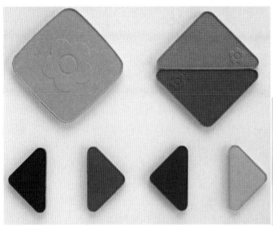

Colour shades

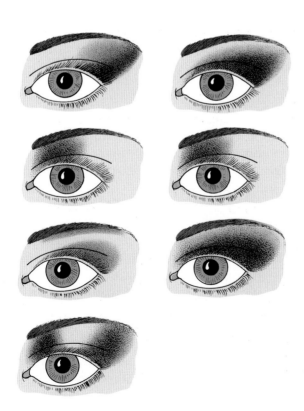

Some eyeshadow effects

REMEMBER

Do not overload the applicator with eyeshadow; besides being wasteful, excess powder could enter the eye or fall onto the face, spoiling the rest of the make-up.

Do not over-stretch the skin around the eyes.

REMEMBER

Tips for applying eyeshadow

- Use clean, sterilised brushes or sponge applicators.
- Support the skin and protect the surrounding make-up with tissue.
- Blend the product well so that no hard demarcation lines are produced.
- Check that the eyeshadow application is 'balanced' on both eyes.
- Make sure the client's eyes are kept closed or that they are not looking directly at a bright light when applying the eyeshadow.
- If applying eyeshadow beneath the eyes, ask the client to look away from the brush to prevent the eyes from blinking or watering.
- Apply pink and lilac eyeshadow colours only when the eyes are bright and clear; these colours emphasise tired eyes and make them look sore.
- Apply soft, muted or pastel colours of eyeshadow to more mature clients; the eyes lose some of their colour with age and stronger colours look too heavy.

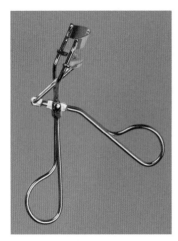

Eyelash curlers

Curling the eyelashes

Many people like to use eyelash curlers even if they are not wearing eye make-up. They help to make the lashes appear longer and are particularly effective for short, straight lashes. It is best to use eyelash curlers before applying mascara as, if used afterwards, the lashes may stick to the curlers and be pulled out when they are released.

To curl the lashes:

- position the upper lashes between the upper and lower pressing edges of the curlers
- squeeze the edges of the curlers together and 'hold' for 10 seconds
- gently release the curlers from the lashes and repeat if necessary.

REMEMBER

If strip false eyelashes are to be worn, they should be applied after the make-up has been completed (see page 293).

HEALTH MATTERS

Eyelash curlers must be cleaned and disinfected before use. Any dirt or debris on the edges could easily enter the eye and cause an irritation or infection.

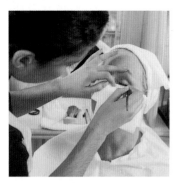

Applying eyeliner

Eyeliner

Eyeliner is used for emphasising the shape of the eye by framing the eyelid and accentuating the lash line. Colours that blend in with the mascara look most natural. Very dark colours of eyeliner are suitable only for people with dark hair or for achieving dramatic fashion effects. An eyeliner that is in the same tone but darker than the eyeshadow will give a softer look.

Cake

Cake eyeliner is the most versatile of the eye-lining products but it is also the most difficult to apply. Cake eyeliners have a similar formulation to pressed powder eyeshadows, but they are wetted before being applied to the eyelids with a fine, tapered brush. The line produced can be made hard or soft by adjusting the amount of water used.

Liquid

Liquid eyeliner is a gum solution containing pigments and is applied with a brush. Liquid eyeliners also come in refillable applicators, which have a soft, pointed tip for precise application.

Pencils

Eyeliner pencils have a basic formulation of oils and waxes with pigments added. They are produced in a wide range of colours and some are soft enough to be blended like an eyeshadow if a hard line is not required.

Kohl (kajal)

Kohl is soft, black and waxy, usually in a pencil that is applied to the inner rim of the lower eyelid. It enhances the white of the eye and produces a sophisticated make-up look.

Lining the eyelid inside the lash line makes the eyes appear smaller; dark eyeshadow and eyeliner are usually applied to the upper and lower lids to compensate for this.

1 Eyes look rounder when the line is deeper in the middle

2 A softened upwardly tapered line provides a more youthful 'lift' to the eye

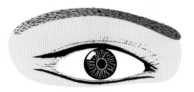

3 A dramatic sweep above and below the eye makes the eye look larger, provided that the lines do not meet and 'close up' the eye

4 The upper and lower line are softened with a clean damp brush – providing more subtle emphasis

5 Fifties 'flick' for a fashionable effect

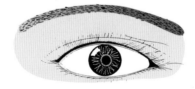

6 A fine tapered line to provide 'natural' enhancement

Different eye-lining effects

Mascara

Mascara is used to accentuate the eyes by darkening and thickening the lashes. Mascaras are produced in standard colours of black, brown and grey, and also in fashion colours such as violet, green, blue and pink.

Block

Block mascara has been available for a long time but became less popular when automatic brush and wand mascaras appeared on the market. Block mascaras are currently regaining their popularity in salons because they are applied with a flat brush which is easy to clean and disinfect. The brush is used wet to work the mascara up into a creamy consistency before applying it to the lashes. The basic formula for a block mascara combines waxes and pigments in a soap base.

Liquid

Liquid mascaras have been modified to produce a wide range of products with special features, for example waterproof, smudge proof, lash-lengthening, extra-thickening, protein enriched. The basic liquid mascara contains pigments and synthetic resins in water or alcohol and water, with castor oil added to prevent the film of mascara from becoming brittle. Lash-building ingredients include filaments of nylon, silk or even cashmere to make the lashes look thicker and longer. The automatic brush applicator supplied with a liquid mascara is not suitable for general salon use as it cannot be cleaned and disinfected effectively. A disposable mascara brush is required; alternatively a client may bring their own mascara to be applied in the salon.

Choosing a colour

The mascara should be the darkest of the eye make-up colours applied. For a natural effect, it should tone in with the hair colour.

HAIR COLOUR	MASCARA COLOUR
White	Grey
Grey	Grey
Blonde	Brown or grey
Auburn	Brown, brownish black
Brown	Brownish black
Black	Black

Tips for applying mascara

- Instruct the client to relax their eyelids when applying mascara to the upper eyelashes.
- Lift the skin of the eyelids from underneath the brow to prevent wet mascara touching the face make-up.
- Apply mascara downwards over the upper lashes, then upwards from underneath to give maximum coverage and curl; do not miss the shorter hairs at the inner corner of the eyelids.
- Place a tissue underneath the lower lashes before applying mascara to them; excess mascara will go on the tissue and not on the skin.
- Instruct the client to look away from the brush when applying mascara to the lower lashes.
- Build up mascara in fine coats that are allowed to dry between each application; this will help prevent the lashes from clogging together.
- Separate the lashes afterwards with an eyelash comb if a more natural effect is required.

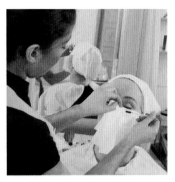

Applying mascara

Do not apply mascara if there are signs of infection or if the eyes are feeling sensitive. Make sure the hand is supported when applying mascara so that you do not penetrate inside the eye area with the mascara.

Eyebrows

Eyebrow cosmetics are used to strengthen the colour of the brows and define their shape. They include pencils, liquids, powders and eyebrow mascara. Eyebrow pencils have a similar formulation to eyeliner pencils, but have to be harder so that they can be sharpened to a point and applied with very fine feathery strokes. Eyebrow pencils are produced in a limited range of hair colours, for example grey, brown and black.

Eyebrow powders have a similar formulation to eyeshadow powders and are applied with a clean brush. They can be used wet or dry depending on the effect required.

Applying eyebrow powder

Do not apply eyebrow pencil in a heavy, unbroken line.

Look at the colour tone of the client's hair before choosing the eyebrow colour: a reddish-brown pencil would not look right on a client with ash blond hair.

Do not apply an eyebrow cosmetic that is too dark as this will spoil the balance of the make-up.

Tips for applying eyebrow cosmetics

- Brush the eyebrows into shape before applying the pencil or powder.
- Sharpen the eyebrow pencil before use.
- Try to simulate the natural hairs by following their direction of growth.
- Choose a colour that looks natural with the hair colour and complements the rest of the make-up.

Corrective eye make-up

As with all corrective work, the main aim is to achieve 'balance'. This means creating the correct proportions between the upper eyelid and the area between the eye socket and the eyebrow. The eyebrow shape must complement the shape of the face and contribute to the overall effect of the eye make-up.

Close-set eyes – picture (a)

Attention needs drawing away from the centre of the face:

- remove excess brow hairs above the bridge of the nose; the space between the eyebrows should be a little wider than normal
- avoid using strong or pearlised eyeshadows on the inner corners of the eyelid; use pale, matt products to 'open up' the space without drawing attention to it
- focus attention from the centre of the eyelid towards and beyond the outer corner of the eye by using darker eyeshadows, eyeliner and eyebrow cosmetics
- create a gentle 'lift' to the eyebrow and apply highlighter underneath
- eyeshadow and eyeliner can be applied underneath and beyond the outer corner of the eye if the condition of the skin is suitable.

Wide-set eyes – picture (b)

Attention needs to be drawn towards the centre of the face:

- use eyebrow pencil skilfully to make the brows appear closer together; do not extend the eyebrow line beyond the outer corner of the eye
- apply strong or pearlised eyeshadow colours on the inner eyelid; use paler matt products from the centre to the outer eyelid
- extend a thin eye line beyond the inner corner of the eye; do not extend the eye line beyond the outer corner of the eye
- eyeliner and eyeshadow can be applied underneath and beyond the inner corner of the eye if the skin is suitable.

Pale matt colours to open up
space between eyes

Highlighter

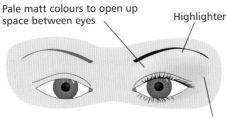

Eyebrows, eyeliner and eyeshadows
extended beyond outer corner of eye

a) Close-set

Eyebrows drawn slightly
inside normal guidelines

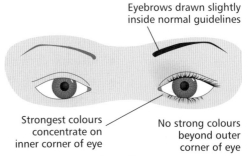

Strongest colours
concentrate on
inner corner of eye

No strong colours
beyond outer
corner of eye

b) Wide-set

Gently tapered eyebrow arch

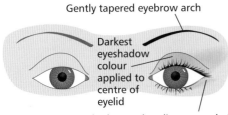

Darkest
eyeshadow
colour
applied to
centre of
eyelid

Eyeshadow and eyeliner extended
beyond outer corner of eye

c) Round or prominent

Highlighter

Darkest eyeshadow blended over fullness of overhanging
lid and blended up to the highlighter with a medium shade

d) Overhanging lids

Highlighter

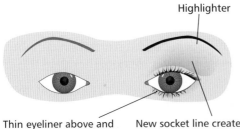

Thin eyeliner above and
slightly below eyelid,
softened with
eyeshadow

New socket line created
with dark shadow slightly
above natural socket line

e) Small or deep-set

Highlighter

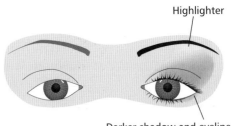

Darker shadow and eyeliner
blended upwards and outwards
inside outer corner of eye

f) Downward slanting

Darker socket line created above
natural socket line, blended up
towards highlighter

Highlighter

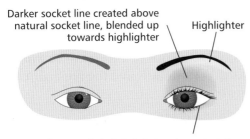

Eyeliner applied slightly below lower lash line,
softened with eyeshadow

g) Narrow

Socket shading above
the natural socket line
creates contour and
depth to the eyelids

Matt neutral eyeshadow
blended above the middle
third of eye socket produces
more rounded effect

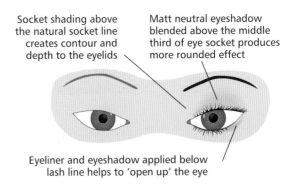

Eyeliner and eyeshadow applied below
lash line helps to 'open up' the eye

h) Oriental

Different eye shapes

Round or prominent eyes – picture (c)

By reducing the depth of the eyelid and creating extra width, the eyes appear more 'sultry':

- avoid creating a 'round' arch to the eyebrow; a gentle tapering curve is more flattering
- use the darkest eyeshadow over the deepest (centre) part of the eyelid
- apply quite a thick eyeliner to the upper eyelid; taper the line upwards and outwards before reaching the outer corner of the eye
- if suitable, extend an eye line below the eye from the centre of the lower eyelid beyond the outer corner of the eye; do not allow this line to meet the upper line
- blend a dark eyeshadow over the lower eye line to soften it
- if appropriate, kohl can be applied inside the lower eyelid
- individual false eyelashes can be attached at the outer corners of the eyes to draw attention to the width rather than the depth of the eyes.

Overhanging lids – picture (d)

The aim of the make-up is to reduce the fullness of skin which creates the 'overhanging' effect:

- create a gentle 'lift' to the eyebrow and apply highlighter immediately below the arch, without spreading it too far, over the area of fullness
- apply a pearlised pale-coloured eyeshadow to the upper eyelid
- use a dark, neutral-coloured eyeshadow to shade the 'fullest' area of skin hanging over the eyelid
- blend the dark colour upwards into the highlighted area beneath the arch of the brow; you may wish to use a slightly paler shade rather than the darkest colour for blending.

Small or deep-set eyes – picture (e)

The shading of the eye socket needs creating above the natural socket line to give the appearance of more depth to the upper eyelid. This is enhanced by creating a new 'lash line' below the eyes:

- create an arch to the eyebrow and highlight underneath to 'open up' the area
- apply a pale colour, which may be pearlised, to the upper eyelid
- ask the client to open their eyes and apply dark eyeshadow above the natural socket line, following the line created by the tips of the eyelashes when the eyes are opened wide; blend the dark shadow upwards into the highlighter, which has been applied below the arch of the brow
- apply a thin eye line to the outer half of the upper eyelid
- if appropriate, create a thin eye line slightly below the natural lash line and soften with a blending of eyeshadow
- build up the lashes with three or four coats of mascara.

Downward slanting eyes – picture (f)

The aim of the make-up is to produce a 'lift' to the outer corners of the eyes, which detracts from the effect of 'droopiness':

- create a 'lift' to the end of the eyebrow and highlight underneath
- apply a pale eyeshadow to the inner third of the eyelid only
- apply a darker eyeshadow to the outer two-thirds of the upper eyelid; blend upwards and outwards before reaching the outer corners of the eyelids
- follow with eyeliner the line created by the eyeshadow
- blend socket shading up and outwards from the outer third of the eye socket
- build up mascara on the lashes located on the outer third of the upper eyelid; do not apply mascara to the lower eyelashes.

Narrow eyes – picture (g)

By enhancing the depth of the eyelids at their 'fullest', the eyes will appear rounder and bigger:

- apply the lightest shade of eyeshadow to the centre of the eyelid
- apply a medium shade of eyeshadow to the inner third of the eyelid and the darkest shade to the outer third
- recreate the socket line above the natural one with a dark eyeshadow; do not extend this shading beyond the outer corner of the eye
- apply a matt, neutral grey or brown shade to the area between the socket line and the eyebrow
- apply a small amount of highlighter below the arch of the brow
- if the surrounding skin is suitable, apply eyeliner slightly below the natural lower lash line; soften with eyeshadow
- build up the lashes with three or four coats of mascara: the lashes may be curled beforehand with eyelash curlers to 'open up' the eyes.

Oriental eyes – picture (h)

The narrow lids are often not apparent because they are deep-set and dominated by the area between the socket and eyebrow. Socket shading needs creating above the natural eye sockets to create contour and depth to the eyelids:

- recreate the socket line above the natural one with a medium to dark eyeshadow; do not extend this shading beyond the outer corner of the eye
- apply a matt, neutral grey or brown shade to the area between the new socket line and eyebrow, concentrating over the middle third of the socket line above the eye; this will help to produce a more rounded effect
- balance the shape and thickness of the eyebrow to produce a gentle arch rather than an angular or rounded eyebrow shape
- apply eyeliner slightly below the lower lash line and soften with a medium, muted eyeshadow colour do not extend this beyond the outer corner of the eye
- use eyelash curlers if the lashes are long enough apply; several coats of mascara to the upper and lower lashes.

Make-up for people who wear glasses

The effects of glasses on the appearance of the face depend on the design of the frames and the colour and type of lenses.

Celebrity, made up, wearing glasses

Mature woman, made up, wearing glasses

Frames

Heavy frames can take bolder eye make-up and a strong lipstick colour to provide balance. Lightweight, steel frames look lost in front of a dark, heavy make-up. Keep eye make-up colours soft but make good use of eyeliner, mascara and eyebrow pencil for defining the eyes and brow shape.

The make-up scheme should complement the colour of the frames. Muted shades of eyeshadow are preferable if the frames are bright.

Lenses

People who are short-sighted wear glasses that enable them to focus at a greater distance; the lenses in their glasses make the eyes look smaller. Long-sighted people wear glasses that help them to focus on closer objects; the lenses in their glasses make their eyes appear bigger. Corrective techniques may be necessary to compensate for the effects of lenses on the appearance of the eyes.

Tinted lenses change the effects of eye make-up colours. Stronger and more contrasting colours may be needed to provide definition.

Make-up for people who wear contact lenses

Some clients prefer to keep their contact lenses in place when having make-up applied. Others would rather take the lenses out and leave them soaking in their special solution until they can be replaced. Whatever the client decides, the therapist should take the following precautions to prevent irritating the eye area:

- be particularly gentle when working on the skin around the eyes
- take care not to touch the eyes with make-up applicators
- avoid using heavy creams around the eyes as these creams could melt and smear the natural lens
- instruct the client to keep their eyes closed when applying powder products
- do not create dust in the atmosphere when transferring powder from the container
- apply only creamy-textured pressed powder eyeshadows, not loose, dry ones
- for extra control, powder eyeshadows can be applied with a slightly damp brush
- use block or liquid mascara which does not have a high alcohol content
- avoid using mascara that contains filaments.

A PRACTICAL GUIDE TO BEAUTY THERAPY

HEALTH MATTERS

It is very uncomfortable to have a small particle of make-up trapped between the natural lens and a contact lens. Make sure you do everything you can to prevent this happening to your client.

Lip cosmetics

These are available as lipsticks, glosses and pencils, and are used to define the mouth by adding colour and enhancing the shape of the lips. The products share the same basic ingredients of oils, fats and waxes, but in different proportions. The vast range of colours of lip cosmetics are derived from pigments that are safe to eat! Lip cosmetics protect the lips against the effects of the environment.

Types of lip cosmetics

Lipstick

The hardness of lipstick is due to its high wax content. Creamy-textured lipsticks contain softening ingredients such as lanolin, mineral oils and petroleum jelly. Mica or bismuth oxychloride is included for a pearlised effect. Lipstick is applied with a brush to outline the mouth and to spread the colour evenly over the lips.

Lip balms are produced in lipstick form. They are softening and moisturising and contain a sun block which helps to prevent the lips from drying or chapping during extremes of weather. Some lipsticks combine colour, gloss, care and protection.

Lip gloss

This has a gel consistency produced by mixing bentonite clay with mineral oils. Lip gloss may be clear or coloured. It gives a temporary 'wet' shine to the lips and can be applied over lipstick or on its own for a more natural look. Lip gloss is also available as a liquid or in lipstick form.

Lip pencil

This may be used to outline the lips before applying lipstick and is a popular retail line. Lip pencils contain a high proportion of hard waxes, which means that they are less likely to smudge than softer lip cosmetics. They are very useful for correcting lip shapes and preventing the lipstick colour from 'bleeding' into the fine lines around the mouth.

Lipstick sealer

Usually produced in liquid form, the colourless sealer is applied with a brush. It is designed to keep the lipstick in place and prevent it from fading and smudging.

GOOD PRACTICE

Always try and link sell lipsticks and nail enamels. Most cosmetic ranges offer them in matching colours, which is ideal for full colour co-ordination.

Choosing a lipstick colour

A lipstick should be chosen which balances the colour scheme of the make-up with the clothes that are being worn:

- strong and vibrant lipstick colours draw attention to the mouth and lower part of the face; they should be avoided if the teeth are discoloured or if the skin around the mouth and chin is blemished
- a deeper colour of lipstick or lip pencil should be used to outline the new lip shape if corrective work is being done
- very pale, pearlised lipsticks give fullness to the lips; lip gloss has a similar effect
- deep blue-toned reds, dark purplish-pinks and bronze shades help to reduce fullness; they are particularly effective when used on black clients.

Corrective lip make-up

Always apply foundation and powder to the lips before carrying out corrective work.

1 Thin lips: draw a lip line slightly outside the natural shape

2 Full lips: blot out natural lip line with foundation and powder. Use dark colours to draw just inside the natural shape

3 Drooping mouth: build up the corners of the upper lip slightly. Join with lower lip line

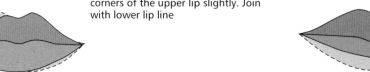

4 Asymmetrical lips: build up lip line where necessary to achieve balance and symmetry

5 Unbalanced lips: draw slightly outside the natural lip line as required

 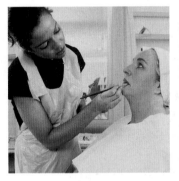 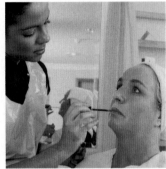

1 *Outlining the mouth*   **2** *Applying lipstick*   **3** *Applying lip gloss*

SELF-CHECKS

Lip cosmetics

1 State three factors that influence the choice of lipstick colour for a client.

2 Give two contraindications to lipstick.

3 State two hygiene precautions which should be taken when using a lip pencil.

4 Explain the procedure for correcting the shape of the mouth with lip make-up.

5 Describe how a lip brush should be cleaned after use.

Make-up for different client groups

**African-Caribbean
(Bello)**

1 *Bello before make-up is applied*

2 *Concealer applied*

3 *Foundation and face powder applied*

4 *Blusher applied*

5 *Eyeshadows applied*

6 *Mascara, eyeliner and eyebrow
powder applied*

7 *Mouth outlined, lipstick and lip
gloss applied*

8 *Evening make-up*

Bello's make-up palette

MAKE-UP ITEM	TYPE	COLOUR	NOTES
Concealer	Cream	Medium beige	Applied above and below eyes to disguise very dark pigmentation. A lighter colour would create too much of a contrast
Foundation	Liquid	Brown blaze	Matches Bello's natural skin colour very well
Face powder	Loose	Deep bronze	Good match for foundation. Bello needs powder, not just to set the foundation but also to counteract the natural shine related to her oily skin type
Blusher	Powder	Mauve passion	The blue tones in the blusher are neutralised by the orange tones in the foundation; the effect is, therefore, no longer 'cold'
Eyeshadow 1	Powder	Pearl grey	Provides the 'backcloth' (base) for the rest of the eye make-up, which appears much paler on Bello than if it was applied on a paler skin. The base colour provides a pale, neutral background which does not interfere with the colour and tones of products applied afterwards
Eyeshadow 2 (highlighter)	Powder	White frost	Applied over the eyelid; acts as a highlighter and helps to 'balance' this area with the space between Bello's eyes and eyebrows. The 'true' colours of the eyeshadows show up better when applied over white
Eyeshadow 3 (main colour)	Powder	Lavender mist	Bello's choice, which complements her clothing and sets the colour tone for the rest of the eye make-up
Eyeshadow 4 (contour)	Powder	Deep taupe	A blue-toned browny colour which adds depth to the eye socket, thereby helping to make the eyes appear bigger and harmonising with the blue tones of the lavender main colour
Eyebrow cosmetic	Powder	Dark brown	Applied with a narrow brush for further definition to balance the rest of the eye make-up
Eyeliner	Cake	Black	A very fine line applied at the base of the lashes emphasises the shape of Bello's eyes and helps make her eyelashes appear thicker
Mascara	Liquid, lash thickening	Black	The best choice for Bello's colouring, it 'frames' the rest of the eye make-up
Lip liner	Pencil	Maple	Chosen to tone in with the preferred main lip colour to avoid an obvious outline
Lip colour	Lipstick	Mocha veil	This colour looks really good on Bello and complements her subtle eye make-up. A brighter colour would 'shout' and spoil the effect
Lip gloss	Gel	Natural	Bello has got wonderful, pearly white teeth, which deserve to be shown off! Natural lip gloss gives an attractive 'wet' shine which does not interfere with the main lip colour

Asian (Vena)

1 *Vena before make-up is applied*

2 *Concealer applied*

3 *Foundation and face powder applied*

4 *Blusher applied*

5 *Eyeshadows applied*

6 *Mascara, eyeliner and eyebrow powder applied*

7 *Mouth outlined, lipstick and lip gloss applied*

8 *Evening make-up*

A PRACTICAL GUIDE TO BEAUTY THERAPY

MAKE-UP ITEM	TYPE	COLOUR	NOTES
Concealer	Cream	Medium beige	Applied around the eyes and along the naso-labial folds to lighten areas of natural shading
Foundation Face powder	Cake/compact N/A	Almond beige	Vena does not usually wear foundation. She is very active (exercise coach), has good skin and likes a 'natural' effect. An all-in-one foundation contains enough powder to set the make-up without Vena feeling 'made up'. It also effectively covers up one or two minor skin blemishes on her cheek
Blusher also	Powder	Sandalwood	This blusher complements the chosen lipstick well and Vena's fabulous dark brown eyes
Eyeshadow 1 (base)	Powder	Spice	This provides the golden undertones for the rest of the eye make-up
Eyeshadow 2 (highlighter)	Powder	Golden light	A very pale golden colour, which emphasises the brow bone
Eyeshadow 3 (main colour)	Powder	Jade	A 'first' for Vena! The rich dark green works well with the other colours and enhances Vena's dark brown eyes
Eyeshadow 4 (contour)	Powder	Terracotta	Appears less 'red' on Vena than it would on a paler client. The effect is warm brown, which gives contour
Eyebrow cosmetic	Pencil	Black	Used only for filling in gaps in Vena's eyebrows to enhance their shape
Eyeliner	Cake	Charcoal	Eyeliner has a significant effect when converting Vena's make-up for evening wear. Eyeliner blended slightly upwards and outwards emphasises the almond shape of her eyes
Mascara	Liquid, lash lengthening	Black	Completes the dramatic effect of the rest of the eye make-up
Lip liner	Pencil	Pumpkin	The nearest shade to the main lip colour. Helps prevent the lipstick 'smudging'
Lip colour	Lipstick	Laser	Vena is feeling quite ambitious and has agreed to a lipstick colour she has not worn before. A reddish brown, brighter than Vena would normally wear but perfect within the overall colour scheme and draws attention to her lovely teeth
Lip gloss	Gel	Natural	Adds a final touch of glamour

Caucasian (Claire)

1 *Claire before make-up is applied*

2 *Concealer applied*

3 *Foundation and face powder applied*

4 *Blusher applied*

5 *Eyeshadows applied*

6 *Mascara, eyeliner and eyebrow powder applied*

7 *Mouth outlined, lipstick and lip gloss applied*

8 *Evening make-up*

MAKE-UP ITEM	TYPE	COLOUR	NOTES
Concealer	Cover stick	Ivory	Claire is very fair and the skin on her chin occasionally 'flares up'. No infection is present so the palest concealer is used to tone down the area
Foundation	Cream	Beige diaphane	A pale beige foundation is best for Claire. Anything warmer will look orange on her fair skin. Beige is a 'flat', neutral colour which provides a good base for other coloured cosmetics
Face powder	Loose	Translucent	A light, transparent powder is applied, which will not add unwanted colour
Blusher	Powder	Soft rose	This soft shade adds warmth to the make-up without providing too strong a contrast to the pale foundation
Eyeshadow 1 (base)	Powder	Ice white	Enhances the eye area and shows up the 'true' colours of eyeshadows applied on top
Eyeshadow 2 (highlighter)	Powder	Rose white	A slight hint of pink softens the highlighting effect when applied to the brow bone and harmonises with the chosen colour scheme
Eyeshadow 3 (main colour)	Powder	Light grape	The colour enhances Claire's lovely, clear blue eyes. It also picks up the pink tones in the blusher and highlighter. The eyeshadow is applied with a damp brush as a precaution against particles falling into her eyes and getting trapped underneath her contact lenses
Eyeshadow 4 (contour)	Powder	Plum	The natural choice for providing 'depth' in the eye socket and beneath the outer corners of the eyes
Eyebrow cosmetic	Pencil	Hazel	The pencil is chosen to match the natural colour of Claire's eyebrows. Any darker would overpower the soft, muted eyeshadow colours
Eyeliner	Cake	Plum	A very fine line is applied in keeping with the colour theme of the eye make-up. A thicker line would virtually cover her lids and make Claire's eyes appear smaller
Mascara	Block	Dark brown	Darker than the eyeshadow colours but not too dark for Claire's colouring
Lip liner	Lipstick	Brick	Applied very carefully with a lip brush, creating a slightly 'fuller' effect to the upper lip by outlining slightly outside the natural lipline
Lip colour	Lipstick	Rose beige	This colour has just enough pink in it to carry through the theme without looking 'too' pink
Lip gloss	Gel	Strawberry pink	A slightly tinted lip gloss adds the finishing touch and Claire looks and feels wonderful!

Oriental (Emmaline)

1 *Emmaline before make-up is applied*

2 *Concealer applied*

3 *Foundation and face powder applied*

4 *Blusher applied*

5 *Eyeshadows applied*

6 *Mascara, eyeliner and eyebrow powder applied*

7 *Mouth outlined, lipstick and lip gloss applied*

8 *Evening make-up*

Emmaline's make-up palette

MAKE-UP ITEM	TYPE	COLOUR	NOTES
Concealer	Cream	Light	A small amount is applied underneath Emmaline's eyes to counteract slight shadows
Foundation	Liquid	Blonde	The foundation matches the colour of Emmaline's fair skin, which is very striking in contrast to her shiny, black hair
Face powder	Loose	Translucent	Emmaline has a flawless skin which shows through the translucent powder
Blusher	Powder	Mauve passion	This colour looks much less 'blue' when applied over the slightly yellow tone of Emmaline's foundation
Eyeshadow 1 (base)	Powder	White frost	Applied with care over the eyelids, which are characteristically narrow, avoiding the space between the eye socket and brow bone
Eyeshadow 2 (highlighter)	Powder	Mint	Palest green applied over the eyelid provides the main colour theme
Eyeshadow 3 (main colour)	Powder	Jade	Blended above the eye socket and underneath the eye, slightly away from the lash line, to help 'open up' the eye
Eyeshadow 4 (contour)	Powder	Teal	Applied sparingly, slightly above the natural socket line, to create contour and depth to the eyelids
Eyebrow cosmetic	Pencil	Dark brown	A well-defined eyebrow shape accentuates Emmaline's beautiful eyes and also helps to take up space in this slightly 'top heavy' area
Eyeliner	Cake	Black	The line on the upper lid is tapered up and out, slightly beyond the outer corner of the eye. Underneath, the eyeliner is applied in the same way, slightly away from the base of the lashes to help 'open up' the eye area. The upper and lower lines must not meet as this will have the opposite effect
Mascara	Liquid, lash lengthening	Black	Framing the eyes with long lashes helps to make the eyes look bigger
Lip liner	Pencil	Maple	The lip liner is the same colour as the chosen lipstick and is used to accentuate the shape of Emmaline's mouth
Lip colour	Lipstick	Maple	There is just a hint of pink in what is, essentially, a light-brown lipstick. This completes the 'colours of nature' theme chosen for Emmaline
Lip gloss	Gel	Strawberry pink	The slightly tinted, high gloss shine puts the finishing touches to the make-up

HEALTH MATTERS

An adverse skin reaction whilst applying the make-up could be caused by an ingredient contained in one of the products. If left untreated, a much more severe reaction could occur.

HEALTH MATTERS

Irritation, itchiness and erythema (redness) are all signs that the product must be removed and a soothing preparation applied. Details of any adverse reactions during treatment must be written on the client's record card with a note of the action taken.

REMEMBER

The Cosmetic Products (Safety) Regulations 1989 are concerned with **product safety**, and require that cosmetics have safe formulations and are tested as being safe for use.

HEALTH MATTERS

In the EU and USA, the law requires cosmetic companies to conduct very strict safety tests on the materials they use to formulate products. Nevertheless, there will always be someone, somewhere, who is allergic to a substance that most other people tolerate without any problems.

Contra-actions to make-up

Occasionally, the make-up treatment has to be interrupted and remedial action taken. These are called **contra-actions to make-up**. Here are some examples of what can happen:

- the client's eyes may start watering
- the client may complain of itchiness and the skin may appear red and blotchy
- excessive perspiration may appear on the face.

Adverse skin reactions

Some of the substances that are known to cause adverse reactions in people who are hypersensitive are:

- *lanolin*: a fatty substance similar to sebum, which coats sheep's wool and is used as a softening ingredient in creams
- *eosin*: a red staining pigment contained in some lip cosmetics
- *mineral oils*: examples are oleic acid and butyl stearate
- *paraben*: an antiseptic ingredient, used as a preservative in cosmetics
- *perfumes*: particularly those containing bergamot, lavender and cedarwood
- *alcohol*: a strong grease solvent and astringent used in cosmetics and skin-care products
- *cobalt blues*: pigments used to produce eye make-up colours
- *pearlising agents*: ingredients that give make-up products an iridescent (light-reflective) effect
- *gums*: adhesive and binding ingredients contained in cosmetics.

Perfume is added to most cosmetics and is a common sensitiser. This means that it can cause an allergic reaction. People who have an allergy to perfume should not buy a product before checking the ingredients on the label or package. From January 1997, manufacturers are required, by law, to list all the ingredients of a product.

Hypo-allergenic cosmetics

Hypo-allergenic cosmetics are available for people who are irritated by, or are very sensitive to, standard make-up products. They do not contain perfume, and fewer pigments and preservatives are used. The colour range of hypo-allergenic cosmetics is usually more limited than with other make-up ranges.

Eye irritation

REMEMBER

Make sure your client does not look directly into the light when having make-up applied. This is another cause of watery eyes.

Very strict testing is carried out to ensure that eye make-up products will not irritate the eye or surrounding skin. Only 'safe' pigments are used, but, even so, some of them may cause a reaction in people who are hypersensitive. If the eyes are watery and the skin of the eyelid is irritated, this indicates an adverse reaction to a cosmetic ingredient. The product must be removed and cotton wool pads soaked in cool water or witch hazel should be applied to soothe the eyes. If there is no skin reaction but the eyes are watery, the cause is more likely to be a small particle of make-up which has entered the eye and caused surface irritation.

HEALTH MATTERS

A small speck of make-up in the eye will usually filter itself out naturally as the eye waters. Sit the client upright, advise them to keep their eyes closed and use a soft tissue, gently, to absorb excess fluid at the inside and outside corners of eye. If this is not effective, use the first-aid treatment for 'objects in the eye' (see page 48).

REMEMBER

Your portfolio should show evidence of your ability to adapt your make-up skills to any age group, skin colour and occasion.

Excessive perspiration on the face

It is important to keep the skin as cool as possible during the make-up. A warm skin interferes with the effects of the make-up application. If your client appears to be perspiring excessively during the make-up treatment, check first that they are not feeling unwell (they might have a temperature). If the client feels fine but rather warm, make them more comfortable by loosening any garments or towels around their neck, increase the amount of cool air into the room if possible and offer them a cool drink. The make-up may be blotted carefully with a soft, fine tissue and the skin cooled by gently pressing cold, damp pads over the face make-up or by spraying with a fine mist of cold water.

SELF-CHECKS

Contra-actions

1 Give two possible causes of skin irritation during a make-up treatment.

2 Explain the procedure to be taken if a client suffers extreme eye irritation during a make-up treatment.

3 Name two pieces of legislation relating to the safety of cosmetics.

4 List three ingredients of cosmetics which are known to cause adverse reactions in some people. Name the type of cosmetic product that may contain each ingredient.

5 Why is it important to keep a record of any adverse reactions experienced by the client during a make-up treatment?

6 How are hypo-allergenic cosmetics different from standard make-up products?

7 Why is it important to keep the skin cool during a make-up treatment?

8 State three ways of preventing the client from getting too warm during a make-up treatment.

9 What action should be taken if a client rings you to complain of an adverse reaction to a make-up product purchased from the salon?

10 A client returns to the salon with a lipstick she purchased from you two days earlier. The barrel of the lipstick is faulty and cannot be used. Who is legally responsible and what action should be taken?

False eyelashes

False eyelashes are used extensively when applying make-up for fashion photography and catwalk modelling. They are also popular for producing glamour effects when the client's natural lashes need more enhancement than can be achieved with mascara or eyelash tinting.

There are two basic types of false eyelashes:

- *temporary*: supplied as pre-shaped strips which are attached with a relatively weak, latex-based adhesive to the edge of the eyelid
- *semi-permanent*: available as individual lashes or in small clusters of two or three which are attached at the base of the natural lashes with a special strong adhesive.

Contraindications to false eyelashes

False eyelashes must not be applied if:

- the client has very sensitive eyes
- the skin around the eyes is dry and flaking
- the eye or surrounding skin is infected
- the eyelid is swollen or inflamed
- the client has previously experienced an allergic reaction to eyelash adhesive.

Choosing false eyelashes

The client must have the confidence to wear false eyelashes so it is important to consult with them first and give appropriate advice. You will need to consider:

- *reasons for use*: there is no point in going through the comparatively lengthy procedure of applying individual lashes if they are intended to be worn only for a single event
- *facial characteristics*: the length and thickness of the lashes must suit the size and shape of the eyes and balance the face shape
- *client's personality*: although most clients prefer their false eyelashes to look natural, more extrovert clients may want a more obvious, glamorous effect
- *glasses*: if the client wears glasses, make sure you choose lashes that will not touch the lenses and cause irritation when moving the eyes
- *personal preference*: clients will know the effects they want and how much trouble they are prepared to take looking after their lashes.

Selection of artificial 'strip' eyelashes

Applying temporary (strip) lashes

Temporary lashes are worn to make the natural lashes look thicker and longer. They are usually applied to the eyelids as complete strips, but the base can be cut down into shorter sections depending on the client's requirements. Lashes on a fine base look more natural than ones on a thicker, heavier base.

Strip lashes are applied at the end of the make-up procedure. This way, they do not need washing as often and they last longer. Applying eyeliner first will help to conceal the base of the strip so that the lashes look more natural.

You will need:

- the chosen set of false eyelashes
- tube of adhesive
- pair of clean manual tweezers
- clean plastic palette
- clean mascara brush
- clean eye bath (in case of an accident)
- tissues
- hand mirror.

You should allow an extra 10 minutes for a make-up involving the application of strip lashes. This gives time for measuring up, trimming and applying the lashes, and for allowing the adhesive to dry. Work from behind the client when applying the lashes.

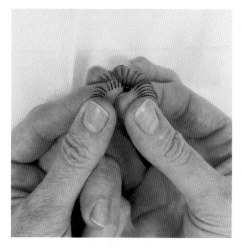

1 *Moulding the base of the strip*

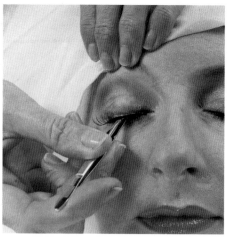

2 *Securing the centre of the strip to the centre of the eyelid*

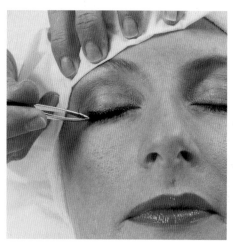

3 *Securing the inner and outer edges of the strip*

4 *Blending the false eyelashes with the natural ones*

5 *The final effect*

1 If the lashes are new, measure the strip against the edge of the eyelid. If necessary, shorten the strip from the outside edge. Avoid removing the shorter lashes from the inner edge which are shaped specially to fit comfortably near the nose.

2 A new strip is easier to apply if it is made more pliable. This is done by moulding the strip into a half-moon shape to fit the eyelid.

3 Place the false eyelashes on a clean tissue with the lashes facing away from you. This will enable you to use the tweezers to pick them up at the correct angle.

4 Apply a small amount of adhesive to the clean palette.

5 Using the tweezers, pick up one set of eyelashes in the centre of the strip on the lash side.

6 Stroke the base of the strip through the adhesive so that a fine line is distributed evenly along its length. Do not get adhesive on the lashes.

7 Using your free hand over a tissue, lift the skin of the eyelid from beneath the brow to ensure a good fit close to the base of the natural lashes.

8 Line up the tweezers with the centre of the eyelid and press the strip gently into place, making sure the lashes follow the direction of natural hair growth.

9 Secure the inner and outer corners of the strip. Do not get adhesive on the tweezers or natural lashes.

10 Apply the second strip in the same way.

11 When the lashes are quite secure (after approximately two minutes), ask the client to open her eyes and gently press the false eyelashes and the natural ones together with clean tweezers.

12 Use a clean mascara brush to blend the false eyelashes with the natural ones.

13 Offer the client a mirror and ensure that they are satisfied with the result.

14 Ensure details of treatment are entered on the client's record card.

REMEMBER

When applying strip lashes beneath the eyes, ask the client to look upwards and secure the lashes in the same way as the upper strip, but applying them underneath the lower lashes.

Removing and cleaning temporary (strip) lashes

You will need to instruct your client how to remove and care for the strip lashes:

- support the skin of the eyelid with one hand and then pull the strip away with the other, from the outer edge towards the inner corner of the eyelid

- remove adhesive by peeling it away from the strip

- replace the lashes in their box until required, attaching them to the preformed ledge which helps keep the base of the strip moulded to the correct shape.

Over time, the lashes will collect dust and traces of mascara. To clean them:

- wipe over the lashes with make-up remover

- wash the lashes in warm, soapy water and rinse well.

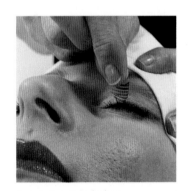

Removing strip lashes

Procedure to curl the lashes

1 Wrap a tissue once around an even-barrelled pencil.

2 Place the clean false eyelashes on the pencil, over the tissue, with the inner edges of the strips together. Make sure the lashes are evenly dispersed along the pencil.

3 Roll the pencil along the rest of the tissue, enclosing the lashes. Secure the tissue tightly at both ends with rubber bands and leave overnight.

4 Return the strip lashes to their container for safe storage.

Applying semi-permanent false eyelashes

Semi-permanent false eyelashes produce a more natural effect than strip lashes and can even be worn without eye make-up. They are applied directly to the client's own lashes and, if treated carefully, will stay in place for about four weeks as long as the supporting eyelashes are secure.

The lashes are attached individually to the client's natural eyelashes, so they take much longer to apply than the strip type. Great care is needed to prevent adhesive or lashes penetrating the eye.

You will need:

- a selection of false eyelashes
- adhesive (transparent or black depending on the colour of the lashes)
- a small glass dish lined with foil
- special eyelash adhesive solvent
- clean tweezers
- clean eye bath and distilled water (in case of accidents)
- a clean head-band
- tissues
- a hand mirror.

Procedure to apply individual false eyelashes

You should allow 20–30 minutes for applying a full set of semi-permanent false eyelashes. Work from behind the client when applying the lashes.

1   Assist the client to a comfortable position on the beauty couch.
2   Secure their hair off the face with the head-band.
3   Ensure that the natural lashes are scrupulously clean and dry.
4   Using the tweezers, remove the lashes individually from the pack and arrange them on a tissue in the order they will appear after attachment. The lashes should be facing away from you. (This is particularly helpful if you are using different lengths and types of lashes for corrective work or for creating special effects. You can see the overall shape emerging as you place and arrange the lashes on the tissue.)
5   Squeeze a little adhesive into the foil-lined dish. The foil helps to keep the adhesive at the correct consistency so that it does not set too quickly.
6   Raise the client's head slightly to reduce the risk of adhesive running into the eye.
7   Select the cluster of lashes which is due to be placed centrally and pick it up with the tweezers so that the knotted end is exposed.
8   Dip the knot into the adhesive making sure that none gets on the tweezers.
9   Ask the client to look downwards but not to close their eyes.
10   Using your free hand over a tissue, lift the brow area to release the fold of the skin from the base of the natural lashes.
11   Carefully locate the false eyelash over a centrally placed natural lash, stroke the knot slightly along its base to distribute the adhesive and then ease it back up the natural lash so that it settles on top. Hold the lash in place for a few seconds while the adhesive dries.

12 Apply the corresponding false eyelash to the other eye and continue in the same way, working alternately between the eyes to achieve a balanced effect.

13 When all of the upper lashes have been applied and the adhesive has dried, ask the client to open her eyes gently and allow a few seconds for her to get used to the lashes. Check that they are comfortable and apply lower lashes if they are required.

14 Offer the client a mirror and ensure that she is satisfied with the result.

15 Enter details of the treatment on the client's record card.

1 *Arranging the lashes in order, ready for application*

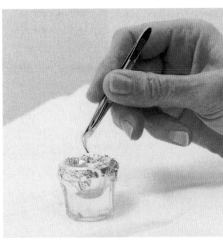

2 *Applying adhesive to the 'knot' at the base of the lashes*

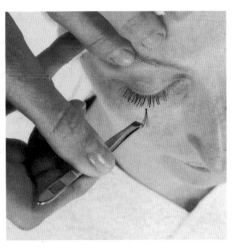

3 *Commencing application in the centre of the eyelid*

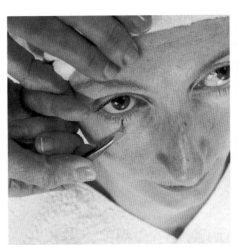

4 *Applying lower lashes beneath the natural lashes*

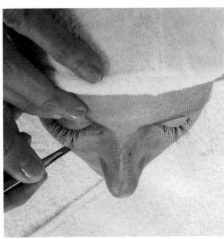

5 *Achieving a 'balanced' effect*

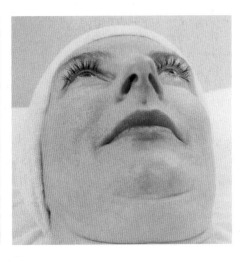

6 *Completed application of lashes*

GOOD PRACTICE

Keep checking the eyes to ensure that the different lengths of lashes have been applied in the right place and that the eyes match.

ACTIVITY

Activity 8.7: False eyelashes

Practise creating different effects with false eyelashes and photograph the results. You could either a) incorporate this activity into your make-up portfolio, or b) use the same model each time so that the effects of different lengths, colours and thicknesses of lashes upon the eyes are more obvious. Adapt the eye make-up according to the effect you are trying to achieve.

Removing individual false eyelashes

The client should be advised never to pull off the false eyelashes, otherwise the natural lashes to which they are attached will also be lost. If many hairs were removed in this way, the eyelids would be left 'bald'. Besides spoiling the appearance of the eyes, this would remove the protection given to them by the lashes.

The procedure for removing semi-permanent false lashes is as follows:

1 Secure eyeshields or dampened preformed cotton wool pads beneath the eyes, close to the base of the lashes.

2 Tip one end of an orange stick with cotton wool and soak it in the special solvent.

3 Ask the client to close their eyes and apply the solvent to the base of the lashes.

4 Allow the solvent to penetrate the adhesive for about 10 seconds and then ease the false eyelashes away with a gentle rolling action of the orange stick.

5 Finally, wipe over the eyelids and lashes with a mild skin freshener.

Contra-actions

There are always risks involved when working so closely around the eyes, particularly when applying chemical adhesive and extensions to the natural eyelashes. You must work with a very steady hand to avoid the following problems:

- *adhesive entering the eye*: do not use an excessive amount of adhesive. Only the knotted base of the false lash should be covered

- *false lash entering the eye*: the client's eyes must be kept still and remain relaxed. The false lashes should follow, exactly, the direction of the natural eyelashes and should never be placed at an angle to them

- *eyes watering*: this may be a reaction to a lash or the applicator penetrating the eye, but can also occur as a reflex action if the client is nervous about you working so close to their eyes. It is up to you to put the client at ease; reassure them beforehand and build up their confidence

- *top and bottom lashes sticking together*: make sure the client does not close their eyes during the procedure and keep the skin above the eye lifted until the adhesive has set

- *irritation or sensitivity to the adhesive*: a patch test beforehand should establish the client's sensitivity to the adhesive. If irritation occurs during the treatment you must not continue. Remove any lashes that have been applied and assist your client with an eye bath. If the irritation persists, apply cool, soothing eye pads soaked in witch hazel.

REMEMBER

When applying lower lashes, ask the client to look upwards; apply the lashes in the same way as the upper set but securing them underneath the natural lashes.

REMEMBER

If the client's eyes start watering during the treatment, sit the client up and ask them to keep their eyes closed. Offer a tissue to dry their eyes. Mild watering without an obvious cause will usually settle down quite quickly and you may proceed as long as the eyes have not become too sensitive. It is not safe to continue the treatment if the eyes remain sore or sensitive.

HEALTH MATTERS

Heavy watering accompanied by intense irritation suggests that the eye has been penetrated, probably by adhesive. You must immediately fill a clean eye bath with distilled water and help the client to flush out the irritant.

Advice for home care

Explain to your client that some of the newly applied false lashes may be lost during the week following application. It is good policy for the salon to replace them at no extra cost to the client.

Give your client the following advice:

- be very careful when removing eye make-up and cleansing the face. Although the adhesive is strong, it does not embed the false lash into the skin. Any rough treatment that dislodges the false lash will also affect the natural eyelash to which it is attached
- use a non-oily eye make-up remover to prevent loosening the adhesive
- keep the use of mascara to a minimum to avoid attracting dust particles that may accumulate in the longer lashes and cause irritation
- do not attempt to remove the lashes by pulling them. This will be uncomfortable and the natural lash will also be lost
- if more lashes are required, the client should return to the salon for an 'infill' treatment
- the client should return to the salon to have the false lashes removed.

Make-up

Compare your answers with those of your colleagues and see if you all agree. Some of the questions have more than one right answer! When that happens, rank them in priority order.

1 The bride should not have a full facial on her wedding day because:
   (a) there is not enough time
   (b) the skin will reject the make-up afterwards
   (c) the massage will make her hair greasy
   (d) the skin will be sensitive after the massage.

2 Stronger make-up colours are required for evening because:
   (a) the make-up wears off more quickly than during the day
   (b) artificial lighting is brighter than natural daylight
   (c) a more dramatic effect is required for evening wear
   (d) artificial lighting is not as bright as daylight.

3 At the end of a make-up lesson, the client is given a make-up chart so that:
   (a) they will know what products have been used and how they should be applied
   (b) they have a record of the make-up products they have bought
   (c) the therapist knows what products have been used during the lesson
   (d) there is a plan to refer to when the client has another make-up lesson.

4 Moisturiser is worn under make-up to:
   (a) even out skin texture and provide a smooth base for foundation
   (b) add moisture to dry skin
   (c) to prevent make-up from drying the skin
   (d) to set the foundation.

5 Nail enamel should not be worn by the therapist during a make-up treatment because:
   (a) it looks unprofessional
   (b) the client may be allergic to the nail enamel
   (c) the nail enamel may chip during the treatment
   (d) the nail enamel may contaminate the make-up.

6 Eye pencils should be sharpened before use because:
   (a) they feel more comfortable on the skin
   (b) a better effect can be achieved if the pencils are sharpened
   (c) a more subtle effect can be achieved if the pencils are sharpened
   (d) for hygiene reasons.

7 Foundation may change colour on the skin because:
   (a) the client is allergic to the foundation
   (b) the pH of the skin is not normal
   (c) the foundation is the wrong colour
   (d) the pH of the foundation is not normal.

8 Mascara may not be applied to the lower lashes when:
   (a) the client has small eyes
   (b) the client has round eyes
   (c) the skin beneath the eyes is lined
   (d) the skin beneath the eyes is greasy.

9 Lipstick should be applied with a brush because:
   (a) better coverage of the lips will be achieved
   (b) it is more hygienic than not using a brush
   (c) the lipstick will stay in place for longer
   (d) it is more hygienic than using a lip pencil.

10 For photographic make-up, the cheekbones may be emphasised by:
   (a) applying blusher above the cheekbones and shader underneath
   (b) applying highlighter above the cheekbones and shader underneath
   (c) applying blusher to the cheekbones
   (d) applying blusher beneath the cheekbones.

You should now understand the following words and phrases. If you do not, go back through the chapter and find out what they mean:

Day make-up	**Evening make-up**	**Contraindications to make-up**
Artificial lighting	**Colour correction**	**Strip lashes**
Foundation	**Contour cosmetics**	**Complementary colour theory**
Highlighting	**Shading**	**Semi-permanent false eyelashes**
Corrective make-up	**Hypo-allergenic make-up**	
Contra-actions to make-up	**Product safety**	

Chapter 9 Depilatory waxing

Remove hair using waxing techniques

After working through this chapter you will be able to:

- describe the different types of hair
- understand the basic principles of hair growth
- describe the structure of hair
- apply and remove waxing and sugaring products
- provide treatment advice
- know about other methods of temporary hair removal and their effect on the waxing and sugaring process
- identify contra-actions and contraindications to waxing and sugaring treatments.

Before you work through this chapter: Be wise and revise!
Revision topics to help you achieve this unit:

Remove hair using waxing techniques

There are many people for whom the appearance of facial or body hair is either a nuisance or extremely embarrassing. Waxing and **sugaring** treatments clear small and large areas of unwanted hair quickly and efficiently. These treatments are very popular in the salon, particularly during the summer months when more of the body is exposed.

Hair growth

Attitudes towards body hair vary between different cultures and also between individuals. In most Mediterranean countries it is considered quite normal for a woman to have dark hair growing above the upper lip. A heavy growth of hair in the underarm region is not considered to be offensive – in fact, quite the opposite!

In the UK, dark or excessive hair growth on the face and body is generally considered undesirable and the preferred look is for smooth, clear skin. Fair-skinned people usually have less hair than those with olive skins who come from Mediterranean and Middle Eastern countries; people with black skins are generally hairier than oriental people but less hairy than caucasian people (those with 'white' skin).

Types of hair

The skin of the face and body is virtually covered by hair. It appears either short and downy (vellus) or longer and coarser (terminal). **Terminal hairs** grow thickly where they are needed for extra protection:

- *eyelashes*: filter out dust and dirt and shade the eyes from excessive sunlight
- *eyebrows*: protect the eye area and 'cushion' the brow bone
- *scalp hairs*: prevent heat loss from the body and protect against injury to the head
- *underarms/pubic area*: protect against friction
- *body hair*: provides some insulation and has a sensory function linked to the production of sebum.

HEALTH MATTERS

Small arrector pili muscles connect the walls of the hair follicles to the base of the epidermis. In cold weather these muscles contract, causing the hairs to stand on end and trap air between them. This is how 'goose bumps' are formed.

Both women and men grow terminal hairs on their legs and arms. Men also grow them on their chests and faces. The hairs that grow on exposed areas of the body have a significant effect on overall appearance, particularly if they are dark or excessive.

HEALTH MATTERS

In women, the normal pattern of hair growth may change during the menopause when the balance of sex hormones is disturbed. It is not uncommon, at this time, for vellus hairs on the face to become strong and terminal, particularly above the upper lip and on the chin.

A PRACTICAL GUIDE TO BEAUTY THERAPY

- Superfluous hair: excess hair, which is not abnormal but may be considered socially undesirable. Superfluous hairs may be removed by **depilation** or **epilation** (see below).
- Hypertrichosis: an excessive and abnormal growth of hair. Strong, terminal hairs appear in areas where **vellus hairs** usually grow.
- Hirsutism: an abnormal condition of male-pattern hair growth on a female.
- Depilation: technically, this means the removal of hair from the skin's surface and refers to methods such as shaving, clipping or using chemical depilatories. The term is, however, commonly used to describe all temporary methods of hair removal, including waxing and sugaring.
- Epilation: this term is used to describe permanent methods of hair removal using an electrical current. In fact the word 'epilation' means the removal of hair completely from the skin (not just partial removal), and should also be used to describe methods such as tweezing, waxing and sugaring where the hairs are removed at their roots.
- Bleaching: dark hairs may be bleached using a commercially prepared cream or paste. Bleaching is usually quite successful when used for lightening vellus hairs, but two treatments may be needed to strip out the reddish tones of very dark hair.

REMEMBER

The basic structure of skin.

- Epidermis: the outer layer of skin.
- Dermis: the layer of skin beneath the epidermis.
- **Hair shaft**: the part of the hair above the surface of the skin.
- **Hair root**: the part of the hair below the surface of the skin.
- **Dermal papilla**: the part of the hair root where the hair starts to grow.
- Blood capillaries: tiny blood vessels bringing nutrients and oxygen to the dermal papilla.
- **Hair follicle**: the pocket in which the hair sits.
- Sebaceous gland: the gland producing sebum, the natural lubricant of skin and hair.
- Sweat gland: the gland producing sweat to cool the body.

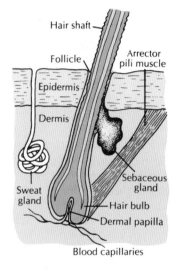

Location of hair in the skin

Each hair grows from a narrow, tube-like depression in the skin called a hair follicle. The base of the hair follicle surrounds the dermal papilla. This area has an abundant supply of blood vessels which bring nourishment to the hair. Each papilla is surrounded by hair germ cells, which develop into a bulb and then grow up the follicle to form a hair. Hairs are soft at the base but gradually harden and die as they approach the surface.

Hair stops growing when it is removed from its source of nourishment. This happens naturally during the normal cycle of hair growth and replacement. The papilla (which contains blood vessels) degenerates, the blood supply ceases and the hair falls out.

Eventually a new hair is formed with an active blood supply and the cycle of events leading to the growth of a new hair is repeated.

REMEMBER

The average lifetime of eyebrow and eyelash hairs is four to five months; scalp hairs may keep growing for up to seven years.

Anagen   Catagen   Telogen   Anagen
Active   Breakdown Resting   Regrowth

The hair growth cycle

Electrical epilation – electric current discharged here will destroy the hair

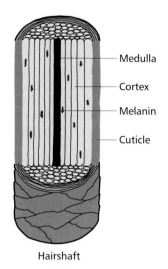

Medulla

Cortex

Melanin

Cuticle

Hairshaft

Longitudinal section of hair

Stages of hair growth cycle

- **Anagen** is the active growing stage which may last from a few weeks up to several years. Hair germ cells reproduce at the matrix and pass upwards to form the hair bulb. They then split and change to form different layers. The anagen stage ends when the hair becomes detached from the dermal papilla and therefore not able to receive nourishment.

- **Catagen** is a transition stage from active to resting. The hair stops growing, the follicle begins to shrink or a new hair begins at the base of the follicle as the old hair moves slowly up the follicle.

- **Telogen** is the resting stage. It does not last long. The blood supply has ceased, the hair bulb closed and the hair prepares to be shed. Meanwhile, a new replacement hair has started to grow at the base of the follicle.

The only way of stopping this cycle permanently is to destroy the structures involved with reproducing hair cells. Treatment with electrical epilation can do this.

An electrical current is passed down a fine needle to the base of the hair follicle. Depending on the type of current used, destruction takes place either chemically or by heat.

Some people cannot tolerate the feeling of the current used in electrical epilation and prefer to use other methods of treating superfluous hair. For others, the long-term effects of the treatment compensate for the patience required and the expense involved.

Structure of hair

The hair that shows above the skin's surface is dead. It is composed mainly of keratin, the same protein that makes up the skin and nails.

A hair is made up of three layers:

- *cuticle*: the tough, outer protective layer of the hair. The cells are translucent and allow colour from beneath to show through. They form scales that overlap towards the hair tip. Chemicals that are applied to lighten or tint the hairs have to penetrate the cuticle in order to work on cells in the deeper layer

- *cortex*: this is the main part of the hair, which contains the colour pigments melanin (brown/black) and pheomelanin (yellow/red). The cells in the cortex contain bundles of fibres. The strength, thickness and elasticity of the hair is determined by the way in which the cells and fibres are held together. Keratin is formed in the cortex

- *medulla*: the middle 'core' of the hair, which is not always present. The medulla does not appear to have a function.

Hair

1 State the main difference between terminal and vellus hairs.

2 List three types of terminal hairs.

3 Why do women sometimes have problems with facial hair around the time of the menopause?

4 Name the part of the hair that is situated below the surface of the skin.

5 What happens at the dermal papilla?

6 Why do some hairs grow coarser than others?

7 Name the three stages of hair growth and explain briefly what happens at each stage.

8 How does electrical epilation affect hair growth?

9 Name the layer of hair that contains the colour pigments.

10 Name the protein contained in hair.

ACTIVITY

Activity 9.1: Test your knowledge of hair

Draw a large, clear, fully labelled diagram of a hair in its follicle. Use colour to show the different structures. Show how the hair is held in place and identify its source of nourishment.

Wax depilation

During a depilatory treatment, wax is heated and applied to the skin so that it grips or sticks to the the hairs. When the wax is removed, the hairs are pulled out completely, leaving the skin soft and smooth.

Waxing is a very profitable salon service:

- only small quantities of products and consumable materials are used
- equipment running costs are low
- only a short amount of time is needed by a skilled operator
- there are opportunities for linked retail sales.

The treatment must be made quick and painless for the client. Wax depilation can be very uncomfortable if adequate care is not taken.

REMEMBER

Cold wax products are available as pre-waxed strips, but these have limited effectiveness and are not used for professional treatments.

REMEMBER

One bad experience may put the client off waxing for ever. Worse still, they may decide to go to a different salon next time so that you lose their custom altogether.

Wax depilatories

There is a wide range of waxing products available. These tend to be categorised by the temperature at which they are used:

- *warm wax*: the wax is maintained at a working temperature of approximately 40–43 °C (104–110 °F)
- *hot wax*: used at a temperature of approximately 48–50 °C (118–122 °F).

Warm wax

Warm wax heater

Warm wax is usually supplied in a tin or firm plastic tub which fits neatly into a special wax heater. Some warm wax products are water-soluble. They are washable and can be microwaved before use.

A low melting-point wax, such as paraffin wax, is used. Synthetic resins and other organic materials are often added to improve the texture and quality of the product. When heated to a temperature of 40–43 °C, the wax becomes warm and clear and can be spread thinly on the skin with a spatula.

'Organic' waxes are very popular; these are based on a glucose syrup or honey. They do not set when cold, but become more fluid when heated. Some warm wax products are available in cream form.

Effects of warm wax

Warm wax creates a sticky coating on the hairs, which makes them adhere to a fabric or bonded fibre strip applied over the top. The hair is depilated when the strip is pulled away from the skin.

Benefits of warm wax

Warm wax depilation is usually preferred to hot wax treatments because:

- the treatments are quick and require very little preparation time
- the equipment is easy to clean and maintain
- the treatments produce a milder skin reaction than hot wax treatments
- warm wax is more comfortable for treating sensitive areas such as the face, underarms and bikini line
- the wax can be reapplied to less sensitive areas without burning the skin
- even very short hairs (2.5 mm) can be removed.

Roll-on applicator systems

Some warm wax systems provide all the necessary equipment and materials in a compact, self-contained unit which takes up very little space. Pre-filled roll-on applicators are available as an alternative to applying wax with a wooden spatula. They are produced in a range of sizes for treating different areas of the body. The applicators are warmed in a special heater which maintains them at a comfortable working temperature. Depending on the system, the applicator heads are either detachable, making them very easy to clean and maintain, or disposable, so that new applicators are used for each client and for each area treated.

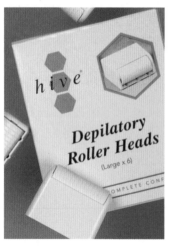

Disposable applicator heads

> **HEALTH MATTERS**
>
> Although warm wax is used at a fairly low temperature, loose surface skin cells are removed, there is mild stimulation of the blood supply and the hair follicles are left more open to infection. This is because their hairs and surface skin coatings have been removed. Sometimes, ingredients such as tea tree oil, witch hazel and allantoin are added to the wax for their healing and antiseptic effects.

The benefits of disposable applicator and roll-on waxing systems are:

- there is minimal risk of cross-contamination during treatment
- the treatments are quick and relatively easy to perform
- there is no mess so equipment is easier to maintain
- the equipment is compact, as everything required is contained in a purpose-built unit
- the treatment is very economical because the amount of wax used is controlled and dispensed by the applicator
- the equipment is safe and there is no risk of spilling the wax or causing burns
- there is very little skin reaction
- clients find the treatments quite comfortable.

Roll-on applicator system

Hot wax

Hot wax depilatories have been available for a long time but they are less popular than warm wax products which have been developed more recently. Hot wax is usually supplied as pellets which contain beeswax and resin. The pellets are melted in a special thermostatically controlled heater. As the wax begins to liquefy, the temperature is reduced to prevent it from getting too hot and to ensure a controllable consistency.

If your hot wax heater is supplied with a filter, ignore it! It is no longer considered acceptable to filter and recycle used depilatory wax. This is because surface skin cells, sebum, sweat and, sometimes, spots of blood become impregnated in the wax. They cannot be removed by filtering. Also, the high temperature that would be needed to sterilise used hot wax would spoil its texture. The wax would become brittle and unsuitable for treatment.

A thermostatically controlled 'hot wax' heater

Effects of hot wax

Beeswax liquefies on heating and coats the hairs when applied with a spatula. As the wax cools, it becomes firmer and contracts around the hairs, gripping them tightly. When the wax strip is removed, so are the hairs that have become set into it. Resin makes the wax pliable so that it can be removed from the skin in a continuous strip without cracking or breaking.

Benefits of hot wax

Some therapists who have originally trained with, and become expert in, hot wax depilation sometimes prefer it to other methods because the strong, gripping action of the wax makes it particularly effective for removing strong, deep-rooted hairs.

Which treatment?

The most suitable treatment for a client is the one that will clear their particular hair problem as quickly, hygienically and efficiently as possible with minimal discomfort and skin damage. All methods of depilatory waxing produce very good results if performed competently. The hairs are removed completely from their follicles, not just from above the skin's surface. It usually takes at least four weeks for new replacement hairs to appear.

HEALTH MATTERS

Because the wax is used at quite a high temperature, the blood supply is stimulated, which causes reddening of the skin. Sometimes, ingredients such as azulene and camphor are added for their soothing effect. Bactericidal agents may also be contained to decrease the risk of infection through hair follicles.

GOOD PRACTICE

Always advise a client who uses a self-tanning preparation that waxing may cause their tan to appear patchy. Self-tanning products contain a chemical, dihydroxyacetone, which reacts with keratin, causing it to change colour. Most of the skin's keratin is contained in the upper layers of the epidermis. When loose epidermal cells are removed with the wax, some of the effects of a 'tan' are lost with them.

HEALTH MATTERS

People with diabetes have skin that is very slow to heal. They should be referred to their doctor for permission to have wax depilation, then be treated with a low-temperature wax. The skin should be checked closely throughout treatment to make sure it does not overreact.

GOOD PRACTICE

When making an appointment for wax depilation, clients should be asked about their reaction to any previous waxing treatment and about the sensitivity of their skin in general. Ideally, new clients should be 'patch tested' to make sure that they will not react adversely to the products.

General contraindications to wax depilation

Depilatory waxing must not be carried out if any of the following conditions are present:

- allergy to the products
- broken skin
- recent scar tissue
- bruising
- warts
- moles
- inflammation, swelling or pus
- rashes
- very thin or crêpey skin
- very sensitive skin
- within 24 hours after sunbathing or sunbed treatment
- immediately before or after a sauna or steam bath.

Specific contraindications to wax depilation

Some specific contraindications to wax depilation are:

- legs: varicose veins
- underarm: mastitis
- lip and chin: cold sores
- eyebrows: styes, conjunctivitis.

Preparing for a wax depilation treatment (all methods)

It is important to have the client's record card and all materials prepared on the trolley before they arrive. If it is the client's first depilatory wax treatment and a preliminary consultation has not taken place, a treatment plan will need to be agreed. This will be based on a visual examination and information supplied when questioning the client.

To give a patch test:

1. cleanse and dry an area of skin on the inside of the client's forearm
2. having tested the temperature of the wax on yourself first, apply a small amount of heated wax to the area you have cleansed
3. remove the wax in the same way as if you were giving treatment
4. note the immediate reaction of the skin to treatment and enter details on the client's record card

5   advise the client to contact you if there is an adverse skin reaction in the patch test area during the next 48 hours. If there is, the depilatory wax treatment must not take place.

When assessing the client:

- cleanse and dry the area and examine it in good light, preferably using a magnifying anglepoise lamp
- identify and note any contraindications which may limit treatment or may need medical referral
- note the pattern of hair growth
- note the length, texture and thickness of the hairs
- get details of the client's home treatment of their condition.

HEALTH MATTERS

Some warm wax products are promoted as being suitable for using over conditions such as varicose veins, which are normally contraindicated. If, after examining the client, you are not sure whether or not it is safe to go ahead, ask the advice of your supervisor. They may decide that it is best to ask the client for their doctor's permission before proceeding with treatment.

REMEMBER

The hairs need to be a minimum of 2.5 mm long for removing with warm wax and 5 mm long for removing with hot wax. This is to ensure that there is sufficient length for the wax to adhere to or grip the hairs prior to removal.

Preparing the treatment area

1   Depending on the waxing system that is used in your salon, you will need to prepare your trolley with all or some of the following equipment and materials:
- thermostatically controlled heating unit
- wax products
- talcum powder
- non-greasy antiseptic skin cleanser, for example a gel or lotion (sometimes surgical spirit, is used but this does not smell very pleasant)
- wax removal strips made from fabric or bonded fibres
- disposable spatulas or applicators (unless using a hygienic, reusable roll-on method)
- a pair of small scissors and tweezers soaking in disinfectant
- after-wax oil: for clients with dry skin, it can also be used for dissolving any wax left on the skin
- after-wax lotion: a calming, soothing lotion, which cools and moisturises the skin
- vinyl gloves
- clean towels
- bed roll
- tissues
- cotton wool.

2   Protect the couch using polythene sheeting followed by a soft paper sheet for the client to rest on. Depilatory wax will make a mess if spilled on bedding, clothing, towels or floors. Water-soluble warm waxes can be removed by washing. Other types of warm wax can usually be cleaned up using a little after-wax lotion. Special wax cleaner or surgical spirit is used for cleaning up after hot wax.

3   Position the wax heater. Place it at a safe distance from the client but near enough to the couch to avoid spills or premature cooling of the wax before it is applied.

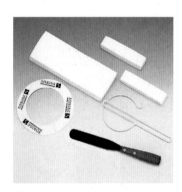

Waxing accessories

GOOD PRACTICE

Warm wax products take between 20 and 30 minutes to heat up to the required temperature. In the salon, the wax heater is usually switched on first thing in the morning and kept on 'standby', so that it can be used at a moment's notice for treating unexpected clients.

Preparing the client

1   Examine the skin and hairs. Do this in good light. Note any contraindications and patterns of hair growth.

2   Protect the client's clothing with a piece of paper bed roll and remove any jewellery from the area to be treated. Hair on the head should be covered with a towel when treating the face.

3   Position the client. Make sure they are comfortable and that the area to be treated is supported well.

4   Wash your hands with an antiseptic cleanser.

5   Prepare the client's skin and hair:
    - wipe over the skin with a special pre-wax cleanser or surgical spirit
    - trim excessively long hair with scissors to reduce the discomfort of hair removal
    - unless advised otherwise, apply a light dusting of talc against the direction of hair growth. This coats the hairs, making them easier to see (this is especially useful if the hairs are fair).

6   Advise the client about what is going to happen. Explain what you are going to do, how it will feel and the probable skin reaction.

Applying and removing warm wax

1. Test the wax. Apply a little of the wax to the inside of your wrist or to the sensitive skin between the thumb and index finger. If the wax feels comfortable for you, it should feel comfortable for the client. Test a small amount of wax on the client's wrist or ankle, whichever is the most convenient.

2. Observe the direction of hair growth. Warm wax is applied in one direction only, that is in the direction of hair growth.

3. Take up some wax on a spatula and twist it round over your free hand to control the drips. Wipe off any excess on the drip bar or sides of the tub containing the wax.

4. Transfer the wax to the skin. Holding the spatula at a right angle (90°) to the skin, spread a very thin film of wax over the whole of the exposed area to be treated. Work in one direction only, i.e. with the natural hair growth, supporting the skin with your free hand. Maintain the 90° angle as much as you can so that only a very thin layer of wax is produced.

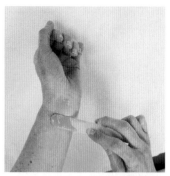

Testing the temperature of the wax

REMEMBER

A thin layer of warm wax is more effective than a thicker one. This is because the wax does not set on cooling. It merely provides a sticky coating to the hairs. A thick layer of wax creates a barrier between the hairs and the removal strip so the treatment is not effective.

5. Press a fabric or bonded fibre strip on to the wax and smooth over it once with your hand in the direction of hair growth. Make sure the strip has a clean, free edge for gripping.

6. Pull the strip away, quickly, from the skin, against the direction of hair growth.

REMEMBER

When removing warm wax, always work methodically from a starting point which provides you with a clean, wax-free area of skin at the 'gripping' edge of the strip. This will help to prevent your hands from getting sticky.

GOOD PRACTICE

Supporting the skin firmly when applying and removing the wax prevents dragging (and stretching) the skin.

7. Apply a little pressure with your hand to reduce the stinging effect which may occur after removing the strip.

8. Work methodically over the whole area, using the same strip for as long as it continues to pick up hairs.

9. When the strip is finished with, fold it up with the waxed sides together and either throw it away (if disposable) or keep it hygienically in a covered container until it can be laundered (some fabric strips may be washed, boiled and re-used if used with water-soluble wax products).

GOOD PRACTICE

Don't struggle to reach awkward areas when applying the wax. It is much better for you to reposition the client so that you can apply and remove the wax efficiently without causing them discomfort.

GOOD PRACTICE

When removing warm wax, the strip should be pulled back on itself quickly, parallel with the skin surface and not vertically from the skin. This is the most efficient and most comfortable way of removing the wax.

Sometimes small spots of blood and tissue fluid appear on the surface of the skin following waxing, particularly after using hot wax. Infections can be carried in blood and other body fluids. If the skin of the therapist's hands is intact, they are not at risk of catching blood borne infections, such as HIV, from a client. If they have open cuts or abrasions on their hands, then they should be very careful. Some therapists choose to wear disposable vinyl gloves for every waxing treatment they provide. Others choose to wear them only when they feel it is essential. The beauty industry professional associations issue guidelines. Refer to your professional association's guidelines and follow them.

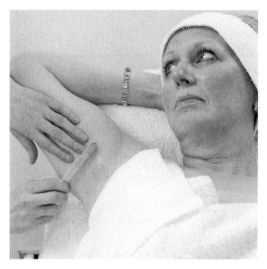

Applying and removing warm wax – underarms

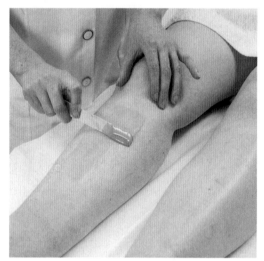

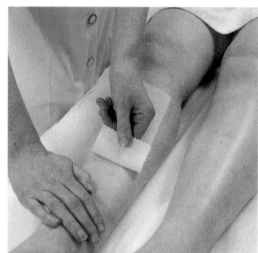

Applying and removing warm wax – legs

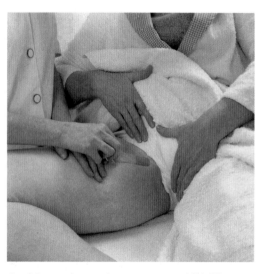

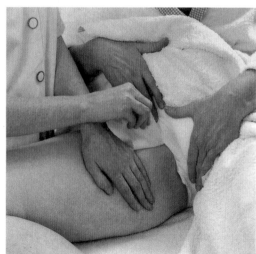

Applying and removing warm wax – bikini line

A PRACTICAL GUIDE TO BEAUTY THERAPY

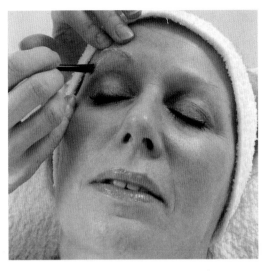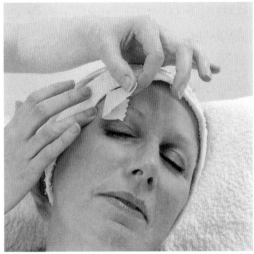

Applying and removing warm wax – eyebrows

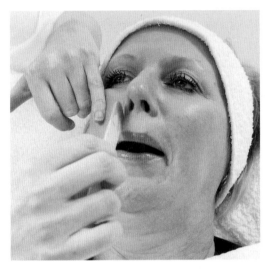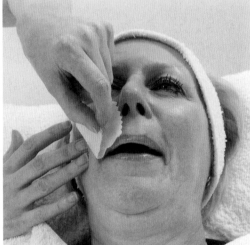

Applying and removing warm wax – upper lip

Waxing strips

REMEMBER

The wax must always be applied and removed in relation to the direction of natural hair growth:

- warm wax: apply the wax with the hair growth and remove it against

- hot wax: apply the wax against, with and against the hair growth and remove it against.

Using a roll-on (warm wax) applicator system

The wax used for this type of system works at a higher temperature than other warm waxes. It is very effective for removing strong hair. Roll-on applicators of different sizes are used to dispense a fine film of wax from a single stroke of the applicator. The procedure is hygienic because the wax is contained and not exposed until rolled on to the skin.

Applying and removing hot wax

1   Test the wax. Apply a little of the wax to the inside of your wrist or to the sensitive skin between the thumb and index finger. If the wax feels comfortable for you, it should feel comfortable for the client. Test a small amount of wax on the client's wrist or ankle, whichever is the most convenient.

2   Observe the direction of hair growth: this influences the procedure for applying and removing wax.

3   Take up some wax on a spatula and twist it round over your free hand to control the drips. Wipe off any excess on the drip bar or sides of the tub containing the wax.

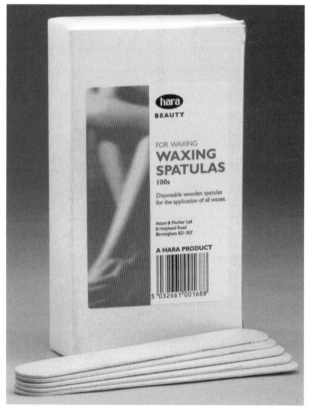

Spatulas

4   Build up layers of wax; apply the wax against, with and then against the direction of hair growth.

5   Use your free hand to stretch the skin so that all hairs in the area get covered by the wax.

6   Adapt the size of the strips to the area that is being treated. (The strips should be no wider than 5 cm or they will be difficult to remove.)

7   Build up the thickness of the strips to approximately 3 mm.

8   Where possible, apply a few strips at a time, working quickly to keep the treatment flowing.

9   Create a thick, strong 'lip' with the wax, which will help you to get a firm grip.

10   When the surface of the wax is dry but still warm, mould the strip to the contours of the area with your fingers.

11   Create the 'lip' by flicking up the lower edge of the strip. Support the surrounding skin while you do this, to minimise discomfort.

12   Grip the wax 'lip' firmly and remove the strip swiftly against the direction of hair growth.

13   Immediately apply pressure to reduce the stinging effect.

14   Remove small patches of remaining wax by pressing the exposed side of the warm strip over the area. It is best to fold the strip with the hairy sides together before doing this.

Waxing different body areas

Here are some guidelines to follow when waxing different areas of the body, whichever method is used.

Front of leg

- The client should be lying down or in semi-reclining position.
- Begin treatment at the bottom of the leg, above the ankle.
- Always bend the leg when waxing over the knee.
- Support the inner thighs well so that the skin is taut when applying and removing the wax.
- Short strips are quicker and easier to work with than long ones.

Back of leg

- The client should be lying down on their front; a magazine may be offered.
- Note the different directions of hair growth on the backs of the legs and thighs; adapt treatment accordingly.
- Begin treatment at the bottom of the leg, above the ankle.
- Do not apply wax over the back of the knee.
- Use short strips until you become more confident at trying to remove longer ones.

Thigh/bikini line

- The client should be in crook-lying position (legs placed in a figure 4), either lying down or semi-reclining.
- A pillow may be offered to support the leg that is bent.
- Use tissues to protect the client's briefs.
- Hairs will probably need trimming before waxing; this is important to minimise discomfort in this sensitive area.
- Treat the area in small sections according to the different directions of hair growth.
- The hairs in this area are strong and likely to produce tiny blood spots when depilated.

Lower abdomen

- The client should be lying down, face upwards.
- Use very small strips of wax when working around the navel.
- You may need your client's help in supporting the surrounding skin if the area is very fleshy.

Underarm

- The client should be lying down or in a semi-reclining position with the hand of the arm to be treated resting behind their head.
- Tuck a protective tissue under the edge of the client's bra.
- Trim long hairs before waxing.
- Ask the client to gently pull their breast tissue away from the area to be treated to make the skin taut and the treatment more comfortable.
- The wax may be applied either in small strips working from the outside of the hair growth in towards the heavier growth in the centre or in two strips, one each side of where the hairs part in the axilla (armpit).

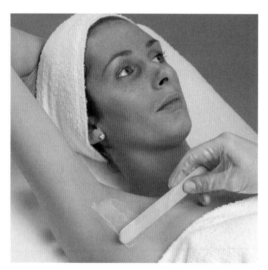 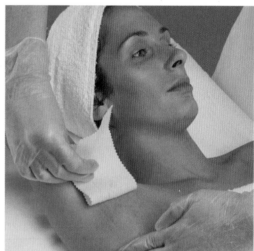

Upper lip and chin

- The client should be lying down.
- All traces of make-up must be removed.
- Do not apply wax over the lip.
- Ask the client to stretch the skin above the upper lip when waxing there.
- Ask the client to tilt their head back so that the skin is pulled taut over the chin when waxing.

Arms

- The client should be semi-reclining with the arms resting beside them on the couch.
- Bend the arms when treating the upper arms and waxing over the elbows.

Eyebrow

- Do not use hot wax for treating the eyebrows; the skin is too thin and sensitive.
- The client should be lying down with their eyes kept closed during the treatment.
- Study the eyebrows before deciding on their final shape.
- Brush the eyebrows and separate the unwanted hair from the line of the other hairs.
- Pull the skin beneath the brow upwards and outwards before applying wax.
- Using a small spatula, apply a thin film of wax and remove it using a clean strip.

Nape of the neck

- The client should be seated comfortably, leaning forwards with their forehead resting on their hands.
- The skin of the neck should be stretched to ensure ease of application and removal of the wax.
- The client's hair should be secured out of the way so that it does not get caught up in the wax.

Toes

- The client should be semi-reclining with the toes bent to pull the skin taut.

Completing wax depilation

1. Assess the results. Check the condition of the skin and look for any remaining hairs that should have been depilated. If there are just one or two hairs left behind, they may be removed by tweezing. Patches of stubborn hairs may need a second application of wax.
2. Provide after-care. Wipe over the skin with an antiseptic, after-wax cleanser. This will remove any sticky residue and help protect the skin from infection.
3. Apply a soothing after-wax lotion. This helps to cool the skin and replace lost moisture.
4. Advise the client on after-care. Explain the special precautions that should be taken by the client until the area has completely settled down.
5. Fill in the client's record card. Record details of treatment and sales.

After-care advice

Clients should be advised to take the following precautions for at least 24 hours after wax depilation and for longer if the skin still feels sensitive:

- apply a soothing after-wax lotion or gel regularly to keep the skin soft and to minimise any redness or irritation
- have only lukewarm showers and baths
- refrain from applying antiperspirant, deodorant or perfumed products to the area
- avoid applying make-up or self-tanning preparations over the area
- avoid sunbathing or having a sunbed treatment
- do not touch the area with your fingers and keep the skin clean.

HEALTH MATTERS

As there is only a very mild skin reaction to warm wax, it is usually quite safe to make a second application to remove stubborn hairs. Treatment with hot wax has a far more stimulating effect on the skin, which means that a second application may not be advisable. Do not reapply wax for at least 48 hours if the skin appears pink and shiny.

REMEMBER

The skin needs extra protection after a depilatory wax treatment. Empty hair follicles provide a route for bacteria.

REMEMBER

It takes between 24 and 48 hours for the skin to stabilise itself after wax depilation. The actual recovery time depends on the sensitivity of the skin, the amount and type of hair that has been removed, and the method of treatment that has been used.

REMEMBER

An after-wax lotion could also be used as a moisturiser, hand lotion or body lotion or for after-sun skin care: sell it!

REMEMBER

Surgical spirit is very effective for cleaning up after hot wax depilation. Wipe over the equipment while it is still warm. Wax is much more difficult to remove once it has cooled and gone hard.

Clearing up

- Dispose of used spatulas, wax, removal strips and waste in a sealed, plastic bag or bin liner.
- Remove used towels.
- Clean the equipment with an appropriate solvent. Some warm waxes are water-soluble and can be wiped clean with a damp cloth. Others require surgical spirit or a special wax remover.

Approximate treatment times. Allowances must be made for filling in the record card, consulting with the client and agreeing a treatment plan

AREA	WARM WAX (MINS)	ROLL-ON/DISPOSABLE APPLICATOR SYSTEM (MINS)	HOT WAX (MINS)
Half leg	15–20	15	20–30
Full leg	30–45	30	45–60
Bikini line	10–15	10	15
Underarm	10–15	10	15
Arm	10–15	10	15–20
Upper lip/chin	10	5–10	15
Eyebrow	10	5–10	10–15
Nape of neck	10	10	10–15
Toes	10	10	10–15

GOOD PRACTICE

Although the client's clothing is protected during a waxing treatment, it is a good idea to advise them not to wear their best underwear when having their underarms or bikini line treated. Some salons issue bikini wax clients with disposable paper briefs, which are included in the cost of the treatment. Alternatively, clients are advised to wear an older pair of high-cut briefs.

Brazilian and Californian waxing treatments

Styles of bikini wax treatments are emerging in response to lifestyle and fashion trends. Particularly during the summer months or in preparation for holidays abroad at different times of the year, clients may have specific requirements dictated by their favourite bikini! The following fashions have reached the UK from the US. If you are asked for one of these treatments and it is the policy of the salon to provide them, make sure that enough time is allowed in the appointment book to cover the extra work involved.

Brazilian

This treatment is becoming very popular and involves total hair removal from the pubic area. The client needs to attend regularly and often to maintain the effects. The treatment is high maintenance and can be painful. At least an extra 15 minutes should be allowed in the appointment book.

Californian

Also known as a 'Mohican', this treatment is not quite total. A small line of pubic hair is left centrally in a vertical line which allows a narrow cut 'thong bikini' to be worn. Again, an extra 15 minutes should be allowed.

Activity 9.2: Wax depilation

1 Working with a partner, try to work out the average profit on a half-leg wax treatment using warm wax. You will need to work out how much it costs to give the treatment and take that amount from the price that is charged to the client. Do some practical work to help you estimate the amount of wax and other consumable items needed for the treatment. When you have managed to agree on an answer, compare your salon's prices with those of other salons in the area. If there is a wide price range, suggest some reasons for this.

2 Using the information you have gained (from 1 above), decide how you could run a special promotion for leg waxing. Consider an appropriate special offer. Design a newspaper advertisement to promote your offer. Use a computer where you can.

The ones that got away!

It is very frustrating to find that some of the hairs you thought you had depilated managed to escape.

Here are some possible reasons for hairs remaining after a wax depilatory treatment:

- the hairs were too short to wax
- the warm wax was applied too thickly for the strip to grip the hairs
- the hot wax was too thick to contract tightly around the hairs
- the wax was applied and removed in the wrong direction
- the wax was removed too slowly
- the skin was not pulled taut and hairs were caught in creases.

Contra-actions

It is important to recognise a normal and abnormal reaction to waxing, and to advise the client appropriately.

Adverse skin reaction

The skin normally looks slightly pink after wax epilation, even when a low-temperature product has been used. However, extreme redness (erythema) and skin irritation suggest an overreaction to the treatment. Possible causes of this could be:

- failing to recognise a sensitive skin and not giving a skin test before treatment
- the wax was too hot
- overlapping applications of hot wax
- applying too much pressure with the side of the spatula when applying warm wax
- pulling off the wax strip upwards rather than back on itself
- failing to pull the skin taut when removing the wax.

The client should follow the after-care advice provided at the end of the waxing treatment.

Burns

If adequate safety precautions have not been taken, a burn may occur, making the skin very sore and red with possible loss of skin from the upper layers of the epidermis. This leaves the skin very open to infection. The first-aid treatment of burns should be followed (see page 48). If the burn does not show signs of healing within three or four days, medical attention should be sought.

GOOD PRACTICE

It is a good idea to give the client an after-care leaflet containing all the necessary information. This will help to remind them what to do at home.

HEALTH MATTERS

Always wear vinyl gloves when releasing ingrowing hairs in case blood or tissue fluid appears on the skin during the procedure.

GOOD PRACTICE

Regular exfoliating treatments and moisturising of the skin will help to prevent ingrowing hairs.

REMEMBER

It is possible that the stimulating effects of repeated wax depilatory treatments could strengthen the follicles and increase their blood supply. This would result in replacement hairs growing back coarser and more firmly rooted.

REMEMBER

Hairs that have been cut or shaved feel thicker because they have blunt ends. After wax depilation a new replacement hair grows, which has a fine, tapered end.

Ingrowing hairs

These usually occur when the mouth of the hair follicle becomes blocked and the hair gets trapped and grows back on itself. Possible causes of ingrowing hairs following wax depilation are:

- increased keratinisation, causing more cells to be produced in the stratum corneum, which block the mouth of the hair follicle
- the wearing of tight clothing over the treated area in the few days following wax depilation
- dry skin caused by inadequate after-care.

Ingrowing hairs can be recognised as:

- a flat thread, which can be seen lying underneath the surface of the skin
- a coiled, ingrowing hair appearing as a small, slightly raised lump with a dark dot on the middle
- an infected ingrowth of hair usually resulting from one of the above. The area appears red and a pustule may be present.

In each case, the hair needs releasing by effectively and hygienically removing the blockage over the mouth of the hair follicle. This is best done with a sterile needle, followed by application of a suitable antiseptic.

Some questions and answers

Q. How long do the effects of wax depilation last?

A. Usually about four to eight weeks, but this varies between individuals. People who have very sensitive hair germ cells produce replacement hairs more quickly than others.

Q. Do depilatory wax treatments make the hair grow back thicker?

A. There is evidence both for and against this theory. Most clients claim that hair growth is more sparse after depilatory waxing. This is probably because the hairs are depilated at different stages of their growth cycle, so the replacement hairs do not appear at the same time.

Q. Is it all right to have wax depilation in between electrical epilation treatments?

A. No, definitely not. Regular depilatory wax treatments can distort the hair follicle and make subsequent treatment with electrical epilation very difficult.

Q. Does depilatory waxing hurt?

A. No, not if it is done properly. When the wax is removed, the feeling is similar to having a plaster pulled off. Any skin sensation soon stops once soothing after-care has been applied.

Q. How long do treatments take?

A. It depends on the amount and type of hair growth and the method of waxing used. As a guideline, the average time for a half leg-wax treatment (ankle–knee) with warm wax is 15–20 minutes. With hot wax, treatment to the same area takes nearer 30 minutes.

SELF-CHECKS

Wax depilation

1 When are particularly good times of the year for promoting wax depilation in the salon?

2 State three ways of ensuring that the temperature of the wax is comfortable for a client.

3 What is a suitable working temperature for warm wax?

4 How are the ingredients of warm wax different from hot wax?

5 Compare the action upon hair of warm wax and hot wax.

6 Give two reasons why the position of the client is important during a depilatory wax treatment.

7 Describe two possible contra-actions to wax depilation.

8 Identify three pieces of health and safety legislation that relate to wax depilation.

9 Why should vinyl gloves be worn when giving depilatory wax treatments?

10 In what direction should warm wax be a) applied, and b) removed?

Sugaring

This technique has been practised for centuries in the Middle East. Sugar, water and lemon juice are cooked together to produce a caramel. The mixture is poured onto a plate and rolled into little balls. It is then pressed firmly onto the skin, spreading it with the thumb and fingers, and then flicked off, taking the hairs with it. The effect of sugaring is similar to warm wax depilation.

Strip sugar and sugar paste

There are two types of professional sugaring products available:

- **sugaring paste**
- **strip sugar**.

Sugaring paste

A pliable paste made from pure sugar and other natural ingredients, this is used to provide traditional hand sugaring treatments. The sugaring paste is supplied in plastic tubs which can be heated safely in either a special heater or microwave. For treatments to be effective, the texture of sugar paste must be soft and pliable without being runny:

- if the paste is too soft it is difficult to handle; the paste sticks to the skin and is difficult to remove

- if the paste is too hard a lot of pressure is needed to spread it: the paste will not stick to or remove the hairs efficiently and the treatment is slow. Bruising and discomfort may result.

Sugaring paste is available as:

- *soft (regular)*: this type of paste is the easiest to work with and does not usually need adjusting

- *hard*: used in warm temperatures or when the hands are hot, also to harden (adjust) regular paste that has become too soft.

GOOD PRACTICE

Always return the lid to the tub of paste immediately after use and store it in a cool, dry place. The texture of sugar paste is affected by temperature and humidity. Heat and moisture soften the paste and make it too sticky.

Strip sugar

Strip sugar is a natural alternative to warm wax and is particularly useful for clients who have previously experienced sensitivity to wax products. Treatments with strip sugar are identical to warm wax treatments. The main benefits of strip sugar are:

- being water-soluble, it is an extremely clean product to work with
- most strip sugar products can be heated in a microwave
- the method of application and removal is identical to warm waxing
- strip sugar is economical to use
- it is effective even on coarse, stubbly hair
- it does not leave a sticky residue on the skin.

Selection of strip sugar products/equipment

Specialist companies provide training in sugaring techniques and offer a range of products and accessories for use with sugar paste and strip sugar:

- *antiseptic pre-wipes*: for cleansing the skin and hair prior to sugaring
- *antiseptic lotion*: for cooling and soothing the skin after hair removal
- *purified talc*: for drying the hairs, preventing the hands becoming sticky and absorbing perspiration
- *moisturising cream*: for softening and smoothing the skin immediately after and between sugaring treatments. This helps to prevent ingrowing hairs
- *body mitt*: for exfoliating the skin when bathing and for treating ingrowing hairs
- *bactericidal hand cleanser and barrier cream*: to protect against cross-infection
- *fabric strips*: for using with strip sugar and for removing any patches of sugar paste remaining on the skin after treatment
- *disposable spatulas and applicators*: for applying strip sugar
- *thermostatically controlled heater*: for maintaining the paste at the required temperature.

Benefits of sugaring

Sugaring companies promote their treatments as being the most comfortable and least painful way of removing unwanted hair from the face and body. A very low temperature is used and the products contain only natural ingredients. This makes the treatments very attractive to some clients.

The main benefits of sugaring are:

- sugar paste sticks to the hair and not to the skin
- sugaring is particularly effective for treating facial hair; it grips coarse hairs, leaving the soft, vellus hairs
- the hairs are pulled out cleanly from their roots
- the low temperature of the paste and gentle removal of the hairs means that treatments can be given quite safely to some clients who would be contraindicated to other methods of hair removal
- even very short hairs can be treated successfully, including recently shaved hairs
- sugar paste is water-soluble and therefore easily removed from the skin and any other surface.

Preparing for sugaring

The treatment area and trolley are prepared in exactly the same way as for depilatory wax treatments, ensuring a suitable range of products for pre-treatment and after-care.

Using sugaring paste

The sugar paste needs to be heated gently in advance of treatment. This can be done either in a special thermostatically controlled heater or in a microwave. If using a heater:

- place the container of paste in the heater approximately 15 minutes before the client is due to arrive and begin to heat up on a medium setting
- when the paste shows signs of melting around the edges, reduce the heat setting to very low
- leave the paste to stand for five minutes before using; this will ensure an even distribution of heat and the correct texture of the paste.

If heating the paste in a microwave:

- place the container of paste in the microwave with the lid on for one-and-a-half to two minutes on a medium setting or one minute on full power
- leave the paste to stand for 5–10 minutes before using to allow the heat to spread evenly throughout the paste.

HEALTH MATTERS

Be very careful when testing the temperature of the paste when it has been heated in the microwave. The microwave heats from the middle of the container towards the outside and can get very hot. If you try testing the paste with your fingers, you could burn them.

Using strip sugar

If using a heater:

- place the container with the lid on in the heater and put on the full power setting for 10–15 minutes
- turn the heater setting down to very low; the paste should be runny but not watery.

If using a microwave to heat the paste, place the container in a microwave with the lid on and set the timer for one to one-and-a-half minutes on full power.

REMEMBER

If the paste overheats in the microwave, the bottom of the container may melt and you may risk spilling very hot wax over yourself. Always set the timer accurately and check how hot the container is before attempting to remove it from the microwave.

Preparing the client

1 Prepare the client exactly as you would for wax depilation, ensuring that all relevant details are entered on their record card.

2 Check for contraindications: these are the same as for wax depilation except for varicose veins, which are contraindicated only if they are enlarged.

3 Position the client appropriately for treatment and ensure all relevant areas are protected and covered.

4 Examine the hair and skin in good light. Note the patterns of hair growth.

GOOD PRACTICE

Always test the texture and temperature of sugaring paste before applying it to the client.

GOOD PRACTICE

It will take longer to heat up a hard paste. Sugaring paste can be kept in the heater on a very low setting.

GOOD PRACTICE

Microwaves vary in power and heating times may need adjusting. The paste will not need as long to heat up if the salon is very warm.

REMEMBER

If you allow the paste to become watery in texture, it will be too hot to apply to the skin.

GOOD PRACTICE

Check the manufacturer's instructions before treating the legs of a client with varicose veins. If you are in any doubt about going ahead with treatment, ask your supervisor for advice. Always ask your client to get written medical approval if you are not sure.

5   Wash your hands with a bactericidal cleanser and, if using the hand method of sugaring, apply a small amount of barrier gel to protect your hands and prevent them from getting sticky.

6   Cleanse and dry the area to be treated and apply a fine dusting of talc.

7   Trim excessively long hairs with sanitised scissors to reduce discomfort during hair removal.

8   Explain to the client exactly what you are going to do, how it will feel and the possible skin reactions.

9   If using sugaring paste, have a small, damp towel or a bowl of water on your trolley so that you can wipe your hands if they become sticky.

> **REMEMBER**
>
> It is important to talc the hairs thoroughly because, if the hairs are not completely dry, they may be difficult to remove.

GOOD PRACTICE

The paste needs to be slightly firmer for treating coarse hairs and softer for finer hairs. The texture of the paste becomes more difficult to work with as it picks up hairs and loose skin cells. When this happens, discard the paste and use a fresh amount.

Procedure for sugaring treatments

The basic rules that apply to wax depilation also apply to sugaring:

- the product is applied with the hair growth and removed against it
- the client is positioned according to the area being treated.

Applying and removing sugaring paste

1   Remove the required amount of paste and, if necessary, adjust the paste while it is still warm. This is done by adding a few drops of water and stretching and folding the paste to make it more pliable. Alternatively, a little strip sugar can be added to soften the paste.

2   Using the special spreading technique, massage the paste with your fingers and thumb on the area to be treated. Stretch the skin to support it and then pull back to release the edge of the paste. You will need to have created a thicker 'lip' to the edge of the sugar paste to provide grip for removing the paste.

3   Remove the paste with a gentle but efficient 'flicking' action.

> **REMEMBER**
>
> You need very nimble fingers and expert tuition to develop the techniques required for applying and removing sugaring paste. Experienced sugaring practitioners offer specialist training in traditional hand sugaring techniques. Your supervisor will be able to tell you which companies offer this type of training.

Applying and removing strip sugar

1   Using a similar technique to applying warm wax, apply the strip sugar in a very thin layer, positioning the spatula at a 45° angle to the skin. Follow the direction of hair growth, covering as much of the area as possible with one application.

2   Apply a fabric or bonded fibre strip using the same guidelines as for warm wax treatments.

3   Remove the strip swiftly against the direction of hair growth, supporting the skin below.

4   Immediately press the treated area with your hand to reduce any stinging effect.

5   Continue with treatment in the same way until all of the area is cleared.

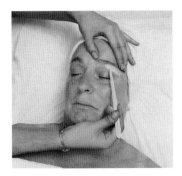

Applying strip sugar to the eyebrow area

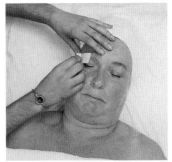

A fabric strip is used to remove the sugar

REMEMBER

Sugar paste is water-soluble and can be removed easily from equipment and other surfaces by wiping over with a damp cloth.

REMEMBER

The rate at which replacement hairs appear varies between individuals. As a general rule, sugaring treatments for body hair should be given every four to six weeks, for facial hair every two to four weeks, and for underarm and bikini line every three to five weeks.

Completing treatments with sugaring paste and strip sugar

1 When the whole area has been covered, wipe the skin with antiseptic wipes followed by a soothing lotion.

2 Wash your own hands.

3 Provide the client with a home care leaflet and explain about possible contra-actions.

4 Record details of treatment and retail sales.

The time required for sugaring treatments varies depending on the type and strength of hair and the size of the area to be treated

Half leg	1/2 hour
Full leg	1 hour
Bikini/underarm	5–10 mins
Lip/chin	5–10 mins
Eyebrow	5–10 mins
Forearm	10–15 mins

Contra-actions

In most cases there is very little skin reaction to sugaring. However, occasionally a client may develop a reaction shortly afterwards, when they have left the salon. It is important for you to explain what to do if any of the reactions listed below occur.

Red, itchy skin
The client should be advised to avoid anything that might heat or irritate the skin:

- avoid hot baths, sunbeds and sunbathing until the redness has disappeared
- avoid wearing tight clothing over the treated area
- apply an antiseptic soothing lotion regularly until the skin has calmed down.

Small whiteheads
These are mainly seen on the upper lip and forearms and are due to an excessive amount of sebum being secreted following removal of hair from the follicle. Minor infections may occur, which disappear after two or three days. The client should be advised to apply antiseptic soothing lotion regularly and avoid squeezing or picking the whiteheads. The spots usually disappear within four days.

Ingrowing hairs

Ingrowing hairs may result from the formation of dry skin over the follicle. The skin should be kept well moisturised and mild exfoliating treatments should be used to remove the skin blockage. When these are not effective, a sterile needle may be used to expose the opening of the follicle.

HEALTH MATTERS

Ingrowing hairs should be dealt with promptly otherwise they can become infected.

SELF-CHECKS

Sugaring

1 State three features that could be used to promote sugaring in the salon.

2 How should sugar paste be stored?

3 Name one advantage of heating sugar paste in a microwave.

4 How do the effects of sugaring compare with those of waxing?

5 State four contraindications to sugaring.

Other methods of hair removal

There are a number of ways of dealing with unwanted hair at home. You need to know about these so that you can advise the client about the advantages of professional treatments. Most professional hair removal systems have a range of complementary retail products which can be promoted in the salon.

Depilatory creams

These products contain a chemical such as calcium thioglycollate, which breaks down the protein keratin and dissolves the hair so that it can be wiped away. Hair is removed from slightly below the skin's surface. Depilatory creams provide a very short-term solution to the problem of unwanted hair.

REMEMBER

Depilatory cream should never be used on the face. A skin test should be undertaken before using it on other areas of the body.

Clipping

Scissors are used to cut the hair at skin level. Clipping removes the tapered end of the hair and leaves it blunt. A smooth finish cannot be achieved as a close cut is not possible with scissors.

Shaving

HEALTH MATTERS

Razors that are not cleaned and stored hygienically are likely to cause a skin infection.

Shaving creates a blunt tip which replaces the natural, tapered one. This gives the effect of a thicker regrowth. If the skin is stretched while shaving, the hair is removed from just beneath the skin's surface. Razors are quick and easy to use, but they cause a stubble and are not hygienic.

Plucking

Plucking is normally done with tweezers and removes one hair at a time from the hair follicle. The hair will not break as long as the skin is prepared properly and the hair is pulled out in the direction of growth. Plucking is only suitable for treating small areas, for example the eyebrows.

Threading

Threading is practised expertly by some Mediterranean and Asian communities. A piece of cotton is wrapped around the fingers, and then twisted and rolled over the skin. The hair is caught up in the thread and is pulled swiftly out of the follicle. While some hairs may be removed completely, it is likely that others are broken off at the skin's surface. When performed skilfully, threading has the same effect as plucking.

Pre-waxed strips

These are strips of cellophane coated with a cold wax. The wax sticks to the hairs, some of which are removed when the strip is pulled off. The basic principles of treatment are the same as for warm wax, but the results are less satisfactory. For depilation to be effective, it is the hairs that need to be coated with wax, not the cellophane! The strips are easy to apply, but quite painful to remove.

Abrasives

A pumice stone or abrasive glove is rubbed over the skin in circular movements and the hair is broken off at the skin's surface. The effects of abrasion on the skin are probably more useful than the effects on hair growth, provided that the skin is not damaged.

ACTIVITY

Activity 9.3: Removing hair using temporary methods

Collect evidence of treatments that you give for removing hair. Make notes on any problems encountered and how you overcame them. If possible, provide copies of your client's treatment plans and record cards. Note any retail sales you made.

Ask your clients to give you written feedback on how well you handled the consultation, treatment and after-care advice.

Treat as many different types of client as possible, ensuring you get practice in removing hair from each of the following areas:

- eyebrows
- face
- legs
- underarm
- bikini line
- forearm.

Depilatory waxing

Compare your answers with those of your colleagues and see if you all agree.

1   The small muscle attached to the hair follicle is called the:
    (a) arrector pili
    (b) dermal papilla
    (c) sebaceous gland
    (d) hair shaft.

2   The layer of hair containing pigment is the:
    (a) medulla
    (b) cuticle
    (c) melanin
    (d) cortex.

3   Resin is contained in hot wax to:
    (a) set the wax
    (b) soften the wax
    (c) grip the hairs
    (d) make the wax pliable.

4   The minimum length of hair suitable for warm wax depilation is:
    (a) 2.5 mm
    (b) 1.5 mm
    (c) 3 mm
    (d) 5 mm.

5   Talc is applied to the hairs before waxing to:
    (a) prevent the wax from sticking to the skin
    (b) to help grip the wax
    (c) to absorb sweat
    (d) to protect against infection.

6   The temperature of the wax should be tested first on:
    (a) the area to be treated
    (b) the client's wrist
    (c) the client's ankle
    (d) the therapist's wrist.

7   Antiseptic after-care is required after wax depilation because:
    (a) empty hair follicles provide a route for bacteria
    (b) waxing spreads infection
    (c) the skin is sensitive after treatment
    (d) the last traces of wax will be removed.

8   Shaved hairs feel thicker because:
    (a) shaving stimulates germ cells
    (b) the hairs have blunt ends
    (c) shaving irritates the cuticle
    (d) shaving splits the hairs.

9   Sugaring is particularly effective for treating facial hair because:
    (a) it grips vellus hair, leaving terminal hairs
    (b) it grips terminal hair, leaving vellus hairs
    (c) it removes hairs from their roots
    (d) it can be used over shaved hairs.

10 The effects of wax depilation usually last:
    (a) 1–2 weeks
    (b) 2–4 weeks
    (c) 4–6 weeks
    (d) 4–8 weeks.

KEY TERMS

You should now understand the following words and phrases. If you do not, go back through the chapter and find out what they mean:

Vellus hair	**Terminal hairs**	**Hot wax**
Depilation	**Hair shaft**	**Sugaring**
Dermal papilla	**Hair follicle**	**Sugar paste**
Hair root	**Cortex**	**Strip sugar**
Anagen	**Catagen**	**Telogen**
Warm wax	**Cuticle**	**Epilation**

Chapter 10 Manicure and pedicure

Provide manicure treatment; provide pedicure treatment

After working through this chapter you will be able to:

- describe the structure of the nail unit and surrounding structures
- appreciate ethnic variations in the structure of nails
- understand the process of nail growth
- know about the different types of products and corrective treatments available
- carry out safe and effective manicure and pedicure treatments
- recognise contra-actions and contraindications to manicure and pedicure.

Before you work through this chapter: Be wise and revise!
Revision topics to help you achieve this unit:

Provide manicure treatment; provide pedicure treatment

It is not difficult to convert clients to regular manicures and pedicures once they have had their first treatment. The hands and feet look and feel so much better afterwards. Manicures and pedicures are known as 'small' treatments: only small amounts of products are needed and the treatments take up a relatively short amount of time. However, they are popular and profitable and provide the opportunity for promoting other salon services. Very often, a manicure can be given while a client is receiving another treatment. This is good for the client and good for business.

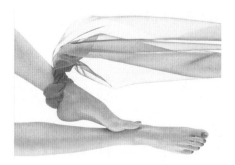

Perfectly groomed hands and feet

Assessing the client for treatment

There are some conditions of the skin and nails which either limit the amount and type of treatment that can be given or contraindicate treatment altogether. You must be able to identify signs of normal and abnormal **nail growth**, and provide appropriate treatment and advice for home care. You must also be able to recognise signs of infection or disease that require medical referral. It is important that the skin and nails are clean so that an accurate assessment can be made. The examination should take place in good light, preferably under a magnifying lamp. Jewellery should be removed from the area to be assessed.

1   Assess the general condition of the skin; note the colour and texture. Is the skin soft and smooth or dry and rough? Look for any cracks or breaks in the skin. Are there any signs of infection?

2   Look at the skin between the fingers or toes; are there any signs of dryness, sogginess or flakiness? Is there any skin irritation where rings have been worn?

3   Inspect the cuticles; notice if they are dry and hard or soft and pliable. Are there any splits or hangnails? Are any of the cuticles excessively thick?

4   Examine the skin around the nails; is the skin intact and are there any signs of infection?

5   Study each of the nails; are they smooth, flexible and slightly pink? Do they look and feel strong or are they all different shapes and sizes? Are there any splits or breaks?

Structure and growth of the nails

The parts of the nails that we can see are dead. They have no blood supply, no nerves and no means of taking in nourishment from the outside. This can sometimes be confusing when products and treatments claim to 'nourish' or 'feed' the nails. The true source of food for the nails is the blood that supplies the 'living' matrix cells just behind the nail fold where the eye cannot see.

Structure of the nail unit

The **nail unit** comprises the nail itself and all the surrounding tissues involved with its growth and development.

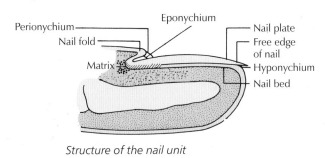

Structure of the nail unit

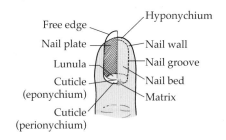

Matrix
This is the only 'living' part of the nail situated behind and underneath the nail fold. The cells are contained in an area of dense fibrous tissue called the mantle. The matrix is the site of nail reproduction and has a good supply of blood and lymph to keep the cells healthy.

Mantle
This is the area of skin tissue that contains the matrix. The mantle helps to protect the matrix cells from damage.

Nail bed
Composed mainly of the dermis layer of skin, the nail bed is a continuation of the matrix, and contains many blood vessels and nerve endings. A thin layer of the stratum germinatum of the epidermis connects the nail bed to the nail plate. If a nail is removed, this layer of the epidermis remains in contact with the nail. Ridges in the nail bed connect with ridges on the underside of the nail to keep the nail firmly in place as it grows. Blood circulating in the nail bed is responsible for the pinkish colour of the nail.

Nail grooves
These are deep ridges underneath the sides of the nail along which the nail moves as it grows. The nail grooves help to direct the nail along the nail bed.

Nail walls
These pads of skin, which surround the nail on three sides, help to cushion the sides of the nail and protect them from external damage. They also help to keep the nail in place.

Nail plate
This is the main body of the nail, made up of specialised cells of the stratum lucidum (clear) layer of the epidermis. Ridges on the under-surface fit firmly into ridges on the underlying nail bed. The cells of the nail plate have an overlapping, stacking arrangement, which, together with the protein keratin, make the nails hard and strong. The layer of cells that adheres to the nail bed is the softest. The external layer is the hardest. The nail plate normally appears pink but may become white or bluish depending on temperature and other physical conditions.

Hyponychium
This is the area of skin that rests directly underneath the free edge, where the nail separates from the nail bed.

Cuticle

The cuticle protects the matrix by forming a barrier between the nail and surrounding skin. It is divided into two parts. The main, outer portion surrounding the nail is the perionychium, which develops from the stratum corneum of the epidermis. It covers about one-fifth of the developing nail. Beneath this lies the less significant eponychium, a thin layer of dead skin tissue which adheres to the nail plate. The cuticle is continually discarding old cells and producing new ones. Unless it is kept soft and pliable, the cuticle can split or grow on to the nail surface where it becomes unsightly.

Lunula

Commonly known as the 'half moon', the lunula is a whitish crescent at the base of the nails which is generally only visible on the thumbs and big toes. The lunula is the only visible part of the matrix. The pale colour is due to the relative looseness of the nail plate at its base, over an area of very dense, fibrous tissue. The cells of the lunula are only partially keratinised, therefore the colour of the underlying blood vessels does not show through.

Free edge

This is the extension of the nail plate, which grows over and beyond the finger tip. It does not adhere to the nail bed, hence its white colour. The free edge is the hardest part of the nail.

Nail growth

The matrix is the site of nail formation. Some of the protein keratin is deposited here, which is then carried in the cells as they travel along the nail bed. During the journey from the matrix to the free edge, the soft, living cells are converted into compacted layers of dead cells, held together with a little moisture and fat.

As the cells move along the nail bed, more keratin becomes deposited in them so that, by the time a free edge has developed, the nails are perfectly structured to perform their protective role.

Without nails, the delicate nerve endings and blood vessels in the fingers would soon become damaged. The nails give support from above, which enables the fingers to perform many important functions. They also concentrate the sense of touch.

Here are some facts about nail growth:

- the average rate of nail growth is between 0.5 and 1.2 mm per week. Toenails grow much more slowly than fingernails. It takes about six months for a fingernail to replace itself and about 12 months for a toenail
- the nails are growing all the time but the rate slows down as you get older
- if you are ill, your nails suffer just like your skin and hair; this is because your blood supply concentrates on those parts of your body that need restoring to good health. As you get better, the state of your nails improves
- if the skin around or underneath a nail becomes inflamed, the rate of growth of that nail speeds up; this is because of the increased blood supply
- the nails of the longer fingers grow faster than those of the thumbs and little fingers.

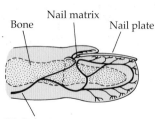

Bone Nail matrix Nail plate

Digital artery

The digital artery divides and subdivides to supply blood to the skin and nail bed

Blood supply to the nail and nail bed

Structure and growth of the nails

1 a) Name the protein in the nail.
   b) What is the function of this protein?

2 Why is it important to keep the cuticles in good condition?

3 How does the nail plate keep attached to the nail bed?

4 Why does illness affect the nails?

5 How does ageing affect nail growth?

6 How are the cells of the nail plate held together?

7 Compare the growth rate of fingernails and toenails.

8 Why are healthy nails a pinkish colour?

9 Why is the lunula white?

10 Name the 'living' part of the nail.

Diseases and disorders of the nails

Nail diseases are conditions of the nail and surrounding skin which result from bacterial, fungal and viral infections. Nail diseases **contraindicate manicure**. A client with a diseased nail should be referred to their doctor for medical treatment.

Nail disorders do not usually create a problem for the beauty therapist. The basic manicure and pedicure procedures can be adapted for most conditions, supported with appropriate home care advice.

Nail diseases

The general signs of disease are inflammation, swelling and pus around, and sometimes underneath, the nail plate. Some conditions show a green, yellow or black discoloration of the nail, depending on the nature of the infection. The main route for infection is through broken skin or damaged cuticle.

Paronychia

This is the most common of all nail diseases; it usually starts off as a torn cuticle or following the loss of cuticle from all or part of the nail. Bacteria enter the 'live' tissue behind the nail fold and a swollen, throbbing condition results with the formation of pus around the nail border. People who have their hands in and out of water a lot can develop an advanced form of the condition which involves infection by a fungus as well as bacteria. A doctor will usually prescribe an anti-fungal ointment and antibiotics to clear the infection.

REMEMBER

You can save your client a lot of discomfort by identifying the early signs of disease and advising them to get prompt medical attention.

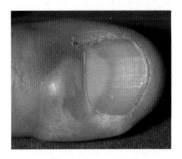

Paronychia

HEALTH MATTERS

The best way of preventing paronychia is to keep the hands dry and the cuticles soft and pliable.

REMEMBER

The warm, moist environment of a shoe creates ideal growing conditions for a fungus. Feet and shoes should be kept as cool and dry as possible.

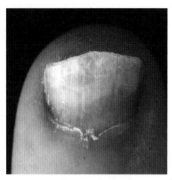

Ringworm of the nail

Ringworm

Ringworm of the nail (onychomycosis or tinea unguium) is a fungal infection that can appear either as whitish patches, which can be scraped off the nail surface, or as yellow streaks, which appear in the main body of the nail. The disease invades the free edge and spreads down to the nail root. The nail plate becomes spongy and furrowed, and is sometimes completely detached. Often, after medical treatment, the nail remains malformed.

Nail disorders

A nail disorder does not usually contraindicate manicure, but special care may be required during treatment to prevent the condition from worsening. If you are concerned about the severity of a disorder and are unsure whether to proceed or not, ask the advice of your supervisor. They may recommend the client to get written permission from their doctor or suggest you omit the affected nail from some or all parts of the manicure procedure.

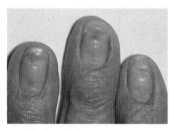

Beau's lines – transverse furrows

Transverse furrows

When caused by ill health, transverse furrows (Beau's lines) appear across every nail as the affected cells emerge from under the nail fold. Of course, the furrows cannot be seen until two or three weeks after the illness. As the general state of health improves, so does the health of the matrix and new, normal cells replace the damaged ones. Bad manicure practices can cause furrows when too much pressure is applied at the base of the nail.

HEALTH MATTERS

Always take care when pushing back and removing excess cuticle from the base of the nail. Too much pressure in this area can disturb the matrix cells situated behind the base of the nail. If the matrix cells are damaged, the resulting nail growth is malformed.

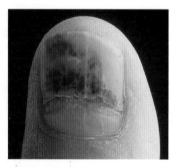

Bruised nail

Bruised nail

A blue–black nail indicates bruising of the nail bed as a result of injury, for example trapping a finger in a car door or dropping a heavy weight on the foot. The injury causes bleeding under the nail plate. As the injury heals, the bruise changes colour and eventually disappears. The finger or toe should be excluded from treatment if the injury is painful. A dark-coloured nail polish may be used to disguise the bruise.

Dry, flaking nails

Fat and moisture keep the nails flexible, and the layers of cells compacted into a smooth plate. Both fat and moisture can be removed easily if the hands are not properly cared for. Dry, flaking nails (onychorrhexis) and chapped skin are usually caused by inadequate protection. Exposure to harsh weather conditions, contact with solvents, and poor diet can all cause dry, flaking nails. Salon treatments and home care focus on smoothing and strengthening the free edge, lubricating the nail plate and softening the cuticles and skin. In some cases, the client's diet may be need to be revised.

REMEMBER

Detergents are designed to dissolve grease, and they are just as effective on skin and nails as they are on dirty dishes and laundry!

Split nails

Split nails are usually brittle nails. The most common causes are excessive use of solvents and detergents, careless filing, poor diet and ill health. If the condition is accompanied by dry hair and skin, there may be a glandular disorder. Regular manicures and a good home care routine are important for preventing split nails.

Pitted nails

A few isolated pits or dimples in the nail are common and do not usually indicate a serious disorder. Deep pitting of the nails may be caused by psoriasis, in which case there is usually an accompanying skin condition.

Longitudinal ridges

Ridges that appear down the length of the nails often accompany the ageing process. They result from irregular keratin production and can also appear as a result of minor external injury. The ridges may split, allowing dirt to enter. As the nail grows, healthy cells replace the damaged ones and the problem disappears.

GOOD PRACTICE

Nail polish should not be applied to nails with severe ridging because it is difficult to achieve a good finish. Buffing with paste helps to smooth ridges and creates an attractive shine. Special basecoats (ridge fillers) help to even out the surface of slightly ridged nails before applying enamel.

Loose nails

Loose nails (onycholysis) may be due to an internal disorder or may accompany certain skin diseases such as psoriasis, eczema and fungal infections. The nail gradually separates from the nail bed until the whole nail becomes loose or sheds completely. Severe nail separation contraindicates manicure and pedicure treatments. Further disturbance to the nail could result in premature shedding of the nail and exposure to infection.

Discoloured nails

Some deeply pigmented nail varnishes produce yellow stains on the nails if worn without a basecoat. The stains are unsightly but harmless. Brown staining of the nails may be evident in people who smoke heavily.

White spots

White spots (leuconychia) usually occur as a result of minor injury to the nail when air becomes trapped between the layers of cells. The spots are harmless and disappear as the nail grows out. White spots present on every nail can indicate a calcium deficiency but you are not likely to come across this in the salon.

Spoon-shaped nails

Some people are born with the condition, but, for others, it can be a symptom of anaemia and, when this is treated, the nail condition disappears. Spoon-shaped nails (koilonychia) are due to an accumulation of cells under the free edge. They sometimes occur in people who have an over-active thyroid gland.

Very thick nails

When present on the fingers, very thick nails (onychauxis) may accompany the ageing process, but they can also be caused by an internal disorder. Very thick, disoloured toenails may be the result of constant irritation by ill-fitting shoes.

Eggshell nails

Eggshell nails are thin, pale and much more flexible than normal nails. They curve upwards easily at the free edge. The usual causes are chronic illness or a nervous disorder.

HEALTH MATTERS

Normally, the nails contain 18 per cent water. If this amount is increased greatly, for example after soaking, the nails become very soft and less effective for protection. If the amount is reduced considerably, the nails become brittle and prone to snapping or splitting.

HEALTH MATTERS

Clients should be advised against 'digging' under the free edge. The area where the hyponychium attaches to the nail plate creates a seal which protects the nail bed. If this seal is broken, minor separation of the nail plate from the nail bed occurs, opening up a route for infection.

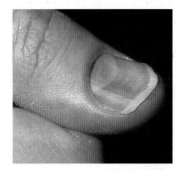

Spoon-shaped nails (koilonychia)

GOOD PRACTICE

Treat eggshell nails as fragile nails. Although they are more flexible than normal, they are also much thinner and therefore not as strong.

Excess cuticle

Some cuticle is necessary to protect the nail matrix, but an excessive amount of cuticle (pterygium) looks unattractive. Most people have a little excess cuticle, which can be removed during a manicure treatment. However, in extreme cases, the whole nail is virtually covered in cuticle skin and medical treatment is required to remove it.

Blue nails

The nails may appear blue when there is poor blood circulation to the fingers. The fingers have a bluish tinge and the hands feel cold. The nails do not actually turn blue, but they lack the healthy pink colour which would normally show through the nail plate.

Dark pigmentation

The nails of black clients often have areas of dark pigmentation which appear in linear streaks or bands. These are harmless and due to clusters of melanocyte (pigment-forming) cells present in the matrix.

Hangnail

A hangnail is a small piece of horny epidermis which has split away from the cuticle and nail walls. Sometimes hangnails 'catch' and tear the skin, providing a route for bacteria. Hangnails are common in nail biters and also occur as a result of dry cuticles.

Ingrowing toenails

The nails of the big toes are the ones most commonly affected. Instead of moving along the nail bed in the nail grooves, the sides of the nail cut into the nail walls causing skin damage. The condition can be very painful. Inflammation, swelling and pus often occur and the condition has to be treated medically. The two most common causes of ingrowing toe nails are a) wearing ill-fitting shoes, which put pressure on the toenails from above, and b) cutting the toenails down their sides instead of straight across; sharp 'spicules' of nail become embedded in the nail walls.

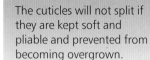
Blue nails

REMEMBER

The cuticles will not split if they are kept soft and pliable and prevented from becoming overgrown.

Ingrowing toenail

GOOD PRACTICE

Always cut toenails straight across and never down their sides; the latter forces them to grow into the skin.

Bitten nails

In most cases, only a small portion of the nails is visible, the edges of which are rough and uneven. The finger tips appear bulbous; there is no free edge. Frequently the cuticles become involved and constant biting causes them to grow thicker and harder. Severe nail biting can lead to hangnails, warts and bacterial infection around the nails. The disturbance of the matrix cells over a long period of nail biting can affect the formation of the replacement nail.

Bitten nails (onychophagy)

HEALTH MATTERS

Treatments that stimulate the blood supply help to improve poor blood circulation. Hand massage and buffing warm the tissues, bringing blood to the surface and improving skin colour.

Bitten nails: how manicures can help

Professional manicures encourage the client by improving the appearance of the nails and making them less easy to chew! This is achieved by:

- filing the nails into a regular shape
- bevelling the split layers together so that the edges become smoother
- softening, lifting and removing excess cuticle from the nail plate (a warm oil treatment is particularly useful before doing this)
- buffing the nails, which helps them to grow and gives them a healthy glow.

Diseases and disorders of the nails

1 State three causes of nail disease.

2 Give two reasons why a client with a nail disease should be referred to their doctor.

3 State three ways in which illness may affect the appearance of the nails.

4 Describe the appearance of paronychia.

5 Name one fungal infection of the nails.

6 Give two examples of how bad manicure techniques can damage the nails.

7 Why are strong solvents bad for the nails?

8 State two ways in which ageing affects the nails.

9 What is the most common cause of 'white spots' in the nail?

10 Why is buffing good for the nails?

Diseases and disorders of the hands and feet

It is not just the nails that are examined before a manicure or pedicure. The condition of the skin, hands and feet also influences the treatment procedures and advice for home care.

Diseases and disorders of the skin

Many skin diseases involve the hands but some are more likely to appear there than on other parts of the body. This is mainly due to them being exposed and in contact with potentially harmful substances or other sources of infection through touch. Most damage to the skin of the feet occurs as a result of pressure, friction and congestion in footwear (which includes shoes, tights, socks and stockings). Problems arise if the toes are not able to move freely and the feet are not adequately ventilated.

Eczema and dermatitis

Eczema and dermatitis have the same symptoms but their causes are different. Both conditions start off with redness or duskiness of the skin. Small lumps appear, which blister and form scales. The skin is very dry and there is usually intense itching.

Eczema is usually caused by factors inside the body or by an inherited or acquired instability of the skin. People suffering from eczema often suffer from asthma or hay fever as well.

Dermatitis results from factors outside the body, for example contact allergies. An allergic dermatitis reaction usually shows up within 24 hours of contact with the offending substance.

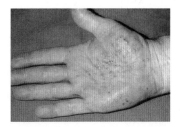
Eczema

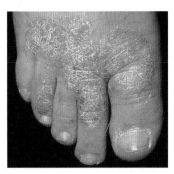

Psoriasis

Psoriasis

Psoriasis appears as irregularly shaped plaques of red skin, covered in waxy, silvery scales. The skin feels very rough and, if the scales are removed, tiny spots of bleeding occur. Psoriasis is thought to be an inherited condition which flares up during times of stress or illness. It is caused by an abnormally rapid rate of cell turnover in the epidermis. Unfortunately, psoriasis can be very itchy and if the scales are disturbed through scratching, bleeding may occur, leaving the skin open to infection. The limbs, elbows and knees are common sites of psoriasis.

HEALTH MATTERS

If the condition is present in a very mild form, the client may have a manicure or pedicure as long as stimulating treatments are avoided and the skin plaques are not disturbed. If the psoriasis is severe, the skin will be particularly sensitive and contraindicated to salon treatments. Psoriasis is not contagious and treatment is medical.

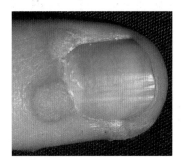

A wart

Warts

Warts occur commonly on the fingers and, less frequently, on the palms of the hands. They are usually skin-coloured or greyish-brown, raised and with a rough surface, which tends to itch. The centre of the wart is often depressed with a dark centre. Warts are due to a virus and contraindicate manicure treatment. Warts occurring on the soles of the feet are called verrucas.

HEALTH MATTERS

Warts are due to a virus and contraindicate manicure because they are contagious. Substances can be bought from a chemist which help to destroy the wart chemically. There are medical treatments for warts, but most tend to disappear spontaneously.

Whitlow

A whitlow is a bacterial infection of the soft pad at the tip of the finger or thumb. There is a build up of pus which cannot escape due to the thickness of the skin. As a result, intense pain occurs which reaches a peak after two or three days.

HEALTH MATTERS

A whitlow contraindicates manicure because of the infection present. Treatment is medical and usually involves lancing the swelling and prescribing a course of antibiotics.

REMEMBER

Never let a client talk you into cutting away a corn. The treatment of corns should be left to a qualified chiropodist.

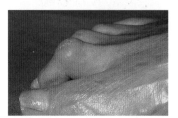

A corn

Corns

Corns consist of a central core surrounded by thick layers of skin. They appear frequently over the **joints** in the toes and the soles of the feet. The skin thickens up in response to friction, then pushes down into the dermis. Corns are not usually infectious. Sometimes, soft corns develop between the toes and these can become infected.

HEALTH MATTERS

Corns are painful due to the pressure put on underlying nerve endings. Special plasters and pads are available which ease the pressure. Ointment can be bought from the chemist which causes the hard skin to peel.

Calluses

These are larger areas of hard skin caused by friction, but they are less painful than corns because they do not push down into the dermis. Calluses often occur on the pads of the toes and the heels, and sometimes on the palms of the hands after doing heavy work. Calluses usually clear up quite quickly once the source of pressure has been removed.

Athlete's foot

Athlete's foot (tinea pedis) is a form of ringworm which affects the skin of the foot. The fungus invades between the toes and spreads to the soles and sides of the feet. The first signs are itching, flaking, cracking and weeping of the skin between the fourth and little toe. Small blisters and rashes occur. When the soles and heels are involved, the skin develops bright red inflammation covered with white scales. Athlete's foot is extremely contagious and is contraindicated to salon treatment.

Athlete's foot (tinea pedis)

Verrucas

Verrucas (plantar warts) are firm and round with a rough surface. They may occur singly or in groups. If the top is scraped off, small dark spots (blood vessels supplying the verruca) can be seen. Verrucas are caused by a virus and are contagious; they are picked up easily by bare feet. Because they occur commonly on the soles of the feet, the weight of the body pushes the verrucas inwards and they become deeply embedded in the skin, which can be very painful.

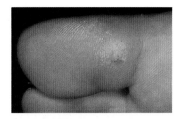

A verruca (plantar wart)

Disorders of the joints

Rheumatism is a general term for pain, with or without stiffness, which affects the muscles and joints. It describes a symptom of a disorder rather than being a disorder itself. Rheumatism covers many conditions including arthritis.

Arthritis

Arthritis is a general term for inflammation of a joint. The condition can follow injury or bacterial infection, but, more commonly, it results from the wear and tear of ageing. The joint swells, stiffens and becomes painful. The overlying skin takes on a red, shiny appearance. When the joints of the hand are affected, in severe conditions, the whole hand appears deformed.

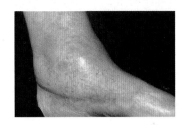

Arthritis

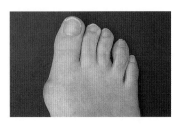

A bunion

Bunion

A bunion is a harmless swelling of the joint of the big toe which is particularly common in middle-aged women. It usually affects both feet. As the joint swells, the skin over it becomes hard, red and tender. The big toe usually becomes displaced, turning inwards towards the other toes.

GOOD PRACTICE

A bunion does not contraindicate pedicure, but care should be taken when massaging the foot if the bunion is painful.

SELF-CHECKS

Diseases and disorders of the hands and feet

1 State the main difference between eczema and dermatitis.

2 Describe the appearance of psoriasis.

3 Why are warts contraindicated to manicure?

4 State two differences between a corn and a verruca.

5 Name four conditions that may result from wearing ill-fitting shoes.

ACTIVITY

Activity 10.1: Ethnic variations

Everybody's nails and skin have the same basic structure, but are there any ethnic variations in their appearance and condition? Find out! 'Ethnic variations in skin structure', covered in Chapter 6, may be helpful.

It might be good for you to work with one or two colleagues on this activity.

1 Identify three people with different ethnic backgrounds, for example one Asian, one Oriental and one African-Caribbean person. Ask them to help you with a small piece of research.

2 Prepare a short questionnaire for each of them about the nails and skin of their hands and feet. Consider things like colour, thickness, strength, suppleness and any specific problems.

3 Inspect their hands and nails closely, and get as much information from them as you can. Remember that you are aiming to find out things that relate to ethnicity rather than anything else. Think of this when preparing your questions.

4 Write up a short report and present your findings to your superviser.

Structure of the hands and feet

Joints make up the main 'engineering' of the hands and feet, enabling them to produce a variety of movements which make everyday activities possible. Joints are formed wherever two bones come into contact. The bones are bound by **ligaments**, which limit their movement and prevent dislocation. The power behind joint movements is supplied by muscles. Each end of a muscle is attached by a strong **tendon** to a bone. One end is called the origin and the other is called the insertion. Muscles are most powerful at the point of their insertion, where movements occur as a result of the muscle contracting and pulling one bone towards the other. Muscles and bones need a good supply of blood to stay healthy. They also need protection from external damage and this is provided by skin that is structured specially to withstand friction and pressure.

Bones of the hand and forearm

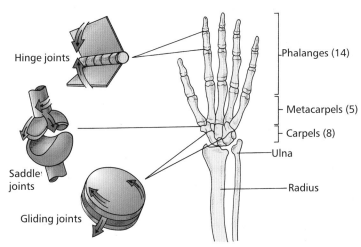

Hinge joints

Saddle joints

Gliding joints

Phalanges (14)

Metacarpels (5)

Carpels (8)

Ulna

Radius

The radius and ulna are the two long bones of the forearm. The ulna is situated on the little finger side of the arm.

There are eight carpal bones in the wrist, arranged in two rows.

The five long bones in the hand are the metacarpels. They are different lengths and each one moves with one of the five digits (fingers and thumb).

Fourteen small bones make up the digits.

There are three in each finger and two in each thumb. These bones are called phalanges.

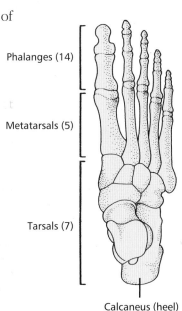

Humerus

Ulna

Radius

Carpal bones

Metacarpal bones

Phalanges

Bones of the hand and forearm

Types of joint

The names of the joints give an idea of the range of movement that occurs there:

- the small bones of the phalanges move at hinge joints; there is limited movement in one direction only
- a saddle joint connects the thumb to the hand and allows it to rotate freely across the palm; this movement is known as opposition. Without this ability, the hand would be just a claw. Its precise movement and powerful grip would be severely limited
- the individual pebble-like bones of the wrist glide over one another in a mainly sideways movement.

Bones of the foot and lower leg

The feet support the body and have to take a considerable strain. The main strength of the foot is in the big toe and the true centre of balance is in the ball of the foot. Damage to either of these affects the natural body posture. The feet are structured specifically to perform their very important functions.

The bones of the feet fit together to form arches, which help to support the weight of the body, absorb the impact of movements such as running and jumping, and maintain balance when walking on uneven surfaces.

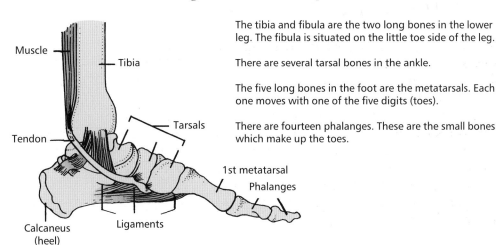

Muscle

Tibia

Tendon

Tarsals

Calcaneus (heel)

Ligaments

1st metatarsal

Phalanges

The tibia and fibula are the two long bones in the lower leg. The fibula is situated on the little toe side of the leg.

There are several tarsal bones in the ankle.

The five long bones in the foot are the metatarsals. Each one moves with one of the five digits (toes).

There are fourteen phalanges. These are the small bones which make up the toes.

Ligaments and tendons support the arches of the foot

Phalanges (14)

Metatarsals (5)

Tarsals (7)

Calcaneus (heel)

Bones of the foot

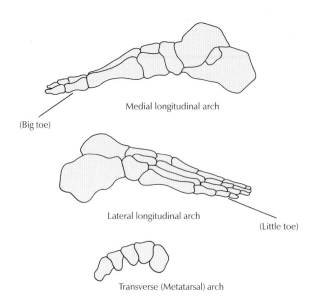

Arches of the foot

Muscles of the hand and forearm

Muscles work in pairs to produce movements at the joints. Muscles are made up of fibres and always pull in the direction of the muscle fibres:

- flexors bend the parts to which they are attached
- extensors straighten the parts to which they are attached
- abductors pull parts away from the centre of the body
- adductors pull parts towards the centre of the body.

The following diagrams identify the main muscles by their actions.

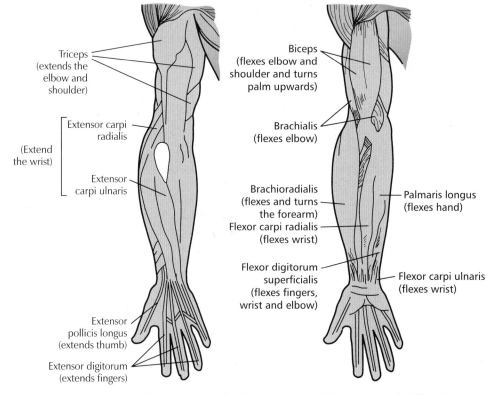

Main arm muscles (back)   *Main arm muscles (front)*

A PRACTICAL GUIDE TO BEAUTY THERAPY

Muscles of the foot and lower leg

Foot movements are produced primarily by muscles in the lower leg. These pull on tendons, which move the feet and toes.

Muscles of the foot and lower leg

Quadriceps group	Extends knee joint
Tibialis anterior	Pulls foot upwards and turns it inwards
Extensor digitorum longus	Pulls toes upwards
Peroneus longus	Tilts foot upwards and outwards
Extensor hallicus longus	Pulls big toe upwards
Gastrocnemius	Pull foot downwards
Soleus	Pulls foot downwards

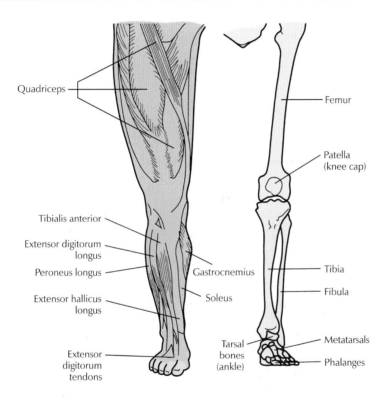

Muscles of foot and lower leg – front

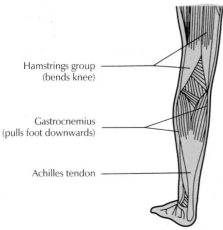

Muscles of foot and lower leg – back

Blood supply to the hands and feet

Living cells need oxygen. The arteries carry blood, which contains oxygen bound to haemoglobin. Haemoglobin is the colouring matter of red blood cells. Blood containing oxygen is bright red. It also contains the breakdown products of digestion, when the food we eat is converted into nutrients which living cells use to keep them healthy.

When the cells have taken up oxygen from the blood and used up the nutrients, they create waste products which are taken away in the veins with carbon dioxide. Carbon dioxide is later converted into oxygen. Blood, which has had its oxygen removed by cells is bluish in colour. Capillaries form a branched network of tiny, thin-walled vessels which link the arteries, tissues and veins and circulate blood around the body.

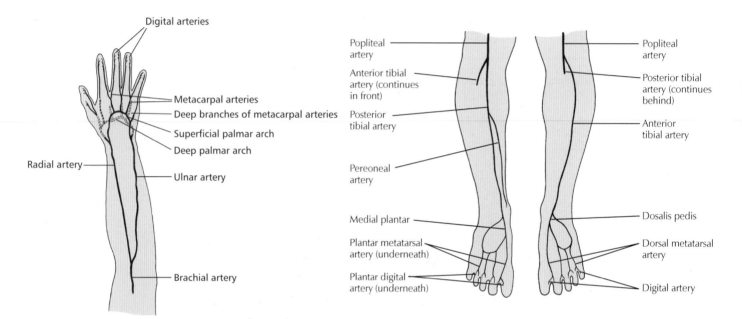

Arteries of the hand and forearm

Arteries of the foot and leg

Skin of the hands and feet

Starting from the top, the skin has three main layers:

- the epidermis, which is the outer, protective covering of the body. The cells at the base of this layer are living; they gradually move up to the surface and die
- the dermis, which is a deeper, fibrous supportive layer made up of different types of protein fibres. This layer contains blood vessels, nerves, hair follicles, sebaceous glands and sweat glands
- the subcutaneous (adipose) layer, which stores fat.

The uppermost layer of the epidermis is called the stratum corneum. It is made up of dead cells containing the protein keratin. The role of the stratum corneum is to protect the deeper, living layers. It is thickest on the palms of the hands and the soles of the feet where extra protection is required against friction.

The skin of the feet is thickest in these areas because of the pressure upon them. Some jobs, such as gardening, cause dirt to become ingrained deep in the streatum corneum. Even after scrubbing, the evidence remains trapped between the cells for

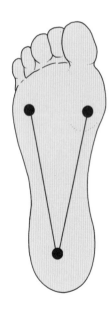

Skin is thickest on the weight-bearing points of the feet

several days until the cells are finally shed. The skin of the palm and the soles is thick, ridged and has no hair or sebaceous glands. It does, however, have more sweat glands than other area of the body. These features help hands and feet to grip and to perform their essential tasks.

Manicure treatments

The main purposes of a manicure are to improve the appearance and condition of the hands and nails whilst providing advice for their healthy maintenance. Routine manicure procedures usually take between 20 and 30 minutes in the salon depending on the length and state of the nails. The more regularly a client attends for manicure, the less time is required. Special hand and nail treatments are available which may require additional treatment time or which can be incorporated into the basic manicure.

Preparing for manicure

The preparation of tools and equipment does not begin minutes before the manicure is due to start. The cleaning and tidying procedures that conclude one treatment help towards preparing the next.

Manicure workstation

Equipment and materials

You may be providing manicure treatments at a purpose-built nail station which incorporates a magnifying lamp, finger bowl, storage drawers and arm rest for your client, or you could be working from a standard beauty trolley or mobile manicure stool with fitted storage trays.

Whatever your working situation, you will need to ensure that the area is spotlessly clean before treatment and covered with a towel and paper sheeting or tissues where the work surface and small tools need protecting.

You will need the following:

- *Nail scissors*: the lightweight, curved blades adapt to the convex shape of the nails. They cut the nails without weakening them. Nail scissors are used to remove excessive length before the nails are shaped with an emery board.
- *Emery boards*: professional emery boards are long, strong and flexible with a coarse side for reducing the length of strong nails and a fine side used for achieving the final shape and smoothing the free edge. 'Combination' files are foam-covered boards which have a medium grit on one side for re-shaping and reducing length, and a fine grit on the other for final shaping and smoothing.
- *Orange sticks*: the bevelled end is used to push back pre-softened cuticles and also for transferring small amounts of cream from pots. The pointed end is always used tipped with cotton wool for cleaning around the nail border, the cuticles and under the free edge. Plastic cuticle pushers are available which can be cleaned and disinfected in the normal way.
- *Cuticle knife*: the straight cutting edge of the knife is sharp and must be used with great care when scraping away eponychium from the surface of the nail plate.
- *Cuticle nippers*: the small pointed blades are used to trim away excessive cuticle in one continuous piece; they are also used to remove hangnails.
- *Nail brush*: used to remove all traces of treatment preparations from the nails and cuticles after soaking.
- *Spatula*: used for transferring hand cream from the jar for massage.
- *Buffer*: covered with chamois leather, it spreads paste polish over the nails and buffs them up to create a sheen.
- *Three or four sided buffer*: an alternative to the traditional chamois-covered buffer, these buffers come in block form. The coarser sides of the buffer are used to eliminate ridges and smooth the nail surface ready for the application of nail polish. The finer sides are used to polish the nails and create a natural-looking shine.

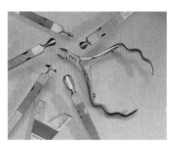

Collection of manicure tools and equipment

GOOD PRACTICE

Good-quality tools will last a long time if you look after them properly:

- use the tools only for their professional purpose
- apply lubricating oil regularly to the screws and hinges of cutting tools
- store cuticle nippers with the spring released
- regularly check the blades of cutting tools and have them sharpened professionally
- store cutting tools in an ultraviolet cabinet or in a clean case wrapped in tissue with the blades well protected.

A PRACTICAL GUIDE TO BEAUTY THERAPY

Other general items you will need for manicures and hand treatments are:

- *disinfectant*: kept in a small jar for soaking the cutting edge of metal tools during treatment
- *tissues*: tools that are not kept in disinfectant are wrapped in or laid on clean tissue until required
- *cotton wool*: used for tipping orange sticks and applying liquid preparations to the hands and nails
- *towels*: for protecting the immediate treatment area and drying the hands
- *three bowls*: one lined with a tissue for the client's jewellery, one for waste and one for the soaking water. The bowl of soaking water is the last item to be prepared before the manicure. A small amount of antiseptic liquid soap is added to very hot water so that, by the time it is needed, the solution has cooled to a comfortable temperature
- *manicure cushion*: to support the client's hands between the various stages of treatment. Alternatively, a towel can be folded into a roll for the same purpose
- *antiseptic*: for cleansing the hands.

Manicure products

Manicure products are safe and effective when used properly, but some require special care when storing and handling them. This is because of some of the ingredients they contain. Before you start giving manicure treatments, remind yourself of the health and safety requirements relating to the Control of Substances Hazardous to Health Act 1988.

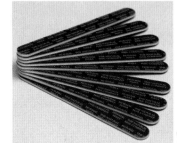

Professional, cushioned emery boards

Collection of manicure products

Nail polish remover

This contains a solvent which dissolves the enamel so that it may be wiped off the nail plate. Acetone is the most frequently used solvent, but it has a very drying effect which can cause the layers of the nail to separate. For this reason, a small amount of oil or glycerol is usually included in the formulation. Acetone-free removers, which are less harsh on the nails, have become popular. They contain solvents such as ethyl, amyl and butyl acetates and toluene.

Nail polish thinner

Ethyl acetate is one example of a solvent used to thin down nail polish which has thickened. A few drops of thinner is added to the enamel at least 20 minutes before the manicure to ensure that it dissolves evenly in time for application. Nail polish removers are not suitable as thinning agents as their oil content causes the enamel to separate and discolour.

Cuticle cream

Cuticle cream is used to make the cuticle pliable so that it can be pushed back and lifted without causing damage or discomfort. White soft paraffin, lanolin and mineral oil are examples of emollients contained in cuticle cream to soften the skin. Dry, flaking nails also benefit from the softening and lubricating effects of cuticle cream. Cuticle oil is available as an alternative to cuticle cream.

Cuticle remover

Potassium hydroxide is alkaline and caustic (it burns). In cuticle remover, it is combined with water, to produce a milky consistency, and glycerol, which is a humectant. Cuticle remover works by breaking down the eponychium so that it can be scraped away gently from the nail plate with a cuticle knife. It can also be used as a nail bleach. Cuticle remover makes the skin dry, sore and irritated if left in contact for too long. Make sure the skin and nails are rinsed well after it has been used.

Buffing paste

Buffing paste is used to smooth out ridges on the nail plate and helps to remove surface stains. Buffing the nails with paste creates a natural-looking polished effect which is sometimes preferred to coloured nail polish. An abrasive ingredient such as stannic oxide is included in the formulation. Other abrasive ingredients that are sometimes used are talc, silica, kaolin and chalk.

Collection of nail polishes

Nail polishes: basecoats, top-coats and coloured enamels

These products share the same basic formula: a film-forming plastic such as nitrocellulose; a plastic resin such as aryl sulphonamide or formaldehyde to give gloss; a plasticiser, usually castor oil, to give flexibility to the plastic film and help prevent the enamel from cracking; and a mixture of solvents, which dissolve all of the other ingredients and evaporates so that the enamel dries on the nail. The most commonly used solvents are ethyl acetate, butyl acetate, amyl acetate, toluene and alcohol. Pigments provide colour, and a pearl effect is achieved by the addition of an ingredient such as guanine or bismuth oxychloride.

Basecoat is applied before coloured nail polish to prevent staining of the nail plate and, also, to provide a smooth adherent surface for the nail polish. Special ridge-filler basecoats are available for using on nails with an uneven surface.

Top-coat seals and protects the coloured nail polish. It helps to harden the surface of cream-textured nail polishes so that they are more resilient to knocks. The extra ingredient contained in pearl enamels has a similar effect so a top-coat is not required.

Hand cream

As well as making the skin feel soft and smell pleasant, hand cream provides 'slip' for the massage; this means that the therapist's hands glide smoothly over the skin without causing friction and discomfort. A typical formulation combines an emollient such as lanolin or glycerol with water, emulsifiers, colour and perfume.

Hand lotion

Hand lotion contains the same basic ingredients as hand cream, but with a higher percentage of water. Pump dispensers are available which prevent contamination of the lotion and minimise wastage during use. Hand lotion spreads easily and does not leave a sticky film on the skin.

Additional items

The following items are extras that may be required for individual clients.

Nail hardener

Nail hardener can be used on fragile nails that have a tendency to split. It is painted on and allowed to soak into the nail. The active ingredient is usually aluminium potassium sulphate (alum), zirconium chloride or formaldehyde resin.

Nail conditioner

An intensive treatment product for strengthening and repairing weak nails. Some nail conditioners contain proteins and calcium.

Nail strengthener

Different types are available for use on brittle, damaged nails to strengthen, condition and protect against breaking, splitting and peeling. Materials used to create sculptured nails and nail extensions may be mixed and applied as a coating to the natural nails to provide additional strength.

Nail glue

Used for the instant repair of torn or split nails as well as for attaching nail tips.

Nail white pencil

This special pencil contains titanium dioxide to help whiten a free edge which has become discoloured. It is moistened before applying to the underside of the nail tip. A nail white pencil can be used to help create a 'French' manicure effect.

Hand lotion

Quick-dry spray

This solvent-based preparation is used to speed up the rate at which the enamel dries on the nail. It is much better for nail polish to be allowed to dry naturally, but, in emergencies, it is useful to have this product available.

Exfoliator

This is a gentle, abrasive, deep-cleansing product for the hands, which helps to remove calluses, rough and dry skin.

Manicure mask

Adapted from their uses in facial treatments, manicure masks draw out impurities in the skin and leave the skin of the hands feeling soft and refreshed.

Manicure mittens

Towelling or electrically heated insulated mittens may be used to cover the hands when paraffin wax or other special treatments have been applied. The mittens help to retain heat, which warms the skin and increases the cleansing and softening effects of the treatments.

Thermal manicure mittens

REMEMBER

Keep your tools, equipment and materials arranged in good order so that you do not waste time having to search for them during treatment.

SELF-CHECKS

Preparing for manicure

1 Which items of manicure equipment are suitable for sterilising in an autoclave?

2 Why is disinfectant required for the manicure?

3 How can the thickening of nail polish be prevented during storage?

4 Explain the difference between a cuticle cream and a cuticle remover.

5 Why is nail polish remover not suitable for thinning nail polish?

6 State three ways of maintaining cutting tools in good working order.

7 Give two reasons for applying a basecoat.

8 Why is a top-coat not required with pearl nail polish?

9 Why should a beauty therapist not wear nail polish when giving a facial treatment?

10 How should manicure tools be stored between uses?

ACTIVITY

Activity 10.3: Preparing for a manicure

1 Visit a wholesaler and study the full range of manicure products and equipment available. Find out if any new products have come on the market. Try to compare the quality of different ranges of tools. See if you can tell the difference between cheaper and more expensive ones. Take away product information leaflets and price lists to keep safely in a file for future reference.

2 Test five of the nail polishes on your manicure tray. Have the necks of the bottles been cleaned before replacing the caps? Are there any signs of the nail polish thickening? If you come across a problem deal with it, making sure you wear rubber gloves when handling solvent. When cleaning the necks of nail polish bottles, saturate the pad of cotton wool with thinner before use so that dry fibres do not stick to the enamel.

Manicure procedure

'Are you sitting comfortably?' This is probably the first question you will ask your client at the beginning of the manicure and it is just as important that you can answer 'yes' as well. The effects of bad posture get worse over the course of a working day, causing premature fatigue and aches and pains.

GOOD PRACTICE

Ensure that the client's hands and arms are free from clothing and jewellery. Offer the client a lightweight gown to protect their clothing. Additional protection may be provided by placing a towel over the client's knees if treatment is not being provided at a manicure station.

The following checklist will ensure comfort both for you and your client:

- sit close enough to your client to avoid stretching and straining arms during the manicure
- sit upright with back straight and shoulders relaxed
- your seating should be firm and at the correct height
- sit with your legs together and not crossed
- make sure you work in good light to avoid 'peering' over the client's hands.

1 Wash and dry your own hands, preferably where the client can see you. Evidence of good hygiene practice is always reassuring for a client and shows that you are working to professional standards.

2 Examine the hands and nails. If nail polish is being worn it will have to be removed before you can make an accurate assessment.

3 While you are checking that there are no contraindications to manicure, note any conditions that may need special attention. If there are signs of neglect they will need discussing with the client and advice should be given regarding home care.

4 Explain the purposes of the manicure relative to the condition of the client's hands and nails. If the client wishes to wear enamel, establish which one they require and check that the texture is suitable for application.

5 Wipe over both sides of the hands with a mild liquid antiseptic on a cotton wool pad. This cleans the hands without softening the nails before filing.

6 Establish whether the client is left-handed or right-handed; proceed on the opposite hand. This ensures that the hand that suffers the most wear and tear has a longer soaking period, which benefits the nails, skin and cuticles.

7 Apply nail polish remover with a cotton wool pad held between your index finger and middle finger. Press the pad firmly on to the nail for a couple of seconds, then slide it off the nail, squeezing gently against the nail plate to remove all traces of dissolved enamel.

8 Pull back the nail walls gently from the sides of the nail plate to expose any enamel which might otherwise be hidden. Use a tipped orange stick and nail polish remover around the nail border so that the nails are left absolutely clean.

9 Nails that are excessively long may need cutting before filing. Apply a little pressure from above with your thumb when using the scissors. This helps to give support and minimises disturbance at the base of the nail.

HEALTH MATTERS

Slouching strains the back, neck and shoulders and restricts proper breathing, reducing the oxygen supply to the body.

REMEMBER

Put the client's jewellery in a lined bowl where it can be seen to be safe.

HEALTH MATTERS

Surgical spirit, unlike many other liquid antiseptics, is tolerated by most skins. It is very effective when used in a manicure. The only drawback is that it smells very clinical. This could 'put off' some clients but reassure others!

REMEMBER

Do not rub the nail with the cotton wool pad and remover, or the nail polish colour may spread over the surrounding skin. This will need treating with more nail polish remover, which is bad for the skin and takes up time during the manicure.

10   Cut across the free edge of the nail, leaving the nail slightly longer than the desired length.

11   Working on the first hand, file the nails from sides to centre towards the nail tip. Hold the emery board as near to the end as possible. This produces long, flowing strokes and gives the nails a smooth edge.

GOOD PRACTICE

Work on building up your speed, using the emery board in the correct way. Find as many volunteers as you can to let you practise. Keep a check on the nail shapes and ask for your clients' comments regarding the final results.

12   Buffing can be done after filing without paste polish to stimulate the blood supply to the nail bed, or with paste polish to help smooth the nail for a later application of nail polish. Use the buffer briskly but lightly, applying approximately 15–20 strokes per nail in one direction only, towards the free edge.

13   Use the blunt end of an orange stick to transfer a little cuticle cream to the client's nails. Massage the cream well into the cuticles, using both of your thumbs.

14   Soak the fingers in the prepared soapy water and repeat the filing and cuticle massage on the second hand. Dry the first hand thoroughly and put the second hand in to soak.

15   Apply cuticle remover with the pointed end of an orange stick tipped with cotton wool. With the flat side of the stick resting on the nail plate, gently push back the cuticles, working around the nail border with small, circular movements.

16   Gently lift and clean under the cuticles with the tipped end of the orange stick and cuticle remover. Use the same stick to clean under the free edge.

17   Use the cuticle knife gently to loosen eponychium from the nail plate. The blade should be used wet and kept as flat to the nail surface as possible to avoid scratching it. Work round the nail border with small circular movements, keeping the cutting edge facing towards the main body of the nail.

GOOD PRACTICE

Never angle the knife so that the cutting edge is vertical. The blade may not look sharp; but it can penetrate the nail if not used carefully.

18   Take the other hand out of soak and dry it thoroughly. Rinse the nails of the first hand and scrub them to remove all traces of debris and cuticle remover. Dry the nails, pushing the cuticles back gently with the towel. Repeat steps 15–18 on the second hand.

19   Use the cuticle nippers to remove any excessive or damaged cuticle. Place the pointed end of the nippers slightly under the lifted cuticle. Squeeze the blades together to ensure a clean cut is made before releasing the blades and moving further along the cuticle.

20　Use the smooth side of the emery board to remove any roughness that may have developed around the free edges of the nails. Stroke the pad of your thumb around the free edge to check that it is smooth.

21　Apply either hand cream or lotion to the hand and forearm and proceed with the massage. Reapply lotion or cream as necessary during the massage to prevent friction. See page 357 for the massage sequence.

22　The massage leaves a film of grease on the nails which must be removed before the next stage of the manicure. Wipe over the nails with nail polish remover on a cotton wool pad.

23　If buffing is required as an alternative to nail polish, apply a tiny amount of paste to the centre of each nail with an orange stick and smooth it towards the free edge with the pad of the ring finger or thumb. Buff the nails until you have created a healthy-looking shine. Take care not to spread paste over the surrounding skin.

24　If nail polish is going to be applied, make sure that the client replaces jewellery beforehand to prevent smudging.

25　Apply a basecoat, then two coats of a coloured enamel and then a top-coat. Pearlised enamels do not require a top-coat.

REMEMBER
Nail polish will not adhere to the nails if grease is present.

REMEMBER
You will not need paste if you use a four-sided buffer. Work from the coarsest to the smoothest side of the buffer to remove ridges and create a natural shine to the nails. All buffers should be used in one direction only, towards the free edge.

Applying nail enamel

REMEMBER
Applying nail polish well is very skilful and needs a lot of practice. The nails are curved so it may be necessary to turn the fingers slightly in either direction to ensure that enamel is applied right up to but not over the nail walls.

REMEMBER
You must be able to produce a smooth, even finish to the enamel, which covers the nail plate without touching the cuticle.

26　Following the application of each coat, lightly touch the tip of the thumb nail to test whether the enamel has dried. It is important to allow each coat to dry before applying another, otherwise the enamel smudges easily and the effect of the treatment is spoiled.

27　While the nails are drying, advise the client about products that may be purchased from the salon for home use.

28　Record details of the client's treatment and escort them to reception.

29　Record details of the client's retail purchases.

GOOD PRACTICE

Practise using no more than four strokes for each nail to avoid 'over-working' the enamel. If your application takes too long, streaks will appear where wet enamel is applied over enamel that has started to dry.

Step-by-step manicure procedure

1 *Apply nail polish remover*

2 *Remove polish from nail border*

3 *File nails from sides to centre*

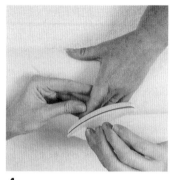

4 *Buff the fingernails*

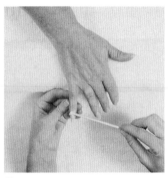

5 *Apply cuticle cream and massage into cuticles (a)*

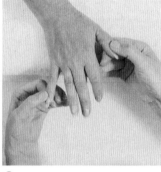

6 *Apply cuticle cream and massage into cuticles (b)*

7 *Soak first hand, repeat filing and cuticle massage*

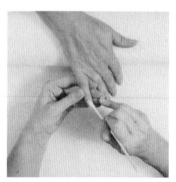

8 *Apply cuticle remover*

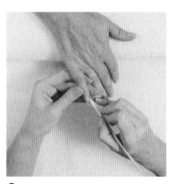

9 *Clean under cuticles*

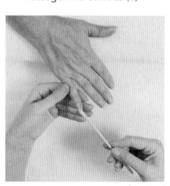

10 *Clean under free edge*

11 *Use the cuticle knife*

12 *Scrub the fingernails*

13 *Push back the cuticles*

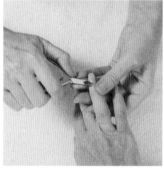

14 *Use the cuticle nippers (a)*

15 *Use the cuticle nippers (b)*

16 *Check the free edge is smooth*

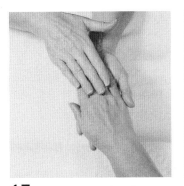

17 *Massage the hands*

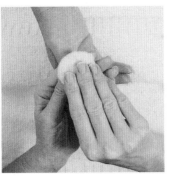

18 *Remove grease from the nails*

19 *Apply nail polish*

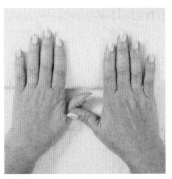

20 *Finished effect*

SELF-CHECKS

Manicure procedure

1 State three ways of avoiding backache when giving a manicure treatment.

2 Give three reasons for examining the client's hands before a manicure.

3 Why should the nail polish colour be chosen at the beginning of the manicure?

4 Why is the orange stick used tipped with cotton wool?

5 How does buffing the nails without paste polish benefit the nails?

6 Why is cuticle cream used before cuticle remover in the massage sequence?

7 State two precautions that should be taken to avoid scratching the nail plate with the cuticle knife.

8 How should the nails be prepared for nail polish after the hand massage?

9 Why is it important to apply nail polish with the minimum number of strokes?

10 What details should be entered on the client's record card after a manicure treatment?

Manicure treatments for men

The male market is becoming increasingly important to the beauty therapy industry. Male grooming has become big business and manicure treatments play their part in that. A male client may attend for manicure treatment either because their occupation means that their hands are continuously on show and they want them to look good, for example they work as a croupier, or because they have become interested as a result of other treatments they are receiving at the salon.

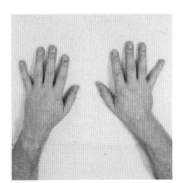

Male manicure

Whatever the motivation of the client, the following guidelines for adapting the manicure procedure apply:

- concentrate on those aspects of the manicure that are designed to produce natural-looking, healthy nails
- file the nails to a short, square shape rather than oval
- push back and remove excess cuticle from the nail plate

- buff with paste to a) remove ridges in the nail plate and b) produce the final, healthy shine
- use unperfumed products throughout
- use an oil or lotion, rather than cream, to massage the hands. This will provide 'slip' and help prevent discomfort when massaging over hairy areas
- use deeper movements during the hand and arm massage.

Hand massage

Massage is not just rubbing hand cream into the skin. If that was the case, the client might just as well be handed the bottle and be told to get on with it! Skilfully applied massage movements help to relax the client, make the joints more supple and leave the skin feeling smooth and refreshed. Besides helping the skin to absorb the hand cream or lotion, the massage increases the flow of blood to the area, providing essential nutrients for the muscles, bones, skin and nails. The removal of waste products from the area is also speeded up. Exercises are included in the sequence which help to ease stiffness and improve the mobility of the joints.

The basic procedure is made up of **effleurage** and **petrissage** massage movements:

- *Effleurage*: long, flowing, stroking movements performed with the fingers and palms of the hand. Very little pressure is used. Every massage sequence begins and ends with effleurage. Effleurage soothes the nerve endings and helps to remove loose surface skin cells.
- *Petrissage*: deeper, rhythmic, localised circular kneading or friction-type movements, which have stimulating effects. Petrissage increases the rate at which blood flows through the skin and underlying muscles, and removes loose surface skin cells and waste matter.

Le Remedi hand treatment programme

SELF-CHECKS

Hand massage

1 Name three beneficial effects of hand massage.
2 Why does the massage sequence begin and end with effleurage movements?
3 Give two effects upon the skin of petrissage movements.
4 Why is a cream or lotion used when massaging the hands?
5 Give two contraindications to hand massage.

ACTIVITY

Activity 10.4: Manicure treatments

You need to get experience of treating as many different clients as possible. This way, you are more likely to come across a range of conditions and problems, and that will help you to apply your knowledge. Always make out a treatment plan and fill in a record card when giving a manicure treatment. These will go towards your portfolio of assessment evidence. Check with your supervisor how many manicure treatments you need to complete.

Massage sequence

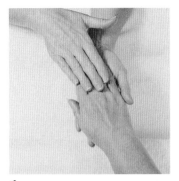

1 *Stroking from fingers to elbow (a) six times with each hand*

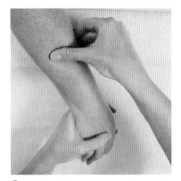

2 *Stroking from fingers to elbow (b) six times with each hand*

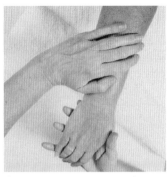

3 *Thumb kneading (petrissage) to forearm*

4 *Thumb kneading (petrissage) to wrist*

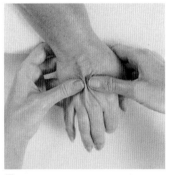

5 *Thumb kneading (petrissage) to back of hand*

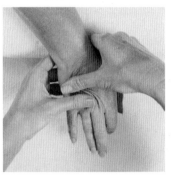

6 *Cross-thumb frictions (petrissage) to back of hand*

7 *Thumb kneading (petrissage) to joints of fingers*

8 *Thumb kneading (petrissage) to joints of thumb*

9 *Pushing against a resistance (exercise) six times to each finger and thumb*

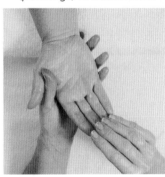

10 *Turning the hand over*

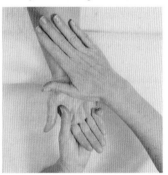

11 *Stroking (effleurage) from fingers to elbow (hand upwards) six times*

12 *Thumb kneading (petrissage) from elbow to palm*

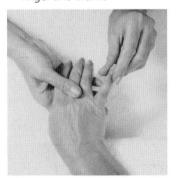

13 *Finger rotation (exercise) six times with each finger and thumb*

14 *Wrist rotation (exercise) six times in each direction*

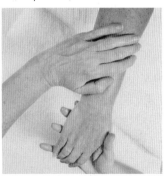

15 *Stroking (effleurage) from fingers to elbow (hand downwards) six times*

Creating nail effects

The length and shape of the nails should enhance the overall size and shape of the hands and should also be practical for the client's occupation. The strength and condition of the nails are also important. Only very strong nails should be worn long. Shorter nails are much less likely to break or split. They are also more hygienic.

Nail shapes

Oval nail
Generally considered to be the most attractive nail shape. Oval nails give the effect of length without producing a fragile point.

Pointed nail
Clients who are impatient for their nails to grow sometimes shape them in to a point so that they look longer. This is the worst thing they could do: a pointed nail will soon snap off.

Square nail
Short, square nails are often preferred by clients because of their jobs, for example people who handle food, and beauty therapists.

Wide nail
Wide nails can be made to appear slimmer by leaving a narrow strip free from enamel at either side of the nail. This creates an illusion of extra length, which draws attention away from the width.

HEALTH MATTERS

Advise your clients never to file down the sides of their nails to make them appear longer. This weakens the bridge of the nail causing it to snap.

REMEMBER

Long square nails flatter long, tapering fingers, but the corners should be rounded off to reduce the risk of them 'catching' and breaking.

Choosing nail polish

The nail polish colour should match the client's lipstick and co-ordinate with the clothes that are being worn. However, there may be times when what seems the perfect nail polish is not the best choice:

- very bright nail polish colours draw attention to the hands and are not suitable if the client suffers from arthritis or has obvious problem skin or a nail condition
- dark enamels make small nails look even smaller
- orange, peach or beige-toned enamels emphasise the bluish tinge of hands with poor blood circulation
- pearl enamels have a reflective quality, which draws attention to any imperfections of the nail.

Chipping and peeling nail polish

There are a number of reasons why the effects of nail polish application may not last for as long as expected. These are mainly to do with inadequate nail preparation, the texture of the nail polish used, and the time and care spent on applying the nail polish. If the nail polish has become chipped or starts to peel, it should be removed.

Causes of chipping:

- flaking nail plate
- grease on nail plate beneath nail polish
- basecoat not used
- enamel thinned down with too much solvent
- 'quick drying' the nail polish instead of allowing it to dry naturally.

Causes of peeling:

- nail polish too thick
- grease on the nail plate beneath the nail polish
- top-coat not used
- insufficient time allowed for each coat of nail polish to dry completely before the next one is applied.

'French' manicure

New make-up looks are designed to complement the seasonal changes in fashion and nails contribute to the total effect. The trend towards good skin care and more natural-looking make-up has made **French manicures** very popular. A clean, natural effect is created by using either white polish, pencil or tape to brighten the free edge, followed by a very pale pink or peach tinted translucent nail polish. Sometimes a stencil is provided for achieving a perfect curve around the flesh line. This is known as the 'smile' line.

French manicure

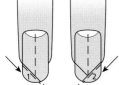

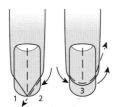
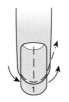

Chevron
The polish is applied down the length of the nail from each side to the opposite corner of the free edge. The point of the chevron sits on the mid line down the length of the nail plate. A diamante may be added later to enhance the chevron.

Rounded chevron
The chevron is applied first and the 'smile line' is created by sweeping the brush across the nail to round off the point of the chevron and produce a soft curve.

Rounded
The smile line is produced in one sweep of the brush, from side to side, dipping slightly in the middle to produce a soft curve. White polish is applied to the rest of the nail tip, working down the free edge in no more than three brush strokes.

Procedure

1 Follow the standard manicure procedure up to and including the application of basecoat.

2 Apply white polish to the free edge using one of the following techniques:

3 Apply the 'natural' coloured nail polish in the usual way.

4 Finish off with top coat.

More advanced nail techniques, involving the use of nail enhancement products and materials, may be used to create a semi-permanent French manicure effect. Some of these are covered at NVQ level 2 (see Chapter 12, Nail technology) and others at level 3.

Nail art

Nail art offers something a little bit different for the more extrovert client wanting to express their individuality. Coloured paints and nail art accessories, including foil, glitter dust and transfers, provide a limitless range of creative possibilities for the beauty therapist or nail technician with artistic talent. Basic nail art techniques at NVQ level 2 are covered in Chapter 11. More advanced techniques, including air brushing, are covered at NVQ level 3.

REMEMBER

Redness and irritation of the skin is called **erythema**.

SELF-CHECKS

Creating nail effects

1 State two important considerations when shaping the client's nails.

2 Why should the nails not be filed to a point?

3 List three factors that influence the choice of nail polish for a client.

4 State three ways of preventing the nail polish from chipping or peeling.

5 What is a 'French' manicure?

HEALTH MATTERS

If a client has an adverse skin reaction to any of the products used during the manicure, remove the offending substance immediately and apply a cooling, soothing antiseptic lotion. Record details on the client's record card with information about the action taken. Tell the client to seek medical advice if the symptoms persist.

GOOD PRACTICE

Always note details of any known allergies on the client's record card. Check the ingredients contained in products before using them on a client for the first time.

Contra-actions to manicure

Some people are particularly sensitive to substances which are tolerated without any problem by the rest of us. Contact with the substance, even for a short time, can cause an adverse skin reaction. In extreme cases, other organs of the body can be affected. Nail polishes and nail hardeners containing formaldehyde resin are the most likely manicure products to cause an adverse reaction (**contra-actions to manicure**). People with very sensitive skin may also react to perfumed products such as hand lotion. The skin will feel itchy and become inflamed.

Allergy to nail polish

The nail plates are dead, so, although they can be affected by nail cosmetics, they cannot become allergic to them. An allergy to nail polish is much more likely to appear on the face or neck as a result of touching the skin and bringing it into contact with the offending ingredient in the enamel. This is why you must never wear nail polish when giving a facial treatment.

A typical allergic reaction appears as dermatitis:

- itchiness
- inflammation
- swelling
- blistering at the site of contact, followed by
- weeping
- dryness
- flaking of the skin.

The most commonly affected sites of an allergy to nail polish are the eyelids, around the mouth, the sides of the neck and upper chest. The symptoms of the allergy may not show up until 24–48 hours after the initial contact.

HEALTH MATTERS

There have been rare cases reported of allergic reactions to nail polish which have affected the nail bed. The cause of these have been deep pigments in poor-quality nail polishes, which have penetrated the nail plate and reacted with the living tissue underneath.

SELF-CHECKS

Contra-actions

1 Describe the first signs of a typical allergic skin reaction.

2 Explain why an allergy to nail polish usually appears on the face.

3 Name two ingredients of a nail polish which are most likely to cause an allergic reaction.

4 What immediate action should be taken if a client has an adverse reaction to a manicure product?

5 Why might an allergy to nail polish not show up during the manicure treatment?

Conditioning treatments for the hands and nails

With a little imagination you can create your own luxury treatments for the hands and nails. Many facial products and treatments can be adapted quite easily.

REMEMBER

The growth and expansion of the 'nail' industry has prompted manufacturers and suppliers to provide new and exciting product ranges to support this developing market. Keep up with new product developments so that regular clients do not have long to wait to try something new. Special promotions can help to attract new clients.

Warm oil treatment

This is given immediately before the hand massage and involves soaking the hands and nails in a good-quality vegetable oil, which has been warmed up in a hot water bath. Almond oil is ideal but it is expensive. Olive oil is also good but its distinctive smell is retained by the skin after treatment. Arachis (peanut) oil is an acceptable, cheaper alternative. Warm oil treatments are particularly beneficial for clients with dry skin and cuticles and flaking, fragile nails.

HEALTH MATTERS

Arachis oil should be avoided if there is a history of peanut allergy.

1   Before beginning the manicure, pour enough oil into a small bowl to cover the nails up to the first joint of the fingers and thumbs. Cover the bowl and place it in a slightly larger container to one side of the manicure table.

2   As the second hand goes in to soak, pour boiling water into the outer container. The heat will gradually transfer to the oil, ensuring that it does not get too hot.

3   When the cuticle work is complete and the free edge has had a final smoothing, remove the inner bowl from the water and position the client's fingers and thumbs so that they are covered with warm oil.

4   Leave the nails in to soak until the oil has cooled down, usually about 10–15 minutes. One at a time, lift the hands out of the bowl and proceed to massage the oil well into the cuticles and the skin of the hand.

Ideally, the remaining fine film of oil should be left to soak into the nails and skin, and nail polish should not be applied. The palms of the hands can be degreased by wiping over with witch hazel. In some manicure procedures, a warm oil treatment substitutes soaking the nails in soapy water. This means that the cuticles have the advantage of being softened by the oil before being lifted and pushed back.

REMEMBER

Electronically controlled thermal mittens help to retain the temperature of the oil and increase the effectiveness of treatment.

Thermal mittens

Paraffin wax treatment

In this treatment, layers of melted paraffin wax are built up to form a glove, which covers the hand and wrist (or the foot). The melted wax is applied to the skin with a brush or by immersion in a special paraffin wax bath. The wax 'glove' is then either wrapped in foil or sealed with 'cling film' and wrapped in a towel or towelling mittens to retain the heat.

Over the next few minutes the temperature of the skin rises enough to stimulate the sweat glands and sebaceous glands. As a result, the skin is deep cleansed and softened. The heat stimulates the flow of blood, which brings nutrients to the skin and underlying structures. At the same time, the nerves are soothed, which has a relaxing effect.

GOOD PRACTICE

For best effects, paraffin wax should be applied immediately before the hand massage or straight afterwards to increase the absorption of hand cream.

Paraffin wax heater and accessories

Paraffin wax is usually purchased in 1 kilo blocks or pellets. A thermostatically controlled heater maintains the wax at a safe temperature range from 52 °C to 55 °C (126°–130 °F).

REMEMBER

Electrically controlled heated mitts help to retain the temperature of the wax for longer, which extends the beneficial effects of the treatment.

GOOD PRACTICE

Wear a disposable plastic apron when giving paraffin wax treatments.

1 Switch the wax heater on at least 30 minutes before you will need it.
2 Test the temperature of the wax on the inside of your wrist before applying it to the client.
3 Immerse the client's hand in the wax to just above the wrist. As you lift the hand out of the bath, a layer of wax sets on the skin.
4 Repeat five or six times until a white wax 'glove' has formed.

Building up the paraffin wax glove

Wrapping the coated hand in foil to retain the heat

Wrapping in a towel to provide further insulation

5 Wrap the wax-coated hand in foil or cling-film and cover with a towel or towelling mittens to keep in the heat.
6 After 20 minutes remove the towel and then the wax film and plastic wrapping in one firm, sliding movement.

Safety precautions

1 Some wax baths have an outer water vessel which heats up like a kettle. The heat is then transferred to an enclosed metal-sided wax container. Always make sure that the water level has been topped up so that the heating element does not burn out.

2 Make sure that the client's skin does not touch the metal sides of the bath. A paper towel placed over the rim of the bath helps to avoid painful contact between the skin and hot metal.

3 Protect the surrounding area with old towels or plastic sheets. Although the wax sets quickly once it is exposed to air, there is a slight risk of spilling or dripping the wax.

4 Used wax and wrappings should be disposed of immediately in a sealed container.

ACTIVITY

Activity 10.5: Paraffin wax heaters

Different types of wax heater will have different operating instructions. Some can be left switched on all day without the wax becoming overheated. Find out about the paraffin wax heaters in your salon. Make notes of any special instructions about using and cleaning the equipment. Keep your notes handy for quick reference when giving a paraffin wax treatment.

Exfoliating treatment

Massaging the skin with an abrasive cream is particularly good for lifting out dirt or stains ingrained in the skin. Removing dead surface skin cells helps to smooth and soften the skin as well as cleanse it. An exfoliating cream is applied in a gentle, circular motion, paying particular attention to areas with rough or dry skin or calluses. Rinse off the cream in warm water or remove it with damp hot towels, ensuring all abrasive ingredients are removed from the skin.

An exfoliating treatment

Hand treatment mask

Lightweight gel masks are available especially for the hands, although facial mask ingredients can be used quite effectively. The mask is applied to the hands with a mask brush. The hands are then placed in towelling mitts or wrapped in a towel for approximately 10 minutes, then the mask is rinsed off or removed with warm, damp towels. The mask is followed with a relaxing hand massage.

Hand treatment mask

Thermal mittens applied over a manicure mask

SELF-CHECKS

Conditioning treatments

1   Which type of oil is the most suitable for giving a warm oil treatment?

2   State three benefits of a warm oil treatment.

3   How does a paraffin wax treatment achieve its beneficial effects?

4   What is the purpose of wearing insulated mittens during a paraffin wax treatment?

5   State three beneficial effects of using an exfoliant on the hands.

6   Describe a) a normal, and b) an abnormal reaction to a skin conditioning treatment.

ACTIVITY

Activity 10.6: Luxury treatments for the hands and nails

1   Design a 'luxury' manicure using products and treatments from your salon. The manicure should be designed for a one-hour appointment. Indicate the estimated time and costs to the salon of each stage of the treatment.

2   Design a special offer 'tear off' voucher for your luxury manicure treatment, to feature in the local newspaper. The voucher should show the price that will be charged for the treatment.

GOOD PRACTICE

Clients have confidence in purchases which are backed up with a trusted professional's recommendation. It is also easier to monitor a client's progress with a home care routine if you are familiar with the products that are being used.

Home care advice

Giving advice on home care is an important part of the professional service and should include selling the client good-quality hand and nail care products from the salon's retail range.

Having convinced your client about the benefits of regular professional manicures, you need to give advice on how the hands and nails can be maintained in good condition between treatments. You should check how well the hands are usually protected from everyday activities and if there are any aspects of the client's job that might affect the condition and appearance of the hands and nails. Here is some general advice for looking after the hands and nails.

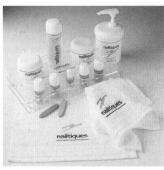

Retail manicure range

Washing

- Use mild soaps or hand cleansers that are not too drying.
- Remove rings before washing the hands so that soap does not build up behind them and irritate the skin.
- Rinse the hands thoroughly with lukewarm water and dry them properly with a soft towel; skin creases that are left soggy crack and become sore.
- Always use hand cream or lotion after washing to lubricate and soften the skin.

Protecting

- Wear household gloves for wet jobs and any activities involving the use of chemicals. When this is not practical, apply barrier cream beforehand. If working with the hands submerged in hot water, rubber gloves should not be worn for longer than 15 minutes at a time as sweat builds up on the hands, which irritates the skin.
- Wear a barrier cream and gloves when going out into cold weather. Use a richer hand cream during the winter months.
- Keep a supply of hand cream close to the kitchen sink and in the bathroom, so that it can be used each time the hands are washed or rinsed.
- Massage the hands with cream each evening just before going to bed.
- Rub cuticle cream into the nails and cuticles at bedtime to keep them soft and pliable.
- Always apply a basecoat under nail polish to protect the nails and prevent them from becoming stained.
- Avoid using nail polish remover too often; acetone-free removers are less harsh on the nails.

REMEMBER

If water or detergent gets inside the gloves while they are being worn, they should be removed immediately and allowed to dry thoroughly before being worn again. Sprinkling talc inside the gloves helps to keep them dry.

GOOD PRACTICE

Wearing a barrier cream when doing dirty jobs makes cleaning the hands afterwards very much easier.

Strengthening

- Eat a balanced diet which contains all of the nutrients essential for good health; they are good for your skin and nails too.
- Use nail strengtheners to reinforce weak nails and make them less likely to break or split.
- Use an emery board to neaten a rough edge or split nails: metal files should be avoided as they create heat in the nails, which dries out the natural moisture and weakens them.
- Buff the nails to a healthy pink shine before going to bed: this stimulates the supply of blood.

REMEMBER

The nails should never be used as tools, for example for prising off lids. This could break the nails, weaken them or cause separation from the nail bed.

HEALTH MATTERS

The health and strength of the nails depends on a good supply of protein, iron, calcium, potassium, vitamin D and iodine. Nibble cheese, celery and carrots when you are feeling peckish. They are much better for you than sweets and crisps!

A PRACTICAL GUIDE TO BEAUTY THERAPY

Exercising at home

Regular exercising improves the circulation, makes joints more supple and increases the strength of the hands. Just a few minutes are needed when the hands are not busy. After a shower or bath is a good time, when the muscles are warm and relaxed. Try them now while you are reading.

The tight squeeze

Grasp a squash ball in the palm of the hand and squeeze it tightly. Repeat until you can feel the strain. Relax your grip and repeat with the other hand.

Fist and flare

Clench both fists very tightly. Hold a second, then flare the fingers out in front of you as wide apart and as stretched as possible. Repeat six times.

Finger spread

Hold arms straight out in front of you with hands forward, palms down and fingers straight and pressed tightly against each other. Thrust the fingers apart, spreading them as much as possible. Repeat six times.

Wrist circling

Let the hands droop, then rotate them from the wrist, making as full circles as possible, 10 times in one direction then 10 times in the other.

Royal waves

Keep the hands relaxed, palms facing downwards, and then move them gracefully up and down, waving slowly from the wrists. Repeat 10 times.

Piano playing

If you are not an accomplished piano player, use the table top instead to rap out the William Tell overture! All the joints in the fingers and thumbs should get exercised, particularly if you play at double speed.

Shake and rest

Finally, with hands and wrists relaxed, shake them vigorously at the same time for about 20 seconds.

Following the exercises, sit comfortably with your hands completely relaxed on your knees for two minutes.

Tight squeeze

Fist flare

Finger spread

Wrist circling

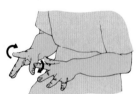
Royal waves

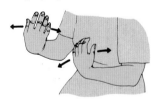
Piano playing

Shake and rest

GOOD PRACTICE

Practise these exercises regularly yourself to help keep your fingers, hands and wrists flexible. You need supple joints for massaging and doing detailed work with your hands.

ACTIVITY

Activity 10.7: Home care of the hands and nails

Collect information about the hand and nail care retail products available in your salon. Design a home care information leaflet which gives general advice to clients but also promotes the salon's retail range. Produce your leaflet on a computer for a professional result.

Pedicure treatments

Feet do not generally get the attention they deserve. This is probably because, for most of the time, they are hidden in shoes and do not contribute to the overall appearance. Neglecting the feet can have quite serious consequences. Many aspects of neglect are actually forms of abuse:

● cramming the feet into shoes that bear no resemblance to the natural foot shape

● buying uncomfortable shoes with a view to 'breaking them in'

● wearing high heels that thrust the body forwards and put the natural body posture out of alignment.

'You'll have to break them in.

People are gradually becoming more informed about the importance of foot care, particularly those who take regular exercise and are concerned about keeping their bodies in good condition.

GOOD PRACTICE

Pedicures should be promoted in the salon throughout the year, not just during the peak summer holiday months. Clients should be advised to care regularly for their feet at home, using products from the salon's retail range.

Preparing for pedicure

The basic pedicure requirements are the same as for a manicure with one or two variations and additions:

● *foot bath*: containing a hot, antiseptic soaking solution for the feet. Sometimes essential oils are added, for example tea tree, menthol, peppermint or eucalyptus, which have a cooling, invigorating effect. A special foaming foot bath can be used to revitalise tired, aching feet

● *foot spray*: the alcohol base has a cooling action, which is offset by propylene glycol to prevent the skin from drying. Essential oils may be contained to refresh tired, aching feet

A foot spa

A PRACTICAL GUIDE TO BEAUTY THERAPY

- *pedicure lotion*: a lightweight gel used for the massage, which is not as greasy as a massage cream or oil and does not leave the feet feeling sticky
- *pedicure exfoliant*: has anti-fungal properties and gently rubs away rough, hard skin, leaving the feet feeling smooth, fresh and revitalised. Deep-cleansing scrubs and rough skin removers are also available to achieve the same effect
- *medicated foot powder*: applied to the soles of the feet and between the toes to absorb sweat, and help to keep the feet and shoes dry. Most foot powders have anti-fungal properties
- *toenail clippers*: these look like a much larger and heavier version of cuticle nippers. They are stronger than nail scissors and more suitable for shortening toenails, which tend to be stronger and thicker than fingernails
- *callus file*: the abrasive action helps to remove a build-up of hard skin
- *hoof stick*: used to push back the cuticles on toenails, the hoof stick is used like an orange stick but it has a shaped rubber end
- *toe separators*: these are made from firm latex and are shaped to keep the toes steady and separated from one another while nail polish is being applied. This helps to prevent smudging.

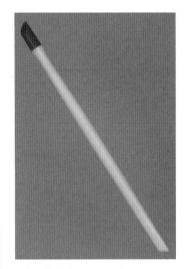

A callus file

A hoof stick

Pedicure procedure

The manicure procedure adapts quite easily for treating the feet, although a basic pedicure usually takes approximately 45 minutes because of the extra work required. Specific differences are explained in the following step-by-step summary.

1. 'Are you sitting comfortably?' The same basic principles of good posture apply. Seating should be adjusted so that the client's foot can be supported comfortably on the therapist's lap for treatment. Reclining seats, footrests and raised footbaths provide extra comfort for the client. A clean towel should be placed conveniently on the floor for the client's feet to rest on between different stages of the pedicure.

2. Wash hands.

3. Examine the feet and nails.

4. Place client's feet in the warm, antiseptic soaking solution. Clients are usually grateful for the opportunity to have their feet freshened up before they are worked on by the therapist, particularly if they are tired and aching.

5. Choose the nail polish colour and check texture.

6. Dry both feet thoroughly and rest them on a clean towel while you replenish the soaking water in the footbath.

7. Remove old nail polish from both feet and examine the nails.

8. Where appropriate, shorten the nails with clippers. Nail clippers are designed to achieve the straight free edge essential for avoiding ingrowing nails.

9. Foot 1: use an emery board to smooth the free edge and achieve the final shape. Thick, strong nails can be bevelled slightly with an emery board to taper the shape of the free edge and complement the convex surface of the shoes.

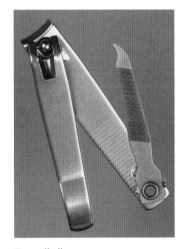

Toenail clippers

10 Use a callus file where there is a build-up of hard skin. Normal sites for this are the heel and pads of the foot. Alternatively, a hard-skin remover, scrub or cream exfoliator can be used.

11 Apply cuticle cream, massage, soak.

12 Repeat stages 9–11 on foot 2.

13 Dry foot 1 thoroughly; pay particular attention to the skin between the toes.

14 Apply cuticle remover. Push back, lift and clean around cuticles and free edge with a tipped orange stick or hoof stick.

15 Use the cuticle knife.

16 Dry foot 2.

17 Foot 1: scrub nails and rinse and dry foot.

18 Repeat stages 14–17 on foot 2.

19 If necessary, use cuticle nippers.

20 File away any rough edges on the nails.

21 Massage.

22 Wipe over the nails with nail polish remover.

23 Separate the toes with pads of rolled tissue.

24 Apply the basecoat, nail polish and top-coat. Some of the toenails are so tiny that only a single stroke of nail polish is required; this is sometimes done across the nail plate.

25 When the nail polish is completely dry, remove the toe separators and apply a light dusting of medicated foot powder to both surfaces of the feet and between the toes.

26 Advise the client about products that may be purchased for home care use and record details of treatment.

27 Assist the client with footwear and escort to the reception.

28 Record details of any retail purchases.

> **REMEMBER**
>
> The toes do not naturally span like the fingers: separating them helps to avoid smudging the nail polish while it is drying.

Step-by-step pedicure procedure

1 *Discussing the treatment plan*

2 *Soaking the feet in the foot spa*

3 *Shortening the nails with clippers*

4 *Smoothing the nail edges with emery board*

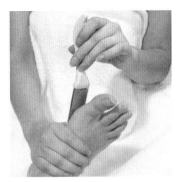
5 *Using a callus file*

6 *Applying cuticle cream*

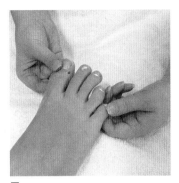
7 *Massaging the cuticles*

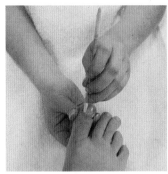
8 *Using a hoof stick to push back the cuticles*

9 *Applying cuticle remover*

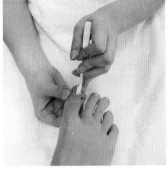
10 *Loosening excess cuticle (eponychium) with a cuticle knife*

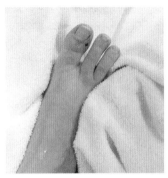
11 *Scrubbing the nails*

12 *Drying the foot*

13 *Using the cuticle nippers*

14 *Smoothing any rough edges*

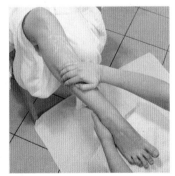
15 *Providing massage*

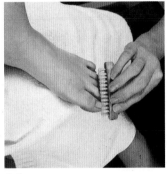
16 *Removing grease from the nails*

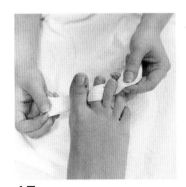
17 *Separating the toes before applying basecoat*

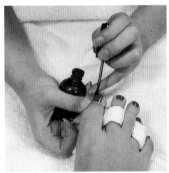
18 *Applying nail enamel*

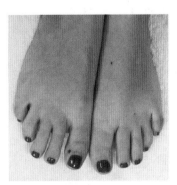
19 *The final effect*

Thermal boots

REMEMBER

The special treatments available for hands can also be provided for the feet. Pedicure masks help to refresh the skin, while heat treatments have a deep-cleansing action and stimulate the circulation, improving blood supply to the muscles and joints. Thermal boots aid the absorption and effectiveness of products applied to the feet.

Foot massage

The basic effleurage and petrissage movements used in the manicure adapt quite easily for treating the foot and lower leg, but an extra type of movement, **tapotement**, is usually included for working over larger muscles.

Tapotement

Tapotement covers a range of percussion movements where the hands work briskly, lightly and alternately on the body. The movements are adapted according to the shape, size and strength of the underlying muscles, the amount of stimulation required and the condition of the skin.

In this massage routine, cupping is performed over the back of the lower leg. This improves the tone of the muscles and skin by stimulating the superficial nerves and increasing the supply of blood to the area.

Contra-actions

The most likely cause of an adverse reaction during a pedicure (**contra-action to pedicure**) is a perfumed product added to the footbath or used for the massage. If the skin appears inflamed and the client complains of a burning sensation or itchiness, rinse the feet (and legs if affected) with cool, clean water, dry the skin and wipe over the inflamed area with witch hazel. A soothing, antiseptic lotion can be applied when the skin has calmed down. As always, enter details of the reaction on the client's record card for future reference. Advise the client to get advice from their doctor if the symptoms persist.

Home care advice

A client who has experienced a professional pedicure treatment will be keen to maintain the benefits for as long as possible. A full retail range of foot care products should be available so that clients can make an immediate and enthusiastic start to giving their feet the attention they deserve!

REMEMBER

The feet should never be restricted in tight footwear. Medicated inner soles and those containing activated charcoal help to absorb odours. These are quite cheap and can be fitted into most types of footwear.

The general aims of home care treatment are to:

- keep the feet clean and dry
- prevent the build-up of hard skin
- minimise the risks of infection
- avoid postural problems
- maintain an attractive appearance.

A PRACTICAL GUIDE TO BEAUTY THERAPY

Step-by-step foot massage procedure

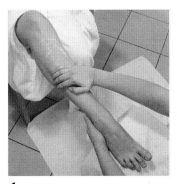

1 *Effleurage from toes to knee six times with each hand*

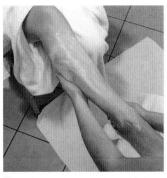

2 *Sliding down back of leg*

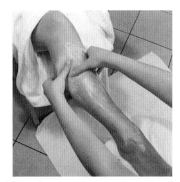

3 *Thumb kneading (petrissage) to front of leg*

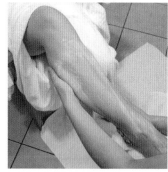

4 *Palmar kneading (petrissage) to calf*

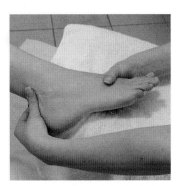

5 *Cupping (tapotement) (a)*

6 *Cupping (tapotement) (b)*

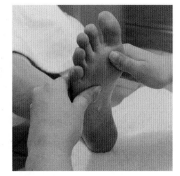

7 *Whipping (tapotement)*

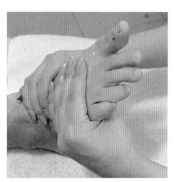

8 *Stroking (effleurage) six times with each hand*

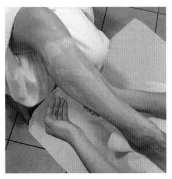

9 *Kneading (petrissage) Achilles' tendon*

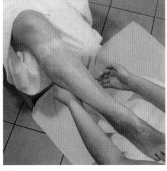

10 *Thumb kneading (petrissage) underneath foot and toes (a)*

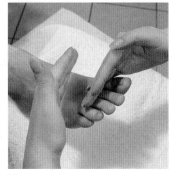

11 *Thumb kneading (petrissage) underneath foot and toes (b)*

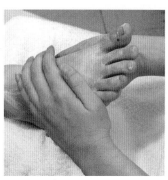

12 *Squeezing (petrissage)*

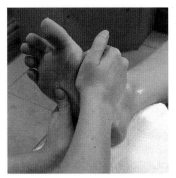

13 *Palmar kneading (petrissage) to medial arch*

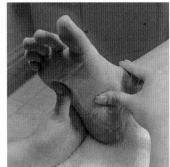

14 *Thumb kneading (petrissage) to medial arch*

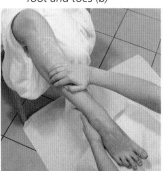

15 *Finishing effleurage*

HEALTH MATTERS

Foot odours tend to be associated with sweaty feet. Sweat actually does not smell, but bacteria that are always present on the skin multiply in a sweaty environment and produce a characteristic, undesirable smell. Regular attention to keeping the feet dry and cool is the best way of tackling the problem.

HEALTH MATTERS

Exercising stimulates the blood circulation, stretches the muscles and loosens the joints. This helps to improve mobility and revitalise tired, aching feet.

You will have explained each stage of the pedicure during the treatment, so the client should have a good idea of techniques which can be practised at home in between visits to the salon. A daily routine should be recommended, with extra tips given on the general care and maintenance of the feet.

1   The feet should be washed at least once a day, finishing with a cold rinse. Care should be taken to dry the skin well, particularly between the toes where it soon becomes warm and moist and vulnerable to infection.

2   Dusting the feet with foot powder after bathing and before putting on shoes helps to keep the feet dry, absorbing sweat from the skin. Foot powder is basically a talc with fungicide added to help resist diseases such as athlete's foot.

3   Excessively sweaty feet should be wiped twice a day with surgical spirit or cologne, which has a cooling, astringent effect on the skin.

4   The regular use of a foot spray throughout the day cools and refreshes the feet.

5   Hard skin can be treated at home with a pumice stone or callus file. The best time to do this is following a bath or shower. Soften the treated area afterwards by massaging in a medicated foot cream or body lotion.

6   Tired, aching feet can be revived at home by soaking in warm water with added footbath salts, sea salt or aromatherapy oils. The salts help by dispersing body fluid in the area and reducing swelling.

7   Shoes should be allowed to ventilate properly when not being worn. If possible, they should be aired for a day before being worn again. This advice is particularly important for synthetic shoes, which are not as absorbent as leather.

GOOD PRACTICE

Keep a list of local chiropodists handy to whom you can refer your clients. They will appreciate your help and you may even get client referrals from the professionals you have recommended.

Exercises for the feet

The feet spend most of their time confined and unable to exercise freely. Most people should be able to find a few minutes a day to perform these simple exercises. Try them yourself!

Foot flexion

Sit barefoot on an upright chair and cross one leg over the other. Stretch the toes downwards as far as they will go, pointing towards the floor. This is called plantar flexion. Stretch the foot back towards you until you can feel a pull on the back of the leg. This is called dorsi flexion. Do the complete exercise six times then swap legs and repeat.

Foot circling

Still sitting down with legs crossed, keep the uppermost leg as still as possible and, with the toes pointed, draw six wide circles in the air with the foot. Repeat the exercise with the other leg uppermost.

Joint stretch

Stand upright and take the body weight on one foot. Raise the heel of the other foot and bend the toe joints at right angles to the sole of the foot. Hold this position for a count of two, then balance the foot on tiptoe for a count of two. Return the foot to the bent position and finally to the floor. Repeat six times for each foot.

Toe toner

Stand on a thick book or step with the toes hanging over the edge. Bend the toes firmly downwards, hold for a count of two, then pull them back strongly upwards, also for two. Repeat the exercise 10 times.

Shake and rest

Finally, stand upright and take the body weight on one foot. Lift the other foot and shake it loosely and vigorously for a few seconds. Swap legs and repeat the exercise.

Following the exercises, sit comfortably for two minutes with your legs relaxed and both feet flat on the ground.

SELF-CHECKS

Pedicure

1 Give three contraindications to pedicure.

2 Give two reasons for using a foot spa during a pedicure.

3 State two ways of removing hard skin from the feet.

4 When is the best time to promote pedicure treatments?

5 State three benefits of exercising the feet.

6 Name two retail foot care products which could be sold in the salon.

7 State the locations and the functions of the arches of the feet.

8 Name the heel bone.

9 Give the common name for ringworm of the feet.

10 State two ways of refreshing tired, aching feet during a pedicure.

11 Why should the feet be dried thoroughly after bathing?

12 What causes foot odour?

13 Over which muscle of the leg is 'cupping' applied during the massage?

14 What would you do if your client has a verruca?

MULTIPLE CHOICE QUIZ

Manicure and pedicure

If you think there appears to be more than one right answer, have a word with your colleagues and supervisor and see if they agree with you.

1 Nails receive nourishment from the:
(a) matrix
(b) blood supply
(c) keratin
(d) nail bed.

2 The cuticle must be kept pliable so that it does not:
(a) bleed
(b) grow too thick
(c) split
(d) look untidy.

Manicure and pedicure

3 The function of the nail grooves is to:
(a) guide the nail
(b) strengthen the nail
(c) protect the nail
(d) straighten the nail.

4 A cuticle knife is used for:
(a) cutting off excess cuticle
(b) loosening eponychium from the nail plate
(c) loosening perionychium from the nail plate
(d) preventing the formation of cuticle.

5 Oil is contained in nail polish remover to:
(a) counteract the drying effect of the solvent
(b) dissolve the nail polish
(c) improve the texture of the nail polish remover
(d) soften the nails.

6 The most common cause of foot problems is:
(a) heredity
(b) ill-health
(c) ill-fitting shoes
(d) physical damage.

7 Corns are caused by:
(a) a virus
(b) bacteria
(c) friction
(d) a fungus.

8 The main vessels supplying blood to the hands are:
(a) the digital arteries
(b) the radial and ulnar arteries
(c) the capillaries
(d) the veins.

9 The correct working temperature of paraffin wax is approximately:
(a) 52°C
(b) 39°C
(c) 62°C
(d) 69°C.

10 Toe nails are shaped straight across in order to:
(a) prevent nail disease
(b) prevent ingrowing toenails
(c) prevent them from rubbing against the shoe
(d) prevent them from bruising.

KEY TERMS

You should now understand the following words or phrases. If you do not, go back through the chapter and find out what they mean:

Nail unit

Nail growth

Joints

Effleurage

Petrissage

Conditioning treatments

Contraindications to manicure/pedicure

Contra–action to manicure/pedicure

Erythema

French manicures

Tapotement

Ligaments

Tendon

Arteries

Chapter 11 Nail art

Provide nail art service

After working through this chapter you will be able to:

- consult with the client
- prepare for nail art treatment
- plan the nail art treatment
- provide nail art treatment
- advise clients about nail art treatment.

Before you work through this chapter: Be wise and revise!
Revision topics to help you achieve this unit:

Provide nail art service

TOPIC	CHAPTER	PAGE
Healthy and Safety at Work Act 1974	1	5
COSHH Regulations 1988	1	9
Public liability insurance	1	10
Sale and Supply of Goods Act 1994	1	15
Communication skills	2	24
Client care	3	52
Treatment hygiene	3	54
Selling treatments and services	5	103
Understanding colour	8	254
Complementary colour theory	8	254
Manicure and pedicure treatments	10	405 and 368
Structure and growth of nails	10	330
Diseases and disorders of the nails	10	333

The nail industry is expanding rapidly. New nail systems and product technology are developing all the time and clients are now very well informed through magazines, the media, salons and other retail outlets, about what is available. They know what is new almost as soon as the professionals and expect to be able to get it! This is increasing the demand for knowledgeable, highly qualified, creative nail technicians and nail artists.

A whole new fashion industry has built up around nails. If you want to be part of it, you need to keep up to date with all the latest trends and designs and practice hard so that you can work with them confidently .

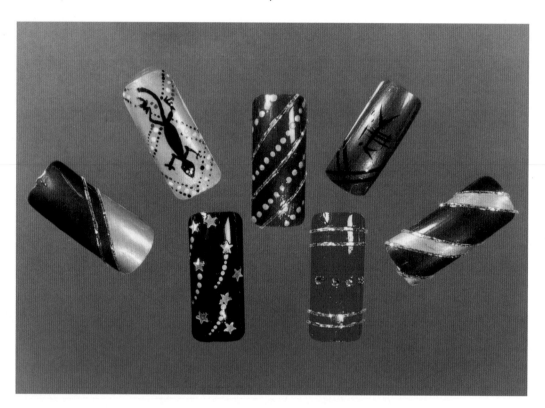

Dramatic nail art

Nail art offers something a little bit different for the more extrovert client wanting to express their individuality

GOOD PRACTICE

If you decide to specialise in nail art, you should read the professional nail magazines and attend as many nail competitions and trade shows as possible. Networking is important in the industry, and you will enjoy and learn a lot from meeting other nail specialists.

ACTIVITY

Activity 11.1: Learning about the industry

Find out as much as you can about what is happening in the nail art industry. Go on the internet, search on 'Nail Art ' and see what happens. Have a look at Melle Stripp's website and see more of her designs. Find details of magazines and other publications for nail professionals and see if they are available in your library or study centre. You might want to consider taking out a regular subscription.

For the therapist or nail specialist with a lot of artistic talent and the patience to practise, there is no limit to the range of creative possibilities. Once you have mastered the basics at NVQ level 2, you will have the opportunity to develop your skills and creativity at NVQ level 3, using more advanced techniques and different specialist equipment.

A PRACTICAL GUIDE TO BEAUTY THERAPY

Preparing for nail art

Nail art involves detailed work so it is important that both you and your client are comfortable and that you have good lighting to work in. A purpose-built nail station or nail desk is ideal as it is designed and shaped specially to avoid stretching during the treatment. Products and equipment can be stored cleanly and safely, and a worktop lamp incorporated into the design can be adjusted as required for close-up work.

A seat with adjustable height and backrest for both you and your client ensures you are seated correctly in relation to one another with appropriate support for your backs. This way, there is no excuse for bad posture and aching backs during or after treatment.

Jenni with client

REMEMBER

'Are you sitting comfortably?' This is probably the first question you will ask your client at the beginning of the nail art treatment and it is just as important that you can answer 'yes' as well. The effects of bad posture get worse over the course of a working day, causing premature fatigue and aches and pains.

HEALTH MATTERS

Slouching strains the back, neck and shoulders and restricts proper breathing, reducing the oxygen supply to the body.

Assorted nail art tools and materials

The following checklist will ensure comfort both for you and your client:

- sit close enough to your client to avoid stretching and straining arms during the manicure
- sit upright with back straight and shoulders relaxed
- seating should be firm and at the correct height
- sit with your legs together and not crossed
- make sure you work in good light to avoid 'peering' over the client's hands
- make sure both you and your client are warm but that there is also adequate ventilation.

In addition to the standard tools and equipment required for manicure (see Chapter 10), you will need a good supply of nail art products and materials, together with hygienically prepared specialist equipment.

REMEMBER

Keep your workstation free from 'clutter'. Besides looking tidier and more professional, the more space you have to work in, the more comfortable you and your client will be. You will also work more efficiently.

Equipment and materials

The quality of your equipment will have a great impact on your work. Buy the finest-quality brushes and collect a good range of shapes and sizes to suit your needs. Test brushes for 'moulting' before buying. The hairs should be fixed firmly in the metal ferrule that holds them in place. Brushes for nail art work are either natural sable or bristle, or synthetic containing nylon or polyester fibres.

GOOD PRACTICE

Be meticulous about cleaning your brushes. Apart from affecting the quality and finish of your work, it will extend their life. Wash brushes with water-based acrylic paints in warm water and use brush cleaner for cleaning nylon brushes. Make sure your brushes are completely dry before use. Once cleaned they can be stored in an ultraviolet cabinet.

Nail art brushes and equipment

Dotting/marbling tool

A stick with a tiny steel ball at each end. Available in different sizes, a **marbling tool** is ideal for creating flowers and other designs requiring either one or a cluster of dots. Simply dip the tool in to the paint and 'dot' on to the nail. Also used to mix different colours together to create a 'marbling' effect. The tool should be cleaned in warm, soapy water and wiped with disinfectant after use.

Fan brush

A **fan brush** has a very wide set of bristles. Ideal for sweeping colour across the nail in a single movement.

Fine detail brush

A small, very fine, pointed brush used for precise, detailed work.

Flexibrush

A **flexibrush** is a **striping brush** in its own bottle of paint. Used for creating lines, wisps and strokes.

Glitter brush

Ideally a sable brush used to apply the mixture of **glitter** and its adhesive. The brush is cleaned with nail polish remover.

Brushes and paints

GOOD PRACTICE

Nail art brushes in constant use will last for 6–12 months if they are looked after properly. Keep all brushes clean and protected. Store brushes either horizontally or vertically with the bristles facing up, never downwards. When brushes start to thin out, dry up and the ends start splaying, it is time to replace them.

Orange stick

The tapered end of an orange stick is useful for picking up **polish secures** and other small items for attaching to the nail.

Palette

A plastic palette for mixing different colours of acrylic paint or thinning the paint down with water. This can be washed and re-used.

Shading brush

A broad, square-headed bristle brush used to shade and float colour on to the nail and create swirl effects.

Striping brush – long

A brush with long, fine bristles used for creating stripes and straight lines on the nail. Dip your brush into the paint and lay it on top of the nail. Pull the brush towards the tip, keeping it flat on top of the nail.

Striping brush – medium

Used for producing thick lines and colour on the nails.

Nail art products and materials

Basecoat

A good, ridge-filling basecoat is essential to provide a smooth nail surface to work on.

Flat stones

Pieces of holographic (three-dimensional) plastic, usually round or hexagonal. **Flat stones** are ideal for encasing on the nail between layers of clear acrylic or pushed gently on to wet nail polish.

Flat stones

Foils

Foils come in various colours and patterns and have a striking, metallic finish. They are attached to the nail with foil adhesive.

Foil adhesive

A specially designed adhesive for using with foils. The adhesive is white when applied and must be left to go clear before applying the foil.

Foils

Glitters

Glitters

Very fine glitter dust can be applied by mixing with a special glitter mixer or top-coat. The glitter can be mixed before application and then painted over the nail or, alternatively, the brush can be dipped in the mixer, followed by the glitter, and then dragged or dotted over the nail. Glitter dust gives a lovely extra sparkle to nail art designs.

Glitter mixer

Mixed with glitter to apply it to the nail.

Nail paints

The **nail paints** used in nail art are usually non-toxic, water-based acrylics. They come in a wide range of colours and are used with different types of brushes to create abstract patterns, lines and scenic designs. Special effects can be produced by diluting the paints and mixing different colours together. The brush used to apply acrylic paint can be cleaned easily after use in liquid soap and warm water.

Nail paints used to create daisy design

Glitters, polish secures and rhinestones create dramatic effects

Rhinestones

Polishes

Nail polish can be used as the base colour for most designs. Matt colours are available for using with striping brushes.

Polish secures (jewellery)

Gold-plated polish secures are flat charms which need to be moulded to the curve of the nail and secured in place between a layer of nail polish and top-coat. Also available as diamonds and pearls, the secures can be glued into place for more stability.

Rhinestones

Rhinestones are tiny, flat-backed crystals, which sit on the nail. They are faceted and give a lovely sparkle.

A PRACTICAL GUIDE TO BEAUTY THERAPY

Striping tape

Supplied in rolls, **striping tape** has adhesive on one side. Striping tape comes in various widths and colours, the most popular being silver and gold. The tape is applied with light pressure over the chosen nail polish and then snipped just short of the edge of the nail. It needs to be sealed well to prevent lifting at the edges.

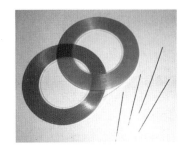

Striping tape

Top-coats

A good top-coat with a soft brush is essential for nail art. Ensure the top-coat is 'floated' over the nail and not dragged, so that your work stays in place.

Transfers

Transfers are available as self-adhesive and water-release 'decals'.

Self-adhesive

These are peeled off the backing sheet and then stuck carefully on to the nail.

Water decals

Water-release 'decals'

These are transfers that detach from their backing sheet when wet and slide over the base colour on the nail. Top-coat needs to be 'floated' carefully over the nail, as decals are very delicate and tear easily.

SELF-CHECKS

Preparing for nail art

1　State two reasons why good posture is important during a nail art treatment.

2　Name and state the function of three different types of brushes used for nail art.

3　State three ways of keeping nail art brushes in good condition.

4　Give two uses of a marbling tool.

5　List three materials that can be applied over nail polish or paint to produce a nail art design.

6　What product is used to 'seal' nail art designs?

7　What is a water-release decal?

8　Give two features of the paints normally used for nail art.

Client consultation

It is important to have a full consultation with the client before applying nail art. This is to assess their suitability and to get all of the information required for planning their treatment. You will need to fill in a record card with all of the relevant details and get the client to sign the card before you begin treatment.

REMEMBER

Many clients are happy with subtle designs on two fingers, with a co-ordinating polish on the rest. Other clients will be happy for you to do exactly what you want and risk the consequences!

In addition to their personal and contact details, you will need the following information:

- *condition of the client's hands and nails*: the treatment may have to be adapted or even refused, depending on the nature of a condition that might be present
- *reasons for treatment*: different occasions may require different sorts of designs, using different products
- *lifestyle*: the client's job, whether or not they have young children and what they do in their leisure time will influence your choice and application of nail art products
- *commitment*: whether the client is willing and capable of maintaining the nail art
- *personal preferences*: it is important not to pressure a client into wearing a design that you like creating but they are not comfortable with.

Assessing the client for treatment

There are some conditions of the skin and nails which either limit the amount and type of nail art treatment that can be given or contraindicate treatment altogether. You must be able to identify signs of normal and abnormal nail growth, and provide appropriate treatment and advice for home care. You must also be able to recognise signs of infection or disease which require medical referral. Diseases and disorders of the hands and nails are covered fully in Chapter 10.

It is important that the skin and nails are clean, so that an accurate assessment can be made. The examination should take place in good light, preferably under a magnifying lamp. Jewellery should be removed from the area to be assessed.

1 *Assess the general condition of the skin*: note the colour and texture. Is the skin soft and smooth or dry and rough? Look for any cracks or breaks in the skin. Are there any signs of infection?

2 *Look at the skin between the fingers*: are there any signs of dryness or flakiness? Is there any skin irritation where rings have been worn?

3 *Inspect the cuticles*: notice if they are dry and hard or soft and pliable. Are there any splits or hangnails? Are any of the cuticles excessively thick?

4 *Examine the skin around the nails*: is the skin intact and are there any signs of infection?

5 *Study each of the nails, run the pads of your thumbs over the nail plates so you can feel any irregularities*: are they smooth, flexible and slightly pink? Do they look and feel strong or are they all different shapes and sizes? Are there any splits or breaks? Are there any signs of nail biting?

6 *Note the natural length and shape of the nails*: these will influence the design of the nail art, for example a design that lends itself to wide, square nails will not necessarily be appropriate for narrow, oval nails.

A PRACTICAL GUIDE TO BEAUTY THERAPY

General contraindications to nail art treatment are:

- inflammation, swelling or pus around the nail, indicating a bacterial infection
- green or black streaking of the nail, indicating a fungal infection
- signs of infection on the skin of the hands, for example warts, which are due to a virus
- severe nail separation
- severe eczema or psoriasis
- severe bruising.

The treatment plan

It is a good idea to promote your designs on artificial nails displayed on a nail art board. Keep the nail tips a realistic length so that clients can try them over their own nails. Display nail tips of different lengths so clients can get a good idea of how the design will look on their own nails.

When you have an idea of the sorts of effects that appeal to your client, you can discuss and recommend nail art treatments suitable for their nail and skin condition. The nail art might have to be applied over false or extended nails to achieve the effect the client wants and this will need building into the treatment plan.

As with all consultations, it is important to use effective questioning techniques in order to establish a suitable treatment plan.

Questions to ask the client

Q. Can the client wear nail art for work?

A. If not, a simple design over French manicure may be suitable.

Q. Does the client have time to maintain the design?

A. Designs with objects on top of the nails, for example rhinestones, will need to have regular applications of top-coat.

Q. Will the client be removing the nail art themselves?

A. Some of the designs will need to be filed off rather than removed by using polish remover. This is best done by a professional to avoid damaging the nail.

Q. Does the client wear bright or subtle colours?

A. This will affect the choice of design and techniques used.

Q. Will the client be able to cope with a design that 'stands off' the nail, for example with rhinestone and glitters which can be quite thick?

It is important that the nails are clean, smooth, dry and nicely shaped and that the cuticles are neat and tidy. A 'mini-manicure' is usually all that is done by way of preparing the nails for nail art. A more extensive manicure involving detailed cuticle work, soaking and trimming is usually done separately a day or two before the nail art treatment.

Once the treatment plan has been agreed, the details are recorded and signed off by the client.

SELF-CHECKS

Client consultation

1 Give three reasons why it is important to examine the hands and nails before nail art treatment.

2 State three ways of ensuring an accurate assessment of the nails.

3 List five things that need considering before recommending a nail art design to a client.

4 Describe three conditions that contraindicate nail art treatment.

5 How should the nail art design be adapted for a client with weak nails?

6 Give two reasons why you might advise your client not to have polish secures.

7 How are the hands and nails prepared for nail art treatment?

8 What advice would you give to a client who requests a nail art design that is unsuitable for their nails?

ACTIVITY

Activity 11.2: Create your own art board

Once you have become confident choosing and applying products, you will soon begin to create your own designs. Help your clients to choose their design by showing them your art work applied to artificial nails displayed on an art board. Provide a good range, combining subtle, understated with more exotic and flamboyant designs. Remember to display different lengths and shapes of nails.

Providing nail art

All nail art treatments start with the application of basecoat. This helps to fill in any ridges in the nail plate and provides a 'key' for the polishes and paints applied over the top. The basecoat also protects the nails and prevents them from becoming stained.

Basic brush work

Your correct choice of brush and the way you use it is important for achieving the desired results. Here are three basic freehand paint techniques which you will use and adapt to build up your portfolio of designs.

Creating even lines and outlining

A 'roll off' technique is used to load the brush evenly with paint and create the tapered point required to produce neat lines:

1 Insert the brush into the paint and lower it onto its side.
2 Pull the brush out of the paint using a rolling motion between your thumb and index finger, rolling away from the paint.
3 Lay the brush flat on the nail, pulling it in the required direction of the lines.

Creating perfect circles

Perfect circles flow into position off the brush. They are not 'painted'. Using a fine detail or medium striping brush:

1 Insert the brush into the paint, keeping it straight and upright.
2 Pull the brush straight upwards out of the paint, leaving an even bead of paint on the end of the bristles.
3 Position the bead of paint on the nail keeping the brush upright.
4 Apply light pressure with the brush to create a small circle and more pressure for a bigger circle.

REMEMBER
Dots can be applied using the end of a marbling tool.

Creating flowers

One method is a 'mixing' technique, using a flat brush and two colours, to create the shaping and shading effects required to create flower petals:

1 Place one-half of the brush into one colour of paint and the other half into another colour.
2 Lift the brush out of the paint, keeping the brush positioned upright.
3 Place the brush on the nail and turn clockwise to create the design, mixing the paints together.

More advanced flowers can be created by using a different mixing technique with a medium striping brush:

1 Pull the brush lengthwise through one colour, then turn the brush over and pull lengthwise through another colour.
2 Draw an oval shape, twirling the brush through your fingers and mixing the paint as you pull down the oval.

REMEMBER
Very intricate patterns require a lot of skill and are usually applied to false nails so that they can be kept for longer.

Applying flat stones

Flat stones are picked up with the dampened tip of an orange stick and then placed onto wet polish or top-coat, which secures the stone as it dries.

You will need:
- basecoat
- coloured polish
- orange stick
- small container of water
- flat stones
- top-coat.

1 Ensure nails and surrounding skin are in good condition.
2 Apply basecoat.
3 Apply two coats of coloured polish.
4 Dampen the tip of the orange stick and use it to pick up a flat stone.
5 Place the stone in position over the wet polish, flat side down.
6 Repeat until the final effect is achieved.
7 Apply two coats of top-coat to seal.

Applying glitter

To apply glitter, you must use a rolling technique with the brush. Roll the brush between your thumb and index finger to take up the glitter mixture and then lift the brush out so that there is an even coating on the brush. Simply dipping the brush into the mixture does not work.

You will need:
- basecoat
- coloured polish
- glitter
- glitter mixer
- sable brush
- top-coat
- nail polish remover.

1 Ensure nails and surrounding skin are in good condition.
2 Apply basecoat.
3 Apply two coats of coloured polish.
4 Dip the brush into glitter mixer and lift out to form a ball on the tip of the brush.
5 Roll the ball of glitter mixer into the glitter to form a small bead of product.
6 Place the bead on the nail and wipe the brush clean on a tissue.
7 Use the tip of the clean brush to create the design with the glitter.
8 Use gentle, circular movements to distribute the glitter and then press the brush, precisely, to produce the required outline.

9 Allowing areas of the base colour polish to show through creates an attractive, stained glass effect.

10 You may use the same brush to apply any number of glitter colours, but make sure to clean the brush thoroughly in nail polish remover between applications.

11 Allow the products to dry thoroughly on the nail.

12 Apply two coats of top-coat to seal.

Applying polish secures

The impact of jewellery in nail art design is extremely effective and relatively easy to achieve.

You will need:
- basecoat
- coloured polish
- polish secure, e.g. charm, pearl, diamond
- top-coat.

1 Ensure nails and surrounding skin are in good condition.

2 Apply basecoat.

3 Apply two coats of coloured polish.

4 Apply top-coat and press the secure into place while still wet.

5 When the first layer of top-coat has dried, apply a second layer to keep the polish secure in place.

Applying rhinestones

Rhinestones are picked up with the dampened tip of an orange stick or an orange stick tipped with blu-tak and then placed onto wet polish or top-coat, which secures the stone as it dries.

You will need:
- basecoat
- coloured polish
- small container of water
- rhinestones
- orange stick
- top-coat.

1 Ensure nails and surrounding skin are in good condition.

2 Apply basecoat.

3 Apply two coats of coloured polish.

4 Dampen the tip of the orange stick and use it to pick up a rhinestone. Alternatively, an orange stick tipped with blu-tak can be used.

5 Place the stone in position over the wet polish, flat side down.

6 Repeat until the final effect is achieved.

7 Apply two coats of top-coat to seal.

Applying transfers

Self-adhesive transfers require nothing more than peeling off the backing sheet, applying to the nails on top of two coats of coloured polish and sealing with two coats of top-coat. Water release decals are slightly more involved.

You will need:

- basecoat
- coloured polish
- small container of water
- scissors
- water release decals
- cotton bud
- top-coat.

1 Ensure nails and surrounding skin are in good condition.
2 Apply basecoat.
3 Apply two coats of coloured polish.
4 Moisten a cotton bud with water and gently rub over the decal. You will notice the water seeping through the transfer.
5 Slide the transfer off the backing sheet with the flat of your thumb.
6 Position it on to the nail and smooth into place.
7 Apply two coats of top-coat to seal.

Blending

Blending can be achieved with a wet mix of acrylic paints. The colours are dragged over each other to form a blend between the colours.

Opalescent blending

This technique produces a glittering rainbow of colours, which is particularly effective on a dark background polish.

You will need:

- basecoat
- coloured polish
- opalescent nail paints
- small container of water
- medium striping brush or fan brush
- palette
- top-coat.

1 Ensure nails and surrounding skin are in good condition.
2 Apply basecoat.
3 Apply two coats of coloured polish.
4 There are two methods of applying the paint before sweeping across the nail:
  (a) apply the chosen colours of paint in dots down either side of the nail and then use the fan brush to gently sweep them from side to side
  (b) apply a thin coat of opalescent paint on to the nail with a striping brush and sweep from side to side, gradually working towards the free edge.

Foiling

Foils are fixed to the nail with an adhesive. Paint the nail or draw a design with your adhesive and wait for it to dry clear. Press the foil firmly on the nail and peel off carefully. The foil will remain attached to where the adhesive has been applied. Foils come in a wide range of matt and transparent colours and designs.

You will need:

- basecoat
- coloured polish
- foils
- foil adhesive
- top-coat
- cotton buds
- scissors.

1 Ensure nails and surrounding skin are in good condition.
2 Apply basecoat.
3 Apply two coats of coloured polish.
4 When the polish has dried, apply foil adhesive. Use sparingly and apply exactly where the foil is going to be fixed. The adhesive will appear white at this stage.
5 When the adhesive has become clear, apply the foil with the pattern facing upwards.
6 Rub the foil carefully with a cotton bud to form a good bond.
7 Lift the excess foil away gently, leaving the required design in place on the nail.
8 Apply two coats of top-coat to seal.

Marbling

Marbling is formed when a mix of two or more acrylic paint or nail polishes are applied to the nail and then pulled and swirled with a marbling tool or tooth pick. White and black may be applied alongside the desired colours.

You will need:

- basecoat
- coloured polish
- two to three contrasting coloured paints
- marbling tool
- top-coat.

1 Ensure nails and surrounding skin are in good condition.
2 Apply basecoat.
3 Apply two coats of coloured polish, ensuring good, even coverage of the nails.
4 Use a marbling tool to apply a drop of each colour paint to the corner of the nail.
5 Clean the marbling tool and, with the large end, swirl the paint colours into one another to create the marbling effect.
6 When the paint has dried, apply two coats of top-coat to seal.

REMEMBER

'Marbleising' kits are available, which work differently. A few drops of the different colours are added to warm water and then mixed with a pin. The client's nail is then pulled gently through and out of the water, creating the marbling effect on the nail. The design is sealed with top-coat.

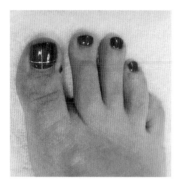

Striping tape on the toes with the addition of a rhinestone

Striping

The self-adhesive striping tape is applied to the nail with light pressure and then trimmed with scissors.

You will need:

- basecoat
- coloured polish
- striping tape
- small scissors
- top-coat.

1 Ensure nails and surrounding skin are in good condition.
2 Apply basecoat.
3 Apply two coats of coloured polish, ensuring good, even coverage of the nails.
4 When polish has completely dried, cut off a length of striping tape slightly longer than the required length and position on the nail, sticky side down.
5 Trim the tape just short of the free edge before securing it to the nail.
6 Apply two coats of top-coat to seal.

Airbrushing

Airbrushing is an advanced nail art technique which you will have the opportunity to study if you progress to NVQ level 3. Airbrush work is subtle and very effective. A small hand-held gun is used, which sprays a fine mist of air and paint onto the nail. Colours can be blended and shaded in a way that is impossible to achieve by any other method. Stencils and masking tape may be used with the airbrush to create intricate-looking designs.

SELF-CHECKS

Providing nail art

1 Give three reasons for applying basecoat during a nail art treatment.

2 How is glitter applied?

3 How is a pearl secured in a nail art design?

4 What is the possible cause of striping tape 'lifting'?

5 Why is particular care required when applying top-coat over a water release decal?

6 State two ways of ensuring a good bond between the foil and nail polish in a nail art design.

7 How should a striping brush be loaded with paint?

8 How are flat stones secured in the nail art design?

REMEMBER

The best way of selling your nail art is by wearing it yourself!

A PRACTICAL GUIDE TO BEAUTY THERAPY

Creating designs

Here are some designs Melle has created to give you experience of using all the basic nail art techniques. Once you have become confident reproducing these, it is time for you to start creating your own designs.

Daisy French

1 Start with a French manicure on all 10 nails.
2 Using a fan brush dipped in gold paint, gently sweep backwards and forwards across the nail.
3 As the paint dries it will give a 'dragged' effect.
4 Using a dotting tool and white, acrylic paint, dot flower petals in circles over the nail plate, leaving a space in the middle.
5 Use the dotting tool and green paint to create leaves around the flowers. Dot and then slightly drag the paint to create the leaf shape.
6 Paint some leaves at the tip of the nail.
7 Use rainbow or crystal rhinestones in the centre of the flowers. Dab a tiny amount of top-coat in the centre of the flower and press the stone into the wet top-coat.
8 At the tip of the nail, create a rhinestone flower with contrasting colours.
9 Place the centre stone first and coloured stones around it. Seal the design with top-coat.

Early stages of Daisy French

Later stages of Daisy French

REMEMBER

Ensure your flower petals and leaves are dry before adding top-coat, otherwise they will be dragged over the nail.

Bright baubles

Stages of Bright baubles

1 Start with your background colour. White is a good base for all colours.
2 Using opaque, brightly coloured, acrylic paints and a small brush, paint circles of different sizes on the nail.
3 Using a thin brush and white paint, highlight each bubble by drawing a curve with a dot underneath on the inside of each bubble, near the edge.
4 Use matching rhinestones over the nail, around the baubles.
5 Seal with top-coat. Ensure your baubles are dry before adding top-coat, otherwise they will drag over the nail.

GOOD PRACTICE

Dip your dotting tool into the paint every two dots, otherwise they will get smaller!

GOOD PRACTICE

Keep each nail design different or you will run into difficulties trying to replicate the same design on the thumb as on the little finger.

REMEMBER

White looks fantastic on toenails.

Tartan French

Stages of Tartan French

REMEMBER

You may choose to lay rhinestones over just one or two of the nails, in which case, for the other nails, use black paint and a striping brush to create thin black lines across the edge of the chevron.

REMEMBER

Ensure your striping brush is not overloaded with paint. You do not want the paint to drip over the nail.

1 Start with a chevron French manicure on the nails. This will help you to produce straight lines and the design will be simpler.

2 Fill the white tip with a cream beige polish or acrylic paint.

3 Using white paint and a striping brush, lay the brush flat on the nail pulling it down the length of the nail tip and then across the nail tip to produce two cross-over lines.

4 Use the striping brush with red paint to create a line down the other side of the nail tip.

5 Use black paint and a striping brush to create straight lines across and down the nail tip.

6 Create thin black lines to edge the two white lines on the inside.

7 Complement the design with rhinestones in red, clear or black. Apply a thin layer of top-coat over the entire nail and lay the stones in the wet top-coat, following the edge of the chevron.

8 Seal the design with another layer of top-coat.

GOOD PRACTICE

Any mistakes can be erased by cleaning and dipping your striping brush into nail polish remover and carefully dragging over the mistake. Go lightly. You do not want to remove any colour that may be underneath.

Union Jack

Stages of Union Jack

1 Paint the entire nail white.

2 Using a thick brush, paint in the red lines. Start with a line down the edge of the nail and then across the middle. The diagonal lines will be simple.

3 Use a smaller brush to paint the blue. Be sure to leave a stripe of white between the red and the blue. Have a good point on your brush to create a clean, sharp angle with the blue inside where the red stripes meet.

A PRACTICAL GUIDE TO BEAUTY THERAPY

4   Use red rhinestones to accentuate the red stripes.

5   This design can be created on one nail only and the rest painted in matching red, white or blue.

6   Seal with top-coat.

Foils and stars

Stages of Foils and stars

1   Paint the nails with a dark base paint. Black was used here.

2   Apply foil adhesive in two stripes across the nail diagonally. Leave a good gap in between.

3   Once the adhesive is clear, press the foil of your choice over the nail and peel away.

4   Apply a top-coat/sealer between the two foil strips and place iridescent or silver stars over the top-coat.

GOOD PRACTICE

Always check with your client that they are satisfied with the finished effect and that it meets the agreed treatment plan. State this on the client's record card.

ACTIVITY

Activity 11.3: Creating 'before and after' designs

Identify three models with different nail shapes and skin colours. Ideally, choose models who are suitable for nail art, but whose own nails are not very long. Agree the main elements of the nail art design and then think of how it might be adapted for: a) applying to the model's natural nails, and b) applying to artificial nails.

The main point of the activity is to adapt your design and techniques for the different lengths and shapes of the nails, according to your model's requirements.

Photograph your model's hands and nails before nail art treatment, without any nail cosmetics, then with the nail art design applied to their natural nails and, finally, with the decorated artificial nails applied. Test the reactions of your models and see which of the designs they prefer. Keep the photos for your portfolio.

Treatment advice

It is important for the client to understand how to maintain and preserve the effects of the nail art treatment. This will ensure they get the best value from their treatment. You should include the general home care advice given after a manicure treatment:

- wear gloves for manual jobs such as gardening and washing up
- try to use the pads of the fingers, not the nails, for performing certain tasks such as using the computer keyboard
- do not use the nails as 'tools'
- use a pen or similar item for dialling a telephone number
- if the nail 'snags' or chips, use a suitable file (purchased from the salon) to smooth the nail
- when on holiday, make sure the hands and nails are dried thoroughly after swimming and any oil or sun cream is washed off the hands
- when bathing, try not to soak the hands for too long and wash off any cream-based bath products
- use a nail brush very gently to remove any dirt or creams from under the free edge
- apply additional layers of top-coat every two or three days to provide further protection for the nail art.

Depending on the type and extent of the nail art, you may recommend retail products that the client may purchase to 'touch up' the nail art design if required.

Removing the nail art

Ideally, your client should return to the salon to have their nail art removed in conjunction with a manicure treatment. Most nail art designs can be removed using nail polish remover. Sometimes filing is required to remove attachments from the nail surface. It is very important that this is done carefully to avoid 'over' filing and thinning the nail plate.

If, for some reason, the client has to remove their own nail art, they should be advised how to do this safely and effectively.

Contra-actions to nail art

The nail plates are dead so, although they can be affected by nail art products, they cannot become allergic to them. Nail polishes, nail paints, adhesives and other nail art products containing solvents might, in very rare cases, cause an adverse reaction. An allergy usually appears on the face or neck as a result of touching the skin and bringing it in contact with the offending ingredient in the nail product. This is most likely to happen at night, during the hours of sleep.

GOOD PRACTICE

Ensure that the cuticles and surrounding skin are kept free from products during a nail art treatment. This reduces the risk of a reaction.

A typical allergic reaction appears as dermatitis:

- itchiness
- inflammation
- swelling
- blistering at the site of contact, followed by
- weeping
- dryness
- flaking of the skin.

The most commonly affected sites of an allergy to nail polish are the eyelids, around the mouth, the sides of the neck and upper chest. The symptoms of the allergy may not show up until 24–48 hours after the initial contact.

HEALTH MATTERS

There have been rare cases reported of allergic reactions to nail polish which have affected the nail bed. The cause of these have been deep pigments in poor-quality nail polishes, which have penetrated the nail plate and reacted with the living tissue underneath.

HEALTH MATTERS

If a client has an adverse skin reaction to any of the products used during the nail art treatment, remove the offending substance immediately and apply a cooling, soothing antiseptic lotion. Record details on the client's record card with details of the action taken. Tell the client to seek medical advice if the symptoms persist.

Nail art removal involving the use of nail polish remover and, sometimes, filing away the nail design, can dehydrate the nail. The client should be advised to use nail conditioners and corrective treatments as part of their regular hand and nail care routine.

GOOD PRACTICE

Always note details of any known allergies on the client's record card. Check the ingredients contained in products before using them on a client for the first time.

SELF-CHECKS

Treatment advice

1 State two pieces of advice that the client should be given about removing their nail art.

2 State four precautions that the client should take to preserve their nail art.

3 Which nail art products are most likely to cause an adverse reaction and why?

4 Why does a reaction to nail art products not show on the nails themselves?

Nail art

Work your way through these questions and discuss your answers with a colleague. Sometimes there may appear to be more than one right answer, in which case decide which one is the most important. Check with your supervisor if there is anything you are not sure about.

1 Straight lines are produced on the nail using a:
 (a) fan brush
 (b) striping brush
 (c) airbrush
 (d) shading brush.

2 Brushes used with water-based acrylics are cleaned in:
 (a) brush cleaner
 (b) nail polish remover
 (c) liquid soap and cold water
 (d) liquid soap and warm water.

3 Small charms applied in nail art are called:
 (a) rhinestones
 (b) polish secures
 (c) flat stones
 (d) foils.

4 Striping tape is applied over:
 (a) wet top-coat
 (b) wet nail polish
 (c) dry top-coat
 (d) dry nail polish.

5 The paints used in nail art are usually:
 (a) non-toxic, spirit-based acrylics
 (b) toxic, spirit-based acrylics
 (c) non-toxic, water-based acrylics
 (d) toxic, water-based acrylics.

6 A nail art board is used to:
 (a) file the nails
 (b) buff the nails
 (c) remove nail art
 (d) display nail art.

7 Top-coat is applied to:
 (a) set the nail art
 (b) harden the nail art
 (c) seal the nail art
 (d) fix the nail art.

8 A marbling tool is used to produce:
 (a) fine lines
 (b) thick lines
 (c) swirls
 (d) dots.

9 Flat stones are applied with:
 (a) a flexibrush
 (b) an orange stick
 (c) a fine detail brush
 (d) a polish secure.

10 An allergy to nail polish usually affects the:
 (a) nail bed
 (b) nail plate
 (c) eyelids
 (d) cuticles.

KEY TERMS

You should now understand the following words or phrases. If you do not, go back through the chapter and find out what they mean:

Marbling tool	**Foils**	**Striping brush**
Flat stones	**Rhinestones**	**Nail paints**
Polish secures	**Flexibrush**	**Transfers**
Blending	**Glitter**	
Fan brush	**Striping tape**	

Chapter 12 Nail technology

Extend and maintain nails

After working through this chapter you will be able to:

- consult with the client to establish their requirements
- identify contraindications and give advice
- prepare for and repair natural nails
- apply artificial nail enhancements using the wrap system
- maintain and repair artificial nail structures using the wrap system
- carry out correct health and safety procedures
- provide home care advice.

Before you work through this chapter: Be wise and revise!
Revision topics to help you achieve this unit:

Extend and maintain nails

Nails have become important fashion accessories and professional nail treatments now make a major contribution to the continuing growth and success of the beauty industry. Almost every high street has at least one specialist nail clinic and many hairdressing and beauty salons employ qualified nail technicians. Artificial nails are big business. They are very profitable and there is considerable scope for associated retail sales.

Good false nails

Artificial nail systems

There are many different artificial nail systems and technology is advancing at such a rate that new, improved methods seem to be appearing all the time. Fortunately, the companies who distribute nail systems in the UK provide very good training, which ensures that technicians keep up to date.

The main aim of research and development in the nail industry is to produce an artificial nail which not only looks natural, but feels and reacts like a strong, healthy natural nail; it should be comfortable, lightweight, resilient and not prone to cracking or splitting. The artificial nail structure may be applied as an '**overlay**' to strengthen the natural nail as it grows or as a '**nail extension**' involving the creation of an artificial **nail tip**.

The NVQ level 2 will qualify you to repair natural nails, apply artificial nails that use the wrap system, and maintain and repair artificial nails that use the wrap system. The more advanced nail extension systems are covered at NVQ level 3. A basic description of them is provided in this chapter to help you develop a wider knowledge which might be useful when working on reception, handling stock, assisting senior nail technicians or discussing nail extensions with clients during other treatments.

The main benefits of artificial nails are that they:

- enhance appearance
- increase self-confidence
- help discourage nail biting
- can be used to reconstruct bitten or misshapen nails
- protect the natural nails as they grow
- allow the natural nails to grow without splitting
- enable nail to enamel last longer, up to two to three weeks.

Sculptured nails

This term describes the process of applying materials such as acrylic or gel to the natural nails, and then lengthening, layering and 'sculpting' them over small pieces of metal or foil nail forms. As the natural nail grows out, the sculptured nails are maintained with regular manicures, during which the area at the base of the nail is 'infilled' with the sculpting material and the artificial nail tip is filed down. This helps to keep the size and shape of the artificial nail in proportion. Eventually the client ends up with just an 'overlay' of sculpting material covering the natural nail.

Nail tips

In these treatments a plastic nail tip is secured to the natural nail with glue and then gel, **fibreglass**, silk or acrylic is applied over the entire nail. As with sculptured nails, the extensions are maintained with regular manicures and infill treatments. Eventually the artificial tips are either filed away or removed by soaking in the recommended solvent under the supervision of a nail technician. White tips are often applied to create a French manicure effect without the use of white nail polish.

Acrylic nails

This method of nail extension involves building up an artificial nail over a nail form or plastic nail tip using a liquid and powder acrylic mixture. Some systems use a drill with an abrasive head to smooth down the hardened compound to the correct thickness and shape. Considerable skill is required to apply and blend in the tips and produce a natural shape. Maintenance work is required every two to three weeks following initial application to compensate for the effects of natural nail growth. This requires 'infilling' the space created at the base of the nail over the area of new, natural nail growth. Acrylic nails look natural and are very strong and resilient. They will withstand normal wear and tear.

Selling points:

- very strong
- natural appearance
- need only a small area of natural nail to ensure a firm attachment
- flexible
- resilient
- can be used to disguise bitten nails long as the nail bed is not exposed and there are no signs of infection
- can be adapted to any size or shape of natural nail
- very good for reconstructing bitten or misshapen nails
- effects last up to two to three months if regular infill treatments are provided
- a full-set application of acrylic nails takes approximately one hour 15 minutes.

Disadvantages:

- more expensive than temporary methods due to the treatment time, products used and costs of maintenance
- 'infilll' treatments required every two to three weeks after initial application
- the treatment products have a pungent smell, which can be unpleasant for the client and the technician

> **REMEMBER**
> Acrylic nails are the strongest and most durable of all the nail overlays, but if they are not applied correctly they look very thick and unmistakably false.

REMEMBER

Acrylic nail products can also be applied as an overlay to protect the natural nails as they grow.

- too 'heavy' for use on weak nails and could cause nail trauma
- are porous, therefore natural moisture can escape but moisture can penetrate the artificial nail causing a fungal infection
- acrylic nails may discolour with prolonged exposure to ultraviolet, going a yellowy colour.

HEALTH MATTERS

If nail extensions are applied and removed correctly, there is very little risk of damaging the natural nails, but equallty the extensions will not make the natural nails any healthier.

Gel nails

These are quite strong, non-permeable and have an attractive, high-gloss finish. Acetone, the solvent that is usually used for removing false nail structures, does not break down gel nails, therefore they have to be removed by buffing. Minimum **lifting** occurs. Gel nails require setting or '**curing**' by either ultraviolet light emitted in a light box, or by brushing or spraying with setting gels.

Nail extensions can be produced by applying the gel over artificial nail tips or nail forms. This system produces longer, natural-looking nails, but re-gelling is required every two to three weeks. The appearance and consistency of the nail produced depends upon the manufacturer and the gel product used for each stage of treatment.

REMEMBER

Gel nails may be recommended for clients with brittle nails to help protect the natural nails as they grow. The gel coating hardens on the nails so the client has to return every three to four weeks to have the small ridge created by new growth buffed away and new gel applied.

REMEMBER

The gel is non-porous and prevents natural moisture from escaping. This can be a problem for fragile nails. It can be used as a top-coat for other nail systems to prevent water from penetrating the artificial nail. Because it is non-porous, gel is very difficult to remove.

Selling points:

- very natural appearance
- do not require nail enamel
- quite strong
- effects last up to two to three months if regular infill treatments are provided
- a full-set application of sculptured gel nails takes approximately one hour.

Disadvantages:

- not as strong as acrylic or fibreglass systems
- more expensive than temporary methods due to treatment time, products used and costs of maintenance
- can weaken the natural nails if **primer** used
- not suitable for people who use a computer keyboard a lot as the typing action can cause the gel seal around the nail to crack.

Fabric overlays and nail extensions (wraps)

Different types of fabric can be used to reinforce the natural nails or create nail extensions by securing false tips. Pieces of fabric are cut to the size of the nail and then eased into position over a layer of resin, taking care to avoid the cuticle. Extra layers are then built up and the resulting 'nail' is buffed smooth until it is transparent. Wraps are most commonly used to strengthen tips.

Fabric products

Materials such as silk, linen and fibreglass are used. The thickness and openness of the fabric mesh determines the strength and resilience of the resulting nail structure. A thick, coarser open mesh material will hold more resin and will therefore set harder and stronger.

- *Silk*: produces the most natural-looking wrap because the material is very thin and flexible; however, it can be too delicate for people with an active lifestyle. Silk is virtually invisible when applied properly, but is the weakest of the wrapping fabrics. Silk is used mainly for repairing natural nails.
- *Linen*: the thickest of the wrapping fabrics, linen is stronger than silk but not invisible when applied, therefore nail enamel has to be worn. Linen provides a strong, durable wrap for someone with weak, damaged nails.
- *Fibreglass*: thicker and stronger than silk but thinner and more flexible than linen, fibreglass combines the best qualities of each of the other materials. The resin applied breaks down the fibreglass so that the detail of the mesh cannot be seen when the product has hardened. The resulting nail structures look and react like strong, healthy natural nails.

> **REMEMBER**
> Fibreglass nails are the least harmful to natural nails because fewer chemical substances are used during the process.

> **REMEMBER**
> Fabric overlays are used to provide strength and rigidity, not length. A narrow fibreglass 'stress' strip can be applied across a natural nail to strengthen the area of weakness. This will help the nail to grow longer without breaking.

Selling points:

- very natural appearance
- very strong and flexible
- extremely light and thin
- can be used effectively for matching odd broken nails
- suitable for clients with weak and brittle nails
- there is less trauma to the natural nail so can be worn for longer periods of time
- a full set of fibreglass nail extensions takes approximately one hour 15 minutes.

Disadvantages:

- quite expensive due to the time involved and the cost of materials
- cannot be used on clients with badly bitten nails due to the relatively small area of natural nail plate available.

Semi-permanent nails (nail tips)

The tips are made of plastic and are attached to the natural nails with resin to provide extra length. The most popular shades are clear, opaque and white. There are different shapes and sizes. It is very important that the nail tips fit snugly without causing discomfort or lifting off. Artificial nail tips appear very natural, but, because they are applied only to the tips of the natural nails, they are not very strong. Extra resin is used to create a seamless join where the false tip is attached to the natural nail. This is the weakest part of the nail extension, which can be strengthened with an overlay of gel, fibreglass or acrylic.

REMEMBER

A much stronger and more long-lasting nail extension can be produced by applying an overlay of gel, fibreglass, acrylic or silk over the natural nail and nail tip.

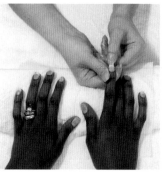
Before

During

After

Application of false nail tips

Selling points:

- very natural effects
- ideal for special occasions when the hands are on show
- can temporarily disguise a broken nail
- good, short-term solution for people who are not normally able to have long nails
- easy to remove
- full-set application takes approximately 45 minutes
- with overlays, treatment takes approximately 1 to $1\frac{1}{2}$ hours.

Disadvantages:

- weakest type of nail extension
- temporary effects (7–10 days)
- easily damaged
- great care needed when doing manual jobs and when hands are near sources of heat.

GOOD PRACTICE

Make sure you keep up-to-date with new nail systems as they come on the market. Clients will want the latest treatments. Keeping up with changing fashion trends and new systems will ensure you are one step ahead of your competitors.

A PRACTICAL GUIDE TO BEAUTY THERAPY

Temporary nails (pre-formed)

For some clients, nail extensions are not practical for everyday wear. Temporary, pre-formed nails are effective for special occasions or one-off events. They are probably the least natural looking of the false nail systems, but they have the advantage of being easily removed after a single wearing if required. Theoretically, they can be worn for up to 7–10 days if applied well and looked after carefully by the client. However, after two weeks, the natural nail has grown sufficiently to create a noticeable gap between the false nail and the cuticle.

Selling points:

- ideal for special occasions when the hands are on show
- relatively inexpensive
- can disguise a broken nail if nail enamel is being applied
- do not weaken the natural nails
- quick results: a full-set application takes approximately 30 minutes.

Disadvantages:

- the least natural looking of all the artificial nail systems
- must be worn with nail enamel
- temporary effects (maximum 7–10 days)
- not very strong
- great care needed when doing manual jobs and when hands are near sources of heat.

Products and equipment

The following are specialist items used for nail technology treatments. Some of these are basic requirements of all artificial nail systems. Others are used only with certain treatments. You need to be familiar with the types of products and equipment used across the range of nail technology treatments, and understand the health and safety implications for their use and storage.

Selection of nail technology products and equipment

Products

Nail sterilisers

These are alcohol based and are usually applied from a spray pump to prevent bacterial or fungal growth occurring between the client's natural nails and the artificial ones. The steriliser should have a 'chalky' white appearance when it has dried, indicating that all grease and moisture has been removed from the nail surface.

REMEMBER

It is important to remove all grease and moisture from the natural nail to prevent the artificial nail from 'lifting' after it has been applied. 'Lifting' describes what happens when the nail glue weakens and the artificial nail structure becomes detached from the natural nail. This creates all sorts of problems if remedial action is not taken quickly. Apart from spoiling the appearance of the nails, artificial nail structures that have 'lifted' provide a haven for water and bacteria, risking damage to both the artificial and natural nails.

HEALTH MATTERS

If water gets trapped beneath an artificial nail structure, the natural nails can develop a fungal infection and turn green/black.

Primer

A primer is used to 'etch' the natural nail chemically. This removes surface oil and bacteria and provides a more adherent surface for the acrylic to stick to. If primer is not used, the acrylic lifts more easily, increasing the risk of infection. When used for infills, primer must not be allowed to run over the surface of previously applied acrylic as it can weaken and discolour it.

HEALTH MATTERS

Primers are highly caustic and should be used with extreme care to avoid damaging the natural nails and the skin. They must not be brought into contact with the nail walls and cuticles. Primers can have an adverse effect on the natural nails which only becomes apparent when the acrylic nail is removed. The over-use of primers causes excessive damage to the nail plate and underlying tissues.

Acrylic liquid

This is used to bond with acrylic powder to create an acrylic nail. Acrylic liquid has a very strong odour which can cause dizziness, sickness and headaches if there is inadequate ventilation. Once the acrylic has set, the fumes disappear.

HEALTH MATTERS

Acrylic does not stick to the skin but it can irritate it, so be careful when handling it.

Acrylic powder

When liquid acrylic and powder are mixed, a chemical reaction takes place, creating a structure that is strong and durable. Acrylic powders come in a range of colours, which produce very natural effects:

- pink and white for a French manicure look

- ivory and peach, which are especially attractive for clients with black skin
- overlay (slightly opaque) for applying over nail tips.

Some powders have smaller particles which allow the acrylic to set more quickly. These are used by more experienced nail technicians.

UV gel
The gel hardens on exposure to ultraviolet light, leaving a sticky residue which must be removed with a finishing wipe or cotton wool soaked in sterilising fluid before buffing to finish.

Fibreglass/silk mesh
This is available either in strips or pre-cut in various sizes. The mesh usually has a sticky backing to aid application. Good-quality meshes should not fray or show through after the application of resin. When resin has been applied, a hard, resilient structure is formed, which either strengthens the natural nail or provides extra support for a nail extension.

Selection of different shapes and sizes of nail tips

Nail tips
Nail tips are made of plastic and are applied to extend the natural nail. Products are then overlaid to give extra strength to the nail extension. Nail tips come in a wide range of shapes, sizes and shades. The size and shape of the client's natural nails must be assessed accurately to ensure a perfect fit. If the nail tip does not fit well, this may cause discomfort or the tip will not adhere well to the natural nail.

Nail forms

Nail forms are used to help create a nail extension if a tip is not being applied. The false nail is built up over the nail form. Care must be taken to ensure a good fit or the acrylic will run underneath and build up the nail incorrectly, resulting in a thick, lumpy edge. Nail forms are available as:

- *re-usable*: metal, plastic or Teflon®-coated forms, which can be shaped to fit any size of nail and finger. They can be sanitised and used again
- *disposable*: paper forms with a sticky under-surface, which come in various sizes and shapes to fit a range of clients. They can only be used once.

Different types of nail forms

Resin glue

Resin glue may be used with a fabric mesh for applying overlays or nail extensions. It sets hard and glossy. Although resin glue will set without using a curing product, it will not be as hard and will take longer to set. The finish will not be as durable.

Resin activator

Resin activator contains **setting agents** that dry and harden the resin so that it becomes non-porous and stronger. The room must be well ventilated when using this product. Spray-on activator should be applied at a minimum distance of 30 cm from the nails to prevent the client experiencing a 'burning' sensation. Brush-on activators are available for technicians who prefer not to use the spray type.

Resin activator being applied to the nail with nozzle applicator

Spray-on resin activator

GOOD PRACTICE

To prevent the nozzle of the resin applicator from clogging up, clean it with solvent regularly and add a little oil to the cap to prevent it from sticking.

Brush cleaner

This helps to extend the life of applicator brushes. The bristles are immersed in the cleaner immediately after use to avoid acrylic setting and hardening on the brush. The brush must be suspended in the cleaner so that the bristles maintain their shape. Brush cleaner can also be used on other items of equipment which come into contact with the acrylic.

HEALTH MATTERS

Brush cleaner must be used and stored with great care as it contains very harsh chemicals that can damage the skin.

Cuticle oil

During a nail extension treatment, the softening and conditioning effects of cuticle oil are particularly important for helping to protect the skin around the nails.

Additionally, cuticle oil is used to:

- prevent damage to surrounding skin during the removal of false nails
- help produce a high shine during the final buffing process
- improve the look (and smell) of the finished 'nail'
- help hide any tiny imperfections.

Nail glue

Nail glue is used to apply a nail tip to the natural nail. The glue is applied carefully and sparingly to the 'well' on the underside of the nail tip. It can also be used in an emergency to apply a false nail that has lifted.

Product remover

Acetone or acetone based removers are used to dissolve artificial nail structures during their removal.

Nail wipes

Lint free, acetone free nail enamel remover pads are used to clean the nails and remove particles of 'dust' created during the treatment. Nail wipes are used in preference to cotton wool. This is to avoid fibres being shed on to the nail extension, which would spoil the finished result.

GOOD PRACTICE

It is a good idea to try out a few different brushes so that you can find out which one is the most comfortable and effective for you.

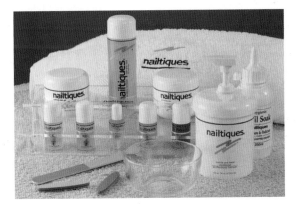

Selection of equipment

Equipment

Brushes

These are sable or nylon, wooden-handled brushes, which come in various shapes and sizes. Slender, shorter brushes give the nail technician more control. Using the wrong brush with the right product makes application difficult.

Files (boards) and buffers

There are various shapes and sizes of cushioned boards and block buffers which are graded according to their '**grit**' size. The coarser the surface, the lower its grit number; 60–200 grit are classed as coarse grade and are used mainly for etching the nail plate, first-stage acrylics and shaping the natural nails. There are different combinations:

- *80/80*: a heavy-duty buffer used for the first stage of acrylics
- *100/100*: for shaping the natural and artificial nails
- *100/180*: for second-stage buffing of acrylics, fibreglass and brush-on gel systems.

180–280 grit are classed as medium grade and are used mainly for smoothing and finishing natural nails and shaping and blending. The combinations found are:

- *100/240*: a buffer for use on strong natural nails and artificial nail extensions
- *180/240*: for shaping natural nails.

280–900 grit are classed as fine grade and are used mainly for blending and smoothing.

1000–2500 grit are classed as micro-abrasive and are used to buff and shape natural and artificial nails.

REMEMBER

Micro-abrasive three- and four way buffers are used to achieve a high shine on any type of nail. They smooth out ridges on the natural nail plate and scratches on the surface of artificial nails.

HEALTH MATTERS

Some files and buffers can be cleaned in water or sprayed with sanitiser before and after use.

GOOD PRACTICE

When files are new, it is a good idea to score over their edges with an old board. This helps to dull the sharp edges before use and reduces the risk of the board cutting the client.

GOOD PRACTICE

To avoid friction heat when buffing, lift the buffer occasionally from the nail surface and do not apply too much pressure.

Cuticle pusher
A plastic hoof stick is used to gently push back the cuticles.

Tip cutters
Tip cutters are specially formulated to cut cleanly through the artificial nail structures without damaging the natural nails. An occasional drop of oil on the screw or spring helps to ensure a smooth cutting action and prevents 'squeaking'.

Scissors
Used for cutting fabric overlays to size. 'Stork' scissors are traditionally used for cutting fibreglass or silk. They should not be used for any other purpose. This is to prevent them from becoming blunt, causing the fabric to tear and fray.

Dappen dish
This is a small glass or plastic dish which is used to hold small amounts of product during the treatment. This avoids contaminating products by using them straight from their container.

UV lamp
This is sometimes used for 'curing' (setting) UV gel and UV acrylics.

Dappen dish

Terminology

Some frequently used terms have a specific meaning in relation to artificial nail treatments.

Porosity

Porosity refers to the ability of the nail or artificial nail structure to absorb substances. The natural nail is porous and absorbs oils and moisture. This is why using oils or soaking the nails before creating extensions causes the product to 'lift'. Some products applied as overlays are porous, which is why they can be removed with solvents.

Friction heat

This is caused by filing and buffing too vigorously or too hard and is very uncomfortable for the client.

Product curing heat

When curing or setting a product, a chemical reaction occurs which creates the hardened finish. Curing products are exothermal. This means they give out heat while curing. This can sometimes be uncomfortable for the client.

Dehydrating

It is important to dehydrate the natural nails before applying nail extensions. Any moisture, oils or bacteria left on the nail plate will become trapped under the product, causing the artificial nail to lift, the nail plate to soften and even mould or fungal growth to appear.

Lifting

Lifting can occur for various reasons, for instance if an overlay has been applied too thickly or if it has been applied over surrounding skin. Glue may be used to repair the lift. This is best done by a nail technician.

GOOD PRACTICE

To avoid friction heat when buffing, lift the buffer occasionally from the nail surface and do not apply too much pressure.

Consultation

A consultation is essential. The receptionist should allow time for this when the appointment is booked. Your client needs to agree the treatment plan and understand what is involved. They need to be fully aware of the necessary after-care and maintenance procedures and their costs.

It is important to choose the system that will best meet the needs of your client. Make sure that you explain what can be achieved so that they have realistic expectations before the treatment begins.

REMEMBER

A thorough consultation ensures that the client knows what to expect and is pleased with the results.

Use open and closed questions to find out the following:

- Why the client wants nail extensions: are they for a one-off occasion, for example a holiday, or are they required for permanent wear?
- Has the client any previous experience of nail extensions? Was it a good or bad experience? Has it made the client sceptical?
- The client's lifestyle: how much time does she have available for looking after her nails? Will she be able to return every fortnight for maintenance? Does she have small children? If she does, she may frequently have 'fiddly' jobs to attend to like fastening buttons, which make long nails impractical.
- Her occupation: the job she has may influence which system and products are used.
- Does the client have preconceived ideas about what can be achieved? Can the desired shape and length really be achieved?

Inspect the natural nails closely in good light and stroke over them with your thumbs to detect any irregularities in the nail surface. Different nails may have different characteristics which you need to note in order to adapt the treatment.

Contraindications to artificial nails

Treating a contraindication risks making the condition worse or causing cross-infection. Do not provide treatments if any of the following are present:

- severely bitten nails
- thin, flaking nails
- nail loss or signs of separation from the nail bed
- any signs of bacterial or fungal infection
- damaged cuticles
- inflammation or swelling in the area
- open wounds, cuts and abrasions
- allergy to nail products
- extreme curvature of the nail.

HEALTH MATTERS

Pain, particularly when pressure is applied, swelling and bruising might indicate that a client with a recent injury has broken one or more of the small bones in their fingers or hand. Treatment may not proceed and the client should be referred to their GP.

REMEMBER

People with a skin condition on their hands often lack self-confidence and want to hide their hands away. Fibreglass nails can be applied to help increase the confidence of a client with a mild skin condition, as long as it is not infectious. Extra-special care should be taken to ensure the artificial nail products do not come into contact with the surrounding skin.

HEALTH MATTERS

In most cases, artificial nail techniques can be used to improve the appearance of splits and ridges in the nails. Where you suspect that the condition of the nails may be symptom of a more widespread, systemic disorder you should tactfully refer your client to their GP.

Applying artificial nails using the wrap system

The following procedure is for applying fibreglass nail extensions using tips and overlay. If there is a lot of work required on the cuticles, this is best done during a full manicure the day before. The treatment area and work station is set up as for a manicure with the addition of the specialist products and equipment required.

Fibreglass products

HEALTH MATTERS

The treatments can take up to 1½ hours. This is a long time for both you and your client to be sitting. Before you start, make sure you are both warm and comfortable, that your seats are at the right height, that you have good light to work in and that there is adequate ventilation. Some of the products have a very strong odour, which, if allowed to build up, can be very unpleasant.

You will need:

- bactericidal hand and nail cleanser
- nail steriliser
- selection of graded files and buffers
- resin and nozzle
- resin activator
- assorted nail tips
- fibreglass mesh
- tip cutters
- fine scissors
- cuticle oil
- nail wipes
- selection of nail enamels, basecoat and top-coat
- record card.

Procedure

1 Prepare the natural nails by removing all traces of nail enamel and wipe over the hands and nails with steriliser.

REMEMBER

The nails should dry to a cloudy finish after the steriliser has been applied. This indicates that all oil has been removed, which would otherwise cause the artificial nail structure to lift. Applying steriliser helps to inhibit bacterial and fungal infections.

2 Check that there are no contraindications.

3 File the nails to an even length of approximately 3 mm and push back the cuticles gently. Aim to expose as much of the nail plate as possible. This will add to the overall appearance of the nails.

4 Check the sizes of the nail tips against the natural nails and line them up in order.

GOOD PRACTICE

Selecting the nail tips
Look closely at the shape of the client's natural nails. Look at their profile and barrel view. The nails will not all be the same shape. Select the tip that will be the most suitable shape and then identify the correct size. Press the tips against the nails to check for fit. Write the number of each tip on the client's record card for future reference.

REMEMBER

The tips have a slight depression called a 'well' designed into their underside at the base. This is where the false nail tapers off and is 'fitted' to the curve of the natural nail. If the client's nails are badly bitten, a tip with a small well will be necessary as the tip should cover only one-third of the client's natural nails. If you only have a limited supply of tips, they must be customised to fit by cutting and filing the well.

GOOD PRACTICE

Choose the size of tip according to your client's requirements and the condition of their nails. For instance, a client trying to give up biting their nails will be able to 'cope' better with their new nails if they wear short tips. Short-to-medium length tips can be adapted to suit most clients. Long tips are for people who really want to make a statement and are prepared to adapt their life style accordingly!

5 Lightly buff the nail plate followed by roughening it slightly with a fine grit file. This will help the false nail to tip to adhere to the nail.

6 Apply resin down the centre of the nail and spread over the nail using the extended nozzle. Leave a free margin around the nail plate so that resin does not come into contact with the cuticle or nail walls.

7 Spray with activator to help speed up the drying time and make the surface non-porous. This helps prevent staining from the pigments in nail enamel or other dyes.

A PRACTICAL GUIDE TO BEAUTY THERAPY

8   Lightly buff the area of the nail plate over which the nail tip will fit.

9   Apply a small drop of resin to where the 'well' of the false nail tip is going to be fitted and no further.

10   Position the nail tip at a 90° angle to the natural nail. Ease the 'well' into position, gently pressing and rocking the tip until it lies flat against the nail surface.

11   Apply a small amount of resin to the seam created between the nail tip and natural nail. This will ensure effective bonding of the nail tip and make blending quicker and easier.

12   Spray with activator or use an ultraviolet light or brush-on activator to set the resin, according to the manufacturer's instructions.

13   Cut the nail tip to the desired length with tip cutters and file to shape with 100 grit file.

Easing the nail tip into position

Lightly tapping the nail tip to make sure it is secure

Using the tip cutters

Filing to shape

14 Blend the seam area using first a coarse file, then gradually finer ones, avoiding too much contact with the nail plate. Finish with a 240 grit file. Do not buff to a shine at this point, as this would prevent further resin from adhering properly. Use a dry tissue or nail wipe to remove excess dust from the nail plate.

15 Apply resin over the entire nail surface, taking care to avoid touching the cuticle and surrounding skin.

16 Spray with activator.

17 Apply the previously cut fibreglass mesh to the whole surface of the nail, leaving a 1–5 mm gap around the cuticle and nail groove area. It does not matter if there is an overlap beyond the free edge as this can be buffed away later. Apply the mesh with the tacky side to the nail plate, ensuring it is smooth with no frayed edges.

Blending the seam area

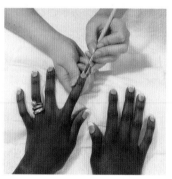
Applying cut fibreglass mesh

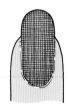
Fibreglass mesh applied over whole nail, leaving a small gap around the edge

REMEMBER

If the fibreglass has frayed through the resin, it is likely that the scissors were not sharp enough or that the fibreglass was not pressed smoothly enough to the nail before the resin was applied.

REMEMBER

Allowing the products to stray over the nail wall or cuticle can cause the products to 'lift'. Too much resin or not enough resin may also cause this problem.

Checking the fibreglass application

18 If too much resin has been applied, remove it now or it may cause lifting.

GOOD PRACTICE

The resin should be allowed to soak into the fibreglass mesh for a few seconds. This helps prevent the mesh showing through the final application.

GOOD PRACTICE

Avoid 'over' buffing, which causes the fibreglass mesh to show through. Should this happen, apply two more coats of resin, set with activator and buff again using less pressure.

19 Set the product using activator.

20 Apply another coat of resin until three layers have been applied. Activate each application.

21 Buff gently with a 240 grit file to remove shine. This increases the effectiveness of the rest of the procedure.

22 Use a four-sided buffer to work up a high-gloss shine, starting with the coarsest side and finishing with the finest.

23 Apply a drop of cuticle oil and massage it into the cuticles, nail walls and over the nail surface to lubricate the skin and create a high-gloss finish.

24 The client may wash their hands to freshen them up and remove any remaining dust particles.

25 Nail enamel may be applied if required. Basecoat is not essential as the artificial nails are not porous.

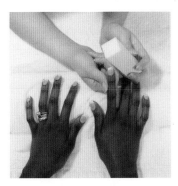

Using a buffer to achieve the final effect

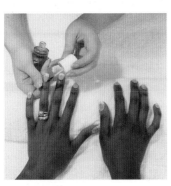

Applying cuticle oil

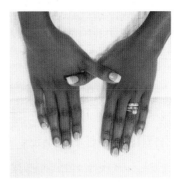

Treatment complete

Maintaining and repairing artificial nails

Make sure your client understands that their new nails are not indestructible! In the event of a heavy blow, they will break. This is much better than the possible damage to the nail bed which could occur if they did not break.

The client needs to know how to care for their new nails. The following advice will ensure they get the best value from her treatment:

● wear gloves for manual jobs such as gardening and washing up

● try to use the pads of the fingers or the knuckles for performing certain tasks such as turning on light switches

● use a pen or similar item for dialling a telephone number

● use only non-acetone nail enamel remover. Acetone damages the surface of artificial nail structures, causing 'lifting'

● if the nail 'snags' or chips, use a suitable file (purchased from the salon) to smooth the nail

● any slight lifting can be resealed with a little glue purchased from the salon. Ensure the nail is clean and dry before repairing, and inform the technician at the next maintenance visit so that the repair can be checked

● do not pull the extensions off. They must be removed properly with the appropriate solvent, preferably followed by a manicure

● when on holiday, make sure the hands and nails are dried thoroughly after swimming and any oil or sun cream is washed off the hands

● when bathing, try not to soak the hands for too long and wash off any cream-based bath products

- use a nail brush very gently to remove any dirt or creams from under the free edge. Dirt can get trapped very easily between the nail extension and the natural nail
- have regular manicures and infills
- always apply a basecoat under nail enamel to prevent 'yellowing' of the artificial nail.

Infills and repairs

Infills will be required every two to three weeks as the nail grows. This helps to prevent lifting and provides regular opportunities for repairing any lifting that has occurred. It is important to avoid unnecessary use of fibreglass and build-up of product in the cuticle area. Sometimes it may only be necessary to apply resin to the area of new growth at the base of the nail.

GOOD PRACTICE

Do not use extra mesh fabric for the first infill as this may cause bulk in the cuticle area. Fibreglass should only be required for alternate maintenance treatments.

Area of new natural nail growth

Area of infill maintenance

Step-by-step infill maintenance procedure

1   Cleanse the hands and nails.
2   Remove nail enamel with acetone-free remover and check that there are no contraindications. If there is infection present, the artificial nails must be removed carefully and the client referred to their doctor.
3   Dehydrate the nails and tidy cuticles.
4   Using a medium grit file, remove any loose or lifting fibreglass, then buff with a fine grit file until the seam becomes invisible.
5   Gently buff the whole nail to take off the shine.
6   Apply a small amount of resin to the growth area and spread it with the nozzle, avoiding build-up of the product over existing resin.
7   Activate the resin and allow it to dry. If necessary, reapply resin.
8   If fibreglass is needed, cut a small piece of the fabric to fit the regrowth area, allowing for a slight overlap with the existing fibreglass.
9   Apply resin over the new fibreglass and activate.
10 Repeat steps 8 and 9, then buff with a fine grit file to remove shine.
11 Use a four-sided buffer to work up a high-gloss shine, starting with the coarsest side and finishing with the finest.
12 Apply a drop of cuticle oil and massage it into the cuticles, nail walls and over the nail surface to lubricate the skin and create a high-gloss finish.

Removing nail enamel

Filing the nails

Applying the resin

Fitting the fabric to the nail

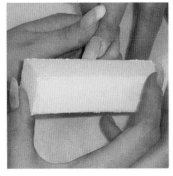
Buffing the nails

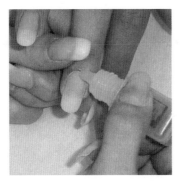
Applying cuticle oil

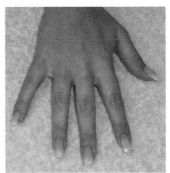
The finished look

HEALTH MATTERS

If the nails do not get appropriate professional after-care, after a few weeks the artificial nail structure becomes 'tip heavy' with product and the untreated area of natural nail growth lacks the strength to be able to support it. If the nail suffers a blow, this puts a strain on the area of stress, which is the line where the untreated nail growth, which is flexible, and the rigid artificial nail structure meet. This can lead to lifting of the product and can cause cracking across the nail plate and bruising to the nail bed. If this happens, the onset of infection is inevitable.

HEALTH MATTERS

There are many products on the market which help to blend the tip into the natural nail. Acetone is effective but must be used with care as it dissolves the plastic tip quickly and can dehydrate the natural nail. Files and buffers can be used on their own without the aid of products, but great care must be taken to avoid mechanical damage to the natural nail.

ACTIVITY

Activity 12.1: Artificial nail systems

1   Conduct a survey of three salons in your area which offer artificial nail treatments. Find out which nail systems they use and see which of them looks the busiest. Compare the prices of the nail technology treatments offered by each of the salons. Note how they promote the treatments and what associated retail ranges they carry.

2   Keep up to date with advancements in nail technology. Read professional journals and visit trade exhibitions. Gather product information and take any opportunity you can to see new nail systems being demonstrated.

Activity 12.2: Quality checks

Use the checklist below to assess your completed work. For each item, award yourself a mark out of five, with one being low and five being high. Give reasons for the marks you award yourself and indicate what you could do to improve on these marks next time.

Upper arch
There should be a gentle, even curve, which runs on the top of the nail from cuticle to free edge. The apex (high point) of the curve should be directly above the stress area (flesh line).

'C' curve
Looking down the barrel of the nail from the free edge, the overlay should be thin and even and straight to the finger.

'Smile' line
There should be a good, even, clear curve to represent the flesh line where the nail bed meets the free edge.

Under the free edge
There should be no resin or dust underneath the nail.

Cuticle and nail walls
The overlay should not be touching the skin. There should be no evidence of excessive filing or buffing.

Free edge
The shape of the free edge must suit the shape of the fingers and hands. The nails must be even and match all the others.

Painting
If nail polish is applied, it should be streak free, have even edges and the smallest margin possible. The nail polish should be applied to the very end of the free edge and none should be visible around or underneath the nails.

Clarity
The overlay should be clear, crisp and with no air bubbles.

Overall appearance
The free edge created should be no longer than the length of the nail bed. Any longer than this and the nails look (and are) unbalanced.

Nail polish will last longer on artificial nails as there are no natural oils or moisture present underneath.

Repairing natural nails

The appearance of split, ridged or broken nails can be improved by adapting the use of the nail extension materials to create the most effective repair. Care must be taken to avoid the repair becoming 'tip heavy' and breaking off. 'Feathering in' of the products during application and timely removal of the repair help to prevent this.

Nail tips

A piece of nail tip, cut to the size and shape of a broken free edge, can be glued into position using the same method as for applying a nail tip. Filing and buffing ensures that the 'jigsaw' repair is blended level with the nail plate, eventually growing out as the free edge is maintained. This type of repair is visible unless nail polish is worn, but, nevertheless, it is simple, strong and effective.

Fibreglass

The application of fibreglass can be adapted to repair cracks or splits in the nail. The fabric is measured and fitted to overlap the edges of the break and cover the width of the nail, leaving a 1–2 mm gap on the undamaged side, but taking it right to the edge of the side of the nail that is split. Layers of fibreglass and resin are then built up using resin activator at each stage to harden and strengthen the repair. The products are 'feathered' with a brush towards the free edge to prevent the tip from becoming 'heavy' and breaking off. The finished effect is achieved by filing and buffing in the usual way.

Fibreglass stress strip

A narrow fibreglass stress strip can be applied across the nail at the junction of the natural nail and false nail tip to strengthen the nail extension. This is where a break is most likely to occur. The stress strip is applied before the main fibreglass mesh application, using the same techniques and taking the same precautions. A stress strip is also useful, applied in the same way, for strengthening long, natural nails.

Gel

This can be used to help protect brittle nails as they grow, building up the layers of gel in the area in greatest need of repair. Gel can also be applied over fibreglass to strengthen a weak or damaged nail.

Acrylic

Once a crack or split has been bonded with glue, acrylic can be applied as an overlay in the usual way and buffed smooth. Alternatively, acrylic can reconstruct areas of 'missing' nail by being sculpted over a nail form or by being applied as an overlay to fibreglass.

HEALTH MATTERS

Always take special care with the products used for artificial nail treatments. Many of them contain chemicals that have strong odours and are potentially hazardous if breathed in or absorbed by the skin. Always store the products correctly when not in use.

Strengthening the natural nails using the wrap system

Fibreglass mesh overlays can be applied to cover the entire surface of the nails to protect and strengthen them as they grow. This is known as 'capping'. The treatment area and work station is set up as for a manicure with the addition of the specialist products and equipment.

You will need:

- bactericidal hand and nail cleanser
- nail steriliser
- selection of graded files and buffers
- resin and nozzle
- resin activator
- fibreglass mesh
- fine scissors
- cuticle oil
- nail wipes
- selection of nail polishs, basecoat and top-coat
- record card.

Procedure

1 Prepare the natural nails by removing all traces of nail polish and wipe over the hands and nails with steriliser.

2 Check that there are no contraindications.

3 File the nails to an even length and push back the cuticles gently. Aim to expose as much of the nail plate as possible. This will add to the overall appearance of the nails.

4 Lightly buff the top of the nail plate followed by roughening it slightly with a 600 grit or finer file. This helps make the nail plate more receptive to the glue.

5 Remove filings with a nail wipe. This also removes any final traces of natural oils which might cause lifting.

6 Cut the fibreglass to fit the size of the nail plate, allowing for a 1.5 mm gap between the fabric and nail border.

7 Apply resin down the centre of the nail and spread over the nail using the extended nozzle. Leave a free margin around the nail plate so that resin does not come into contact with the cuticle or nail walls.

8 Spray with activator to help speed up the drying time and make the surface non-porous. This helps prevent staining from the pigments in nail polish or other dyes.

9   Apply the previously cut fibreglass mesh to the whole surface of the nail, leaving a 1–5mm gap around the cuticle and nail groove area. It does not matter if there is an overlap beyond the free edge as this can be buffed away later. Apply the mesh with the tacky side to the nail plate, ensuring it is smooth with no frayed edges.

10 If too much glue has been applied remove it now or it may cause lifting.

11 Set the product using activator.

12 Apply another coat of resin until three layers have been applied. Activate each application.

13 Using a 240–260 grit file, blend the **nail wrap** seam area into the natural nail. Be careful when filing to avoid damaging the natural nail.

14 Use a four-sided buffer to work up a high-gloss shine, starting with the coarsest side and finishing with the finest.

15 Apply a drop of cuticle oil and massage it into the cuticles, nail walls and over the nail surface to lubricate the skin and create a high-gloss finish.

16 The client may wash their hands to freshen them up and remove any remaining dust particles.

GOOD PRACTICE

Avoid 'over' buffing, which causes the fibreglass mesh to show through. Should this happen, apply two more coats of resin, set with activator and buff again using less pressure.

Remove all residues and sanitise the surface by scrubbing the nail plate with a lint-free pad and a one-step nail prep solution.

File the nails to an even length

fabric#

Cut the fibreglass to fit the size of the nail plate

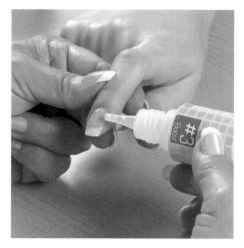

Apply resin over the centre of the nail and spread

Use the spray-on activator

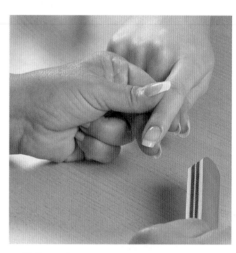

Buff the nails

fabric #

After-care

The follow-up treatment and maintenance of nail wraps is the same as for fibreglass nail extensions (see page 417). Infills will be required every two to three weeks as the nail grows. Buff the area closest to the cuticle to blend in with the natural nail. It may only be necessary to apply resin to the area of new growth. Do not use extra mesh fabric for the first infill as this may cause bulk in the cuticle area.

Removing artificial nail structures

Clients should be advised to return to the salon to have their false nails removed by a technician. This will ensure that products and equipment are used safely with minimal damage to the natural nails.

You will need:

- nail polish remover
- artificial nail solvent (acetone)
- cuticle oil
- two non-plastic bowls, e.g. glass or porcelain
- nail clippers
- orange stick
- medium grit file
- **three-way buffer**
- strong tissues or cotton pads.

Procedure

1 Ask the client to wash and dry their hands.
2 Remove nail polish.
3 Use nail clippers to remove excess length from the false nail.
4 Buff the nail extensions to create a rough surface. This encourages absorption of the solvent by the nail.
5 In each of the bowls place enough artificial nail solvent to cover the nails. A teaspoon of vegetable oil can be added to help counteract the drying effect of the acetone.
6 Ask the client to place their fingertips in the bowls and allow them to soak for five minutes.
7 Working alternately between the hands, remove the fingers from the bowl and wipe over the surface of them with a tissue or pad soaked in solvent. An orange stick can be used to gently 'tease off' the product.
8 Continue to soak and wipe over the nails every two to three minutes until the nails are completely free from product. This should take 10–15 minutes.
9 Ask the client to wash their hands and scrub their nails thoroughly.
10 When the hands are dry, reshape the nails and massage cuticle oil into the nails and cuticles. Finish off by using the three-way buffer to smooth the surface of the nails and create a shine. Alternatively, a full manicure may be given.

GOOD PRACTICE

This is a good time to recommend the purchase of nail conditioning and nail strengthening products for the client to use at home, in between artificial nail treatments or manicures.

Contra-actions

The following adverse reactions may occur following application of an artificial nail structure. Some will only be detected when the false nail structure has been removed:

- Thinning of the natural nail plate, caused by excessive filing and buffing when preparing the nails and blending in a nail tip. Removing the nails incorrectly can also be a cause. The nails should be kept short and the client advised to have regular manicures and use a nail strengthener. False nails should not be applied again until the natural nails have grown back strong.

- Allergy to one of the many chemical products used during the process. Inflammation and irritation of the skin around the nails, or areas of face touched by the nails, suggests an allergy to the products. The nails should be removed immediately by the technician and, if the reaction is severe, the client referred to their doctor.

- Bacterial or fungal infection caused by inadequate hygiene procedures or incorrect home care. This can appear as inflammation and pus around the nail, separation of the natural nail from the nail bed or dark green/black spots between the artificial nail plate and the natural nail. The nails must be removed immediately by the technician and the client referred to their doctor for treatment of the infection.

- Softening of the natural nail plate as a result of prolonged exposure to harsh products such as nail primer. The condition needs to be allowed to 'grow out'; in the mean time manicures and the regular use of nail strengthener will help. False nails may not be applied until the condition of the nails has improved.

- Physical damage to the nail plate, nail bed or cuticle showing as bruising, ridges in the nail plate and skin damage to the cuticles and nail walls. These signs indicate 'heavy handed' techniques and incorrect use of equipment during a treatment, for which there is no excuse.

ACTIVITY

Activity 12.3: Contra-actions to nail technology treatments

Design a questionnaire and conduct a survey of people who have had artificial nail treatments to tra-actions either during or after their treatment. Identify the most common problems highlighted by your survey. Suggest how these problems could have been avoided and the solutions.

Artificial nail structures

1 Why should all grease and moisture be removed from the nail surface before applying an artificial nail?

2 Explain the purpose of resin glue.

3 Give three selling points when recommending fabric overlays.

4 a) Select the coarsest grade file from the following: 180 grit, 80 grit and 280 grit.
   b) Compare the uses of a coarse grade, medium grade and fine grade file.

5 State two retail products that could be recommended to a client following application of fibreglass nails.

6 Why is cuticle oil used when applying nail extensions?

7 Give two reasons why an overlay may 'lift' within a few days of nail extensions being applied.

8 What are 'infill' treatments and why are they necessary?

9 State three factors that influence the choice of nail tips for a client.

10 State three factors that influence the choice of artificial nail system for a client.

11 State two possible reasons for a nail extension becoming discoloured.

12 Why is good ventilation important when applying nail extensions?

13 Why should clients be advised to use acetone-free nail polish removers on their artificial nails?

14 State three advantages of using fibreglass as an overlay.

Nail technology

Work your way through these questions and discuss your answers with a colleague. Sometimes there may appear to be more than one right answer, in which case decide which one is the most important. Check with your supervisor if there is anything you are not sure about.

1 The hands should not be soaked in water before applying nail extensions because:
(a) the extensions will not adhere to the natural nails
(b) the water will dilute the resin
(c) a fungal infection may occur
(d) the natural nails will be softened.

2 Fibreglass overlays are applied to short, natural nails to:
(a) make them appear longer
(b) produce a high gloss
(c) smooth out ridges
(d) provide strength.

3 A fungicide is contained in nail primer to:
(a) prevent disease
(b) help the nails to stick
(c) harden the natural nails
(d) harden the false nails.

Nail technology

4 Resin activator is used to:
(a) apply the resin
(b) sterilise the resin
(c) set the resin
(d) dissolve the resin.

5 Nail extensions should be applied:
(a) immediately after a full manicure
(b) a week after a full manicure
(c) during a full manicure
(d) the day after a full manicure.

6 The natural nails are buffed with an abrasive file to:
(a) ensure good adhesion between the natural nail and nail extension
(b) reduce the thickness of the nails
(c) reduce the length of the nails
(d) remove surface dirt and stains.

KEY TERMS

You should now understand the following words or phrases. If you do not, go back through the chapter and find out what they mean:

Resin glue	**Resin activator**	**Setting agent**
Nail sterilisers	**Nail tip**	**Three-way buffer**
Nail wrap	**Lifting**	**Porosity**
Fibreglass	**Curing**	**Nail extension**
Overlay	**Grit**	**Primer**

Chapter 13 Ear piercing

Pierce ears

After working through this chapter you will be able to:

- understand the importance of hygiene when piercing ears
- identify contraindications and contra-actions to ear piercing
- carry out ear piercing safely and correctly
- advise on the range and use of after-care products
- know the law relating to ear piercing.

Before you work through this chapter: Be wise and revise!
Revision topics to help you achieve this unit:

Pierce ears

Ear piercing has become a very popular salon service, probably because clients know they will receive a professional treatment with high standards of hygiene and safety. These are essential for ensuring that the ear does not become damaged or infected. Ear piercing is a quick and profitable service which can attract new clients to the salon. This provides an ideal opportunity for you to promote and recommend the other treatments that are available.

Ear piercing systems

The most modern **ear piercing systems** allow the whole procedure to take place quickly and efficiently without any direct contact between the hands and the stud fastenings. This is important because, during the treatment, the ear lobe is punctured, increasing the risk of infection.

Sterile, disposable systems virtually eliminate any risk of spreading infection from person to person. Pre-sterilised gold **studs and clasps** are loaded into a gun with a disposable cartridge. The cartridge contains and protects the stud throughout the loading procedure. A trigger mechanism causes the stud to pierce the ear lobe quickly and painlessly.

Other ear piercing 'gun' systems are available on the market. They use the same trigger action, but the studs and clasps are not contained in a disposable cartridge and are, therefore, more exposed during the loading procedure. Clean plastic guards protect the metal surface of the gun from becoming contaminated by the pierced ear lobe. Treatments with this method are generally not regarded as being as safe as those using a sterile, diposable system, even when strict hygiene procedures are followed.

Ear piercing and the law

Under the Local Government (Miscellaneous Provisions) Act 1982, there can be very serious consequences for a salon that does not take the necessary precautions when giving ear piercing treatments. The Act is currently under review and it is expected that even tighter controls will be introduced. This coincides with a review of the EC regulations on 'invasive' procedures. Throughout Europe, the spread of infectious diseases such as hepatitis and AIDS has increased public attention on controls for avoiding cross-infection.

European Nickel Directive

In 2000, the European Nickel Directive was made law in the UK. This is because nickel, which is present in some fashion accessories, jewellery and clothes fastenings, has been shown to be the most common cause of skin contact allergy in Europe. The Directive does not totally ban the use of nickel, but items containing nickel must have a coating that lasts a minimum of two years, and that is designed to stop corrosion and the releasing of nickel 'ions' onto the skin. Manufacturers of ear piercing systems have had to consider the implications, for them, of the Directive and some have made slight revisions to the production processes of their studs and other jewellery items to provide even safer treatments for clients.

What you must do:

- use only equipment that is approved by your local Environmental Health Department
- do not provide treatment where there is a health risk
- maintain high standards of personal hygiene
- maintain high standards of treatment hygiene
- dispose of waste correctly
- give the appropriate advice for after-care.

Health Authorities now recognise the advantages of **pre-sterilised disposable systems** and are actively encouraging salons to adopt one of these methods. In the future, the law may require **ear piercing guns** to be autoclaved between treatments to achieve complete sterilisation.

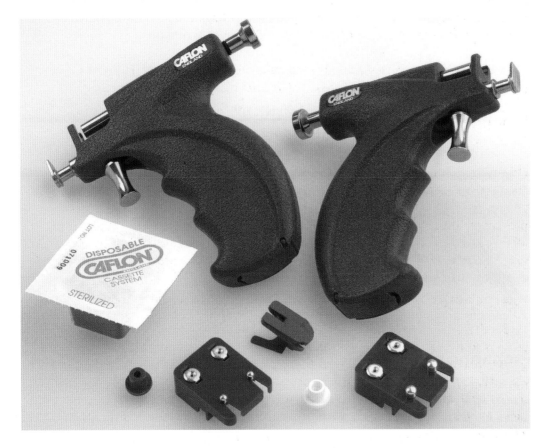

Ear piercing system and accessories

ACTIVITY

Activity 13.1: Costing ear piercing treatments

1 Visit your local wholesaler and find out the cost of two different ear piercing systems. Look at what is included in the price. The gun might be sold separately or there could be a number of other items included, for example medicated cleansing swabs, pre-packed studs and clasps, after-care lotion. Work out the cost to the salon of providing 10 ear piercing treatments, using each of the systems. Do not forget to allow for VAT.

2 Find out from two or three salons the prices charged to customers for ear piercing, using the systems you have researched. Work out the gross profit using the costs of the materials and the selling price for each treatment.

3 Work out the net profit taking into account the additional costs of providing treatment, for example staff time and overheads.

REMEMBER

Treatments involving disposable equipment usually cost more for the salon to provide and this is reflected in the price to the customers. If the health and safety benefits of a sterile disposable system are explained to the clients, they are usually willing to pay a little extra for the service.

Preparing for ear piercing

Clients attending for ear piercing may be nervous about their treatment. Many will be expecting it to be painful. A warm, relaxing environment with good ventilation should help. Although the procedure is fairly straightforward, accuracy is essential. You only have one chance to get it right, so make sure that you will be working in good light.

Equipment and materials

Prepare your trolley before the client arrives. Check that the gun you are going to use is working properly by testing the plunger and trigger mechanism. If you have stored your gun in an ultraviolet cabinet, you may leave it there until required for treatment. Otherwise, it can be placed on the trolley, covered with a clean tissue. There are advantages in keeping the gun out of sight if the client is nervous!

You will need:

- a clean, water-based marker pen
- an ear piercing gun which complies with health and safety requirements
- sterile ear studs; a range of styles allows the client some choice
- a mirror
- medicated swabs (impregnated with 70 per cent isopropyl alcohol) or surgical spirit
- soothing, medicated after-care lotion
- a towel
- a clean, covered bowl containing cotton wool
- a clean hair-band or hair clips
- a prepared record card plus a consent form signed by a parent or guardian if the client is under 18 years of age.

Preparing the client

You will need to assess the client's suitability for treatment and to ensure the hygienic preparation of the skin for ear piercing. Use this time to put your client at ease. They will feel reassured if you appear confident and in control throughout the treatment.

1 Make sure the client is seated comfortably with head supported in the upright position.

2 Place a towel across the shoulders and, if necessary, secure the client's hair away from the face with a head-band or clips.

3 Wash and dry your hands. You may want to put on a pair of hygienic, lightweight, disposable gloves.

4 Examine the ears and surrounding areas to check that there are no contraindications.

5 Discuss the client's requirements and offer a choice of studs for selection. Keep the studs in their sterile pack until needed for treatment.

6 Cleanse the ear lobes, front and back, with a medical swab or surgical spirit applied on cotton wool. This will remove any harmful bacteria, which could invade the pierced skin.

7 Allow the ear lobes to dry. This will prevent the water-based marker pen from smudging with the moisture.

8 Using a mirror, discuss the positioning of the studs with the client and agree where they should be placed. Mark each of the ear lobes in the agreed place with a small dot of the marker pen.

9 The ears may not be level. Take time to line up and check the position of your markings so that you achieve a balanced effect.

10 Gain the final agreement of the client. You are now ready to pierce the ears.

Group	Regular	White	Triangle
Heart	July	Star	November
Pearl	Black onyx	Sapphire	December

A range of studs

Contraindications to ear piercing

The following are contraindications to ear piercing and prevent treatment from taking place:

- inflammation or swelling
- bruising
- cuts and abrasions
- lumps, moles or scar tissue in the area to be pierced
- any signs of infection or open wounds
- circulatory disorders
- infection by hepatitis or HIV
- diabetes (because of the poor healing quality of the skin)

GOOD PRACTICE

Make sure you record that you have checked for contraindications in case the client returns with a problem later on.

- epilepsy (because of the possible effects of anxiety)
- small ear lobe, where it is not possible to use the equipment and position the stud safely because of the size of the area available.

The following contraindications require medical referral:

- systemic medical conditions
- serious localised infections
- ear infections.

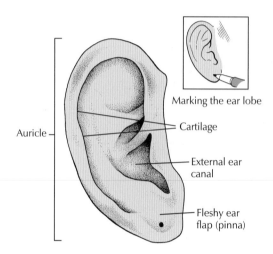

Deciding where to pierce

Deciding where to pierce

The ear should be pierced in the centre of the fleshy part of the ear lobe. Above this, the ear is made up of fibrous cartilage covered by firmly adherent skin. Piercing through cartilage is very painful and can lead to a condition called 'cauliflower ear', where the damaged ear appears large and deformed. Cartilage takes longer to heal and infected cartilage is difficult to treat.

Piercing the ears

Always follow the manufacturer's instructions when loading the gun and lining up the stud and clasp with the markings on the ear lobes. The following procedure is for a pre-sterilised disposable system. The details may be slightly different for the system used in your salon.

Procedure

1   Peel off the backing paper from the sealed pack containing the studs. Make sure you do not drop the cartridge, otherwise you will have to throw it away and use a new one.

2   Holding the gun firmly, pull back the plunger until it is fully extended. Listen for a 'click' that lets you know the plunger is resting in the correct position.

3   Remove the plastic cartridge from the pack, holding it by the plastic mount. Avoid touching the stud or backing clasp.

4 Position the back clasps in the gun by sliding the cartridge down as far as it will go into the appropriate slot.

5 Position the cartridge, holding the studs against the stud barrel of the gun. This automatically places a protective plastic ring around the barrel of the gun and the stud.

6 Carefully pull the holder upwards, allowing the stud to slip neatly into the barrel.

7 Gently support the ear lobe with your free hand and slide the gun into position.

8 Hold the gun horizontally and position the stem of the stud accurately over the ear marking.

9 Give a gentle squeeze of the trigger until it stops and make a final check that the stud is aligned correctly with the ear lobe.

10 Finally, squeeze the trigger. The ear should now be effectively pierced with the back clasp secured on the stem of the stud.

11 Still supporting the ear lobe, slide the gun out of position and, holding it downwards, discard the plastic ring directly into a lined waste bin.

12 Pull back the plunger and load the gun with the remaining back clasp and stud. You will need to remove the back-clasp holder from the gun and reverse it so that the clasp is in the correct position.

13 Pierce the other ear, using the same procedure.

14 Make a final check and wipe over the ear and around the clasp and stud with a soothing antiseptic, after-care lotion.

15 Offer the client a hand mirror so that they can approve the finished result.

16 Provide after-care instructions for your client and allow them a few minutes to relax while you complete the record card.

Solution

Stud packs

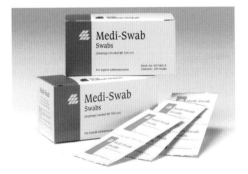

Swabs

GOOD PRACTICE

If your client attends the salon regularly for treatments, use your records to help check up on how well the skin is healing and to confirm that the correct after-care procedures are being followed.

REMEMBER

It is not unusual for the treated ear lobe to appear pink and feel warm after ear piercing. This is a normal reaction. There is an increase in the supply of blood to the area as the deeper skin tissue is penetrated by the stem of the stud. As the skin calms down, the pink colour and warm sensation disappear.

ACTIVITY

Activity 13.2: Problem solving

What is the best action for you to take in each of the following circumstances? Work through these problems with one or two colleagues and discuss your answers with your supervisor.

1   Despite the fact that you have tested it beforehand, there is a malfunction of the ear piercing gun during treatment and the stud and back clasp do not fasten together, although the ear has been pierced.

2   Having loaded the gun successfully, you make the mistake of pointing it downwards and the studs fall out.

3   You are giving the client after-care advice following ear piercing and she tells you that she is going on holiday in three weeks and does not really want to have to keep her studs in all the time she is away. She wants to be able to wear fashionable earrings when she goes out at night.

4   When checking your client for contraindications, she admits to having epilepsy but stresses that the condition is controlled by medication. She has not experienced a fit for six years.

After-care

HEALTH MATTERS

Advise the client to use the correct strength of liquid antiseptic if using a proprietary brand. Using undiluted antiseptic can irritate the skin, causing a burning sensation.

REMEMBER

After six weeks, the studs should be replaced with gold or silver earrings. Other types of metals may cause an infection or skin irritation if worn too soon after ear piercing. Avoid wearing cheap, 'wired' earrings for at least three months after ear piercing and, after then, wear them only for short periods of time.

The holes that have been formed must be kept clean and the studs kept in place for at least six weeks. After this time, healing should be complete and the studs can be replaced with earrings of the client's choice. The client should be given the following advice for after-care.

To prevent infection:

- avoid unnecessary touching of the ears and studs; don't fiddle!
- do not replace studs with other earrings during the initial six-week period
- bathe the ear lobes twice a day with a liquid antiseptic or after-care lotion, ensuring that the lotion seeps behind the stud and clasp
- wash hands before touching ears and studs
- do not allow soap or shampoo to build up behind the stud or clasp; rinse well after washing
- cover ears when spraying perfume, antiperspirant and hairspray.

To prevent holes from closing:

- do not take studs out for at least six weeks
- turn studs at least twice daily while bathing the ears with antiseptic or after-care lotion
- continue to wear earrings after the original studs have been removed
- for the first six months, do not go longer than 24 hours without wearing earrings.

If infection or irritation occurs:

- bathe the area regularly with warm salt water
- contact the salon for specific advice
- contact own doctor if the problem becomes serious.

GOOD PRACTICE

It is a good idea to give the client an after-care leaflet to take home. This will remind them of some of the points you have discussed which may be forgotten once they have left the salon. Make a note on the record card that you have provided the after-care leaflet and ask your client to confirm this by signing the card.

REMEMBER

Inflammation, swelling and 'weeping' of the skin are all signs that the ear lobe may have become infected. This will almost certainly be the result of inadequate after-care. Explain this to your client to reinforce the importance of being patient and thorough with after-care procedures in the six weeks following ear piercing.

Contra-actions

You need to be able to deal with adverse reactions that may develop after ear piercing.

Infection

The client should be advised to contact the salon immediately if they suspect that the ear lobe has become infected. You should refer to your original instructions on after-care. A visit to the salon may provide the client with extra reassurance and also give you the opportunity to have a close look at the ear and to treat the problem yourself. If the problem continues or becomes more serious, the client should be referred to their own doctor for advice.

GOOD PRACTICE

You should make a note on the client's record card of any discussions and follow-up treatment you provide, together with the date and details of any additional advice offered. As with all other salon treatments, it is important to do this to 'cover' yourself for insurance purposes.

Inflammation and irritation

A stud that fits too tightly will not turn readily in the ear lobe and there may be problems with healing. A client with fat ear lobes should be advised of the risk of friction and irritation causing damage to the underlying skin and blood vessels. If the client experiences discomfort, the studs should be removed and hygienic after-care procedures continued until the skin has healed. Inflammation and irritation may also be signs of an allergic reaction where the body cannot tolerate a foreign object in the skin. The client is unable to wear earrings designed for pierced ears. The studs must be removed and hygienic after-care continued until the skin has healed.

Keloids

Some clients have the type of skin which easily forms **keloid** scars at the site of skin damage. A keloid is a lumpy overgrowth of skin tissue which forms during the healing process. Keloids are not harmful, but clients who are prone to them should be advised against having their ears pierced more than once. A further build-up of keloid tissue on the ear lobe would be undesirable.

Secondary ear piercing

A client may ask for two or more studs (a **secondary ear piercing**) to be fitted in the same ear during an ear piercing treatment. This is not recommended for the following reasons:

- Although treatments are safe if the correct procedures are followed, the ear lobe does experience a small amount of trauma when it is pierced and a period of healing is required; the fitting of additional studs in the same treatment would increase the trauma and delay the healing process.

- The previously fitted stud would have to remain in place while the additional ones are fitted; this would be uncomfortable for the client and would create extreme difficulty for the therapist using the ear piercing gun. The safety and effectiveness of the treatment could not be guaranteed.

- Effective after-care would be more difficult if the client had more than one site of healing to attend to; there is a risk that effective cleaning would not take place because of the close positioning of the studs.

- A client may be allergic to the studs and the effects of the allergy would be more serious where more than one stud had been fitted.

Additional studs should not be fitted until the client's ears have completely healed from the previous ear piercing treatment.

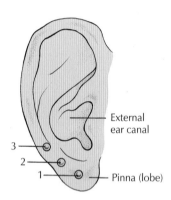

3
2
1

External ear canal

Pinna (lobe)

The position of studs for second and third ear piercing treatments

Preparing for secondary ear piercing treatment

The treatment area is prepared exactly the same for every ear piercing treatment. The preparation of the client is also the same. Studs and earrings must be removed before the area is cleansed and assessed for treatment. Follow the procedures described on page 426.

Deciding where to pierce

When piercing an ear for the second or third time, be careful to avoid piercing through cartilage. Not all clients are suitable for secondary ear piercing because of the relatively small area of fleshy ear lobe available.

- First piercing: place stud in the centre of the lobe.
- Second piercing: follow the natural line of the ear lobe and place approximately 1 cm from the first hole.
- Third piercing: follow the natural line of the ear lobe and place approximately 1 cm from the second hole.

Treatment and after-care

Follow the same procedures for secondary ear piercing as you did with the first treatment. Repeat the after-care advice and provide your client with another after-care leaflet.

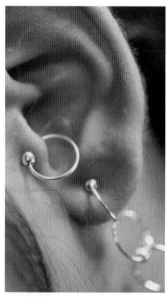

Secondary ear piercing

Body piercing

The salon systems available for ear piercing are not suitable and cannot be adapted for treating other areas of the body. Your professional insurance cover for ear piercing does not extend to treating other areas of the body, for example tongue, cheek, navel, lip, and your NVQ in beauty therapy does not qualify you to offer these treatments.

There are currently no laws regulating **body piercing**, just a voluntary code. Health professionals generally feel that far stricter controls are needed to prevent body piercing clients being infected with serious diseases. The UK Government has pledged to introduce legislation to regulate body piercing following the death of a teenager from septicaemia after having a ring fitted to his lip. It is envisaged that the legislation will give all local authorities specific powers to regulate body piercing businesses.

HEALTH MATTERS

Body piercing can cause a range of problems including serious bleeding and excess scar tissue. If the piercer uses non-sterile equipment, clients are also at risk of life-threatening infections including hepatitis C, HIV and septicaemia.

SELF-CHECKS

Ear piercing

1   (a) State three legal requirements when carrying out ear piercing.
    (b) Name the legislation that relates to ear piercing treatments.

2   Give three ways of putting the client at ease before an ear piercing treatment.

3   Which part of the ear lobe is suitable for being pierced?

4   Explain why a client with diabetes is contraindicated to ear piercing.

5   Why might a client with small ear lobes not be suitable for ear piercing?

6   Give two reasons why only one stud should be fitted in each ear during an ear piercing treatment.

7   What is the likely consequence of removing studs too soon after ear piercing?

8   What information should be entered on the record card of a client attending for ear piercing?

9   Why is record keeping necessary?

10 (a) State three ways in which infection may be spread during an ear piercing treatment.
    (b) Give four precautions that should be taken to avoid cross-infection during an ear piercing treatment.

11 Describe the possible contra-actions that may occur after ear piercing. State the advice that should be given in each case.

12 What is the normal skin reaction following ear piercing?

Pierce ears

There may appear to be more than one correct answer. Read each question carefully before making your final decision. Discuss your answers with your colleagues and see if you all agree. If you don't, talk through the issues raised.

1 Keloid is a type of:
(a) scar
(b) ear infection
(c) skin infection
(d) skin tissue.

2 The 'age of consent' for ear piercing is:
(a) over 18 years
(b) under 18 years
(c) 18 years
(d) any age.

3 The 'use by' date on a pack of ear studs identifies the length of time the manufacturer can guarantee the:
(a) safety level of nickel in the studs
(b) safety level of the procedure
(c) sterile condition of the pack
(d) sterile coating on the studs.

4 During ear piercing, a medical swab is used to:
(a) cleanse the ear lobes after piercing
(b) cleanse the ear lobes before ear piercing
(c) wipe away blood produced during ear piercing
(d) wipe away tissue fluid produced during ear piercing.

5 The position of the studs is identified using a:
(a) spirit-based marker pen
(b) sterile stud
(c) cartridge
(d) water-based marker pen.

6 The ear lobe may feel warm after ear piercing because the:
(a) ear lobe has become infected
(b) ear lobe has swollen
(c) nerve endings have been stimulated
(d) blood supply has been stimulated.

7 The studs fitted during an ear piercing treatment should remain in place for:
(a) two weeks
(b) six weeks
(c) three months
(d) six months.

8 Following ear piercing, the skin should normally heal within:
(a) two weeks
(b) six weeks
(c) three months
(d) six months.

KEY TERMS

You should now understand the following words or phrases. If you do not, go back through the chapter and find out what they mean:

Ear piercing	**Ear piercing gun**	**Secondary ear piercing**
Ear piercing system	**Keloid**	**Body piercing**
Pre-sterilised disposable systems	**Studs and clasps**	

Chapter 14 Hydrotherapy and heat treatments

Assist with spa treatments

After working through this chapter you will be able to:

- prepare work areas for water, temperature and spa treatments
- clean, maintain and monitor the spa environment
- assist with monitoring water, temperature and spa treatments
- assist with the shutdown of treatment areas.

Before you work through this chapter: Be wise and revise!
Revision topics to help you achieve this unit:

Assist with spa treatments

In an increasingly hectic world, spa treatments provide the ultimate experience for people wanting to escape the hustle and bustle of everyday life. People who feel good generally look good, and a whole new industry has built up around the development of specialist treatments and services to help clients 'renew' their minds and bodies and improve their sense of well-being. Some of the treatments may be offered as an extension of beauty salon services. Others require more space and equipment than a salon can provide and are available at day spas, fitness centres, gyms, health resorts and leisure clubs, often situated within four or five star hotels. The treatments are provided in a calm, peaceful environment, allowing clients to relax, be pampered, unwind and emerge looking and feeling healthier.

Swimming pool at Manchester Airport Marriott Hotel

REMEMBER

A beauty salon may only be able to provide a sauna, steam cabinet and relaxation area, but if these are backed up with individualised treatment programmes using specialist techniques and beautiful spa products, the salon can become as much as a haven to its clients as a large spa offering a wider range of services.

Selection of spa products

A PRACTICAL GUIDE TO BEAUTY THERAPY

Spa treatments

The two main types of treatment that make up the 'spa experience' are **hydrotherapy** and heat treatments. Other specialist treatments, for example **body wrapping**, may also be offered.

Hydrotherapy is the word used to describe therapeutic treatments using water and comes from the Greek words *hydro* meaning water and *therapeia* meaning healing.

Examples of hydrotherapy treatments are:
- **spa pools** (jacuzzis™, whirlpools, hydro pools)
- aerated baths (**hydrotherapy baths**, hydro-oxygen baths)
- **foam baths**
- **floatation** treatments.

Heat treatments include **sauna** and steam, each of which is therapeutic in its own right, but even more so when combined with other spa treatments.

Assisting and monitoring water, temperature and spa treatments

The NVQ 2 unit 'Assist and monitor water, temperature and spa treatments' accredits the work of people who work in a spa environment, supporting the work of the professionals qualified to carry out the treatments. You could be one of those 'qualified professionals' if you progress to NVQ level 3!

Your main responsibilities as an NVQ level 2 assistant are:
- preparing the work areas for water, temperature and spa treatments
- cleaning, maintaining and monitoring the spa environment
- assisting with and monitoring water, temperature and spa treatments
- assisting with the shutdown of treatment areas.

In order to do these effectively, you need to follow the procedure set out below.

Before treatment
Ensure that everything required for treatment is available in the right condition, in the right place, at the right time, according to legal and organisational requirements.

What you should know:
- your organisation's standards and procedures in terms of cleaning, preparing and maintaining the treatment area
- the equipment required and how it should be cleaned and maintained to keep it in good working order, including any accessories
- how the equipment and accessories should be prepared for treatment and how much time to allow for preparing them
- the consumables required, where they are located and any special instructions for mixing or preparing them for treatment.

What you must do:

- always follow the organisation's standards and procedures when selecting and using cleaning products
- until you are sufficiently experienced, read and follow the written instructions regarding the correct cleaning, preparation and use of equipment and accessories
- inspect equipment and accessories before treatment and report faults or breakages promptly to the relevant person
- if a timer is required, check that it is not damaged and that it is in correct working order
- when switching on heating equipment, make sure that enough time is allowed before treatment to get it to the right temperature
- check stock levels of consumables and replenish as necessary. Check contents of containers to ensure sufficient quantities of product are available for treatment
- report to the relevant person when consumables need re-ordering
- always wear the recommended protective clothing when cleaning and preparing the treatment area.

During treatment

Assist the therapist as required and ensure the health, safety and well-being of clients during treatment, according to legal and organisational requirements.

What you should know:

- the specific tasks you are required to do in order to assist the therapist with treatment
- the limits of your responsibilities when assisting with treatment
- the organisation's standards and procedures in terms of maintaining and monitoring the treatment area and equipment
- the possible contra-actions that may occur during treatment and necessary follow-up actions
- the relevant person to whom problems that occur during the treatment should be reported.

What you must do:

- monitor the treatment area and equipment at regular intervals
- monitor the clients at regular intervals, checking that they are comfortable and not experiencing any contra-actions to treatment
- take immediate action if you suspect there is a problem
- maintain the client's modesty and privacy at all times.

After treatment

Ensure that treatments are 'shut down' according to legal and organisational requirements.

What you should know:

- the correct procedures for shutting down treatment
- the person with whom you should liaise regarding the completion of duties.

GOOD PRACTICE

Depending on the nature of the spa treatment, the client will either be wearing very little or nothing at all. Some clients may feel embarrassed by this. Keep the focus of your attention on their eyes when you are speaking to them so that they do not feel uncomfortable.

A PRACTICAL GUIDE TO BEAUTY THERAPY

What you must do:

- shut down the equipment according to instructions
- shut down the treatment area according to legal and organisational requirements
- dispose of waste safely and correctly
- make sure the treatment area is left in perfect condition for the next treatment
- liaise with appropriate colleagues to confirm the completion of 'shut down' duties.

Health and safety in the spa area

- All equipment should be serviced regularly according to the contract with the supplier and follow-up servicing agreements. This is the responsibility of the spa manager.
- The manufacturers' instructions should always be followed. These should be made available to all staff concerned with maintaining health and safety in the spa area.
- Hygiene is of the utmost importance. All equipment should be cleaned and maintained according to the manufacturers' instructions.
- Written instructions on the correct use of equipment should be displayed. This is particularly important in public areas of the spa environment where clients have more control of their treatments.
- Floors in the spa area should be non-slip with adequate drainage.
- No glass should be allowed in the pool areas.
- Outdoor shoes should not be allowed in the pool areas.
- Spillages should be cleared up immediately.
- There should always be sufficient supplies of clean towels and gowns, which are replenished regularly.
- Laundry baskets containing soiled gowns and towels should be emptied regularly.
- Stocks of soaps, shampoos and body lotions should be maintained in the shower areas.
- Clients must always be checked for contraindications before treatment.
- Clients should be monitored for contra-actions throughout treatment and appropriate action taken.
- Records of treatments and equipment usage should be maintained.

REMEMBER

The local Environmental Health Department has the right to inspect premises offering heat and water treatments. They will expect to see records of treatments and equipment use and evidence that regular testing, as required in the local by-laws, has been carried out appropriately by an authorised person.

REMEMBER

Your employer is responsible for ensuring implementation of the local by-laws in relation to water, temperature and spa treatments. These should be reflected in the organisation's standards and procedures. Failing to follow procedures can sometimes amount to breaking the law.

Monitoring the client

This includes keeping a visual check on the client and asking, at regular intervals, if they are comfortable.

The more the client understands about their treatment and its effects, the more likely it is that they are going to be able to let you know if something is wrong. Take time to explain what is involved, how the treatment should feel and how it should not feel. Encourage the client to ask questions and take time to answer them fully.

Contra-actions

People in good health and without contraindications should not normally experience any adverse effects to hydrotherapy, heat or spa treatments. However, occasionally problems can occur. When they do, your first priority is the health and safety of the client. Your second priority is ensuring that the person with overall responsibility is informed as quickly as possible. They will then take control of, and responsibility for, the follow-up actions.

The contra-actions most likely to occur are due to the relatively high temperature and humidity levels of the spa environment, particularly if clients stay for too long in the sauna or steam rooms. They may get too hot, causing them to sweat excessively and suffer from **dehydration**. This may cause nausea, the sensation of feeling 'queasy' and wanting to be sick. Their **blood pressure** may fall, making them feel dizzy and as if they are going to faint. Cramp may occur and possibly nose bleeds in those people who are prone to them. The hot, dry environment of the sauna may cause breathing difficulties if the amount of moisture in the air (humidity) is allowed to fall below a certain level. Skin irritation, for example stinging, tightness or itchiness, may result in reaction to the hot, dry temperature of the sauna or to chemicals in the spa pool.

HEALTH MATTERS

Know and understand the signs:

- **Nausea:** anything that can cause vomiting can also cause nausea, either before or instead of vomiting. Nausea is felt as 'heaviness' in the throat or upper middle region of the abdomen and may come in waves. The person may feel cold and sweaty. The many different things that can cause nausea do so by affecting the 'vomiting centre' in the brain.

- **Dizziness and feeling faint:** caused by a slight lowering or raising of blood pressure or sudden change in position, for example from lying to standing. The client feels as if their head is spinning and their face may become pale. They may lose consciousness altogether and faint. When this happens, there is a reduction in the flow of blood to the head, causing a lack of oxygen in the brain.

- **Cramp:** a sharp, muscular pain, which occurs most commonly in the abdomen and muscles of the legs and feet. The affected muscle suddenly contracts and goes into spasm. Cramp is caused by poor circulation or long periods of repeated movements, for example 'writer's cramp'. It happens when lactic acid, the substance that makes muscles contract, is produced by the body more quickly than it is used up.

- **Nose bleed:** blood may appear from the nostrils if blood vessels in the nose become ruptured.

- **Breathing difficulties:** in order to breathe comfortably, the respiratory tract needs to be kept moist. If the humidity level in the sauna is allowed to fall too low, the hot, dry air breathed in can dry out and irritate the respiratory tract and even 'scorch' the lungs. This is painful and can cause breathlessness.

- **Skin irritation:** the combination of heat and perspiration may result in a heat rash which appears as inflammation and minute, itchy red pimples. These are caused by the effects upon the skin cells, blood capillaries and superficial nerve endings of 'histamine', the substance produced by the body to deal with damage from the outside. A similar rash may occur in reaction to other irritants such as chemicals in the spa pool.

REMEMBER

The risks associated with individual hydrotherapy, heat and spa treatments should be explained to the client in detail at the initial consultation. This is particularly important in relation to the communal use of spa pools, saunas and steam rooms, where individual clients are not under the direct supervision of a qualified therapist. Written instructions and warnings should be provided in the form of information sheets and notices displayed where clearly visible in the relevant spa areas.

Follow-up actions

Here are the actions that should be taken to assist a client with a contra-action.

Nausea

- Move the client to a quiet area.
- Help them to either sit down or lie down, slightly propped up.
- Offer sips of non-acidic, sweetened liquids to help calm the stomach.
- Stay with the client until they are recovered.

Dizziness and feeling faint

- Move the client to a cool area.
- Help the client to lie down with their head low and their legs raised. Alternatively, they may sit with their head between their knees. This helps the flow of blood back to the brain.
- Moisten their lips with cold water.
- Stay with the client and provide reassurance. Advise them not to get up too quickly. They should sit up for a few minutes before standing up. If they get up too fast, they might faint.
- When they have recovered, offer drinks of water.
- Get medical assistance if required.

Cramp

Hold the affected muscle in a stretched position until the cramp subsides.

Nose bleed

- Sit the client down with their head held forwards. Do not let the head tip back.
- Advise them to breathe through their mouth and pinch their nose just below the bridge with their thumb and index finger for up to 10 minutes. During this time the client should avoid speaking, swallowing, coughing or sniffing.
- If the bleeding continues, medical advice should be sought.

Breathing difficulties

- Move the client to a quiet area and sit them down.
- Encourage them to relax and restore their natural rhythm of breathing. This should take only a few minutes.
- Offer them drinks of water.
- Wipe over their forehead, face and neck with cold water.
- If breathing difficulties persist, seek medical advice.

Skin irritation

- Advise the client to take a cool shower to reduce skin temperature and/or remove the irritating substances.
- If the irritation persists the client should seek medical advice.

HEALTH MATTERS

Clients are advised to spend some time in the relaxation area following hydrotherapy and heat treatments. This is to give time for the normal body temperature and blood pressure to be restored before leaving the spa. Drinks of water should be taken to replace body fluids lost during the treatment.

ACTIVITY

Activity 14.1: Health and safety in the spa area

The jacuzzi™ is a good place from which to observe all that is happening in the spa area. Book in at your local leisure centre or health club, take up your position in the jacuzzi™ and look closely around you to check out what you have learned about health and safety in the spa so far. Watch the staff, the clients, their behaviour and the general activities going on. Have a good look at your surroundings, the condition of the water, furnishings and equipment. Does everything seem in order? Decide if this is a place where you would like to work.

Hydrotherapy treatments

REMEMBER

'Holistic' means dealing with the whole person, not just treating an individual condition.

Two thousand years after a Greek physician identified the powers of water as part of a 'holistic' regime for counteracting disease, the value of spa treatments and water based therapy has become widely recognised in the health and beauty industry. The ancient Greeks advocated the physical and psychological benefits of taking baths alongside a proper diet, exercise and massage, to restore the body to health. Places with naturally occurring mineral springs became popular health resorts for public bathing and the concept gradually spread to other parts of the world.

REMEMBER

Although a spa is technically 'a place where there is a curative mineral spring', today the word is used generally to describe places that offer professional, water-based treatments in an environment of peace and calm.

Today, in the UK, with the renewed interest in health and water treatments, spa towns that have become places of historical interest are enjoying renewed popularity, not least of all Bath, probably the most famous of British spa towns, due to the revival of its hot thermal waters.

ACTIVITY

Activity 14.2: Spas

There is a wealth of information about spas and spa treatments on the internet. Key in 'spas' in the search window and see what happens. You will be able to browse some of the most beautiful and luxurious spas in the world. Compare what is on offer and learn more about the treatments. Print off details about the three that most appeal to you and keep their details to explore the opportunity of a work placement!

Spa pools (whirlpools, hydro pools)

One of the most popular attractions in any health or leisure facility is the spa pool, commonly referred to as a 'jacuzzi'™. Jacuzzi™ is the name of the American manufacturer who brought whirlpools to commercial success. Varying in size and shape, the 'shell' of the pool is made of synthetic materials, able to withstand chemicals and the velocity (flow) of the water. The prefabricated, one-piece design incorporates a seating area to a central depth of approximately 1 metre. Larger pools can fit up to eight people.

Spa pool (jacuzzi™) in a health spa

A spa pool usually has its own self-contained filter and pump, chemical dosing equipment and fresh-water supply. In order to maintain hygienic bathing conditions, the spa water is continuously drawn off by the main circulating pump and recirculated through the treatment system, where it is filtered, heated and chemically treated.

The main benefits of the spa pool are produced by its hydro-massaging effects. Compressed air, flowing through small holes at the base of the pool, produces a gentle massaging effect. A more stimulating massage is created by jets of air located around the sides of the pool, which pummel the skin from all directions. The combination creates a turbulent, fast-moving stream of warm, bubbling water, which is, at the same time, both relaxing and exhilarating.

Checking the jacuzzi™ filter

A spa pool is usually located near the swimming pool, allowing clients to move easily between the two and benefit from both.

Main effects of the spa pool

- Stimulates the circulation, thereby increasing the supply of nutrients and removal of waste products from the body.
- Stimulates the skin and aids desquamation.
- Increases the rate of metabolism.
- Eases tension in the muscles and joints, thereby renewing flexibility and relieving stiffness.
- Relieves aches and pains.
- Creates a sense of general health and well-being.
- Relaxes and helps relieve anxiety.

Member of staff punching in code to enter the plant room – note the safety signs

Team work in the plant room

Maintenance of the spa pool

A number of safety factors will have been considered when having the spa pool installed.

The floor will have been:

- reinforced to take the heavy weight of the pool when filled with water
- fitted with a good drainage system.

The **plant room**, which houses the master controls of the pool, will have been:

- provided with a suitable power supply
- located within 5 metres of the pool
- equipped with a good ventilation system.

The pool will have been fitted with:

- a filtration system
- a heavy-duty control panel to withstand constant use.

Surrounding surfaces will be:

- easy to clean
- resistant to heat and moisture
- anti-slip.

Thereafter, the reliability, cleanliness and safety of the pool will depend on ongoing monitoring and maintenance in line with the manufacturer's instructions, the legal health and safety requirements and the organisation's procedures.

Assist and monitor spa pool treatment

In a public spa pool environment, your main duties will be related to spa pool maintenance and keeping your eye on the clients. Any problems that might occur need identifying and dealing with as soon as possible.

The essential components of spa pool maintenance are:

- the constant feed of an effective sanitiser
- the maintenance of appropriate chemical ranges
- the periodic, complete draining of spa water and refilling with fresh water.

There will be strict procedures regarding the nature and frequency of the tasks that contribute to maintaining the spa pool. These must be followed at all times and accurate records kept for future inspection.

Water balance

'Balancing the water' is the first step in keeping the spa pool clean and clear. Water that is not balanced can cause skin and eye irritation, cloudy water and may damage the spa pool's 'shell' and inner workings. Water balancing involves checking the pH (acidity/alkalinity)of the pool. The water should be sufficiently alkaline to neutralise the acid and keep the pH level within the proper range. The acceptable pH of a spa pool lies within the range 7.2–8.00.

Water cleanliness

Spa pools require the use of sanitisers and purifiers to keep the water clear and healthy. When added to the water, they kill bacteria and odour. The most common agents used to sanitise and purify spa pools are based on chlorine and bromine, although mineral based purifiers are available.

> **REMEMBER**
>
> Different chemicals need different temperatures and conditions to be effective. The main tests for a swimming pool and 'plunge' (cold water) pool are pH and chlorine. In a jacuzzi™, the water is warmer and the main tests are bromine and pH.

GOOD PRACTICE

Most pools have an automatic 'dosing' system which releases the chemicals regularly into the water. Although there is very little risk of the dosing system breaking down, checks are usually made approximately every three hours to ensure the correct balance and make manual adjustments if required.

Clarifiers work on the bacteria, oils and other organisms that sanitisers cannot destroy in water. They work in one of two ways:

- they coagulate liquid bacteria into a solid which can then be captured by the pool's filter. One disadvantage is that the coagulated materials tend to collect on the shell of the pool, forming an unsightly 'scum line' along the water line
- they break down organisms by converting them into gas before they can interfere with the sanitiser's performance. They do not form a scum line.

Stain and scale preventers help to control any staining or discolouring of the water caused by minerals. They also help to prevent scale from forming on the shell's surface.

Undesirable foaming of the spa pool can sometimes occur as a result of soap residue from bathing suits, shampoo, body oils and cosmetics. Special products are available which, when added to the pool, get rid of the residue. Residual foam occurring after the spa pump has been turned off indicates a more serious problem. The foam harbours bacteria which float on the sanitised spa water, threatening contamination of the spa pool. The pool should be drained and refilled with fresh water.

Pool test – testing for chlorine (swimming and plunge pool), bromine (jacuzzi™) and pH levels

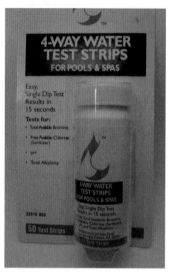

Water testing kit

Water testing

Water testing is an essential part of pool maintenance. Chemical reactions are taking place all the time and water is constantly evaporating, increasing the concentration of chemicals in the water. Even where the pool has an automatic chemical control system, this can periodically go out of calibration and it is still necessary to carry out regular testing.

Water testing kits are available for checking the balance of the water and its chemical content. The tests are usually conducted 5–6 times per day and consist of taking a sample of pool water, colour matching it against colour standards and/or using chemical reagents.

Always follow the manufacturer's guidance on conducting the tests and using the chemical reagents:

- Wash and dry your hands before starting the test.
- Always take the water sample from the same place in the pool.
- Make sure the water sample is sufficient to carry out the required tests in one operation.
- Always use a clean plastic jug or bottle for taking the water sample. Never take glass into the pool area.
- Carry out the tests away from the pool area in a suitable location.
- On completion of the tests, rinse out containers thoroughly in fresh water.

GOOD PRACTICE

Always follow your organisation's procedures for checking water quality and filters. These will have been based on:

- the manufacturer's guidance
- health and safety legislation regarding the frequency of testing and follow-up actions.

Water temperature

The temperature of the spa pool should be maintained between 30 °C and 40 °C. This creates an environment that minimises the risk of bacterial infection and is most comfortable and safe for the clients. The temperature of the spa pool is tested using a thermometer.

GOOD PRACTICE

Clients should be monitored closely in the spa pool. High temperatures can cause drowsiness, which may lead to unconsciousness, resulting in drowning.

Monitoring clients

The aeration of the spa pool works off a pre-set timer. Clients are able to extend their treatment by resetting the timer using the control panel. They are, therefore, in control of their own treatment. You should maintain ongoing monitoring of the pool to ensure that:

- all of the clients look comfortable
- the pool does not become overcrowded
- the water is in good condition
- you can provide assistance if required.

Taking a shower before entering the spa pool

ACTIVITY

Activity 14.3: Assist and monitor spa pool treatment

Using a computer, create an advice sheet for clients using the jacuzzi™. The advice sheet should contain all of the information needed to help them understand both the benefits and risks associated with the treatment. When they have read the advice sheet, they should know how to get the most out of their jacuzzi™ treatment, and the health and safety aspects. Give your advice sheet a title and think what else you might include to help promote other treatments and products offered by the spa.

Hydro baths

Hydro bath treatments are usually offered in specialist health resorts. The effects of the baths are similar to spa pools but the baths are smaller and designed to provide customised treatments for individual clients. The inside of the hydrotherapy bath is shaped to conform, generally, to the shape of the body and there are grab handles to help the client to get in and out. The bath is filled with water, a selected essence is added and the compressor is switched on, allowing air to aerate the bath gently through holes in a duck board located in the base of the bath. The client is assisted in to the bath and a hose, attached to the bath, directs the flow of air over the main muscle groups for approximately 20 minutes.

Main effects of hydro baths:

- body temperature is raised
- perspiration is induced
- circulation is increased
- muscle fibres are relaxed
- metabolism is increased.

Contraindications to hydrotherapy bath:

- heart conditions
- infectious skin diseases
- circulatory disorders
- following a heavy meal or after drinking alcohol
- athlete's foot
- verrucas
- pregnancy.

Conditions requiring medical approval:

- diabetes
- epilepsy.

Hydro bath with client in situ

Steps in the treatment

1 The client is greeted at reception and escorted to the changing facilities where they are provided with a clean gown, disposable slippers and bath towel.
2 Advice is given regarding the removal of contact lenses, spectacles and jewellery and the safe keeping of personal items.
3 The client is requested to shower in order to remove deodorant, fragrances and body lotion. They are then accompanied to the treatment area.
4 The compressor on the bath is switched on to produce gentle aeration of the water.
5 The water is checked to ensure it is a comfortable temperature.
6 The client is helped with the removal of their gown and then settled into a semi-reclining position in the bath.
7 The hose is then switched on and guided over the client's body for approximately 15–20 minutes.
8 On completion of treatment, the hose is switched off, followed by the compressor, and the client is assisted out of the bath.

9 When dry, the client is advised to spend a little time in the relaxation area and to have a drink of water.

10 On completion of treatment, the record card is completed, signed and returned to the files.

Assist and monitor hydro bath treatment

During this treatment, the therapist is present all the time providing the hydro massage. Your main responsibilities are to ensure that everything required for treatment is available, on time, in the treatment area, and that the bath and treatment room are left clean and tidy afterwards.

Preparing the treatment area
- Ensure that there are adequate supplies of clean towels, gowns and consumables as appropriate in the treatment and shower areas.
- Fill the bath with warm water and add the required essence.

During the treatment
- Maintain regular checks to ensure the client is looking and feeling comfortable.
- Keep the floor area around the bath and shower dry to prevent the client from slipping.
- Assist your supervisor as required.

After treatment
- Remove used towels and waste from the bath treatment and shower areas.
- Ensure switches on the bath are in the 'off' position.
- Clean and disinfect the bath ready for the next treatment.

Hydro-oxygen baths

In this treatment, the client reclines in a bath-type cabinet which contains jets that are used to 'blast' their body with hot water and to diffuse oxygen into the cabinet. The treatment is extremely stimulating, leaving the client feeling refreshed and invigorated.

Foam baths

In this treatment, the foam produced acts as an insulator, which prevents heat from escaping. As a consequence, the client's body temperature increases with the associated beneficial effects.

HEALTH MATTERS

The bath should be cleaned between each treatment, using a special sterilising fluid recommended by the manufacturer.

Single-unit foam baths contain a plastic duck board which allows compressed air to be forced through hundreds of tiny holes into the bath water. Only a small amount of water is needed, approximately 10–15 cm, to cover the duck board. The water is heated to between 37 °C and 43 °C, depending on the individual client. Concentrated foam essence such as seaweed is added to the water prior to the compressor being switched on. The compressor pumps air from beneath the duck board and then forces its way through the perforated holes to aerate the water. The compressor is left on until the foam created by the aeration of the water and foam essence reaches the top of the bath. The client relaxes in the foam in a semi-reclined position with their head supported on the back of the bath, above the foam.

Main effects of foam baths:
- body temperature is raised
- perspiration is induced
- circulation is increased
- muscle fibres are relaxed.

Contraindications to foam baths:
- infectious skin diseases
- verrucas
- athlete's foot
- sunburn
- within a few hours of consuming alcohol.

Conditions requiring medical approval:
- diabetes
- epilepsy
- respiratory conditions
- circulatory conditions.

Steps in the treatment
1 The client is greeted at reception and escorted to the changing facilities where they are provided with a clean gown, disposable slippers and bath towel.
2 Advice is given regarding the removal of contact lenses, spectacles and jewellery and the safe keeping of personal items.
3 The client is requested to shower in order to remove deodorant, fragrances and body lotion. They are then accompanied to the treatment area.
4 The temperature of the water is checked and then the client is assisted into the foam bath, ensuring that they are relaxed and comfortable.
5 When the treatment is finished, usually after 15 minutes, the client is helped out of the bath and is offered a warm shower.
6 When dry, the client is advised to spend a little time in the relaxation area and to have a drink of water.
7 On completion of treatment, the record card is completed, signed and returned to the files.

Assist and monitor foam bath treatment
During this treatment, the therapist is not required to be present all the time, therefore you must be readily available to assist the client should they need you and to monitor them regularly throughout. You will also be required to ensure that everything required for treatment is available, on time, in the treatment area and that the bath and treatment room are left clean and tidy afterwards.

Preparing the treatment area

- Ensure that there are adequate supplies of clean towels, gowns and consumables as appropriate in the treatment and shower areas.
- Fill the bath with enough warm water to cover the duck board.
- Choose an appropriate foam essence, for example seaweed, and add to the water.
- Switch on the compressor to aerate the water.
- When the foam is level with the top of the bath, switch off the compressor. The foam bath is now ready for use.

During the treatment

- Maintain regular checks to ensure the client is looking and feeling comfortable.
- Keep the floor area around the bath and shower dry to prevent the client from slipping.
- Assist your supervisor as required.

After treatment

- Remove used towels and waste from the bath treatment and shower areas.
- Ensure switches on the bath are in 'off' position.
- Clean and disinfect the bath ready for the next treatment.

Safety matters when providing bath treatments

All hydrotherapy baths should be maintained well and serviced regularly. Between each treatment they should be cleaned using a sterilising fluid recommended by the manufacturer. Hoses and other accessories should be checked each time the bath is cleaned to make sure they are in good condition.

General precautions:

- Ensure electrical safety in the treatment area.
- Always check for contraindications before treatment.
- Ensure that the standing area around the bath and shower is dry. A shower mat or duck board should be provided to prevent slipping.
- Provide clean gown and towels for each client and place within their easy reach.
- Discard used paper towels immediately and replace with new ones.
- If soap is provided, it should be kept in a soap dish which is cleaned regularly to prevent the build-up of slimey soap deposits.
- Liquid soap dispensers should be wiped over regularly and the nozzles kept clean to prevent them from becoming blocked.
- Clean the shower regularly with a special cleansing agent designed to prevent the build-up of limescale, soap deposits, mould and mildew.
- If something obviously needs repairing or replacing, either deal with it immediately if you have the authority to do so, or report it to your supervisor.
- Do not ignore puddles of water on the floor in wet-treatment areas. Attend to them immediately to prevent accidents.

Floatation treatments

These are often offered as part of a rejuvenation and relaxation package at health resorts or other types of natural-health retreat. They provide the ultimate total mind and body relaxation experience.

Wet floatation

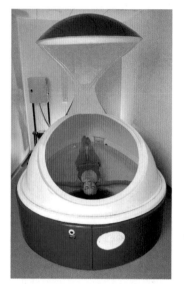

Wet float treatment

In this treatment, the client floats, effortlessly, in a bath or pool of warm, shallow water to which mineral salts have been added. Lighting within the treatment area is dimmed or blocked out entirely and soothing music is played to help create an environment of peace and calm. As the combined effects upon the senses take over, the body 'yields' to the gentle, comforting support of the water, releasing tensions and creating a sensation of intense well-being.

Wet floatation tanks are usually made from moulded fibreglass and vary in size. The most modern ones resemble a small capsule with a sliding, overhead cockpit-style door, enabling the client to easily adjust the space to their own comfort requirements.

State-of-the-art floatation tank

The more traditional designs are small rooms or walk-in cabinets containing a bed-sized tank or pool. The interior colour is often blue to help create the right ambiance. Other features include an in-tank light switch with external control and dimmer, an in-tank audio control to adjust the volume of the music, an in-tank alarm or call button in case of an emergency and an intercom system allowing checks to be made on the client's comfort and well-being during the treatment. The floatation tank is usually contained in a separate room with access to a shower and quiet relaxation area.

Steps in the treatment

1 The client is greeted at reception and escorted to the changing facilities where they are provided with a clean gown, disposable slippers and bath towel.

2 Advice is given regarding the removal of contact lenses, spectacles and jewellery and the safe keeping of personal items.

3 The client is requested to shower in order to remove deodorant, fragrances and body lotion. They are then accompanied to the treatment area.

4 Petroleum jelly is offered to the client to cover any small abrasions which might sting if brought into contact with the salt water.

5 The client is escorted to the floatation tank and provided with ear plugs and a neck cushion if desired.

6 The client's robe is removed and they are assisted into the floatation tank or pool. The internal light should be on at this stage.

REMEMBER

Ear plugs help prevent water entering the ear canals, while the support provided by a neck cushion helps the client relax and float more confidently.

7   The various safety and comfort features are pointed out and the client is reassured that they will be closely monitored during the treatment.

8   The client is instructed to lie back with their neck supported with a neck cushion if desired. They are then advised to try and relax totally so that they float on the salt water. Once the effects of floatation have taken over, all of the superficial muscles become relaxed and tension is released from the body.

9   When the client is settled, the door of the tank is closed gently and the client switches off the interior light when ready.

10 An intercom system may be used to monitor the client.

11 The volume of the music may be adjusted so that it fades into the background when the client is at their most relaxed and reintroduced towards the end of the floatation period so that the client experiences a gentle 'awakening'.

12 The client is assisted out of the tank and escorted to the shower to remove brine from their skin and hair.

REMEMBER

As the client enters the tank, note the time and estimate and record the end of treatment time, 45 minutes later.

REMEMBER

A short period of 'recovery' in the relaxation area helps the client prepare for re-entering the 'real world'!

GOOD PRACTICE

People who have not experienced floatation therapy may sometimes have concerns which should be anticipated and addressed at the initial consultation.

Question: I can't swim. Is there any risk of me drowning in the floatation tank?
Answer: No. The water is only 30 cm deep and the concentration of salts in the tank creates such buoyancy that it is impossible to sink. Floating becomes effortless. In fact there's nothing else you can do except float!

Question: How hygienic is the floatation tank?
Answer:The very high mineral salt content keeps the water sterile and the filtration system, used after each user, ensures maximum hygiene standards.

Question: Will I feel 'trapped' in the tank? I don't want to feel claustrophobic.
Answer: You shouldn't do. The sooner you relax, the sooner you can start benefiting from the treatment and the sooner you will forget where you are! If it helps, you can leave the door partially open for the first few minutes. Even after you have switched off the internal light, a small amount of external light is still visible from the outer room through the door frame and ventilation hole. The outer room lighting will not be switched off until you are ready.

REMEMBER

The water in the tank is maintained at the same temperature as the body. This feels very comforting and helps the client relax and enjoy the treatment.

Main effects of wet floatation

- Relieves muscle tension.
- Reduces blood pressure and heart rate.
- Stimulates the circulation and increases energy levels.
- Increases the supply of oxygen and nutrients to the cells.
- Increases the rate of removal of waste products
- Restores the body's chemical and metabolic balance, strengthening its resistance to illness and injury.
- Reduces the levels of stress-related chemicals in the body.
- Provides relief from aches and pains.
- Creates a feeling of inner calm and well-being.

HEALTH MATTERS

During floatation, the buoyancy of the water creates a feeling of weightlessness, which provides relief from aching joints and muscular pain.

The effects on the brain of floatation are similar to those of hypnosis and deep meditation. The activity of slower brain waves called theta waves is enhanced, improving brain co-ordination and the ability to learn and recall information. People generally feel more confident and creative after a floatation treatment.

Contraindications to wet floatation:

- claustrophobia
- very nervous client
- severe cuts or abrasions
- recent scar tissue
- infectious skin diseases
- severe eczema or psoriasis
- verruca
- athlete's foot
- immediately after a meal or after drinking alcohol.

REMEMBER

People who suffer from epilepsy or who have a heart condition must obtain the written permission of their doctor before having a wet floatation treatment.

Assist and monitor wet floatation treatment

During this treatment, the therapist is not required to be present all of the time. Therefore, you must be readily available to assist the client should they need you and to monitor them regularly throughout. Your other main responsibilities are in relation to the maintenance of the wet floatation tank.

Routine cleaning and maintenance of the tank and shower areas is undertaken between each treatment. Regular water testing is also required:

- ensure the tank is clean without any trace of oil, scum or hairs
- check the area above the water line regularly and clean at least twice a week to prevent a build-up of surface matter on the sides of the tank
- the water in the tank should be filtered between treatments and the temperature checked
- the water level should be checked between clients
- daily testing of the pH of the water is required (pH 7.6 is the recommended norm)
- the level of bromine should not rise higher than 2 ppm (parts per million) and this should be checked at least once per week.

Dry floatation

The term 'dry floatation' is rather misleading. Although the client appears to be floating, their body is either suspended in water on a board or resting on a waterbed mattress, which, itself, is floating on the water. The principles of treatment are similar to wet floatation except that the skin is usually coated in a treatment mask before the client is lowered into the tank which is then covered with vinyl. The temperature of the pre-heated water is maintained throughout treatment.

Although dry floatation treatments are relaxing and enjoyable, they do not have the same effects as wet floatation on theta wave brain activity or stress reduction. These two major benefits are thought to be related directly to the contact that is made between the body and skin-temperature water during a wet floatation treatment. Dry floatation can, however, have additional benefits as a result of the active ingredients contained in body products applied beforehand.

Some health spas provide facials during dry floatation treatments.

Main effects of dry floatation:

- aids relaxation
- relaxes muscles
- eases aches and pains
- creates a general feeling of well-being.

Contraindications to dry floatation:

- infectious skin conditions
- severe respiratory conditions
- a heavy cold or high temperature.

Steps in the treatment

1 The client is greeted and prepared as for wet floatation.
2 They are then taken to the treatment area where a body product may be applied. They are assisted on to the board and lowered into the tank and covered with vinyl.
3 The treatment lasts for approximately 40 minutes. During this time, the client is monitored regularly, every five minutes, to check that they are comfortable.
4 On completion of treatment, the control button is used to raise the board and lift the client to the top of the tank. The vinyl cover is then removed.
5 The client is assisted out of the tank and escorted to the shower. Help is provided removing the body product if required.
6 The client then finishes off in the relaxation area and has a drink of water.

Assist and monitor dry floatation treatment

During this treatment, the therapist is not required to be present all of the time. Therefore, you must be readily available to assist the client should they need you and to monitor them regularly throughout.

Your other main responsibilities are in relation to the preparation and closing down of the treatment area and the maintenance of the dry floatation tank.

Preparing the treatment area

- Ensure that there are adequate supplies of clean towels, gowns and consumables as appropriate in the treatment and shower areas.
- Before the client arrives, pre-heat the water using the temperature control switch and ensure the board is raised to the top of the tank. The board may be covered with paper roll.
- If a clay-based treatment preparation is going to be used, place a protective covering on the floor area between the tank and the shower.

During the treatment

- Maintain regular checks to ensure the client is looking and feeling comfortable.
- Keep the floor area around the tank and shower dry to prevent the client from slipping.
- Assist your supervisor as required.

After treatment

- Remove any used towels and waste from the bath treatment and shower areas.
- Ensure switches on the tank are in the 'off' position.
- Clean and disinfect the tank ready for the next treatment.

Maintaining the dry floatation area

- Routine cleaning and maintenance of the tank and shower areas is undertaken between each treatment.
- The vinyl sheeting is cleaned, dried and kept protected between treatments.

SELF-CHECKS

Hydrotherapy treatments

1 Why is a spa pool also called a 'whirlpool'?

2 State four beneficial effects of a spa pool treatment.

3 Name two chemicals used for testing the water in a spa pool.

4 State three precautions that should be taken when using the water testing kit.

5 List four beneficial effects of a hydro bath.

6 What is the main difference between a hydro bath and a foam bath?

7 a) What essential ingredient is added to the water in a wet floatation tank?
   b) Why is this ingredient essential?

8 Give two reasons why good ventilation is important in the hydrotherapy treatment area.

9 State four general contraindications to hydrotherapy treatments.

10 What happens in the 'plant room' situated near the pool?

Sauna and steam treatments

Sauna and steam are probably the most popular heat treatments offered in a spa environment. Beauty therapy salons providing body treatments may also offer sauna and steam, even if they do not have the space for an extended range of spa treatments.

The main benefits of sauna and steam are due to their effects on the blood circulation. Blood plays an essential role in the maintenance of health. The treatments stimulate the cardiovascular system, increasing the rate at which blood circulates around the body. The blood vessels in the skin expand to help cope with the increased blood flow. This brings blood closer to the surface, causing redness of the skin known as hyperaemia. Oxygen and nutrients are transported to the cells and tissues and waste products are taken away. The whole body benefits.

The amount of pressure exerted on the arteries as blood flows through them is called blood pressure. Blood pressure that is too high or too low can be a problem. High blood pressure increases the risk of heart disease, kidney disease and having a stroke. Low blood pressure can cause symptoms such as dizziness and feeling light-headed. People who have high or low blood pressure are contraindicated to sauna and steam treatments.

HEALTH MATTERS

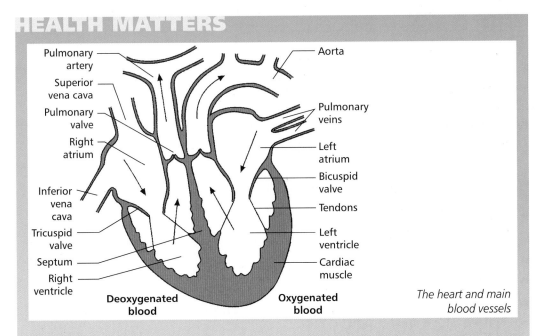

The heart and main blood vessels

The cardiovascular system consists of:

- the heart
- blood
- blood vessels.

The heart is made up of powerful cardiac muscle which 'pumps' blood around the body. The blood that passes through the left side of the heart is rich in oxygen. The blood that passes through the right-hand side is deoxygenated; it carries very little oxygen. The blood vessels that transport oxygenated blood away from the heart are called arteries. The ones that return deoxygenated blood to the heart are called veins. Oxygenated blood is red. Deoxygenated blood is bluish. The organs and tissues in the body rely on a good supply of oxygen and nutrients in the blood circulation to keep them healthy. They also rely on the efficient removal of waste products and harmful substances via the lymph system, which is closely related to the blood circulation.

REMEMBER

During a sauna or steam treatment the skin temperature rises to 40 °C and the internal body temperature to 38 °C.

REMEMBER

Thirty per cent of body waste passes through the skin. The profuse sweating that occurs during sauna and steam treatments enhances the detoxifying capacity of the skin by opening the pores and flushing out impurities.

As body temperature increases, so do the activities of the sweat (suderiferous) and sebaceous glands. The pores dilate, releasing sweat and sebum on the surface of the skin, which has cleansing and softening effects. It is not surprising that people look so youthful, flushed and healthy after a sauna or steam treatment! The effect can last for several hours after treatment.

REMEMBER

During a sauna or steam treatment, blood flow to the skin increases from 5–10 per cent of cardiac output to 50–70 per cent, bringing nutrients to the surface tissues.

Taking a pulse

REMEMBER

Sauna and steam treatments are very good pre-treatments before massage because they relax the client and make the muscles and skin more supple. Sometimes the treatments may be recommended after massage rather than before, to help rid the body of toxins released during the treatment.

HEALTH MATTERS

A temporary, slight lowering of blood pressure is to be expected during a sauna or steam treatment due to the effects of increased temperature on the superficial blood vessels. A follow-up shower, rest and drinks of water in the relaxation area help to restore normal temperature and blood pressure before the client leaves the spa environment.

HEALTH MATTERS

During a 20-minute treatment, the pulse rate (rate at which the heart pumps blood through the arteries) of an average person increases from 60–80 beats per minute to 100–150 beats. This is what causes the increase in blood flow during sauna and steam treatments.

HEALTH MATTERS

The pulse can be taken by placing the fingertips in the hollow located at the wrist, beneath the thumb joint, pressing lightly over the artery beneath. The number of beats per minute that make up the 'pulse' should be counted using a watch with a 'second' hand. A normal, healthy average adult pulse will provide 72 regular, strong beats per minute. An increase in the pulse rate may be due to stress, illness, injury, exercise or as a result of drinking alcohol.

Main effects of sauna and steam

- Increases body temperature.
- Stimulates blood circulation.
- Stimulates lymphatic circulation.
- Increases heart rate.
- Increases pulse rate.
- Induces perspiration.
- Deep cleanses and softens the skin.
- Relaxes tired, aching muscles.
- Relieves stress and tension.
- Helps rid the body of impurities.
- Induces a deeper and more relaxing sleep.
- Creates a general feeling of well-being.

Contraindications to sauna and steam:

- circulatory disorders
- heart conditions
- respiratory conditions, for example asthma
- high or low blood pressure
- epilepsy
- athlete's foot
- verrucas
- infectious skin diseases
- sunburn
- menstruation
- heavy colds/fever
- migraine
- after a heavy meal or alcohol
- recent scar tissue
- severe bruising.

A PRACTICAL GUIDE TO BEAUTY THERAPY

Conditions requiring medical referral:

- diabetes
- pregnancy.

The choice of sauna (dry heat) or steam (wet heat) treatment is very much a matter of client preference. Both treatments leave the client looking and feeling clean, healthy, toned and relaxed. Many clients will combine both treatments in the same visit to the spa. Others may prefer one to the other, based on their tolerance of high temperatures and humidity.

Relative humidity

Relative humidity is the measurement of moisture content as a percentage of the maximum that can be held at that temperature; 60–70 per cent is the normal, comfortable relative humidity level. If the temperature rises without a proportionate increase in the amount of moisture available, then the relative humidity level drops and the atmosphere becomes drier. If the temperature rises and proportionately more moisture is made available, the humidity level can rise up to a maximum 100 per cent, at which point the air is said to be 'saturated' with moisture. When the air is relatively 'dry', sweat evaporates freely, thereby cooling the body. When the air is 'humid', the sweat produced cannot evaporate. The skin remains moist and the body does not cool.

Humidity is measured using a hygrometer.

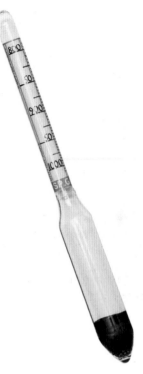

A hygrometer

Sauna

Saunas work on the principle of high heat and low humidity. The working temperature of the sauna is usually 70 °C to 110 °C, although it can range between 50 °C to 120 °C, with a relatively low humidity level of 5–10 per cent.

The sauna is basically a wooden cabin made of pine panels which are packed together with insulating material to prevent heat loss and help keep the air dry. The air inside the sauna is heated by an electric stove containing coals that get hot and are protected by a guard. The coals are a special type made from dolerite rock which can withstand rapid heating and cooling without splintering. They have to be replaced from time to time as they eventually lose their capacity to absorb and retain heat.

The cabin is ventilated through air inlets at floor level and an outlet near the top. Wooden seating at different levels allows the client to experience different temperatures. Heat rises, so the sauna is hotter at the upper level. A thermometer positioned near the top of the sauna measures the temperature and an egg timer is usually fitted on the wall nearby. Alternatively, a clock is clearly visible through the window of the sauna so that clients can monitor the length of their treatment.

Built-in safety features allow water to be ladled over the coals during treatment to create steam and maintain humidity inside the cabin. This makes breathing more comfortable. An essence such as mint, eucalyptus or cinnamon may be added to the water, creating a beautiful, therapeutic fragrance when the water is sprinkled on the coals.

The sauna takes a lot of power and works off mains supply electricity.

REMEMBER

Pine is an ideal wood for a sauna because it is porous and 'breathes' in response to heat and humidity.

Relaxing in the sauna

Steps in the treatment

1　The client has a shower and then enters the sauna with a towel to sit on. Most people start their sauna sitting at a lower level.

2　A little water is ladled over the hot coals on top of the stove to increase the humidity. The client will immediately feel the warmth penetrating their skin as the air inside the cabin 'quivers' with the heat.

3　After a few minutes, when the skin is perspiring freely, it is time for another shower. The pores are open at this stage so the effects of the shower are very deep cleansing.

4　The client returns to the sauna to relax and unwind, returning occasionally to the shower to cool down.

5　After 20–30 minutes, the treatment is concluded by ladling plenty of water over the coals, allowing the body to benefit from the effects of the steam produced.

6　Following the sauna, the client has a cleansing shower and then reduces their temperature with either a cool shower or a cold water plunge.

7　They then spend a little time in the relaxation area, enjoying the after-effects of the sauna and drinking plenty of water to replace that lost from the body during treatment.

At a temperature of between 21 °C and 50 °C, the water in the plunge pool feels very cold indeed, particularly after a sauna or steam treatment!

Assist and monitor sauna treatment

Preparing the treatment area

Depending on where you are working, you may be preparing a small sauna cabin in a beauty salon for treating an individual client or a larger sauna cabin for communal bathing, for example in a health spa.

The basic procedures will be the same. Ask your supervisor if there is anything you are not sure about.

1　Switch on the sauna at the mains.

2　Switch on the sauna stove, allowing enough time for the temperature to build up as required for treatment. A large sauna will take approximately an hour to heat up, a smaller sauna about 30 minutes.

3　Open up the air vents to allow air to circulate.

4　Fill a pine bucket with clean water and place with ladle inside the sauna, near the stove. Add fragrant essence as instructed.

5　Ensure adequate supplies of clean towels, gowns and consumables, as appropriate, in the sauna and shower areas.

6　Ensure the egg timer and thermometer inside the sauna are working.

7　Check the temperature using the thermometer.

8　Check the humidity using the hygrometer.

During the treatment

1　Maintain regular checks to ensure clients are looking and feeling comfortable.

2　Ensure that regular ladling of water on the coals is taking place.

3　Keep the floor area outside the shower dry to prevent clients from slipping.

4　Assist your supervisor and colleagues as appropriate.

After treatment

1 Remove any used towels and waste from the sauna and shower areas.
2 Top up water in the wooden bucket and add essence as required.

At the end of the working day

1 Switch off the sauna at the mains.
2 Scrub the seating and floor of the sauna with disinfectant products recommended by the manufacturer.
3 Empty any remaining water out of the bucket.
4 Leave the sauna door open to allow air to circulate and prevent the build-up of stale odours in the cabin.

Steam

Steam baths are available as single-unit cabinets for treating individual clients or steam rooms for communal bathing in a larger health spa environment.

Steam cabinet

A steam cabinet is made of moulded fibreglass and has a front-opening door through which the client enters and leaves the bath. An adjustable seat inside houses a water tank. Different sizes of water tank are available, the larger ones providing several treatments without needing to be refilled. When the steam bath is switched on, an electrical element in the tank heats the water to boiling point (100 °C), at which stage steam is produced. The steam mixes with air in the cabinet to produce water vapour, which circulates inside the cabinet. A comfortable temperature of 45–55 °C is maintained throughout treatment. This is monitored on a temperature gauge attached to the cabinet. The relative humidity of the air inside the steam cabinet is usually 92–97 per cent, which means it is virtually 'saturated' with moisture.

One advantage of a steam cabinet is that the client's head remains outside the bath during treatment so that the air they breathe in is taken from the room rather than from inside the cabinet. Some clients prefer this.

Steam room

The warm, moist environment of a steam treatment area is potentially a breeding ground for bacteria, therefore the materials used to construct a steam room must be water resistant, heat resistant, non-porous, smooth and easy to clean.

The steam room can be of any size. A large one may be situated near a swimming pool and be serviced by the same water supply.

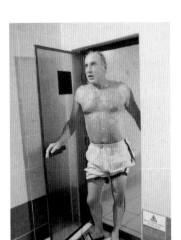

Emerging from the steam room after treatment

Water heated to 100°C in a boiler is converted into steam that passes through tubes into the steam room. The steam mixes with air to form water vapour which circulates inside the steam room, maintaining relative humidity at 92–97 per cent. A good ventilation system ensures the constant, efficient production of steam and, eventually, of water vapour.

Steps in the treatment

For communal bathing in a steam room, the treatment progresses similarly as for a sauna, except that the relatively high level of humidity produced constantly throughout means that perspiration does not evaporate but remains on the skin and trickles off the body. While some clients enjoy the feeling of 'sweating it out', others prefer to take regular cool showers or a cold water plunge during the treatment.

For individual clients having their treatment in a steam cabinet:

1   The client has a shower and is then assisted in to the steam cabinet. A towel is placed over the seat for their comfort.
2   The height of the seat is adjusted if necessary.
3   The cabinet door is closed.
4   A towel is draped around the neck of the steam bath to protect the client and avoid steam escaping from the cabinet.
5   The timer is set for 15–20 minutes.
6   At the end of the treatment time, the client is helped out of the cabinet and takes a cool shower.

They then have a follow-up body treatment or spend a little time in the relaxation area, enjoying the after-effects of the steam bath and drinking plenty of water to replace that lost from the body during treatment.

Assist and monitor steam treatment

Preparing the treatment area

Depending on where you are working, you may be preparing a steam cabinet in a beauty salon to treat an individual client or a larger steam room for communal bathing, for example in a health spa.

The basic procedures will be the same. Ask your supervisor if there is anything you are not sure about.

1   Switch on the steam bath at the mains.
2   Fill the tank with water. It is essential that the heating element is covered.
3   Ensure adequate supplies of clean towels, gowns and consumables, as appropriate, in the steam treatment and shower areas.
4   Set the temperature gauge to maximum to heat up the bath and turn on, allowing enough time for the temperature to build up. A steam room will take approximately one hour to heat up depending on its size. A steam cabinet takes about 15 minutes depending on the capacity of its water tank.
5   When the maximum temperature has been reached, reduce to the required temperature, usually 45–55 °C for a steam cabinet and 40 °C for a steam room, by adjusting the temperature gauge.

A PRACTICAL GUIDE TO BEAUTY THERAPY

During the treatment

1 Maintain regular checks to ensure clients are looking and feeling comfortable.

2 Keep the floor area outside the shower dry to prevent clients from slipping.

3 Assist your supervisor and colleagues as appropriate.

After treatment

1 Remove any used towels and waste from the steam treatment and shower areas.

2 Ensure all switches on the steam cabinet are in the 'off' position.

3 Clean and disinfect the cabinet after each treatment to remove grease and prevent the build-up of body odours.

At the end of the working day

1 Switch off the steam bath at the mains.

2 Clean all internal surfaces with disinfectant products recommended by the manufacturer.

3 Leave the steam bath door open to allow air to circulate and dry out the bath thoroughly.

Body wrap treatments

Body wraps are often referred to as 'slimming' or 'inch loss' treatments (1 inch = 2.5 cm). They are also believed to help reduce cellulite. During treatment the body is wrapped with porous cotton or elastic-type bandages or a large sheet of plastic material underneath which special products have been applied to the skin, often in the form of a 'mud' mask or contour gel. These usually contain extracts from natural ingredients such as seaweed, essential oils, vitamins and minerals, which have anti-cellulite, stimulating properties. They help to tighten and tone the skin.

REMEMBER

Anti-cellulite products help to release the 'trapped' fat, fluid and toxins responsible for the characteristic 'orange peel' appearance of cellulite.

Body wrap

Applying a mud mask before body wrapping

Main effects of body wrapping

- Help to motivate people who are dieting.
- Improve and firm the skin after pregnancy or weight loss.
- Help to tighten stretch marks and make them less noticeable.
- Help reduce cellulite.
- Provide a 'quick fix' inch loss for special occasions.
- Detoxify the body.
- Reduce specific areas, helping to improve the shape of people who are not overweight.
- Improve a dry or rough skin condition.

How body wrapping works

The main aim of body wrap treatments is to increase the blood and lymphatic circulation, thereby detoxifying the body by removing excess fluid and waste.

- The pressure and warmth of the wrap helps introduce the products into the skin's surface cells. The heat-retaining properties of the bandages help to open up the skin pores, allowing the 'active' ingredients in the products to penetrate the skin more easily. Once the bandages are in place, the client is wrapped in a pre-warmed blanket, foil or thermal suit, which retains the heat, thereby intensifying the levels of absorption, inch loss and detoxification.
- Because the bandages are contoured firmly to the body, cellulite fat is compressed and the removal of toxins is speeded up. The tension produced by the body wrap helps to remove excess waste from the skin and muscle cells.

There are usually perceptible improvements in the skin, particularly in the appearance of cellulite and inch loss, after just one treatment. However, body wraps are usually recommended in courses where they tend to be combined with some form of heat treatment and body exfoliation or body 'polishing'. The client usually remains in wraps for approximately 45 minutes, the whole treatment taking up to 1½ hours, and they eventually emerge from the treatment feeling refreshed and invigorated.

The number of body wrap treatments required depends on several things:

- how many inches the client wants to lose
- the number of inches lost per wrap
- how much loose skin the client has
- the client's commitment to dieting and exercising alongside the treatments.

REMEMBER

Body wraps are more effective if done regularly, at least once or twice per week. More intensive courses can be undertaken safely to achieve short-term results, for example for a special event.

REMEMBER

Body wrap treatments are particularly effective when combined with home care products and dietary and exercise advice.

REMEMBER

The inch loss provided by a body wrapping treatment will last for up to five days. A course of treatments will usually provide more lasting results.

GOOD PRACTICE

Although the basic principles of body wrapping treatment are the same, systems do vary. Always check the manufacturer's instructions before using a system you are not familiar with.

A PRACTICAL GUIDE TO BEAUTY THERAPY

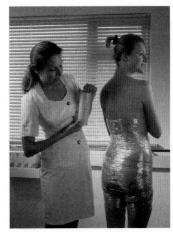

HEALTH MATTERS

A full consultation is always given to check the medical history and general health of the client. Some conditions are not suitable for treatment.

Steps in the treatment

1   The client is greeted at reception and escorted to the changing facilities where they are provided with a clean gown, disposable slippers and bath towel.

2   Advice is given regarding the safe keeping of personal items.

3   The client is requested to shower in order to remove deodorant, fragrances and body lotion.

4   They are provided with paper pants and a shower cap to wear during the treatment and advised to go to the toilet as this will be their last opportunity for some time!

5   The client is weighed and their details entered on their record card. They are then ready for treatment.

GOOD PRACTICE

Weighing the client at each treatment helps to monitor the client's progress with their diet.

6   The client is measured. Up to 18 different measurements may be taken depending on the treatment. It is important that the measurements are taken in exactly the same place each time so that the results are reliable.

GOOD PRACTICE

The measurements are recorded on the client's treatment chart, together with notes of where they want to lose inches or change their shape.

7   An appropriate body product is applied and then wrapping commences according to the manufacturer's instructions, usually upwards towards the heart.

8   Extra amounts of product are added as appropriate.

9   Once all of the bandages/wrapping medium are in place, the client confirms that they are comfortable.

10   Depending on the system used, they are then wrapped in a thermal blanket, thermal suit or covered in foil. This helps to sweat out impurities while they relax. Alternatively, they might undertake gentle exercise, for example on a toning table.

A body wrap treatment

REMEMBER

It is important for the client to stay warm during the treatment.

11   After approximately one hour, the bandages/wrapping medium are removed swiftly in the reverse order of application. Excess treatment product remaining on the skin is removed. The client is remeasured and their results entered on their record card. The '**total inch loss**' is calculated.

12 Depending on the specific treatment procedure, the client is escorted to the shower.

13 Some systems recommend a massage after body wrapping.

14 Home care advice is provided and the date and time of the next appointment is confirmed.

Assist and monitor body wrap treatment

Preparing the treatment area

There are many different types of body wrapping treatment and your supervisor will have received specific training in the system used where you work. They will advise you of the specific requirements and what help they need from you during the treatment. The following is a general guideline.

1 The following items are required:
- body wraps/bandages
- the active treatment product/s
- heating equipment for warming the bandages and, possibly, the treatment product
- pair of tongs for handling the hot bandages, which are placed in a bowl to cool slightly before using on the body
- full-size mirror and measuring tape
- thermal blanket, thermal suit or foil
- bath towels
- laundry basket to keep the clean bandages in
- large plastic bowl for collecting soiled bandages when they are unwrapped

2 Prepare the bandages/wrapping medium. The wraps are pre-heated either in hot water, in a special warming oven or in a microwave set at defrost. They may be soaked in a solution containing ingredients such as herbal extracts, collagen solutions or amino acids, before being applied to the body.

During the treatment

1 Maintain regular checks to ensure clients are looking and feeling comfortable.

2 Keep the floor area outside the shower dry to prevent clients from slipping.

3 Assist your supervisor as appropriate.

After treatment

1 Remove any used towels and waste from the treatment and shower areas.
2 Clean and sterilise the wrapping mediums according to the manufacturer's instructions.
3 Roll up the bandages and store as required.
4 Leave the treatment area clean and tidy.

Home care advice

The beneficial effects of the treatment are more likely to be maintained if the client follows a healthy diet and takes regular exercise.

Clients should be advised to:

- drink 8–10 glasses of water per day to help flush toxins from the system
- avoid eating after 6.30 pm when possible
- limit dietary intake of salt, sugar and caffeine
- avoid fizzy drinks, sweets and starchy foods
- cut down on animal fats
- take fibre regularly in the diet
- exercise at least three times per week
- exfoliate the skin daily, for example by body brushing in the shower. Use a loofah or long-handled bristle brush to give the body a brisk all-over massage, which stimulates the circulation and nerve endings and smoothes the skin.

Contraindications to body wrap

- Pregnancy.
- Open sores or wounds.
- Recent surgery.
- New scar tissue.
- Signs of infection.
- Inflammation and swelling.
- Medical disorders, for example emphysema, phlebitis.

Contra-actions

If the client experiences a tingling sensation or loss of feeling they should be unwrapped immediately. They are either unsuitable for treatment or the wraps have been applied too tightly.

> **HEALTH MATTERS**
>
> The client should be asked to provide written consent from their doctor if they have a heart condition or suffer from epilepsy.

> **HEALTH MATTERS**
>
> There are some areas, which, if wrapped too tightly, can cause loss of feeling in the hands and feet. This is because the underlying blood vessels and nerves are very near the surface. Extra care should be taken when applying wraps to:
>
> - behind the knees
> - the groin area
> - lower lumbar area of the back
> - inside the elbow.

Body wrap treatments

1 Give three reasons for recommending body wrap treatments to a client.

2 How long should be allowed in the appointment book for a body wrap treatment?

3 How frequently should body wrap treatments be given?

4 Identify two different types of wrapping medium that can be used for body wrap treatments.

5 What is the purpose of the product applied to the skin before body wrapping?

6 What is the purpose of the heating device used to cover the client after body wrapping?

7 How many wraps (bandages) are usually required for a body wrap treatment?

8 How is 'total inch loss' calculated after a body wrap?

MULTIPLE CHOICE QUIZ

Hydrotherapy and heat treatments

Work your way through these questions and discuss your answers with a colleague. Sometimes there may appear to be more than one right answer, in which case decide which one is the most important. Check with your supervisor if there is anything you are not sure about.

1 Hyperaemia is:
(a) reddening of the skin
(b) itchiness of the skin
(c) pigmentation of the skin
(d) sensitivity of the skin.

2 The cause of a hyperaemia is:
(a) stimulation of the nerve endings
(b) stimulation of the sweat glands
(c) stimulation of the blood supply
(d) stimulation of the sebaceous glands.

3 The treatment temperature of a sauna is:
(a) cooler than a steam bath
(b) hotter than a steam bath
(c) the same as a steam bath
(d) the same as a spa pool.

4 A thermometer is used to measure:
(a) chlorine
(b) humidity
(c) pH
(d) temperature.

5 The acceptable pH of a spa pool lies within the range:
(a) 3.0–5.0
(b) 6.5–7.5
(c) 7.2–8.0
(d) 8.5–9.5.

6 Water testing kits check:
(a) the temperature of the water
(b) the relative humidity of the water
(c) the warmth and humidity of the water
(d) the balance of the water and its chemical content.

7 The effects of a steam bath on the sweat glands are described as:
(a) relaxing
(b) stimulating
(c) cleansing
(d) sensitising.

Hydrotherapy and heat treatments

8 The effects of a sauna on the blood circulation are described as:
(a) relaxing
(b) stimulating
(c) cleansing
(d) sensitising.

9 The beneficial effects of a wet floatation treatment are due to:
(a) the addition of essence to the water
(b) the temperature inside the tank
(c) the humidity inside the tank
(d) the addition of mineral salts to the water.

10 Air that is 'saturated' with moisture is:
(a) humid
(b) dry
(c) hot
(d) cold.

11 One effect of becoming dehydrated is:
(a) feeling faint
(b) feeling hot
(c) excessive perspiration
(d) excessive stimulation.

12 The main water tests for a spa pool are:
(a) bromine and pH
(b) chlorine and pH
(c) bromine and chlorine
(d) pH and alkalinity.

13 The temperature of a spa pool should be maintained at:
(a) 30–40 °C
(b) 20–30 °C
(c) 30–40 °F
(d) 40–50 °C.

14 During a foam bath treatment, the foam acts as:
(a) an activator
(b) a compressor
(c) an aerator
(d) an insulator.

15 During a hydro bath treatment, air is directed over the main muscle groups using a:
(a) duckboard
(b) compressor
(c) hose
(d) pump.

16 The depth of water in a wet floatation tank is:
(a) 30 cm
(b) 60 cm
(c) 1 metre
(d) 30 mm.

17 The blood vessels that transport oxygenated blood away from the heart are called:
(a) veins
(b) arteries
(c) capillaries
(d) lymph vessels.

18 During a sauna or steam treatment, blood flow to the skin increases from 5–10 per cent of cardiac output to:
(a) 10–20 per cent
(b) 50–70 per cent
(c) 90–100 per cent
(d) 20–40 per cent.

19 The pulse rate of an average person is:
(a) 40–60 beats per minute
(b) 50–70 beats per minute
(c) 60–80 beats per minute
(d) 70–90 beats per minute.

20 The working temperature of a sauna is usually:
(a) 70–110 °C
(b) 40–80 °C
(c) 50–90 °C
(d) 100–110 °C.

A PRACTICAL GUIDE TO BEAUTY THERAPY

Index

A PRACTICAL GUIDE TO BEAUTY THERAPY

A PRACTICAL GUIDE TO BEAUTY THERAPY